Catholic Christianity

with Islam and Judaism

Revision Guide

 RECAP   APPLY   REVIEW   SUCCEED

Andy Lewis
Waqar Ahmad Ahmedi

OXFORD
UNIVERSITY PRESS

OXFORD
UNIVERSITY PRESS

Great Clarendon Street, Oxford, OX2 6DP, United Kingdom

Oxford University Press is a department of the University of Oxford. It furthers the University's objective of excellence in research, scholarship, and education by publishing worldwide. Oxford is a registered trade mark of Oxford University Press in the UK and in certain other countries

British Library Cataloguing in Publication Data
Data available

978-0-19-842279-2

10 9 8 7 6 5 4 3 2

Paper used in the production of this book is a natural, recyclable product made from wood grown in sustainable forests. The manufacturing process conforms to the environmental regulations of the country of origin.

Printed in India by Manipal Technologies Limited

Links to third party websites are provided by Oxford in good faith and for information only. Oxford disclaims any responsibility for the materials contained in any third party website referenced in this work.

Please note that the practice questions in this book allow students a genuine attempt at practising exam skills, but they are not intended to replicate examination papers.

Acknowledgements

The publisher would like to thank Cathy Hobday, Paul Rowan and Cavan Wood for their work on the Student Book on which this Revision Guide is based, and Mary Cunniffe, Peter Jurczak and Laura O'Boyle for reviewing this Revision Guide.

We are grateful to the authors and publishers for use of extracts from their titles and in particular for the following:

Scripture quotations taken from The Revised Standard Version of the Bible: Catholic Edition, copyright © 1965, 1966 the Division of Christian Education of the National Council of the Churches of Christ in the United States of America. Used by permission. All rights reserved.

Excerpts from Catechism of the Catholic Church, http://www.vatican.va/archive/ccc_css/archive/catechism/ccc_toc.htm (Strathfield, NSW: St Pauls, 2000). © Libreria Editrice Vaticana. Reproduced with permission from The Vatican.

Excerpts from The Qur'an OWC translated by M. A. S. Abdel Haleem (Oxford University Press, 2008). © M. A. S. Abdel Haleem 2004, 2005. Reproduced with permission from Oxford University Press.

Excerpts from The Stone Edition of the Tanach (Mesorah Publications, 2010). © ArtScroll / Mesorah Publications, Ltd. Reproduced with permission from ArtScroll / Mesorah Publications, Ltd.

Excerpts from GCSE (9-1) Religious Studies A: Faith and Practice in the 21st Century, Sample Assessment Materials https://qualifications.pearson.com/content/dam/pdf/GCSE/Religious%20Studies/2016/Specification%20and%20sample%20assessments/SAMs-GCSE-L1-L2-Religious-Studies-A-June-2016-Draft-4.pdf (EDEXCEL, 2016). © Pearson Education Limited 2016. Reproduced with permission from Edexcel and Pearson Education Ltd.

Excerpts from Specimen paper 1RA0/1C (EDEXCEL, 2016). © Pearson Education Limited 2016. Reproduced with permission from Edexcel and Pearson Education Ltd.

Excerpts from Specimen paper 1RA0/4A (EDEXCEL, 2016). © Pearson Education Limited 2016. Reproduced with permission from Edexcel and Pearson Education Ltd.

Excerpts from Specimen paper 1RA0/3A (EDEXCEL, 2016). © Pearson Education Limited 2016. Reproduced with permission from Edexcel and Pearson Education Ltd.

Excerpts from Specimen paper Mark Scheme 1RA0/3A (EDEXCEL, 2016). © Pearson Education Limited 2016. Reproduced with permission from Edexcel and Pearson Education Ltd.

D. Birnbaum: Jews, Church & Civilization, (New Paradigm Matrix Publishing, 2012). Reproduced with permission from D. Birnbaum, Jews, Church & Civilization, New Paradigm Matrix Publishing.

Dietrich Bonhoeffer: The Cost of Discipleship, translated by R H Fuller, with some revision by Irmgard Booth (Touchstone, 1995). Copyright 1959 by SCM Press Ltd. Reproduced with permission from Simon & Schuster, Inc.

British Humanist Association: A Humanist Discussion of... Family Matters, http://humanismforschools.org.uk/pdfs/ Family%20Matters.pdf (British Humanist Association, 2016). Reproduced with permission from the British Humanist Association.

Church of England: Medical Ethics & Health & Social Care Policy: Contraception, (Church of England, 2016). © Archbishops' Council 2016. Reproduced with permission The Archbishops' Council.

Congregation for the Doctrine of the Faith: The Nicene-Constantinople Creed Formula to adopt from now on in cases in which the Profession of Faith is prescribed by law in substitution of the Tridentine formula and the oath against modernism, 17th July 1967, (The Vatican, 1967). © Libreria Editrice Vaticana. Reproduced with permission from The Vatican.

W. Jordan: The Sistine Chapel Ceiling is the Greatest Work of Art Ever Made, According to Brits, January 4, 2015, https://yougov.co.uk/news/2015/01/04/sistine-chapel-ceiling-greatest-work-art-ever-made/ (YOuGov, 2014). Reproduced with permission from YouGov.

Mother Teresa: A Simple Path, edited by Lucinda Vardey (Rider & Co. 1995). copyright © 1995 by Lucinda Vardey. Reproduced in the United States and Canada with permission from Ballantine Books, an imprint of Random House, a division of Penguin Random House LLC UK Copyright holder not established at time of going to print.

Cardinal V. Nichols: Preparing my Funeral, http://rcdow.org.uk/att/files/liturgy/funeral%20liturgy/preparing%20my%20funeral.pdf (Diocese of Westminster, 2017). Reproduced with permission from H.E. Cardinal Vincent Nichols, Archbishop of Westminster.

Pope Paul VI: Sacrosanctum Concilium, Constitution on the Sacred Liturgy, 4th December 1963 (The Vatican, 1963). © Libreria Editrice Vaticana. Reproduced with permission from The Vatican.

Pope Paul VI: Lumen Gentium, Dogmatic Constitution on the Church, 21st ovember 1964 (The Vatican, 1964). © Libreria Editrice Vaticana. Reproduced with permission from The Vatican.

We have made every effort to trace and contact all copyright holders before publication, but if notified of any errors or omissions, the publisher will be happy to rectify these at the earliest opportunity.

Cover: Baloncici/iStockphoto

Artworks: QBS Learning, Jason Ramasami

Photos: p15 (T): TerryHealy/Getty Images; p15 (B): Tatjana Splichal/Shutterstock; p18: Peter Barritt/Alamy Stock Photo; p22: jorisvo/Shutterstock; p32: Peter Macdiarmid/Getty Images; p35 (BL): graja/Shutterstock; p35 (TL): Tatjana Splichal/Shutterstock; p35 (R): Zvonimir Atletic/Shutterstock; p44: e X p o s e/Shutterstock; p46: Ishara S.KODIKARA/AFP/Getty Images; p52: Nemeziya/Shutterstock; p57: Sa-nguansak Supong/Shutterstock; p58 (T): Alejandro Mendoza R/Shutterstock; p58 (TM): Justyna Pszczolka/Alamy Stock Photo; p58 (BM): Alexander Mazurkevich/Shutterstock; p58 (B): MarioPonta/Alamy Stock Photo; p59 (L): Avalon_Studio/Shutterstock; p59 (R): Grzegorz Galazka\Archivio Grzegorz Galazka\Mondadori Portfolio via Getty Images; p60: Federico Rostagno/123RF; p61: SuperStock/Getty Images; p62: Steve Skjold/Alamy Stock Photo; p63 (B): Thoom/Shutterstock; p64 (L): PURPLE MARBLES YORK 1/Alamy Stock Photo; p64 (R): Kippa Matthews/REX/Shutterstock; p65: Spencer Grant/Alamy Stock Photo; p72: MuMuV/iStock; p76 (T): destinacigdem/123RF; p76 (B): Samuel Borges Photography/Shutterstock; p77 (L): DNY59/Getty Images; p77 (M): Ditty_about_summer/Shutterstock; p77 (R): Hadi Y Djunaedi/123RF; p78: sirtravelalot/Shutterstock; p87: Romolo Tavani/Shutterstock; p96: graphixmania/Shutterstock; p97: Samuel Perry/Shutterstock; p100: Moses (Approaching Mt. Sinai), 1905-07 (oil on canvas), Ury, Lesser (1861-1931) / Tel Aviv Museum of Art, Israel / Gift of Georg Kareski / Bridgeman Images; p102: irisphoto1/iStock; p105: Jim West/Alamy Stock Photo; p106 (B): Fulcanelli/Shutterstock; p107 (T): Ira Berger/Alamy Stock Photo; p113: pryzmat/Shutterstock; p114: Israel images/Alamy Stock Photo; p121: emyerson/Getty Images; p124: LuVo/iStock; p124: Craevschii Family/Shutterstock; p131: Peter Horree/Alamy Stock Photo; p134: EyeEm/Alamy Stock Photo; p135: MasPix/Alamy Stock Photo; p142: Chris Clark/Alamy Stock Photo; p143: Marmaduke St. John/Alamy Stock Photo; p146: Godong/Alamy Stock Photo; p149: Eyal Bartov/Alamy Stock Photo; p155: aquariagirl1970/Shutterstock; p161: PRISMA ARCHIVO/Alamy Stock Photo; p164 (T): Adam Jan Figel/Shutterstock; p164 (TM): Skylines/Shutterstock; p164 (M): Fresnel/Shutterstock; p164 (BM): Gino Santa Maria/Shutterstock; p164 (B): Linda Bucklin/Shutterstock; p169: Ekkachai/Shutterstock; p171: Isaac gil/Shutterstock; p171 (TL): Maslov Dmitry/Shutterstock; p171 (BL) & p172: pzAxe/Shutterstock; p171 (TR): S. M. Beagle/Shutterstock; p171 (BR): VAV/Shutterstock; p174: Peter Treanor/Alamy Stock Photo; p176: Colin Underhill/Alamy Stock Photo; p178: St. Peter Preaching in Jerusalem (detail of 63197) c.1427 (fresco), Masolino da Panicale, Tommaso (1383-c.1447)/Brancacci Chapel, Santa Maria del Carmine, Florence, Italy/Bridgeman Images; p179: DEA PICTURE LIBRARY/Getty Images; p180 (L): Studio-Annika/Getty Images; p180 (R): Lisa S./Shutterstock; p181 (T): Granger Historical Picture Archive/Alamy Stock Photo; p181 (B): Tim Graham/Alamy Stock Photo; p182: ASIF HASSAN/AFP/Getty Images;

Contents

How **exam-ready** are you?

☹   😐   ☺

Area of Study 3:
Philosophy and Ethics*   130

Area of Study 4:
Textual Studies *St Mark's Gospel** 155

*You will study **either** Islam **or** Judaism and **either** Philosophy and Ethics **or** Textual Studies.

Introduction

What will the exams be like?

If you are studying the **full course**, you will sit **three** separate exams:

- Catholic Christianity – 1 hour 45 minutes
- Judaism or Islam – 50 minutes
- Philosophy and Ethics or Mark's Gospel – 50 minutes

If you are studying the **short course**, you will sit **two** exams, each 50 minutes long. One exam will cover the first two chapters of content in this book (on Catholic Christianity), and the other will cover a second faith option (either Islam or Judaism).

You must answer all of the questions on each exam paper.

What is the exam structure?

- The **Catholic Christianity** paper will be divided into **four** parts.
- The **Judaism** or **Islam** paper will be divided into **two** parts.
- The **Philosophy and Ethics** or **Mark's Gospel** paper will be divided into 2 parts.

Remember that each part has four questions – (a), (b), (c) and (d).

What will the exam questions look like?

The (a) question

The (a) question will always start with the words 'Outline three...' or 'State three...', and a maximum of **3 marks** will be awarded.

For example:

> 1 (a) Outline **three** features of the Trinity. (3)

The (b) question

The (b) question will always start with the words 'Explain two...' or 'Describe two...', and a maximum of **4 marks** will be awarded.

For example:

> (b) Explain **two** Catholic beliefs about the Bible. (4)

The (c) question

The (c) question will always start with the words 'Explain two...', and will ask you to refer to a **source of wisdom and authority**. A maximum of **5 marks** will be awarded.

For example:

> (c) Explain **two** reasons why the resurrection is important to Catholics. In your answer you must refer to a source of wisdom and authority. (5)

The (d) question

The (d) question will always start with a statement of opinion that you are asked to **evaluate**. These questions will sometimes be out of 12 marks, and sometimes be out of 15 marks (if you are being tested on Spelling, Punctuation and Grammar).

For example:

> (d) 'Christianity solves the problem of evil and suffering.' Evaluate this statement considering arguments for and against. In your response you should:
>
> - refer to Christian teachings
> - refer to different Christian points of view
> - reach a justified conclusion. (15)

What is a source of wisdom and authority?

This could be a reference to the Bible, the Catechism, the words of a prayer (such as the Lord's Prayer or the Hail Mary), or a quote from a saint, pope or bishop. For Judaism you could refer to the Torah, Tenakh, Talmud, or other rabbinical teaching. For Islam, you could refer to the Qur'an, Hadith, or Sunnah.

How will the exams be marked?

What are the Assessment Objectives?

	Students must:	Weighting
Assessment Objective 1 (AO1) – questions (a), (b) and (c)	Demonstrate knowledge and understanding of religion and belief, including: • beliefs, practices and sources of authority • influence on individuals, communities and societies • similarities and differences within and/or between religions and beliefs.	50% of the marks in your exam
Assessment Objective 2 (AO2) – question (d)	Analyse and evaluate aspects of religion and belief, including their significance and influence.	50% of the marks in your exam

In the Apply sections of this Revision Guide, the **first question** will always test **AO1** and the **second question** will always test **AO2**.

TIP

Ensure you get your timing right! The exam board suggests:
Question (a) – 3 minutes each
Question (b) – 4 minutes each
Question (c) – 4 minutes each
Question (d) – 15 minutes each
TOTAL – around 26 minutes per part

This means for the Catholic Christianity paper you will have about 5 minutes left to check your answers at the end.

Marking the (a) question

'Outline/State' questions require you to provide three facts or short ideas; **you don't need to explain them or express any opinions.** You can even write these as three bullet points to make it really clear you have three separate ideas. For example, in answer to the question 'Outline **three** features of the Trinity', your three responses could be:

> 1. *There is one God in three persons.* **(1)**
>
> 2. *Each person is fully God.* **(1)**
>
> 3. *Each person is different from the other persons.* **(1)**

For each response, you would receive 1 mark. You are not expected to spend time explaining what the Trinity is: the question only asks you to give three features.

Marking the (b) question

These questions start with 'Explain' or 'Describe', which means you will need to show **development** of ideas. Therefore you need two clearly developed points. For example, if the question is 'Explain **two** types of evil' you might think you just need to state the two types, but you would only be awarded **a maximum of 2 marks** for this.

> *Type 1: One type of evil is called natural evil.* **(1)**
>
> *Type 2: Another type of evil is called moral evil.* **(1)**

The types given above are correct, but you would only score 2 marks out of 4. In order to fully **explain** these points, you need to show some **development**. For example:

> *Type 1: One type of evil is called natural evil,* **(1)** *which means evil caused by nature, e.g. earthquakes.* **(1)**
>
> *Type 2: Another type of evil is called moral evil,* **(1)** *which means evil caused by humans, e.g. murder.* **(1)**

Each of the above points are now developed, and would receive 2 marks each, totalling **4 marks.** It is a good idea to write these points as two small paragraphs, signposted with *Firstly…, Secondly…* or similar.

Marking the (c) question

These questions are very similar to (b) questions, but they have one crucial difference. For an extra mark, you are expected to include a reference to a **source of wisdom and authority**, which could be a quotation from/reference to the Bible or another important source within Christianity. For example, here is a student answer to a (c) question:

(c) Explain **two** reasons why the resurrection is important to Christians. In your answer you must refer to a source of wisdom and authority. (5)

Christians believe that Jesus' resurrection allows their sins to be forgiven. **(1)** *Therefore, they can have a true relationship with God again.* **(1)** *This is made clear when Jesus explains that if Christians repent, they will be forgiven (Luke 24:47).* **(1)**

Jesus' resurrection means that death is not the end; **(1)** *this means that he showed that death could be overcome and he paved the way for Christians to be with God.* **(1)**

You need to write **two** developed points, one of which needs to be supported by a source of wisdom and authority. Setting out your writing in two paragraphs makes it clear that you are giving two developed points. You could directly quote a source, paraphrase it (put it in your own words), or you could just include the reference (as in the above student answer).

Marking the (d) question

These questions specifically ask you to evaluate a statement. Evaluating a statement means that you are weighing up how important, useful, valuable or effective it is. This will enable you to evaluate the statement and make a reasoned judgement. The best way to do this is to consider different opinions on the matter and then summarise which one you agree with more and why in your conclusion. This is exactly what the question asks you to do. When planning your answer, you need to remember to do the following:

- Refer to Christian teachings such as core beliefs and important sources of wisdom and authority.
- Ensure that different viewpoints are included, either from within Christianity or non-religious views, and ensure that relevant ethical or philosophical arguments are referred to if appropriate (the question will make it clear which of these will be required in your answer).
- Ensure that you include a justified conclusion – in other words, your final decision on the matter having considered different viewpoints. You must explain *why* you have come to that decision, using evidence to support your view.

If you don't refer to different viewpoints, **you cannot get more than half of the marks**.

The examiner will mark your answer using a mark scheme, similar to the one below.

TIP

Atheism and Humanism are both non-religious views but atheism rejects God more firmly. The atheist by definition excludes God from any explanation of a miracle, whilst a humanist emphasises the importance of human reason for working out the evidence.

Level 1 (1–3 marks)	• Basic information or reasons about the issue are identified and can be explained by some religious or moral understanding. • Opinions are given but not fully explained.
Level 2 (4–6 marks)	• Some information or reasons about the issue are loosely identified and can be explained by limited religious or moral understanding. • Opinions are given which attempt to support the issue but are not fully explained or justified.

Level 3 (7–9 marks)	• Information given clearly describes religious information/issues, leading to coherent and logical chains of reasoning that consider different viewpoints. These are supported by an accurate understanding of religion and belief. • The answer contains coherent and reasoned judgements of many, but not all, of the elements in the question. Judgements are supported by a good understanding of evidence, leading to a partially justified conclusion.
Level 4 (10–12 marks)	• The response critically deconstructs religious information/issues, leading to coherent and logical chains of reasoning that consider different viewpoints. These are supported by a sustained, accurate and thorough understanding of religion and belief. • The answer contains coherent and reasoned judgements of the full range of elements in the question. Judgements are fully supported by the comprehensive use of evidence, leading to a fully justified conclusion.

Spelling, Punctuation and Grammar (SPaG)

You will be assessed on the quality of your written communication in certain questions
- **Catholic Christianity**: 1(d) and 3(d)
- **Judaism** or **Islam**: 1(d)
- **Philosophy and Ethics** or **Mark's Gospel**: 1(d)

- **0 marks** are awarded if there are considerable errors or irrelevant information, or if nothing is written.
- **1 mark** is awarded for reasonable accuracy and limited use of religious terms.
- **2 marks** are awarded for considerable accuracy and a good number of specialist terms.
- **3 marks** are awarded for consistent accuracy and a wide range of specialist terms.

Good written communication is always important, but you will only receive marks for it in the questions mentioned above. Therefore, you should allow yourself time in your exam to check these particular answers carefully and amend any errors.

it's ALL in your -hands.

Review Your Skills

AO1 – (a), (b) and (c) questions

(a) questions

- **Recall information**
  - Learn key words, memorise short, useful quotes, and ensure you can clearly identify religious teaching.

- **Select appropriate information**
  - Often you will have 'more than enough' information. You need to pick relevant information wisely to best answer the questions.

(b) questions

- **Write about different viewpoints**
  - This is only in (b) questions that begin 'Describe' - carefully structure your paragraphs as indicated on page 9.

- **Write a developed point**
  - PEE – Point, Example, Explain can be a useful format to ensure a developed point.

(c) questions

- **Explain beliefs correctly using a source of wisdom and authority**
  - See above to see what counts – this is necessary in (c) questions, but could be the development of a point in (b) questions

- **Write a developed point**
  - PEE – Point, Example, Explain can be a useful format to ensure a developed point.

AO2 – (d) questions

- **Break down the question**
  - Make sure you pick out each of the key words in the question. Do you know what skills you need to use and which specific content you need to write about?

- **Plan a response**
  - Taking a minute to plan out an essay can be essential to ensure you answer the question being asked. A simple FOR/AGAINST table can be a useful planning tool.

- **Identify arguments for and/or against a statement**
  - It is important to work out what the two sides of an argument are – creating a table may help you do this. You need to know what the Church teaches on topic so that you can identify the Catholic view.

- **Identify divergent views**
  - There may not be divergent views within Catholicism, but there could be among different Christian groups. There is certainly difference between Christians and non-religious people!

- **Begin an essay with a strong line of argument**
  - Responses do not need to be equally balanced, especially where there are multiple bullet points to cover. You may find it easier to begin with an opinion (your conclusion) and then justify it, evaluating and dismissing any criticisms.

- **Write a well-argued paragraph**
  - Words such as 'therefore', 'in addition', 'however', 'in contrast' can help show a chain of reasoning

- **Write a developed point**
  - PEE – Point, Example, Explain can be a useful format to ensure a developed point.

- **Evaluate a statement**
  - An evaluation is making a judgement. The analysis will have usually come before this, looking at strengths and weaknesses of arguments and counter arguments. These are summed up in an evaluation statement, which must include justification or reasoning.

- **Write a justified conclusion**
  - Highlight which argument you think is most convincing. Justifying means giving an explanation for your view and it should be based on the analysis you've already written. The word 'because' is a good indicator that you have justified your response!

For all questions, you should:

- **Organise and clearly signpost an answer**
  - Two separate paragraphs are useful in (b) and (c) questions. Use openings such as 'Firstly', and 'Secondly' to help make your separate points clear.

- **Improve an answer**
  - Being able to identify what is wrong with an answer can help you improve your own.

How to revise using this book

This Revision Guide takes a 3-step approach to help you revise effectively.

RECAP

This is an overview of the key information. It is not a substitute for the full Student Book, or your class notes. It should prompt you to recall more in-depth information. The three bullet points at the top of each topic are real essentials. Diagrams and images are included to help make the information more memorable.

APPLY

Once you've recapped the key information, you can practise applying it to help embed it. There are two questions after each Recap section. The first question will help you rehearse some key skills that you need for the questions on the exam that test your knowledge (the (a), (b) and (c) questions). The second question will help you rehearse some key skills that you will need for the (d) question, which tests your evaluative skills.

There are suggested answers to the Apply activities at the back of the book. Practising exam questions is also a key part of revision.

REVIEW

Once you have attempted the Apply activities, check your answers. You need to work out exactly what it is you don't know – is it knowledge that needs work or do you need to practice a skill?

In addition, at the end of each chapter you will have a chance to review what you've revised. The Exam Practice pages contain sample answers for each question type. For some of the longer question types, there are writing frames that you can use to structure your answer, and to remind yourself of what it is that the examiner is looking for.

When you've answered the questions you can use the mark schemes at the back to help you work out how you've done. You can review your progress to find out if there are areas that you need to revise in more detail. And you can turn back to the pages here for guidance on how to answer the exam questions.

TIP

The Apply activities often feature exam-style questions and all activities provide the opportunity to practice and refine the skills that you will need for the exam. You can either complete the structured activities or go straight to the full exam question!

 COMPARE AND CONTRAST

Compare and Contrast features appear in units 1.8, 2.2, 5.8, 6.3, 7.8 and 8.4 of this Revision Guide. In your exam you may be required to compare Christian beliefs and practices regarding these topics to another religion you are studying. You should consider the similarities and differences between them.

Useful Terms are made orange in the text. All of these key terms are provided in a glossary at the end of this guide.

Effective revision

According to experts, how you revise can have a big impact on how much information you can remember and how you develop your exam skills. The following techniques have been found to have a much better impact than simply reading or highlighting your notes. Why not try some of them for yourself?

Technique	How it works
Start early	Space out your revision over the longest time possible. It's never too early to start! Try to regularly revisit previous topics you have studied.
Practice your recall	Don't use your revision guide or notes straight away – try to recall the information yourself. Can you bring to mind the key information you need for a question? The more you do this, the better you will get… then when you have to do it in the exam hall, it won't be as difficult.
Remember the details	You need to be able to explain and describe ideas in as much detail as possible. A concept map or spider diagram may help do this. Start with a key idea such as Trinity, Incarnation, or Creation and build around it. Keep asking yourself '*why?*' when you are describing and explaining the concept.
Break your revision up	Break topics into smaller chunks and then switch between them in your revision schedule. It is far better to revise a number of smaller topics rather than a big block at once. Around 30 minutes at a time per topic generally works well. Creating a revision timetable will allow you to make sure you cover all topics.
Have examples ready	Ensure you have clear examples of sources of wisdom and authority (including the Bible and Catechism) which you can draw on. You can also use stories of saints, places of pilgrimage, significant Christians, and artworks. Make sure you can link these to key concepts.
Get creative	Creating infographics, timelines, cartoons, or diagrams could help you remember complex topics. Some topics lend themselves to this better than others.

Practice Testing	• Write quiz-style questions as you revise – if these are short answer questions or multiple choice it is easy to get someone else to test you.
	• Attempt exam questions – this is the best way to see if you know enough for the actual GCSE exam.
	• Break exam practice up, for example:
	   • Spend 25 minutes revising 'Topic B'.
	   • Spend 25 minutes doing exam questions on 'Topic A' in exam conditions.
	   • Review your answers with the mark scheme.
	   • Identify areas you were not clear on.
	   • Remember to schedule an exam question on 'Topic B' for next week!

TIP

Be aware that sometimes if we review some material and then do a related exam question straight away, we may have only stored the information in our short-term memory. So, it may be better to actually attempt the question the next day, or even the next week!

RECAP

Essential information
- God is a Trinity of three persons in one God.
- The Nicene Creed declares this belief.
- The Trinity features in baptism and the celebration of the **Eucharist** today.

The Trinity is three persons (Father, Son, and Holy Spirit) in one God. Each person is fully God, and each person is different from the other persons.

The Trinity in the Nicene Creed

The **Nicene Creed** (The Christian declaration of faith) says:

❝ I believe in one God, the Father almighty…

I believe in one Lord Jesus Christ…

I believe in the Holy Spirit… ❞

It is both an **individual declaration of faith** and a **shared statement** that unites Catholics as one body and Church.

The Father is God: 'Our father who art in heaven' (*Matthew 6:9*)
The Son is God: 'The Word became flesh' (*John 1:14*)
The Holy Spirit is God: 'the Spirit of God descending like a dove' (*Matthew 3:16*)

The Oneness of God

Revelation means something that is revealed by God to humans. The Trinity **reveals** something of the mystery of God to Catholics:

- **Outside** as Father and creator
- **Beside** as Son and saviour
- **Inside** as strengthening Holy Spirit

The unity and oneness of God is an idea made clear in the Old Testament: 'Hear, O Israel: the Lord our God is one Lord' (*Deuteronomy 6:4*).

- This is the beginning of the Shema – the most important prayer for Jewish people (see p.117).
- It is also part of the Great Commandment given by Jesus (*Mark 12:28–31*).

The Trinity in Catholic worship today

Baptism: ceremony using water, performed in the name of the Father, Son, and Holy Spirit

Eucharist: sacrament involving bread and wine; begins with sign of the cross, Eucharistic prayer gives thanks to God and makes Son present in the consecrated bread and wine, through the Holy Spirit

 **APPLY**

AO1 Can you write a second developed point to answer this exam question? The student answer is currently worth 3 marks as it is a developed point plus a source of wisdom and authority.

  c. Explain **two** ways the Trinity reveals the oneness of God. In your answer you must refer to a source of wisdom and authority. (5)

  John's Gospel makes it clear that 'the word was made flesh', which means that Jesus is the Son of God. This shows a clear oneness of these two aspects of the Trinity.

TIP

When answering a (b) or (c) question, your structure can really help make it clear you are providing a full mark answer. Start your second point on a new line, like a new paragraph.

 **REVIEW**

Answers: Mark your answers using p.187 and note areas for improvement.
AO1: This question is testing your ability to write a developed point. For help with this skill, see p.12.

RECAP

Essential information

- The **doctrine** (belief held by the Church) of the Trinity is found in the Creed (formal statement of belief).
- The baptism of Jesus revealed all persons of the Trinity in the same moment.
- The Council of Nicaea ended disagreement about Jesus' nature, while the Council of Constantinople clarified belief in the Trinity.

What is a doctrine?

Not everything was written down in the Bible, particularly about the early Church. There is much teaching and doctrine that has been passed on from the earliest of times through the Catholic Church. This is called the Apostolic Tradition.

What is a creed?

- From the Latin *credo*: 'I believe'; a formal expression of what the Church believes
- Originally written to formally correct a mistake in teaching.

TIP
It is really useful to memorise parts of the Nicene Creed (see 1.1 The Trinity) – it can be used as a source of wisdom and authority in various areas of the exam.

History of the doctrine of the Trinity

600 BCE (approx.)
Old Testament
Teaching on 'One God' – found in Jewish prayer, the Shema

270 CE–325 CE
Arian controversy
Arius claimed Jesus was not actually God, just a prophet

325 CE
Council of Nicaea
Nicene Creed written to clarify the divine nature of Jesus

400 CE (approx.)
Bible (as we know it) compiled
This was a reflection of Apostolic Tradition and beliefs of early Church

150 CE

0 CE

30 CE (approx.)
Life of Jesus
Trinity revealed at the Annunciation and present at Jesus' baptism

32 CE onwards
Early Church
Trinity was the lived experience of the Christians, passed on through the **Apostolic Tradition**

300 CE

381 CE
Council of Constantinople
Meeting to clarify belief in Trinity – to underline Holy Spirit also is God

450 CE

Jesus' baptism

— God the Holy Spirit

❝ <u>The Spirit of God descending like a dove</u>, and alighting on him; and lo, <u>a voice from heaven</u>, saying, "<u>This is my beloved Son</u>" ❞ *(Matthew 3:16–17)*

God the Father ⟶

God the Son

TIP
This story from Matthew's Gospel is a vital source of wisdom and authority for the Trinity – make sure you learn it!

APPLY

AO1 Can you develop these two basic points to correctly answer this question?

b. Explain **two** sources for the Catholic Church's teaching on the Trinity. (4)

> One source was the decisions made at the Council of Nicaea, which...
>
> Another source was the Apostolic Tradition, which...

AO2 Read the following exam question. Using your revision from 1.1 and 1.2, create a table with arguments 'for' and 'against'.

d. 'The Trinity is the most essential belief about God.' Evaluate this statement considering arguments for and against.
In your response you should:
- refer to Catholic teachings
- reach a justified conclusion. (15)

REVIEW

Answers: Mark your answers using p.187 and note areas for improvement.
AO1: This question is testing your ability to write a developed point. For help with this skill, see p.12.
AO2: This question is testing your ability to identify divergent views. For help with this skill, see p.12.

RECAP

Essential information

- There are two accounts of Creation in Genesis.
- John's Prologue (*John 1*) describes the role of the Word (Jesus) in the process.
- Catholics believe God created the universe and only God has the power to do this.

Creation in Genesis 1:1–2:3

In this account, God created the universe in six days and rested on the seventh.

Day 1: Heavens, earth, light, dark   **Day 2**: Water, sky   **Day 3**: Land, plants   **Day 4**: Sun, moon, stars   **Day 5**: Fish, birds   **Day 6**: Land animals, humans

Creation in Genesis 2:4–3:23

God

- Said Adam and Eve could eat fruit from all trees but one
- Said if Adam and Eve ate the fruit from the tree of the knowledge of good and evil, they would have to leave the garden.

Adam and Eve

- Were tempted by the snake to eat the fruit from the forbidden tree
- Became afraid and hid from God
- Had to leave the garden.

TIP
This links to evil and suffering (9.7 and 9.8).

Divergent Christian interpretations

A literal interpretation	A metaphorical interpretation
• The Creation accounts are an exact retelling of how Creation occurred – a 'word for word' truth • Genesis is a historical and scientific account • This view is often called 'Creationism'.	• The Creation accounts are symbolic, sacred stories • Genesis is a meditation on the nature and purpose of the universe • This view incorporates modern science.

Most Catholics see the stories as metaphorical and use science to help them understand the universe better.

Significance of the Creation account for Catholics

Creation is significant for Catholics because it reveals four key characteristics of God:

- **God as Creator:** "Let there be light" (*Genesis 1:3*)
- **God as benevolent (loving and good):** 'God saw that the light was good' (*Genesis 1:4*)
- **God as omnipotent (all powerful):** "Let the waters… be gathered… and let the dry land appear." (*Genesis 1:9*)
- **God as eternal:** 'In the beginning was the Word…' (*John 1:1*)

APPLY

AO1 Complete the following question. One point has already been made for you.

  a. Outline **three** features of the Creation account in Genesis 1–2. (3)

> *On the first day God said 'Let there be light'.*

AO2 Create an essay plan for the following question.

  d. 'The Creation story is just a metaphor.' Evaluate this statement considering arguments for and against. In your response you should:
- refer to Catholic teachings
- refer to different Christian points of view
- reach a justified conclusion. (15)

REVIEW

Answers: Mark your answers using p.187 and note areas for improvement.
AO1: This question is testing your ability to select appropriate information. For help with this skill, see p.12.
AO2: This question is testing your ability to identify arguments for and/or against a statement. For help with this skill, see p.12.

RECAP

Essential information
- Catholics believe human beings alone are created in the image of God.
- This means they have a conscience and can relate to God.
- Humans should take care of the earth (stewardship) and rule over it (dominion).

What is humanity?
Catholics believe humanity is created *imago Dei* (in the image of God).

> 66 Let us make man in our image, after our likeness; and let them have dominion 99 (*Genesis 1:26*)

How can humanity bear the image of God?

Characteristic	Explanation	Significance for Catholics
Rational	Humans are intelligent and can find their way to God	Engaging in debate about faith
Free will and conscience	Humans can choose right or wrong; a conscience is the voice of God within	Making moral choices that uphold the values of the Gospel
Relate to God	Humans are able to enter into a relationship with God	Going to weekly Mass; daily prayer
Give and receive love	Humans can only find happiness within a community of love	Accepting the vocation of marriage
Answerable to God	Humans are accountable to God for their actions	This will happen in the next life

TIP
This links to 1.8 Eschatology.

Dominion and stewardship interpretations
- Catholics believe humanity is given **dominion** over creation, which means God-given authority to rule
- Catholics also believe humanity should be **stewards** of creation, which means this authority is expressed in a loving care and cultivation of creation.

How might humans act if they only focused on dominion?	How might humans act if they *also* focused on stewardship?
• Over-farming to feed humans • Cutting down forest for our paper/wood needs • Burning fossil fuels to create electricity	• Managing farming and fishing to ensure a balance in nature • Recycling where possible • Using 'green' energy such as wind or solar power
A minority of Christians believe this – some conservative evangelical Christians claim they do not need to worry about the environment as Jesus will soon return, and that will mean the end of the world anyway.	The majority of Christians take this view. Pope Francis wrote about care for the environment in his encyclical *Laudato si* (2015). Non-religious people do not believe God granted humans dominion over the earth, but many would argue that humans have a moral responsibility to care for the planet.

 APPLY

AO1 This response only has two basic points. Can you develop each one?

b. Explain **two** ways Catholics believe human beings bear the image of God. (4)

> *Humans have free will.*
> *Humans can give and receive love.*

AO2 The arguments for why Christians *should* care for creation are usually quite clear. What would you include as the counter-argument in a question which contains the following statement? Pick one of the sentence starters underneath it and write a full paragraph.

'Christians should make the care of creation a priority.'

> *However, there is a minority of Christians who focus more on dominion. This idea suggests...*
> *OR*
> *However, some Christians would argue that sometimes you do need to prioritise care of other humans over the environment...*

 REVIEW

Answers: Mark your answers using p.187 and note areas for improvement.
AO1: This question is testing your ability to write a developed point. For help with this skill, see p.12.
AO2: This question is testing your ability to write a well-argued paragraph. For help with this skill, see p.12.

RECAP

Essential information

- The Incarnation refers to God becoming a human being in Jesus.
- Jesus is the God-man: fully God and fully human.
- The Incarnation is made clear in scripture and continues today in the life of the Church.

Jesus as incarnate Son

Catholics believe:

- Jesus (also called 'the Word' in John's Gospel) is the Son of God
- Jesus is God incarnate
- Incarnation means 'enfleshment' or 'making flesh', in this case Jesus was 'God made flesh'.

> 66 The Word became flesh and dwelt among us. 99 (*John 1:14*)

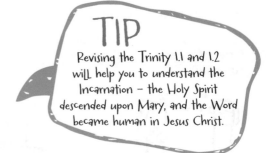

TIP

Revising the Trinity 1.1 and 1.2 will help you to understand the Incarnation – the Holy Spirit descended upon Mary, and the Word became human in Jesus Christ.

How can Jesus be fully human and fully God?

Fully human

- Born of Mary (*Luke 2:7*)
- Died on the cross (*Matthew 27:50*)
- Got tired (*John 4:6*)
- Cried at his friend's death (*John 11:35*)

Fully God

- Mary was a virgin after having her son announced via the Angel Gabriel (*Matthew 1:23*)
- Claimed to be the 'I am' (*John 8:58*) – God's name as revealed to Moses
- 'My words will not pass away' (*Matthew 24:35*)
- He miraculously healed people – e.g. paralysed man (*Matthew 9:2*)

Issues with the Sabbath and the Law

Jesus was accused of **blasphemy** (being disrespectful to God) by the Jewish authorities several times. They believed he was falsely claiming to be God. Two examples of this were:

- Healing and forgiving the paralysed man – Jewish people believed only God could forgive sins (*Matthew 9:2–3*)
- He allowed his disciples to pick corn on the Sabbath – considered to be work – when they were hungry (*Matthew 12:8*).

Why is the Incarnation important for Catholics today?

- Catholics believe God became human so they can be transformed by grace and share Jesus' life through the Church.
- The Incarnation continues through history as humans share the life of Jesus through the sacraments (see 2.1) and the life of the Church.

TIP

You can 'signpost' your answer by beginning each point with 'Firstly...' or 'Secondly...', for example.

APPLY

AO1 When answering (b) questions, you should make it clear that you have written two clear points. Rewrite this answer into two short paragraphs, tweaking the start of each point to signpost them.

b. Explain **two** reasons why Christians believe that Jesus is fully human and fully divine. (4)

> *Mary was Jesus' mother. He was born to a human being, which means he is also fully human. John's Gospel says 'the Word became flesh' which means that Jesus became flesh, God in human form.*

AO2 Try to write a fully developed paragraph using this sentence starter.

d. 'The Incarnation makes it clear that Jesus was fully God and fully human.' Evaluate this statement considering arguments for and against. In your response you should:
- refer to Catholic teachings
- reach a justified conclusion. (15)

> *Jesus was clearly fully God and fully human because he was born to a human...*

REVIEW

Answers: Mark your answers using p.187 and note areas for improvement.
AO1: This question is testing your ability to organise and clearly signpost an answer. For help with this skill, see p.12.
AO2: This question is testing your ability to write a well-argued paragraph. For help with this skill, see p.12.

 **RECAP**

Essential information
- Human beings are saved from sin by the whole work of Jesus, but especially by the Paschal Mystery.
- The Paschal Mystery is the Passion, death, resurrection, and ascension of Jesus.

The Paschal Mystery and salvation
The Paschal Mystery refers to the following events, which can be found in *Luke 23–24*:

Jesus' **Passion** (arrest, trial, and suffering)

Jesus' death on the cross

Jesus' **resurrection** (rising from the dead in a transformed body)

Jesus' t (the moment the resurrected Jesus is taken up to heaven)

Paschal is the Hebrew name for Passover (the Jewish celebration of the Israelites being led to freedom by Moses). There are similarities between the Old Testament account of Moses and the New Testament accounts of Jesus.

Redemption, justification, and redemptive efficacy
- **Redemption**: Jesus' life was redeemed (exchanged) for the freedom from sin for all humans.
- **Justification**: Only just (righteous, holy, loving) people can enter into a relationship with God.
- **Redemptive efficacy**: How does the Paschal Mystery bring about human salvation? It saves humans from eternal death and separation from God. The Passion and death of Jesus allowed the redemption (saving) of humanity.

What does the Catholic Church teach?
Jesus' life, death, resurrection, and ascension are all important in helping both early Christians and Christians today understand exactly who Jesus was. Most followers of Jesus did not realise at the time he was the Son of God.

Why did the 'Word become flesh'?	Why did Jesus die?	Why is the resurrection so important?	What does the ascension mean?
• To save (*CCC 457*) • To know God's love (*CCC 458*) • To model holiness (*CCC 459*) • To share the grace of God (*2 Peter 1:4*).	• To show how to respond to cruelty: 'Father, forgive them' (*Luke 23:34*) • Jesus erased the sins of the world with God's mercy – God himself died on the cross.	• It is the foundation of the Church • It proved that Jesus is God – only God can conquer death • It is a present event – 'I am with you always' (*Matthew 28:20*).	• It prepares the way for humans to follow Jesus to heaven • It was the 'letting go' of Jesus, ready for the arrival of the Holy Spirit at Pentecost.

TIP
Remember that you don't need to give a full chapter and verse reference for a source of wisdom and authority as long as you make sure it is explicit and recognisable.

TIP
Jesus' resurrection was physical; Catholics believe life after death will not just be spiritual – see 1.8.

 APPLY

AO1 Try this one on your own! Remember you need two developed points to get 4 marks, and a reference to a relevant source of wisdom and authority to gain a fifth mark.

c. Explain **two** reasons why the Paschal Mystery is significant for Catholics today. In your answer you must refer to a source of wisdom and authority. (5)

AO2 List the four parts of the Paschal Mystery in order of importance. Explain your reasoning for each. This would provide a good starting point for writing a response to the following question.

d. 'The resurrection is the most important part of the Paschal Mystery.' Evaluate this statement considering arguments for and against. In your response you should:
- refer to Catholic teachings
- reach a justified conclusion. (15)

 **REVIEW**

Answers: Mark your answers using p.187 and note areas for improvement.
AO1: This question is testing your ability to answer a (c) question. For help with this skill, see p.12.
AO2: This question is testing your ability to plan a response. For help with this skill, see p.12.

Essential information

- Catholics believe humans cannot save themselves from sin, but can choose to accept salvation.
- Catholics today continue to participate in the Paschal Mystery through the life of the Church.
- The Eucharist is the most important expression of the Paschal Mystery in the Church today.

The Holy Spirit as God's grace

- The Holy Spirit empowered the apostles for their mission (*Acts 2*) when the Holy Spirit descended at Pentecost. This is seen as the beginning of the Christian Church. It is an expression of God's grace and helped Christians live out the salvation brought about by the Paschal Mystery.
- Peter understood Jesus and the Paschal Mystery far better in *Acts* than he did in the Gospels. The Holy Spirit gives wisdom and understanding to both the early Christians and Christians today.
- Understanding the Holy Spirit and its role is vital to understanding the Trinity.

Choosing to accept salvation

The Catholic Church teaches that humans cannot save themselves from sin. However, they can choose to accept salvation; it is **offered** to everyone by God.

If individuals accept the offer of salvation, this does not mean they have saved themselves; they have accepted that Jesus has saved them from sin through his sacrifice.

> **"** For God sent the Son into the world, not to condemn the world, but that the world might be saved through him. **"** (*John 3:17*)

The significance of salvation and grace

The sacramental life of the Church is the source for experiencing and receiving the grace necessary to continue Jesus' saving mission today:

Baptism	**Confirmation**	**Eucharist**	**Matrimony**	**Holy Orders**	**Reconciliation**	**Anointing of the sick**
Humans are freed from sin and become children of God	Humans receive fresh outpouring of grace through the Holy Spirit to strengthen them	Catholics receive Christ's body and blood, just as at the Last Supper	Graces provided for loving relationships and procreation	Graces provided for ordained ministers of the Church	Repentance of sins restores the relationship with God	God's healing grace unites the suffering person with Jesus' Passion

- The **Eucharist** is the most important expression of the Paschal Mystery in the Church today.
- Participation in the Eucharist is a sign of accepting God's offer of salvation.
- It offers strength to the individual in their life of faith and love.

> **TIP**
> It's vital that you know these seven sacraments – see 2.1 and 2.2.

AO1 **Outline** means you have to write more than just a one-word answer. Expand these one-word answers to ensure you get full marks – this is currently worth 1 mark.

a. Outline **three** ways the Holy Spirit works in the Church. (3)

> Sacraments, charity, counsellor

AO2 You don't necessarily need to put your conclusion at the end of an essay – you can also begin with a statement put forward to be proven, and then justify it – ensuring you still evaluate both sides. Write a short statement to start an answer to this question, then plan how you will continue.

d. 'The Holy Spirit was needed to bring about salvation in the Church.' Evaluate this statement considering arguments for and against. In your response you should:
   - refer to Catholic teachings
   - reach a justified conclusion. (15)

Answers: Mark your answers using p.187 and note areas for improvement.
AO1: This question is testing your ability to answer 'outline' questions. For help with this skill, see p.12.
AO2: This question is testing your ability to write a justified conclusion. For help with this skill, see p.12.

 RECAP

Essential information

- **Eschatology** is the Christian study of the last things in human life: death, judgment, heaven, hell, and purgatory.
- Catholic eschatology is rooted in the Paschal Mystery.
- Catholics believe that how they live in this life affects what happens after they die.
- Catholics believe they can earn their place in heaven by obeying God's will; loving God, and other people as themselves.

Life after death

- For Catholics, life after death is explained in the Paschal Mystery.
- They believe they will be resurrected, like Jesus was.
- Jesus referred to eternal life in his teaching, saying there would be a reward for those who had pleased God.
- This was also made clear by St Paul:

> 66 I am the resurrection and the life; he who believes in me, though he die, yet shall he live, and whoever lives and believes in me shall never die. 99 (*John 11:25–26*)

> 66 For we must all appear before the judgment seat of Christ, so that each one may receive good or evil, according to what he has done in the body. 99 (*2 Corinthians 5:10*)

What is judgment?

- **Particular judgment**: After death a person will go to heaven, purgatory (and then heaven), or hell.
- **General or Last judgment**: This is at the end of time. Everyone, living and dead, will be resurrected and a final and eternal judgment will take place.

What is the nature of resurrection?

- Not all Christians agree on this – is it just the soul that is resurrected, or the physical body too?
- The Catholic Church teaches that resurrection is when a person's soul is reunited with their 'glorified' body (*CCC 997*).
- In his post-resurrection appearances, there was something familiar but also unfamiliar about Jesus – some people didn't recognise him immediately. The Church states that only God knows how resurrection will happen; not everything can be explained (*CCC 268*).

What are heaven, hell, and purgatory?

- **Heaven**: Eternal life with God; a life of love and indescribable joy (*CCC 1027*).
- **Purgatory**: A stage of purification; this enables people to reach the holiness required to get into heaven (*CCC 1030*).
- **Hell**: This is not a punishment from God, it is the absence of the love, generosity, and community of God.

Why is this important for Catholics?

Catholics believe that death reminds us of the importance of life. Death, judgment, and resurrection are reminders for Catholics about how they should live day-to-day. Every choice they make has a consequence.

 TIP

You could be asked to compare and contrast this topic with the view of other Christians, or with members of your second religion in Paper 2. For help with this, see pages 23, 78 and 108 for example.

 **APPLY**

AO1 Can you answer the following question using the writing frame provided?

b. Explain **two** Catholic beliefs about life after death. (4)

> One Catholic belief is... This means that...
> A second Catholic belief is... This means that...

AO2 Have a go at planning and then answering the following question.

d. 'Belief in purgatory is very important.' Evaluate this statement considering arguments for and against.
In your response you should:

- refer to Catholic teachings
- refer to different Christian points of view
- reach a justified conclusion. (15)

 REVIEW

Answers: Mark your answers using p.187 and note areas for improvement.
AO1: This question is testing your ability to organise and clearly signpost an answer. For help with this skill, see p.12.
AO2: This question is testing your ability to answer a (d) question. For help with this skill, see p.12.

 **RECAP**

What is a compare and contrast question?

There are a few areas of the exam specification where you can be asked to compare and contrast two religions, or two groups within a religion. For example, you might get asked to compare Catholic Christianity with other Christian denominations, or to compare Christianity with a second religion, such as Judaism or Islam.

In this paper, Paper 1, you will only be asked to compare Catholic Christianity with other Christian denominations, and you will only be asked to compare them on two possible topics: eschatology and worship (see p.31). Here, you can revise for eschatology.

How is eschatology different for Catholics and other Christians?

	Catholics	Other Christians
Heaven, hell, and purgatory	Catholics believe in the reality of heaven, hell, and purgatory. They believe that : • heaven is an eternity in the presence of God • hell is an eternity outside of the presence of God • purgatory is a place of purification.	• Some Christians would deny that an all-loving God would allow hell to exist, and so believe that everyone (not just Christians) will live together forever in heaven. This is called **universalism**. • Many other Christians believe purgatory does not exist, claiming it is not biblical.
Judgment	Catholics believe in two kinds of judgment: **particular** judgment (which happens when you die) and **final** judgment (which happens at the end of time).	Some Christians place more emphasis on the final judgement, where they believe God will judge all people and give them the afterlife they deserve.
Resurrection	Catholics believe physical resurrection happens after final judgment; it is not just spiritual.	Some Christians believe in just a spiritual resurrection, not a physical one.

⚙ **APPLY**

You could be asked to compare and contrast in (b) questions (but being able to talk about different viewpoints within Christianity is also a useful skill in (d) questions!) For example, here is a question you could be asked:

b. Describe **two** differences in beliefs about life after death between Catholic Christianity and other forms of the main religious tradition of Great Britain. (4)

Here is an example of how you could structure an answer to this question:

Give one belief in Catholic Christianity.	*The first difference is that Catholic Christians believe in the idea of hell, a place of punishment for those who reject God,*
Give a contrasting belief elsewhere in Christianity.	*whereas some other more liberal Christians believe that because God is all-loving everyone will go to heaven forever.*
Give a second belief in Catholic Christianity.	*Secondly, in Catholic Christianity, there is both a physical and spiritual resurrection after death.*
Give a contrasting belief elsewhere in Christianity.	*Yet for some other Christians, the resurrection after death is purely a spiritual one.*

TIP
Remember, when the exam says 'the main religious tradition of Great Britain', it is referring to Christianity.

TIP
Words like 'whereas', 'yet', and 'however' will signal to the examiner that you're making a comparison.

Now have a go at answering the same question yourself, using the grid below to help you. Try to choose **different** points from those given in the answer table above.

Give one belief in Catholic Christianity.	*The first difference is that in Catholic belief...*
Give a contrasting belief elsewhere in Christianity.	*whereas in other Christian traditions...*
Give a second belief in Catholic Christianity.	*Secondly, in Catholic Christianity...*
Give a contrasting belief elsewhere in Christianity.	*Yet for other Christians...*

Exam Practice

Test the 3 mark question (a)

1 State **three** of the religious traditions, other than Christianity, in Great Britain.

(3 marks)

> *Judaism (1)*
>
> *Islam (1)*
>
> *Buddhism (1)*

2 Outline **three** ways that human beings reflect God's image, according to Catholic belief.

(3 marks)

> *Human beings can give and receive love. (1)*
>
> They can pray to God
> Love God

3 Outline **three** features of the Paschal Mystery.

(3 marks)

> That you will go to heaven
> hell or purgatory.

Test the 4 mark question (b)

1 Explain **two** reasons why Catholics believe that Jesus is the Son of God.

(4 marks)

• **Explain one reason**	*One reason is that it is a key part of the beginning of John's Gospel,*
• Develop your explanation with more detail/an example/a reference to a religious teaching	*where it says the Word (Jesus) 'became flesh and dwelt among us'.*
• **Explain a second reason**	*Another reason is that it is shown in the baptism of Jesus,*
• Develop your explanation with more detail/an example/a reference to a religious teaching	*when the voice from heaven says that Jesus is the Son of God.*

2 Explain **two** reasons why the Incarnation is important for Catholics.

(4 marks)

• **Explain one reason**	*Firstly, it meant that God lived on earth,*
• Develop your explanation with more detail/an example/a reference to a religious teaching	*and was then able to sacrifice his life for the benefit of humanity.*
• **Explain a second reason**	*Secondly...*
• Develop your explanation with more detail/an example/a reference to a religious teaching	

3 Explain **two** ways the Trinity is reflected in Catholic worship.

(4 marks)

Exam Practice

Test the 5 mark question (c)

1 Explain **two** Catholic teachings about the Trinity. In your answer you must refer to a source of wisdom and authority. **(5 marks)**

● **Explain one teaching.**	*Firstly, the Trinity allows people to experience the oneness and unity of God.*
● Develop your explanation with more detail/an example.	*This can help affect and deepen their relationship with God,*
● **Either:** Add a reference to a source of wisdom and authority here.	*as shown in the Nicene creed 'I believe in one God'.*
● **Explain a second teaching.**	*Secondly, the Trinity helps Catholics to experience each person of God.*
● Develop your explanation with more detail/an example.	*These three persons help Catholics to understand God's presence on earth.*
● **Or:** Add a reference to a source of wisdom and authority here.	

TIP
Remember, you don't need the chapter and verse when quoting a source of wisdom and authority, as long as it is accurate, specific, and clearly recognisable.

2 Explain **two** ways the Creation account helps Catholics understand the nature of God. In your answer you must refer to a source of wisdom and authority. **(5 marks)**

● **Explain one way.**	
● Develop your explanation with more detail/an example.	
● **Either:** Add a reference to a source of wisdom and authority here.	
● **Explain a second way.**	
● Develop your explanation with more detail/an example.	
● **Or:** Add a reference to a source of wisdom and authority here.	

TIP
You could talk about God as creator, and God as omnipotent. Can you make an explicit link to Genesis 1–2 or the Creed?

TIP
Remember, these questions need a source of wisdom and authority to be included in the answer. It can't be simply a development – it must be an additional point.

TIP
If you can include a source of wisdom and authority for both ways, you give yourself the best chance of achieving full marks, but it is not compulsory.

3 Explain **two** ways the Paschal Mystery demonstrates God's grace. In your answer you must refer to a source of wisdom and authority. **(5 marks)**

Test the 15 mark question (d)

1 'The nature of humanity makes humans superior in Creation.'
Evaluate this statement considering arguments for and against.
In your response you should:
- refer to Catholic teachings
- refer to different Christian points of view
- reach a justified conclusion.

TIP

In a 15 mark question 3 of the marks available are awarded for correct spelling, punctuation, and grammar. You should check your answer thoroughly.

(15 marks)

ARGUMENTS IN SUPPORT OF THE STATEMENT	
• **Explain why some people would agree with the statement.** • Develop your explanation with more detail and examples. • Refer to religious teaching. Use a quote or paraphrase of a religious authority. • **Evaluate the arguments.** Is this a good argument? Explain why you think this. Use words such as convincing/strong/robust/weak/unpersuasive/unsuccessful within your reasoning.	Genesis 1:26 makes it very clear that humans are indeed superior in Creation, as they are granted dominion. The fact that they were created last shows that they are the most important part of the Creation process. According to Catholic belief, dominion means that they have the authority to rule, however the nature of the world as a garden suggests this should be a loving cultivation and care. A strength of the Catholic line of argument is that humans have free will and reason, which is a key indicator of their superiority. **TIP** This student has used words and phrases like 'on the other hand' and 'however' to show a logical chain of reasoning.
ARGUMENTS SUPPORTING A DIFFERENT VIEW	
• **Explain why some people would support a different view.** • Develop your explanation with more detail and examples. • Refer to religious teaching. Use a quote or paraphrase of a religious authority. • **Evaluate the arguments.** Is this a good argument? Explain why you think this. Use words such as convincing/strong/robust/weak/unpersuasive/unsuccessful within your reasoning.	On the other hand, this can cause conflict within Christianity as a whole, as a superior domination, over stewardship, leads to some minority Christians not caring for the environment. This approach does not take both principles (dominion and stewardship) from the Bible into account, however. Most non-religious groups would have similar views to many Catholics on care of the environment. They believe that it should be protected, but not as God's creation, just that it is in the best interests of humanity. However they may not believe that humans are superior, and see an equality in nature. **TIP** This student has gone beyond the demands of the question in referring to non-religious views.
CONCLUSION	
• **Give a justified conclusion.** • Include your own reasoning. • Use words such as convincing/strong/robust/weak/unpersuasive/unsuccessful to weigh up the different arguments for and against. • Do not just repeat arguments you have used without explaining how they apply to your reasoned opinion/conclusion.	In conclusion, I agree with the Catholic view that both dominion and stewardship are important because otherwise creation is not properly cared for and the environment will be damaged in the long term. The minority Christian argument seems to be weaker as it does not weigh up both biblical principles. **TIP** This student has justified their conclusion – they have given a reason why they came to their conclusion.

Exam Practice

2 'Belief in hell is very important.' Evaluate this statement considering arguments for and against.
In your response you should:

- refer to Catholic teachings
- refer to different Christian points of view
- reach a justified conclusion.

(15 marks)

> **TIP**
> Ensure you are clear on the exact Catholic teachings on eschatology.

ARGUMENTS IN SUPPORT OF THE STATEMENT ● **Explain why some people would agree with the statement.** ● Develop your explanation with more detail and examples. ● Refer to religious teaching. Use a quote or paraphrase of a religious authority. ● **Evaluate the arguments.** Is this a good argument? Explain why you think this. Use words such as convincing/strong/robust/weak/unpersuasive/unsuccessful within your reasoning.	
ARGUMENTS SUPPORTING A DIFFERENT VIEW ● **Explain why some people would support a different view.** ● Develop your explanation with more detail and examples. ● Refer to religious teaching. Use a quote or paraphrase of a religious authority. ● **Evaluate the arguments.** Is this a good argument? Explain why you think this. Use words such as convincing/strong/robust/weak/unpersuasive/unsuccessful within your reasoning.	
CONCLUSION ● **Give a justified conclusion.** ● Include your own reasoning. ● Use words such as convincing/strong/robust/weak/unpersuasive/unsuccessful to weigh up the different arguments for and against. ● Do not just repeat arguments you have already used without explaining how they apply to your reasoned opinion/conclusion.	

> **TIP**
> Remember that in order to access more marks you must consider different viewpoints within the religious tradition as instructed by the question.

3 'The Incarnation of Jesus is the most important Catholic belief.'
Evaluate this statement considering arguments for and against.
In your response you should:

- refer to Catholic teachings
- reach a justified conclusion.

(15 marks)

> **TIP**
> Of course, Incarnation is an important belief, so for this question, consider alternative Catholic beliefs as most important.

 **REVIEW**

- Check your answers to these exam questions on p.188, correct your answers with annotations, and note down any general areas for improvement.
- If you don't feel secure in the content of this chapter, you could reread the Recap sections.
- If you don't feel secure in your exam technique, you could revisit the exam support section on pp.7–14.

2.1 The sacramental nature of reality

RECAP

Essential information

- A **sacrament** is a religious ritual performed in the life of the Church that brings people into holiness. There are seven sacraments.
- The 'sacramental nature of reality' means finding the grace of God in the physical world.
- Each sacrament brings Catholics closer to God in a different way.

What is a sacrament?

Visible or accessible to the senses

The Catholic Church believes Christ introduced the seven sacraments

God's life, presence, or holiness

❝ An outward sign of an inward gift, instituted by Christ, in order to give grace to a human being. ❞

	Sacrament	What happens? *It is worth looking at the symbolism in the words and actions that take place.*	Why is it important? *This is the grace it bestows and the effect it has on Catholics.*	Source of wisdom *These are not listed on the specification but they may be useful in justifying the importance of the sacrament.*
Initiation	**Baptism** The ceremony that welcomes a person into the family of God	• Parents and godparents say vows. • Priest pours water over infant's head in the name of the Father, and of the Son, and of the Holy Spirit (Trinity). • Infant is anointed with Oil of Chrism. • Infant receives white garment and candle lit from Paschal Candle.	• Person becomes a son/daughter of God and member of the Church, taking on a new identity in Christ. • Person is freed from original sin, by sharing in the new life that comes from the Paschal Mystery. • Person receives strength from God to continue Jesus' mission.	'Go therefore and make disciples of all nations, baptising them…' (*Matthew 28:19*)
	Confirmation Receiving the Gifts of the Holy Spirit to encourage a faithful life; literally confirming (Latin for 'strengthening') the faith	• Candidates renew their baptismal promises. • They are anointed with Oil of Chrism: 'Be sealed with the Gift of the Holy Spirit'. • They take a new name.	• It strengthens faith ready to become a mature, active Catholic. • Candidates receive the Seven Gifts of the Holy Spirit.	'the Holy Spirit, whom the Father will send in my name, he will teach you all things' (*John 14:26*)
	Eucharist Receiving the body and blood of Christ	• Bread and wine are transformed into the body and blood by the priest. • It is received weekly or even daily. • Preparation is undertaken (catechesis) before receiving it for the first time.	• Receiving the real presence of Christ in a physical way. • Uniting the Catholic community through the Mass.	'This is my body… This is my blood' (*Mark 14:22, 24*) The 'Sacrament of sacraments' (*CCC 1211*) 'The source and summit of the Christian life' (*CCC 1324*)
Healing	**Reconciliation** The forgiveness of sins	• Contrition: genuine repentance for sins. • Confession: admitting to the sins. • Absolution: forgiveness from God. • Penance: act to show repentance.	• Removes spiritual illness of sin. • Restores relationship with God and community. • Offers mercy, forgiveness, and advice to the penitent. • Sins are forgiven.	'When he had said this, he breathed on them, and said to them, "Receive the Holy Spirit. If you forgive the sins of any, they are forgiven; if you retain the sins of any, they are retained"' (*John 20:22–23*)
	Anointing of the sick Healing and forgiveness of sins in preparation for the journey into the next life	• Priest lays hands on person who is ill or near death. • Sins are absolved. • Anointing with oil takes place. • Viaticum (Eucharist – 'food for the journey') is given.	• Gives strength in sickness and suffering. • Prepares an individual for death. • Shows God's presence and love throughout their life.	The disciples 'cast out many demons, and anointed with oil many that were sick and healed them'. (*Mark 6:13*)

Vocation				
Matrimony The joining together of two people as one in marriage 	• Solemn promises (vows) made. • Exchange of rings. • Signing of register (legal part of ceremony).	• Two people give themselves permanently and exclusively. This is the only sacrament in which the people give the sacrament to each other. • They are then open to the possibility of procreation and new life. God is present through the couple's lifelong love and commitment.	'So they are no longer two but one. What therefore God has joined together, let not man put asunder.' (*Matthew 19:6*)
Holy Orders The giving of a distinct mission within the Church	• Laying on of hands. • Prayer of consecration. • Given paten and chalice to celebrate the Eucharist. • Bishop is given mitre, ring, and pastoral staff.	• Priesthood establishes Christ's presence throughout the ages in the sacraments, above all the 'Sacrament of sacraments', the Eucharist (*CCC 1211*).	'And he appointed twelve, to be with him, and to be sent out to preach' (*Mark 3:14*) 'Do this in remembrance of me' (*Luke 22:19*). Following on from the Institution of the Eucharist by Jesus

The sacramental nature of reality

- This means finding the grace of God in the physical world.
- God is invisible but can communicate with humans through everything he has created, for example: bread, wine, water, oil, words, hands upon the head, songs, gestures, movements, books, debates, buildings, music, work, love, sport.

Divergent attitudes

- Not all Christians recognise seven sacraments (see table below). Not recognising a sacrament means they do not believe it was instituted by Jesus – but they might still perform it (e.g. marriage might be carried out in all denominations, but only considered a sacrament by some).
- Not all Christians believe the sacraments are a communication of God's grace, but rather they are expressions of faith.

Is it a sacrament?							
	Baptism	**Confirmation**	**Eucharist**	**Reconciliation**	**Anointing of the Sick**	**Matrimony**	**Holy Orders**
Catholic	✓	✓	✓	✓	✓	✓	✓
Orthodox	✓	✓	✓	✓	✓	✓	✓
Most Protestant Christians (including Church of England, Pentecostal)	✓	✗	✓	✗	✗	✗	✗
Some Protestant Christians (including Quaker, Salvation Army)	✗	✗	✗	✗	✗	✗	✗

APPLY

TIP
Remember, don't just give one-word answers to an 'outline' question. Write a short sentence for each point you make.

(AO1) In an (a) question, you could be asked to outline the key features of any of the seven sacraments. This is quite a challenge! Use the table on pp.28–29 to help you prepare answers to the following question. Can you write three short sentences about each sacrament?

a. Outline **three** key features of _____. (3)

(AO2) Create a basic plan for an answer to the following exam question, by answering each of the five questions underneath.

d. 'The seven sacraments should be recognised by all Christians.' Evaluate this statement considering arguments for and against. In your response you should:
- refer to Catholic teachings
- refer to different Christian points of view
- reach a justified conclusion. (12)
  1. Which Christians **do** participate in all seven sacraments?
  2. WHY?
  3. Any sources of wisdom and authority to back it up?
  4. Which Christians **do not** participate in all seven sacraments?
  5. WHY?

REVIEW

Answers: Mark your answers using p.188 and note areas for improvement.
AO1: This question is testing your ability to recall information. For help with this skill, see p.12.
AO2: This question is testing your ability to break down the question and plan a response. For help with this skill, see p.12.

RECAP

Essential information

- **Liturgical worship** is the structured public service of worship in Catholic churches.
- In the Eucharist, Catholics encounter Jesus, and remember his sacrifice.
- The Eucharist helps Catholics worship God and be given his grace.

What is liturgical worship?

- Structured, public service of worship.
- Set out by the Catholic Church.
- Humans take part in the work of God.
- Helps Catholics grow in holiness and be saved from sin.

What is the Mass?

- **Mass** (central act of worship) is celebrated nearly every day in the Catholic Church (not on Good Friday, or on Easter Saturday before the Vigil). Catholics are expected to attend Mass weekly.
- There are four main parts of the Mass:

Introductory Rites Gathering, Greeting, Penitential Rite, Gloria, Collect	Liturgy of the Word	Liturgy of the Eucharist	Concluding Rites
• Community around Jesus formed • Call to mind sins and ask forgiveness in preparation for receiving the Eucharist	• Readings from the Old and New Testaments including the Gospels • Homily (commentary on the meaning of God's Word) • Nicene Creed (Sundays and feast days) • Prayers of Intercession	• Meeting Jesus • Bread and wine are brought to the altar • Eucharistic prayer transforms these by the power of the Holy Spirit • This becomes the actual body and blood of Jesus (transubstantiation) • Received by the congregation	• The priest greets, blesses, and sends out the people to build the Kingdom of God

The place of the Eucharist

Jesus began the celebration of the Eucharist at the Last Supper. He said, 'Do this in remembrance of me' (*1 Corinthians 11:24*). From the earliest of times, Christians have gathered and broken bread in Jesus' name.

Lumen Gentium makes clear that consuming the Eucharist:

- makes individuals part of Jesus' body, the Church
- makes Catholics part of one another
- creates the Church, the Body of Christ.

> 66 …in the breaking of the Eucharistic bread, we are taken up into communion with Him and with one another. 99 (*Lumen Gentium*)

Divergent Christian attitudes to liturgical worship

Catholic	Some Protestant	Other Protestant
Mass: • Structured • Ordered • Signs and symbols link back to Apostolic Tradition • Transub-stantiation	Eucharistic service: • Similar structure to Catholic Mass • Eucharist is important but does not have same meaning, i.e. the bread and wine are symbolic	Eucharistic service: • Is symbolic • Less structured worship, which many believe is important for a less restricted connection with God • May include spontaneous involvement from members • Varied music

All Christian groups recognise the importance of God's Word in the Bible and sharing that in community.

APPLY

TIP
Make sure there are 'links' in your chain by using words like 'additionally', 'however', 'therefore', 'finally'.

AO1 Answer this question with two developed points, adding one of the quotations from the Catechism of the Catholic Church as your source of wisdom and authority.

c. Explain **two** reasons why Catholics consider the Eucharist to be the most important sacrament. In your answer you must refer to a source of wisdom and authority. (5)

AO2 The marking criteria for this question type encourage students to show a 'chain of reasoning'. Try to complete these six sentences, and then consider how you would order them into a 'chain'.

d. 'Worship should always be formal in structure.' (12)

- The Catholic Church believes…
- The Catholic belief is based upon…
- Additionally…
- However, in other Christian Churches…
- This is appealing to Christians who…
- Finally…

REVIEW

Answers: Mark your answers using p.188 and note areas for improvement.
AO1: This question is testing your ability to explain beliefs correctly using a source of wisdom and authority. For help with this skill, see p.22.
AO2: This question is testing your ability to organise and clearly signpost an answer. For help with this skill, see p.22.

 **RECAP**

What is a compare and contrast question?

There are a few areas of the exam specification where you can be asked to compare and contrast two religions, or two groups within a religion. For example, you might get asked to compare Catholic Christianity with other Christian denominations, or you might be asked to compare Christianity with a second religion, such as Judaism or Islam.

In this paper, Paper 1, you will only be asked to compare Catholic Christianity with other Christian denominations, and you will only be asked to compare them on two possible topics: eschatology (see p.23) and worship. Here, you can revise for worship.

How is worship different for Catholics and other Christians?

	Catholics	Other Christians
Liturgical/ non-liturgical	• The Mass has a formal and structured order to the liturgy. • The Mass contains signs and symbols linking back to Apostolic Tradition and the teachings of the Bible and magisterium. • As part of the Mass, the Nicene Creed is recited by the people. • Other forms of popular piety extend, but do not replace, the Mass. • The priest, or other clergy, leads the Mass.	• The Church of England has a book of Common Prayer to guide worship. • Some Christians, such as evangelical Christians, believe formal liturgy can restrict or inhibit a Christian's connection to God. • The Nicene Creed is recited less often in Protestant churches, and sometimes not at all. • Some Christians feel spontaneous involvement from the congregation, guided by the Bible and Holy Spirit, can help them connect to God.
Importance of Eucharist	• Celebration of the Eucharist is the 'source and summit' and 'Sacrament of sacraments' (*CCC 1324, 1211*). • Catholics believe they receive the actual body and blood of Christ (transubstantiation). • Eucharistic adoration – where Catholics adore the presence of Jesus in the bread and wine.	• Some Christians do not see one form of worship as superior to others; they believe there are equal ways to communicate with and praise God. • Some Christians do not celebrate the Eucharist. • Protestants do not believe the bread and wine transform to become the body and blood of Jesus. • The Eucharist is believed to be symbolic.

APPLY

You could be asked to compare and contrast in (b) questions (but being able to talk about different viewpoints within Christianity is also a useful skill in (d) questions!) For example, here's a question you could be asked:

b. Describe **two** differences in forms of worship between Catholic Christianity and other forms of the main religious tradition of Great Britain. (4)

Here is an example of how you could structure an answer to this question:

● Give one form of worship in Catholic Christianity.	*The first difference is that in Catholic worship the Eucharist is central, with communion offered at Mass,*
● Give a contrasting form of worship elsewhere in Christianity.	*whereas some other Christians do not celebrate the Eucharist at all.*
● Give a second form of worship in Catholic Christianity.	*Secondly, in Catholic Christianity worship follows a strict pattern and includes structured liturgy*
● Give a contrasting form of worship elsewhere in Christianity.	*yet for other evangelical Christian traditions worship is more charismatic, focusing on the Bible and guidance from the Holy Spirit.*

TIP
Remember, when the exam says 'the main religious tradition of Great Britain', it is referring to Christianity.

TIP
Words like 'whereas', 'yet', and 'however' will signal to the examiner that you're making a comparison.

Now have a go at answering the same question yourself, using the grid below to help you. Try to choose **different** points from those given in the table to the left.

● Give one form of worship in Catholic Christianity.	● Give a second form of worship in Catholic Christianity.
The first difference is that in Catholic worship...	*Secondly, in Catholic Christianity...*
● Give a contrasting form of worship elsewhere in Christianity.	● Give a contrasting form of worship elsewhere in Christianity.
Whereas in other Christian traditions...	*Yet for other Christians...*

RECAP

Essential information

- For Catholics, life on earth is a journey towards eternal life with God.
- The funeral rite refers to the ceremonies carried out when a Catholic dies.
- The community comes together to pray for the deceased and remember that they share in eternal life.

Liturgical celebration

- The funeral rite is a liturgy. It has formal practices set out by the Church.
- Although sorrowful, a Catholic funeral is also seen as a celebration because the individual has begun their journey to eternal life:

> 66 I look forward to the resurrection of the dead and the life of the world to come 99 (*The Nicene Creed*)

Practices in the home, church, and cemetery

The home		In Ireland it is common to have a Vigil of Prayer in the home (time spent awake to keep watch or to pray). This may take place in the church if the body is laid out the night before.
The church		Requiem Mass (Mass to remember someone who has died) or just a Liturgy of the Word. Most priests encourage Mass so that the Eucharist is celebrated.
The cemetery		Rite of Committal and Commendation takes place at the cemetery or crematorium. People say their goodbyes with hope in their hearts that they will meet again in the next life.

'Preparing my funeral' by Cardinal Vincent Nichols

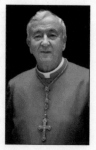

- Encourages those approaching death to plan their funeral:
  - Which readings?
  - Which hymns?
  - Vigil of Prayer the night before?
- The aim is also advice and support.

> 66 Our great hope is that we will be redeemed from death by Christ's great victory 99 (*'Preparing my funeral', by Cardinal Vincent Nichols*)

The aims of the funeral rite

Communion with the deceased: to support the deceased person on their journey into the next life with efficacious prayer (prayer to help and encourage the deceased person).
Significance: Catholics are reassured that they can support the deceased after death, and forgive them for any wrongdoing.

Communion of the community: to show how the people gathered are still connected to the deceased person in the Church, the Body of Christ.
Significance: Catholics are reassured they remain in connection with one another through prayer and the Eucharist.

Proclamation of eternal life to the community: to remind people that death is not the end of life but the passage from this world to life with God.
Significance: Catholics are given hope for the future and can refocus on their own life and priorities.

APPLY

(AO1) Answer the following question. There are three points you could select from the above table. Select two that you could write about in your own words.

b. Explain **two** reasons why the funeral rite is important to Catholics. (4)

(AO2) Answer this question on your own!

d. 'Funeral rites are for the benefit of the living not just the dead'. Evaluate this statement considering arguments for and against.
In your response you should:
- refer to Catholic teachings
- reach a justified conclusion. (12)

TIP
Remember to use **connectives** to ensure both of your points are fully developed. Examples of connectives include: because, and, this means that, therefore.

REVIEW

Answers: Mark your answers using p.188 and note areas for improvement.
AO1: This question is testing your ability to select appropriate information. For help with this skill, see p.12.

 **RECAP**

Essential information
- **Prayer** is communication with God.
- Catholics should pray regularly with both formal and informal prayer.
- The **Lord's Prayer** is the prayer that Jesus gave to his disciples.

What is prayer?

Prayer is 'The raising of one's mind and heart to God' (*CCC 2559*). It can be:

- private or public
- carried out silently or with words
- carried out alone or with others
- speaking to God (active) or listening to God (receptive).

Different types of prayer and their importance

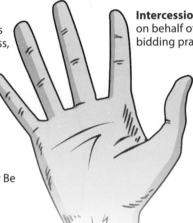

Repentance: Acknowledging their sins and asking for forgiveness, e.g. the I Confess

Intercession: Praying on behalf of others, e.g. bidding prayers at Mass

Thanksgiving: Expressing love and gratitude to God, e.g. Grace before meals

Petition: Asking God for your own personal needs, e.g. a prayer before an exam

Adoration: God is God, e.g. the Glory Be

Formal and extempore prayer

Type of prayer	Why would it be used?
Formal prayer: Formulaic, words from the Church's tradition	Connection to the history of the Church, uniting with other Catholics.
Extempore prayer: Informal, using one's own words, without planning	Moments of great need, helping develop a personal relationship with God.

The Lord's Prayer (the 'Our Father')

In Matthew 6, Jesus teaches his disciples some key principles about prayer:

- It is not for show and shouldn't use empty words. It should be heartfelt and sincere and should seek a deeper relationship with God.

Then, Jesus teaches them the Lord's Prayer:

> 66 Our Father who art in heaven, hallowed by thy name. Thy kingdom come, thy will be done, on earth as it is in heaven. Give us this day our daily bread; and forgive us our debts, as we also have forgiven our debtors; and lead us not into temptation, but deliver us from evil. 99
> (*Matthew 6:9–13*)

The Lord's Prayer:

- is believed by Catholics to be 'the most perfect of prayers' (*CCC 2763*)
- reminds Catholics to honour God, to ask for what they need each day, and to repent and forgive others
- unites all Christians and states key Christian beliefs.

Why is it important to have different types of prayer?

- Different stages of life.
- Different needs and moments – sometimes private, other times public.
- Different locations – at home, in church, at work.
- Different moods or feelings.

 **APPLY**

TIP
Use the hand diagram above to help you with this question. Try to use your own words.

(AO1) Answer the following exam question. One point has already been made for you.

a. Outline **three** types of prayer for Catholics. (3)

> One type is giving thanks to God for his blessings.

(AO2) Starting your answer with a conclusion can help give your essay a strong, clear line of argument. An example is given here, along with a follow-up point. Complete both points.

d. 'Daily prayer is the most important part of Catholic life.' Evaluate this statement considering arguments for and against. In your response you should:
- refer to Catholic teachings
- reach a justified conclusion. (12)

> For Catholics, daily prayer is naturally an essential part of life. This is because...
>
> Some may claim that attending Mass on a Sunday is more important, however....

 **REVIEW**

Answers: Mark your answers using p.188 and note areas for improvement.
AO1: This question is testing your ability to answer 'outline' questions. For help with this skill, see p.12.
AO2: This question is testing your ability to begin an essay with a strong line of argument. For help with this skill, see p.12.

 **RECAP**

Essential information

- **Popular piety** is worship that is not part of the formal liturgy of the Church.
- Forms of popular piety are encouraged by the Church and help Catholics pray in different ways.

What is popular piety?

- Popular piety is worship that does not follow a strict pattern set out by the Church (it is **non-liturgical**).
- Examples include the Rosary (prayer using a string of beads), **Eucharistic adoration** (worship of the presence of Jesus in the bread and wine), and the **Stations of the Cross** (prayers that honour the suffering and death of Jesus).
- The Catechism supports liturgical and non-liturgical worship, but popular piety should not replace Church liturgy:

> ❝These expressions of piety **extend** the liturgical life of the Church, but **do not replace it**❞ (CCC 1675)

> ❝the religious sense of the Christian people has always found expression in the various forms of piety ... the stations of the cross, religious dances, the rosary, medals, etc.❞ (CCC 1674)

 TIP
This source of wisdom and authority would be a useful one to learn for (c) and (d) questions about popular piety and non-liturgical/ liturgical worship.

TIP
If you visit a church building, look around to see what you can see that may be used for prayer outside the formal liturgy of the Church.

The Rosary, Stations of the Cross and Eucharistic adoration

	Description	Significance	Divergent views
The Rosary	• Used in private prayer at home, in church, walking from one place to another, in front of a statue of Mary, evening before a funeral, preparation for Mass. • The person will pray focusing on the 'Mysteries of the Rosary', which are key events in Jesus' life. • Beads help the person count the prayers.	• Meditation on the grace of God, focus on different parts of Jesus' life, honouring Mary.	• Most other Christians do not use the Rosary as it is connected to the elevated status of Mary. They do not share many Catholic beliefs about Mary's significance in prayer and worship.
Stations of the Cross	• 14 stations around the walls of a Catholic church honour the suffering and death of Jesus. • Usually consist of a cross and image showing a scene from Jesus' Passion and death. • People move between them with different prayers, meditations, and reflections.	• Link Catholics to the sites of Jesus' death and suffering in Jerusalem that were visited by early Christians; reminder of Jesus' suffering, but also of the salvation they share in.	• Most Protestants do not use the Stations of the Cross, although they do regularly meditate on the suffering of Jesus. There are also fewer images and statues in many Protestant churches. Some Christians may object to the stations as some of the scenes are not based on the Bible.
Eucharistic adoration	• Adoration in front of the Blessed Sacrament (the real presence of Jesus in the consecrated bread and wine). • Usually placed in a monstrance (a decorative frame).	• Focusing of prayer. Link to Jesus when he commanded his disciples to 'watch and pray' in Gethsemane.	• As Protestant Christians do not believe the bread and wine transform to become the body and blood of Jesus, they do not believe it is his real presence, so would not carry out Eucharistic adoration.

The Blessed Sacrament in a monstrance

Rosary beads

One of the Stations of the Cross

Why is it important to have different types of worship?

- Different ways of doing the same thing: connecting Catholics to God through prayer.
- Certain forms focus more on praying in community, others on praying individually.

TIP
Learn in detail the difference between formal and informal worship and be able to give examples.

APPLY

AO1 This student's answer is a bit jumbled. Can you rewrite it into two clear points?

c. Explain **two** benefits of the forms of popular piety for Catholic Christians. In your answer you must refer to a source of wisdom and authority. (5)

> Jesus' suffering and death are retold in each of the four Gospels. The Stations of the Cross are used as a reminder of this. Also in the church, the Blessed Sacrament might be put out for people to pray in front of. The stations help Catholics reflect on the suffering of Jesus, maybe helping in their time of need. Adoration is beneficial as Catholics pray in front of the physical body of Jesus.

AO2 Complete the following table to help you plan an answer to this exam question. Try to include convincing arguments as to why Catholics would use each form, and then a possible reason why other Christians might not.

d. 'All Christians should use forms of popular piety.' Evaluate this statement considering arguments for and against. In your reponse you should:
- refer to Catholic teachings
- refer to different Christian points of view
- reach a justified conclusion. (12)

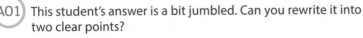

	The Rosary	Stations of the Cross	Eucharistic adoration
Catholics			
Other Christians' view			

REVIEW

Answers: Mark your answers using p.189 and note areas for improvement.
AO1: This question is testing your ability to organise and clearly signpost your writing. For help with this skill, see p.12.
AO2: This question is testing your ability to plan a response. For help with this skill, see p.12.

 **RECAP**

Essential information

- A **pilgrimage** is a journey to a special place of religious significance.
- It is usually connected to the lives of Jesus, Mary, apostles, or saints.
- Examples include Lourdes, Rome, Walsingham, and Jerusalem.

The nature, history, and purpose of pilgrimage

- ~40 CE: people started visiting Bethlehem.
- 4th century: pilgrimage to Jerusalem and Holy Land common, churches built at key sites.
- 4th century: pilgrimage to Rome also began to visit sites including tombs of SS Peter and Paul.
- 16th century: many places of pilgrimage destroyed as part of the Reformation in Europe.
- 19th century: resurgence in pilgrimage as transport improved.

Why pilgrimage is important for some Christians today

- Provides time and space for prayer.
- Connection to other Christians.
- Allows Christian to 'journey' closer to God.
- Response to busy life and world.

The significance of places of pilgrimage

Types	Examples	Significance
Life of Jesus	Holy Land	Pray at sites important in Jesus' life, understand the Gospel better
Mary	Lourdes in France, Fatima in Portugal, Knock in Ireland, Guadalupe in Mexico	Places where Mary has appeared, miraculous occurrences
Apostles	Santiago de Compostela in Spain, St Peter's in the Vatican	Connection to key saints
Other saints	Croagh Patrick in Ireland, Basilica of St Francis of Assisi in Italy	Personal devotion to particular saints
Ecumenical	Walsingham in the UK, Taizé in France	Bringing people of different Christian denominations together
Spiritual	Iona and Buckfast Abbey in the UK	Retreat and prayer

❝ Pilgrimages evoke our earthly journey toward heaven and are traditionally very special occasions for renewal in prayer. **❞** (*CCC 2691*)

Key sites: divergent Christian understandings

	Jerusalem	Rome	Lourdes	Walsingham
Description	Place of Jesus' death and resurrection	Centre of the Catholic Church; home of the Pope	Mary appeared to Bernadette 18 times in 1858; many healings have taken place	In 1061 a noblewoman had three visions of the house where the angel Gabriel visited Mary and built a replica here
Divergent views	A common place of pilgrimage for all Christians as it is based on life of Jesus	As they do not recognise the authority of the Pope, non-Catholic Christians do not regard Rome with the same importance	Mainly a place of Catholic pilgrimage as other Christians do not elevate Mary in the way Catholics do	There are both Catholic and Church of England shrines here

Some Protestant denominations do not place as much emphasis on pilgrimage. While journeying and praying for the sake of God is something they might encourage, pilgrimage is not considered by them to be a central part of Christian life.

 **APPLY**

AO1 In 'outline' questions it is tempting to give one-word answers, but you actually need to write a more complete point. Could you improve this answer?

a. Outline **three** reasons why a Christian would go on pilgrimage. (3)

> To worship...   Illness...   It's not just the journey...

AO2 Read the planning notes in the table. Then, have a go at writing a **justified conclusion** for this essay.

d. 'Going on pilgrimage is vitally important for Christians today.' Evaluate this statement considering arguments for and against. In your response you should:

- refer to Catholic teachings
- refer to different Christian points of view
- reach a justified conclusion. (12)

Important	Barriers to pilgrimage	Not important
• Gets closer to God • Meets other Christians • Seeks healing (spiritual or physical) • Wants connection with saints	• Great expense • Ill health	• Protestant Christians do not see it as a religious requirement • Not all sites have the same significance for Christians

 **REVIEW**

Answers: Mark your answers using p.189 and note areas for improvement.
AO1: This question is testing your ability to answer 'outline' questions. For help with this skill, see p.12.
AO2: This question is testing your ability to write a justified conclusion. For help with this skill, see p.12.

 **RECAP**

Essential information
- The Church works universally for the love of neighbour as well as love of God.
- Catholic Social Teaching promotes justice, peace, and reconciliation.
- CAFOD is a Catholic charity working in England and Wales to help those overseas.

Love of neighbour

Jesus taught that people should love their neighbour:

> ❝Love your neighbour as yourself❞ (*Mark 12:31*)
> ❝Go and do likewise❞ (*Luke 10:37*) [Good Samaritan]

The Catholic Church gives seven themes to its Social Teaching:

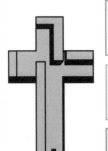

1. Sacredness of life and the dignity of the human person

2. Call to family, community, and participation

3. Human rights and the responsibility to protect them

4. Preferential option for the poor and vulnerable

5. Dignity of work and the rights of workers

6. Solidarity with all people as one family

7. Stewardship and care for God's creation

Justice, peace, and reconciliation

Catholic Social Teaching is concerned with how society should provide:

- **Justice:** promoting justice and eliminating or limiting injustice
- **Peace:** encouraging harmony among all human beings; preventing or resolving war and conflict
- **Reconciliation:** protecting the dignity and rights of the human person wherever they may be.

> ❝The mere fact that some people are born in places with fewer resources or less development does not justify the fact that they are living with less dignity❞ (*Evangelii Gaudium Ch4:190*)

Actions of individual Catholics

Catholics can show love of neighbour through the following:

- **Corporal (bodily) works of mercy:** for example, feeding the hungry, sheltering the homeless, visiting the sick.
- **Spiritual works of mercy:** for example, comforting the sorrowful, forgiving offences, praying for people.

These are influenced by the Parable of the Sheep and Goats:

> 'The King will answer them, "Truly I say to you, as you did it to one of the least of my brethren, you did it to me."' (*Matthew 25:40*)

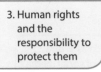

Global neighbours fighting injustice and poverty

Rooted in the Catholic Community

Working for social justice

CAFOD (Catholic Agency for Overseas Development)

Raising awareness and educating Catholics

Helping people to help themselves

There in a crisis: short-term or emergency aid such as after a natural disaster

Facing the toughest challenges e.g. war

TIP
Two key sources in this topic are the Good Samaritan (*Luke 10:25–37*) and the Parable of the Sheep and Goats (*Matthew 25:31–46*). Can you summarise them in bullet points?

 **APPLY**

AO1 Answer the following exam question. Remember, use three full sentences!

a. Outline **three** ways CAFOD shows love of neighbour. (3)

AO2 Plan and write an answer to the following question from scratch.

d. 'Individual Catholics have a responsibility to live out Catholic Social Teaching in their daily lives.' Evaluate this statement considering arguments for and against. In your response you should:
- refer to Catholic teachings
- reach a justified conclusion. (12)

 **REVIEW**

Answers: Mark your answers using p.189 and note areas for improvement.
AO1: This question is testing your ability to answer 'outline' questions. For help with this skill, see p.12.
AO2: This question is testing your ability to plan and write an essay. For help with this skill, see p.12.

2.8 Catholic mission and evangelism

RECAP

Essential information

- Mission is the idea that a person is sent to others to help them, or bring them something of benefit.
- **Evangelism** (or 'evangelisation') is to proclaim and live out the Gospel.
- Jesus sent the apostles to go into the world to proclaim and live out the Gospel.

Mission and evangelism

A brief timeline of the Church's mission:

- God the Father sent the Son on a visible mission to save the world.
- Jesus sent the apostles into the world on a mission to 'make disciples of all nations' and baptise them (*Matthew 28:19*).

- The apostles and their successors continued to send people to continue this work – this is called evangelism.
- Missionaries continued to travel around the world sharing the Gospel:
  - 5th century: St Benedict helped bring Christianity to the Western world
  - 15th century: Catholicism taken to South America
  - 19th century: Catholicism taken to Africa.

- For Catholics, evangelism does *not* mean trying to convert people to the Christian faith.
- Instead, evangelism is about sharing and living out a message. People may wish to find out more, but that is a personal choice.

How does the Church engage in the new evangelisation?

Since Pope Paul VI's *Evangelii Nuntiandi* (1975) and Pope John Paul II's *Redemptoris Missio* (1990) there have been references to a 'new evangelisation' to the Western world (as opposed to evangelism in places that have not heard the Gospel before).

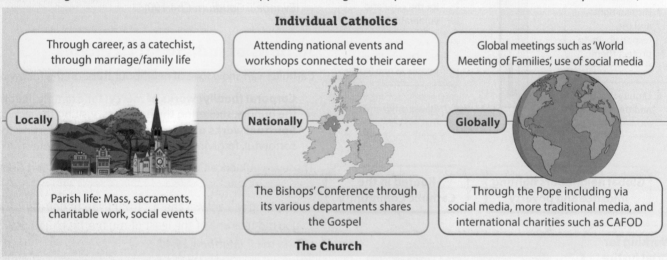

Individual Catholics

Locally	Nationally	Globally
Through career, as a catechist, through marriage/family life	Attending national events and workshops connected to their career	Global meetings such as 'World Meeting of Families', use of social media
Parish life: Mass, sacraments, charitable work, social events	The Bishops' Conference through its various departments shares the Gospel	Through the Pope including via social media, more traditional media, and international charities such as CAFOD

The Church

How about more traditional evangelisation?

Some people still undertake missionary work by travelling the world to spread the Gospel in their words and actions. They may travel to South America, Africa, or Asia, as missionaries have done for a long time. The Catholic Church still plays a vital role around the world in providing education, health care, and other services, often through religious orders.

APPLY

AO1 Can you add to these answers so that they are detailed enough for an 'outline' question?

a. Outline **three** ways the Church engages in evangelism. (3)

> Parish...
>
> Bishops' Conference...
>
> Social media...

AO2 Complete an essay plan for the following question. You could use the table opposite to help you.

d. 'Individual Catholics are better placed to evangelise than the Church.' Evaluate this statement considering arguments for and against. In your response you should:
- refer to Catholic teachings
- reach a justified conclusion. (12)

Individual Catholics are better placed	The Church is better placed

REVIEW

Answers: Mark your answers using p.189 and note areas for improvement.
AO1: This question is testing your ability to answer 'outline' questions. For help with this skill, see p.12.
AO2: This question is testing your ability to plan a response. For help with this skill, see p.12.

Test the 3 mark question (a)

1 Outline **three** practices associated with the Catholic funeral rite.   **(3 marks)**

The Vigil of the Deceased the night before, when the coffin is laid out in the church. (1)

The funeral liturgy, which might be a Requiem Mass. (1)

The Farewell or Commendation at the graveside or crematorium. (1)

2 Outline **three** features of the sacrament of reconciliation.   **(3 marks)**

The penitent confesses their sins. (1)

_____

_____

TIP
This answer includes the events before and after the actual funeral liturgy. This is permitted as the question asks for practices **associated** with the rite.

3 Outline **three** reasons why Catholics pray.   **(3 marks)**

_____

_____

_____

Test the 4 mark question (b)

1 Explain **two** forms of popular piety.   **(4 marks)**

• **Explain one form.**	*One form of popular piety is when Catholics pray using the Rosary,*
• Develop your explanation with more detail/an example/reference to a religious teaching.	*which can be used in different situations to meditate on events from Jesus' life.*
• **Explain a second form.**	*Another form is when Catholics take part in Eucharistic adoration in church*
• Develop your explanation with more detail/an example/reference to a religious teaching.	*where Catholics adore the presence of Jesus in the Blessed Sacrament.*

2 Explain **two** ways CAFOD demonstrates Catholic Social Teaching.   **(4 marks)**

• **Explain one way.**	
• Develop your explanation with more detail/an example/reference to a religious teaching.	
• **Explain a second way.**	
• Develop your explanation with more detail/an example/reference to a religious teaching.	

3 Explain **two** reasons why the Mass is so important for Catholics.   **(4 marks)**

TIP
Remember that the Mass is the 'source and summit' (CCC) for Catholics, it is the most important thing they do!

Exam Practice

Test the 5 mark question (c)

1 Explain **two** reasons why Catholics think it is important to show love of neighbour.
In your answer you must refer to a source of wisdom and authority.

(5 marks)

● **Explain one reason.**	Firstly, Catholic Social Teaching instructs Catholics to work for peace and justice.
● Develop your explanation with more detail/an example.	This means they show love for the poorest and most oppressed around the world.
● **Either:** Add a reference to a source of wisdom and authority here.	This teaching is reflected in the writings of Evangelii Gaudium.
● **Explain a second reason.**	Secondly, in the Parable of the Sheep and Goats it says that if someone helps anyone in need, they are caring for God himself,
● Develop your explanation with more detail/an example.	which means they should see the presence of God in all other human beings and show love to them as a neighbour.
● **Or:** Add a reference to a source of wisdom and authority here.	This is shown in Matthew 25:40: 'The King will answer them, "Truly I say to you, as you did it to one of the least of my brethren, you did it to me."'

> **TIP**
> Here, the student has referred to a second source of wisdom and authority. You are free to do this, though you are only required to refer to one.

> **TIP**
> In questions about love of neighbour, you could also talk about *Imago Dei*, or the Good Samaritan, to make links to wider areas of the course.

2 Explain **two** ways that the sacraments communicate God's grace to Catholics.
In your answer you must refer to a source of wisdom and authority.

(5 marks)

● **Explain one way.**	
● Develop your explanation with more detail/an example.	
● **Either:** Add a reference to a source of wisdom and authority here.	
● **Explain a second way.**	
● Develop your explanation with more detail/an example.	
● **Or:** Add a reference to a source of wisdom and authority here.	

> **TIP**
> 'Grace' is a difficult word. You might want to look it up in a dictionary, or reread the Recap section, to ensure you are clear on its meaning before answering this question.

3 Explain **two** reasons why Catholics believe evangelisation is important. In your answer you must refer to a source of wisdom and authority.

(5 marks)

Exam Practice

1 'Formal worship is central to the life of a Christian.' Evaluate this statement considering arguments for and against. In your response you should:

- refer to Catholic teachings
- reach a justified conclusion.

(12 marks)

ARGUMENTS IN SUPPORT OF THE STATEMENT	
• **Explain why some people would agree with the statement.** • Develop your explanation with more detail and examples. • Refer to religious teaching. Use a quote or paraphrase of a religious authority. • **Evaluate the arguments.** Is this a good argument? Explain why you think this. Use words such as convincing/strong/robust/weak/ unpersuasive/unsuccessful within your reasoning.	For Catholics formal worship or liturgy is clearly central to their lives. The Eucharist is 'the source and summit of the Christian life' (CCC/Lumen Gentium), which means it is a special source of grace. By receiving the Eucharist weekly, or even daily, Catholics believe their relationship with God is strengthened as they are receiving the actual body and blood of Christ. It also enables Catholics to join with all other Catholics in being the Body of Christ, the Church. The Church's teaching on formal worship is clear, and so is convincing to faithful Catholics.
ARGUMENTS SUPPORTING A DIFFERENT VIEW	
• **Explain why some people would disagree with the statement.** • Develop your explanation with more detail and examples. • Refer to religious teaching. Use a quote or paraphrase of a religious authority. • **Evaluate the arguments.** Is this a good argument? Explain why you think this. Use words such as convincing/strong/robust/weak/ unpersuasive/unsuccessful within your reasoning.	However, some Christians would argue that it is more important to participate in pilgrimage. They believe that God will judge based on actions rather than following rituals. They may feel popular piety is more important than attending Mass. They may also belong to a church that has a more informal worship that enables a closer relationship with God. There are diverse views within Christianity about what is most important, hence some Christians will not agree with Catholics.
CONCLUSION	
• **Give a justified conclusion.** • Include your own reasoning. • Use words such as convincing/ strong/robust/weak/unpersuasive/ unsuccessful to weigh up the different arguments for and against. • Do not just repeat arguments you have already used without explaining how they apply to your reasoned opinion/conclusion.	In conclusion, it may well depend on the teachings of the particular Christian Church you belong to. For Catholics, formal worship, in the Eucharist, is fundamental. This is made clear in the CCC. I find this argument more convincing.

2 'Mission is the most important activity in Catholic life.' Evaluate this statement considering arguments for and against. In your response you should:

- refer to Catholic teachings
- refer to different Christian points of view
- reach a justified conclusion.

(12 marks)

ARGUMENTS IN SUPPORT OF THE STATEMENT	Some Christians/Catholics/people would agree with this statement because...
● **Explain why some people would agree with the statement.** ● Develop your explanation with more detail and examples. ● Refer to religious teaching. Use a quote or paraphrase of a religious authority. ● **Evaluate the arguments.** Is this a good argument? Explain why you think this. Use words such as convincing/strong/robust/weak/unpersuasive/unsuccessful within your reasoning.	
ARGUMENTS SUPPORTING A DIFFERENT VIEW	On the other hand, some Christians/Catholics/people would hold a different point of view...
● **Explain why some people would disagree with the statement.** ● Develop your explanation with more detail and examples. ● Refer to religious teaching. Use a quote or paraphrase of a religious authority. ● **Evaluate the arguments.** Is this a good argument? Explain why you think this. Use words such as convincing/strong/robust/weak/unpersuasive/unsuccessful within your reasoning.	
CONCLUSION	Having considered both sides of the argument, I would say that...
● **Give a justified conclusion.** ● Include your own reasoning. ● Use words such as convincing/strong/robust/weak/unpersuasive/unsuccessful to weigh up the different arguments for and against. ● Do not just repeat arguments you have already used without explaining how they apply to your reasoned opinion/conclusion.	

TIP
It is vital to understand divergence – what do different Christians believe about mission?

TIP
Consider what else could be most important. What about prayer or the sacraments?

3 'Daily prayer is an essential part of life.' Evaluate this statement considering arguments for and against. In your response you should:

- refer to Catholic teachings
- reach a justified conclusion.

TIP
Remember there is formal daily prayer as well as informal prayers.

(12 marks)

 **REVIEW**

- Check your answers to these exam questions on p.189, correct your answers with annotations, and note down any general areas for improvement.

- If you don't feel secure in the content of this chapter, you could reread the Recap sections.

- If you don't feel secure in your exam technique, you could revisit the exam support section on pp.7–14.

 RECAP

Essential information

- The Bible is not one book, but a collection of many books, by many authors.
- The Old Testament contains a wide variety of literary styles that include law, history, prophecy, and poetry.
- The New Testament contains accounts of Jesus' life (the Gospels) as well as the letters documenting the growth of the early Church.

The origins, structure, and different literary forms of the Bible

- The Bible was written by approximately 40 authors.
- It was written across approximately 1500 years.
- It was written originally in three languages: Hebrew, Aramaic, and Greek.
- The books of the Hebrew Old Testament were written from around 1400 to 400 BCE.
- The books of the Greek New Testament were written from around 45 to 85 CE.

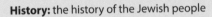

Old Testament
Law: includes the 613 commandments revealed to Moses
History: the history of the Jewish people
Prophets: prophecies are messages from God – often warnings and calls for repentance
Writings: the Poetic and Wisdom writings told stories, and educated about the nature of God, reality, and virtue

New Testament
Gospels: the 'Good News' telling the story of Jesus. For Catholics, 'The Gospels are the heart of all the Scriptures' (*CCC 125*)
Letters: formal letters to individuals and groups that document the development of the early Church
Revelation: a book that describes the end of the world ('apocalyptic')

Divergent content of the Bible

- Not all Christians recognise the same books of the Bible.
- The Catholic Bible includes seven deuterocanonical books that are not in the Protestant Bible.
- The inclusion of these seven books was affirmed at the Council of Trent in 1545.
- Some Eastern Orthodox Churches include additional scriptures that are not recognised by the Catholic Church.

TIP
Learn useful terms *canonical* and *deuterocanonical* and how to use them to express different views.

TIP
You shouldn't just list three books, nor just three types – you need to *outline*, which means you need to give a little more detail than simply one-word answers.

 APPLY

 (AO1) Answer the following exam question. One point has already been made for you.

a. Outline **three** features of the Old Testament. (3)

> *One feature is that it includes writings about the history of the Jewish people.*

 (AO2) Using the essay plan below, write a response to the following exam question. Try to really focus on accurate spelling, punctuation and grammar in your answer.

d. 'All Christians should use the same version of the Bible.' Evaluate this statement considering arguments for and against. In your response you should:

- refer to Catholic teachings
- refer to different Christian points of view
- reach a justified conclusion. (15)

Agree	Disagree
• The Church has added seven Deuterocanonical books for a reason.	• 'The Gospels are the heart of all the Scriptures' (*CCC 125*).
• Affirmed by Council of Trent in 1545.	• These books are rarely read or used by many Catholics.
• Helps understand period of history between Old Testament and New Testament.	• Many versions of the Bible don't include them.

 **REVIEW**

Answers: Mark your answers using p.190 and note areas for improvement.
AO1: This question is testing your ability to answer 'outline' questions. For help with this skill, see p.12.
AO2: This question is testing your ability to plan and write an essay. For help with this skill, see p.12.

 **RECAP**

Essential information
- The Bible is interpreted in different ways by different Christians.
- Some take it literally, others interpret it more liberally.
- Catholics believe the Bible is God's message in human words.

TIP
This perspective has links with 1.3 Creation. Creationists interpret the Creation accounts in a literal way.

Three different ways to interpret the Bible

The inspired Word of God	The literal Word of God	The liberal view
• This is the Catholic view: the Bible is the inspired Word of God, written down by human writers. • 'All scripture is inspired by God' (*2 Timothy 3:16*). • God is the primary author, as human authors were inspired by the Holy Spirit. • There is truth in the message of the Bible, e.g. God created the world, spoke through the prophets, came to earth as Jesus.	• Some Christians believe the Bible is true, word for word. • There are no mistakes, and it must be taken literally. • If there is a contradiction, this is deliberate and there is a reason for it. • If there is a contradiction with science, science must be wrong.	• Some Christians believe the Bible was written by humans who were inspired like any other writers. • The Bible contains spiritual, not literal truths. • The Bible invites closeness with God by sharing human experience. • There is much symbolism and poetry in the Bible, resulting in a range of beliefs. • Some parts of the Bible are outdated and irrelevant to modern life.

Noah's Ark is a tourist attraction located on Ma Wan Island, Hong Kong. Its overarching theme is a creationist narrative

A source of guidance and teaching
- Catholics do not read the Bible like any other book: reading is often a prayerful activity.
- It is meant to be read and understood as a whole text, with no part taken out of context.
- The tradition and teaching of the Church guide Catholics in how to interpret the Bible.
- The lectionary provides approved readings for use in worship and liturgy.
- Catholics are encouraged to read and study outside of Mass, and the Bible has many uses in the home: family prayers, readings after meals, children's books.
- It is a source of guidance and comfort in times of need.

The implications for Catholics today
- Most Catholics are not literalists and accept the teaching of science without rejecting the spiritual truths of Genesis.
- Faith in the Bible comes second to faith in Jesus.
- When interpreting the Bible, Catholics must consider the time and culture, the literary genres, and the different ways of communicating that are found in the Bible, with the guidance of the Holy Spirit (*CCC 110*).

TIP
2 Timothy 3:16 would be an ideal source to incorporate: 'All scripture is inspired by God.'

 APPLY

AO1 Answer the following exam question. Can your two points refer to two of the different ways of interpreting the Bible covered in this unit?

c. Explain **two** reasons why the Bible is believed to be the Word of God. In your answer you must refer to a source of wisdom and authority. (5)

> *Firstly, (literal)...*
>
> *Secondly, (inspired)...*

 AO2 After carefully reading this sample conclusion, consider what your justified conclusion would be to this exam question.

d. 'The Bible is best understood as the literal Word of God.' Evaluate this statement considering arguments for and against. In your response you should:
- refer to Catholic teachings
- refer to different Christian points of view
- reach a justified conclusion. (15)

> *In conclusion, despite the advantages of taking the Bible literally, for example _____, it is clear that many Christians decide to take a different approach because...*

 **REVIEW**

Answers: Mark your answers using p.190 and note areas for improvement.
AO1: This question is testing your ability to write about different viewpoints. For help with this skill, see p.12.
AO2: This question is testing your ability to write a justified conclusion. For help with this skill, see p.12.

 **RECAP**

Essential information

- The Pope is the head of the Catholic Church and the Bishop of Rome.
- The teaching authority of the Church is called the **magisterium** (*magister* is Latin for 'master'). This authority is held by the Pope and his bishops.
- The role of the magisterium is to interpret and protect the Bible and Apostolic Tradition for Catholics in the modern world.

Leaders and leadership in the Church

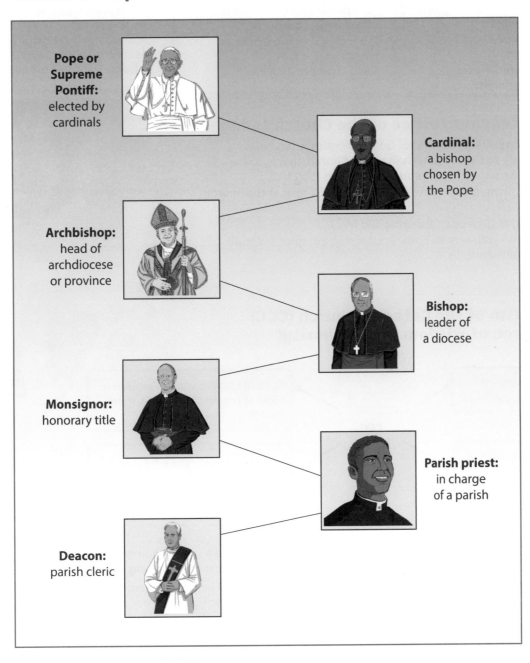

Pope or Supreme Pontiff: elected by cardinals

Cardinal: a bishop chosen by the Pope

Archbishop: head of archdiocese or province

Bishop: leader of a diocese

Monsignor: honorary title

Parish priest: in charge of a parish

Deacon: parish cleric

The Catholic Church can be likened to a three-legged stool, supported by scripture, Apostolic Tradition, and magisterium

Scripture · Apostolic Tradition · Magisterium

The magisterium of the Church

Jesus gave authority to the apostles, with the power of the Holy Spirit at Pentecost.
This authority is called the magisterium and is exercised by the Pope and his bishops.

The ordinary magisterium	The extraordinary magisterium	
	Conciliar	Pontifical
• Everyday teaching of the Church • Found in writings and speeches of bishops and popes • Examples include letters, homilies, exhortations, etc. **These can be useful sources of wisdom and authority.**	• Through an ecumenical council • Pope calls all bishops to meet to settle or explore new questions • The Second Vatican Council is an example • There have been 21 of these	• There have only been two *ex cathedra* ('from the chair') declarations of the Pope – Immaculate conception and Assumption of Mary were declared infallible (can't be wrong)

The living, teaching office of the Church today

Pope Francis is the 266th Pope

- The task of interpreting the Word of God authentically has been entrusted **solely to the magisterium of the Church**, that is, to the Pope, and to the bishops in communion with him (*CCC 100*).
- The magisterium needs to address issues that didn't exist at the time of Jesus.
- Examples include genetic engineering and IVF.
- It is the supreme authority for Catholics, helping interpret scripture and tradition authentically.

The Catechism of the Catholic Church (CCC) – a key source of wisdom and authority!

A doctrinal manual – a book of Catholic teaching

First published in 1566 at the Council of Trent

CCC

Current English version written in 1992 at request of Pope St John Paul II

Used by Catholics to inform their faith and understanding

 **APPLY**

(AO1) Can you write a second point to answer the following question?

b. Explain **two** reasons why the magisterium is important for Catholics. (4)

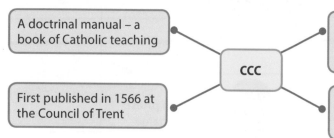
Firstly, it is considered the living, teaching office of the Church today that helps interpret the Bible and Apostolic Tradition for Catholics. This helps them make decisions about issues such as IVF, genetic engineering, etc.

(AO2) Make a list of arguments for and against the following statement.

d. 'The magisterium is important for Catholics because of the guidance given on matters of faith and belief'. Evaluate this statement considering arguments for and against. In your response you should:
- refer to Catholic teachings
- reach a justified conclusion. (15)

TIP
Links to 3.4 The Second Vatican Council will also be useful in your answer.

REVIEW
Answers: Mark your answers using p.190 and note areas for improvement.
AO1: This question is testing your ability to write a developed point. For help with this skill, see p.12.
AO2: This question is testing your ability to answer a (d) question. For help with this skill, see p.12.

RECAP

Essential information

- The Second Vatican Council (Vatican II) was a large ecumenical council held in the Vatican to discuss teaching and belief in the modern world.
- Some of the major changes include the Mass being said in the local language rather than Latin.
- Other changes included guidance on poverty and social justice in the world, and how to work with other Christians and non-believers.

The nature, history, and importance of the Second Vatican Council

- Opened: 11 October 1962 by Pope John XXIII
- Closed: 8 December 1965 by Pope Paul VI
- Held at St Peter's Basilica in the Vatican
- Published:
  - Four Constitutions (the most important, lengthy documents)
  - Three Declarations and nine Decrees (shorter documents answering specific questions).

TIP
You don't need to know both the Latin and English names – one is enough!

The Four Constitutions

Sacrosanctum Concilium (The Constitution on the Sacred Liturgy)	*Lumen Gentium* (Dogmatic Constitution on the Church)	*Dei Verbum* (Dogmatic Constitution on Divine Revelation)	*Gaudium et Spes* (Pastoral Constitution on the Church in the Modern World)
Reform of liturgy	**Beliefs about the Church**	**Scripture**	**Humanity and society**
• More participation by the laity (non-ordained Catholics) in the Mass • Mass could be celebrated in local language • Eucharist could be received in both forms • Revision of the lectionary so more of the Bible used in Mass	• Possibility of salvation for non-Christians and even non-theists • Encouraged bishops to work together more • References to *priesthood of the faithful* and *universal call to holiness* for all Catholics • Explanation of the role of Mary • Emphasis on importance of the laity	• The Word of God is not a book, but a person, Jesus • Bible and tradition are equally important • The Bible is the Word of God, written by humans, inspired by the Holy Spirit • Gospels are particularly important	• Covers economics, poverty, social justice, culture, science, technology, and ecumenism (unity among Christian denominations) • Highlighted impact of science and technology • Reflected on importance of talking with non-believers and other Christians
66 Active participation in [the liturgy] by the Christian people is their right and duty. 99 (*Sacrosanctum Concilium 14*)	66 It is the noble duty of pastors to recognise the services and charismatic gifts of the laity. 99 (*Lumen Gentium 30*)	66 Jesus perfected revelation by fulfilling it through his whole work of making Himself present. 99 (*Dei Verbum 4*)	66 The joys and hopes, the grief and anguish of the people of our time … are the joys and hopes, the grief and anguish of the followers of Christ as well. 99 (*Gaudium et Spes 1*)

 APPLY

AO1 This student answer is worth just 2 marks. Can you rewrite it to ensure it is worth 4 marks?

b. Explain **two** changes to the Church after the Second Vatican Council. (4)

> Mass no longer in Latin.
> Eucharist received in both forms.

AO2 Try to complete the planning table to answer this exam question. Once the table is done, attempt writing your answer in full – perhaps time yourself?

d. '*Lumen Gentium* (Dogmatic Constitution on the Church) is the most important document that was produced by the Second Vatican Council.' Evaluate this statement considering arguments for and against. In your response you should:
- refer to Catholic teachings
- reach a justified conclusion. (15)

Why is it the most important?	• _____ • _____ • _____
Why might other documents be more important?	SC: DV: GeS:
Conclusion	

 **REVIEW**

Answers: Mark your answers using p.190 and note areas for improvement.
AO1: This question is testing your ability to write a developed point. For help with this skill, see p.12.
AO2: This question is testing your ability to plan and write an essay. For help with this skill, see p.12.

 **RECAP**

Essential information
- The Body of Christ means the individuals who form the Christian community.
- The People of God means the group of people who have found faith in Jesus.
- Each member has a responsibility to contribute to the Church in different ways.

The Church as the People of God
- People who have come to Jesus in faith and through baptism.
- They are part of a 'chosen race ... a holy nation' (1 Peter 2:9) belonging to God.

The Church as the Body of Christ

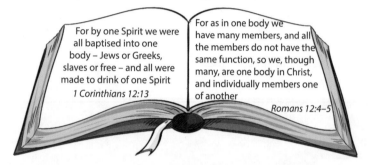

> For by one Spirit we were all baptised into one body – Jews or Greeks, slaves or free – and all were made to drink of one Spirit
> *1 Corinthians 12:13*

> For as in one body we have many members, and all the members do not have the same function, so we, though many, are one body in Christ, and individually members one of another
> *Romans 12:4–5*

- Strength of individuals joining together as one community.
- Jesus is the head that leads the body.
- United through baptism.
- The work of Jesus is continued on earth as the living body, spreading the Gospel.

The importance of this unity for Catholics today

> 66 the body is one and has many members 99
> (*1 Corinthians 12:12*)

Individual Catholics are different parts of the 'body', and they are joined together as one. After the ascension, each person has a crucial role to play in following Jesus' example on earth.

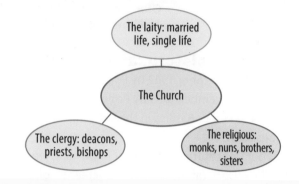

The laity: married life, single life

The Church

The clergy: deacons, priests, bishops

The religious: monks, nuns, brothers, sisters

> 66 Christ has no body but yours 99 (*St Teresa of Avila*)

There are many different ways to show love of God and to neighbours.

Divergent attitudes
Who is the head of the Body of Christ? The answer depends on your definition of the Body of Christ...

	Who is the head?	Who is the Body of Christ?
Catholic	• Pope	Catholics
Orthodox	• Do not recognise the Pope as head of the Church • Authority from councils of bishops or patriarchs working together with the agreement of the people	Orthodox Church
Protestants	• Do not recognise Pope as head of the Church • Most believe the Bible as God's Word is sole authority • Some also believe Church leaders have God-given authority to lead communities	All Christians

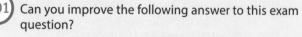
TIP
Structuring your answer into two clear lines or paragraphs helps make it clear that you have made two developed points.

 **APPLY**

(AO1) Can you improve the following answer to this exam question?

b. Explain **two** reasons why the Body of Christ is an important term for Catholics today. (4)

> It is important to help show love to God. It is also important to remember there are different ways to be part of the Body.

(AO2) Complete the planning table to help you answer this exam question.

d. 'The Body of Christ is a term that helps unify the Christian Church.' Evaluate this statement considering arguments for and against. In your response you should:
- refer to Catholic teachings
- refer to different Christian points of view
- reach a justified conclusion. (15)

Agree – how is the Church unified?	Disagree – how is the Church not unified?
•	•
•	•
•	•

 REVIEW

Answers: Mark your answers using p.190 and note areas for improvement.
AO1: This question is testing your ability to improve an answer. For help with this skill, see p.12.
AO2: This question is testing your ability to plan a response. For help with this skill, see p.12.

Essential information

- The four marks are: one, holy, catholic, and apostolic.
- They are found in the Nicene Creed.
- They are part of the Catholic declaration of faith.

The four marks of the Church

66 We believe in one holy catholic and apostolic Church. 99
(*The Nicene Creed* – see 1.2)

TIP
Remember that the Creed can be a useful source of wisdom and authority.

Mark	What does it mean?	Why is it important?
One	• One body, one Church • Unity of the Trinity • Catholic Church united through one Mass	• Division exists within Christianity with many denominations • Ecumenism an important part of Vatican II (see 3.4) • Duty to pray for and talk to other Christians
Holy	• Set apart for a special purpose • Jesus is source of all holiness • Church is a visible sign of this holiness	• Church gives opportunity for regular prayer and the sacraments • Get to know and love God through these opportunities • Saints give a good example of holiness
Catholic	• Meaning 'universal' • Jesus universally present	• History gives evidence to the strength, permanence, and unchanging nature of the Catholic Church • Church has, and continues, to suffer from persecution and attack. Catholics can take personal strength from the Church in these times.
Apostolic	• Living tradition of the apostles • Authority passed down by Pope and bishops – Apostolic Succession	• Magisterium guides Catholics today on issues such as nuclear war, euthanasia, and IVF • Duty to preserve, teach, defend, and pass on the faith

APPLY

(AO1) Try to answer the following question using the writing frame provided.

b. Explain **two** reasons why the marks of the Church are important today. (4)

Firstly, 'One' is important for Catholics, as it means working towards unity and this is important because...

Secondly, 'Apostolic' is important as it provides a way for Catholics to be guided by the magisterium on today's issues, for example...

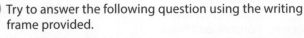

TIP
You can pick any of the four marks – write about the ones you know best!

(AO2) Use the table below to plan an answer to this question.

d. 'The marks of the Church are less significant for Christians today.' Evaluate this statement considering arguments for and against. In your response you should:
- refer to Catholic teachings
- refer to different Christian points of view
- reach a justified conclusion. (15)

	One	Holy	Catholic	Apostolic
Agree				
Disagree				
Conclusion				

REVIEW

Answers: Mark your answers using p.190 and note areas for improvement.
AO1: This question is testing your ability to organise and clearly signpost an answer. For help with this skill, see p.12.
AO2: This question is testing your ability to plan a response. For help with this skill, see p.12.

3.7 Mary as a model of the Church

RECAP

Essential information

- Mary is seen as a model for the Church because of her faith, trust in God, **discipleship** (following the teachings of Jesus), and charity.
- She is a personal role model for Catholics: open to God and willing to accept his requests despite the difficulties.
- There are many feast days, special prayers, and places of pilgrimage dedicated to Mary.

How is Mary a model of the Church?

- Her life reflects the value, teaching, and beliefs of the Catholic faith.
- She is a role model, but this is separate to her role as a model of the Church.
- She is the embodiment of what it means to be Catholic.

Do you know the difference?
- **Immaculate Conception:** Mary was born without sin, so she could give birth to Jesus without sin
- **The Virgin Mary:** She conceived without sexual activity

Joined with Jesus	Discipleship	Faith and charity
• Doctrine (teaching) about Mary is also about Jesus (Immaculate Conception, Assumption). • She is the mother of the Church since she is the mother of Jesus (the Church is the Body of Christ).	• She is sometimes called the first disciple – she had faith in Jesus from the moment of conception. • This is why she is a model for the Church, not just discipleship, as her sacrifice and service began before Jesus' birth.	• She accepted the risk of bearing Jesus. • She obeyed the command in Joseph's dream to flee Egypt. • She is seen as charitable by encouraging Jesus to solve the problem of a lack of wine at the wedding in Cana. • She watched Jesus at the foot of the cross.
❝Mary's role in the Church is inseparable from her union with Christ and flows directly from it.❞ (CCC 964)	❝And Mary said, 'Behold, I am the handmaid of the Lord; let it be to me according to your word.❞ (Luke 1:38)	❝By her complete adherence to the Father's will, to his Son's redemptive work, and to every prompting of the Holy Spirit, the Virgin Mary is the Church's model of faith and charity.❞ (CCC 967)

The implications of this teaching for Catholics today

- Most churches have statues of Mary, or even separate Lady Chapels.
- She has many titles including Theotokos (Mother of God) and Madonna.
- There are many Marian solemnities (important feast days) – see table below.
- Hymns, prayers, and poems are dedicated to Mary – see table below.
- The Rosary (see 2.5 Forms of popular piety).
- There are religious orders dedicated to Mary such as the Marist Fathers.
- Marian apparitions have led to shrines and places of pilgrimage – see table below.

These devotions show the implications of this teaching for Catholics.

TIP You don't need to memorise all of these, but they can help you better understand the person of Mary and demonstrate why Mary is so important to Catholics.

Feast days	Special prayers	Places of pilgrimage
1 January: Mary, the Holy Mother of God 25 March: The Annunciation of the Lord 15 August: The Assumption of the Blessed Virgin Mary 8 December: The Immaculate Conception of the Blessed Virgin Mary	The Hail Mary The Magnificat The Rosary The Hail Holy Queen The Angelus	Lourdes, France Knock, Ireland Fatima, Portugal Guadalupe, Mexico

 ## APPLY

AO1 Change these one-word answers into full sentences – it's currently worth 1 mark.

a. Outline **three** ways a Catholic may show devotion to Mary. (3)

> Rosary
> Feast of Immaculate Conception
> Lourdes

AO2 What would be your justified conclusion to this question?

d. 'It is important to give Mary a significant role within the Church.' Evaluate this statement considering arguments for and against. In your response you should:
- refer to Catholic teachings
- reach a justified conclusion. (15)

 ## REVIEW

Answers: Mark your answers using p.190 and note areas for improvement.
AO1: This question is testing your ability to improve an answer. For help with this skill, see p.12.
AO2: This question is testing your ability to write a justified conclusion. For help with this skill, see p.12.

 **RECAP**

Essential information

- Jesus is seen as a role model for Christians when making moral decisions.
- Jesus gave clear examples of forgiveness, being servant-like, and how to fight for social justice.
- Natural law and virtue ethics can help inform the conscience for Catholics.

Jesus as a source of authority for moral teaching

Morality is doing what is right, and not doing what is wrong. Christians believe that the Gospels give clear examples of how to behave that can still inspire Christians today.

Love for others	Forgiveness
<ul><li>Care for the poor, outcasts, ill, etc.</li><li>'Tough love' to rich young man (see 12.3 The story of the rich man)</li><li>Golden Rule and self-sacrifice (*Matthew 7:12*)</li></ul>	<ul><li>Key to salvation (*Matthew 6:14*)</li><li>Jesus even forgave those who crucified him (*Luke 23:33–35*)</li></ul>
Servanthood	**Social justice**
<ul><li>Given title 'Servant King'</li><li>Showed disciples at the Last Supper how to love each other (*John 13:4–5*)</li><li>Crucifixion was ultimate act of servanthood</li></ul>	<ul><li>Jesus cared for physical as well as spiritual needs</li><li>'preach good news to the poor' (*Luke 4:18*)</li><li>Parable of the Sheep and Goats (*Matthew 25:37–40*)</li></ul>

Jesus as fulfilment of the Law

Jesus helped people to understand the Law, not change or abolish it. Jesus was a faithful and obedient Jew:

> **❝** Do not think that I have come to abolish the Law or the Prophets; I have not come to abolish them but to fulfil them **❞** (*Matthew 5:17*)

Sources of personal and ethical decision-making for Catholics

Catholics do not refer to just one source when making personal and ethical decisions:

> They use their conscience.

> They are informed by scripture and tradition.

> They are under the authority of the magisterium.

Natural Law	Virtue	Primacy of Conscience
• A discoverable moral law that provides set rules for all • The Catholic Church follows the teachings on natural laws found in St Thomas Aquinas' writings • Most basic element is 'do good, avoid evil'	• A virtue is a moral excellence • **Virtue ethics** consider the moral character of a person to help analyse their ethical decisions • St Thomas Aquinas referred to **cardinal virtues** (prudence, justice, temperance, and fortitude) and **theological virtues** (faith, hope, and charity)	• Catholics have a **sacred obligation** to follow an informed conscience • Must be informed by the Bible and tradition, as interpreted by the magisterium

Divergent implications

• 'Do good, avoid evil' can be interpreted in different ways as it is not specific.

• Issues such as abortion, fertility treatment, contraception, euthanasia, pre-marital sex, etc. can have wide and diverse interpretations.

• Other Christians also do not accept the tradition of the Catholic Church or magisterium and so can make personal decisions based on their own study of scripture and guidance from their own Church traditions.

A fully developed conscience helps Catholics to pick the right path

APPLY

AO1 Use the structure, 'Firstly...' [development]; 'Secondly...' [development], to answer this question.

   b. Explain **two** reasons that Natural Law is considered important for Catholics. (4)

AO2 Fill in the top part of the plan opposite in response to this question.

   d. 'An informed conscience enables Christians to make clear personal and ethical decisions.' Evaluate this statement considering arguments for and against. In your response you should:
   • refer to Catholic teachings
   • refer to different Christian points of view
   • reach a justified conclusion. (15)

An informed conscience DOES enable clear decisions	
An informed conscience DOES NOT enable clear decisions	• Other Christians do not see 'informed' as meaning following Apostolic Tradition and the magisterium. • The Bible can appear contradictory in places. • The Bible does not cover many of the modern issues (abortion, IVF, etc.) that Christians may struggle with. • There isn't agreement between other Christians on certain moral and ethical issues.

 REVIEW

Answers: Mark your answers using p.190 and note areas for improvement.
AO1: This question is testing your ability to answer a (b) question. For help with this skill, see p.12.
AO2: This question is testing your ability to plan a response. For help with this skill, see p.12.

Test the 3 mark question (a)

1 Outline **three** features of the New Testament. **(3 marks)**

Most of the New Testament was composed soon after Jesus' death. (1)

The Gospels were written to provide a record of Jesus' words and actions. (1)

The early Church decided what should be included in the New Testament. (1)

2 Outline **three** principles Catholics might apply when making ethical decisions. **(3 marks)**

Natural Law, which basically means 'do good and avoid evil'. (1)

_____

_____

3 Outline **three** Catholic beliefs about Mary. **(3 marks)**

_____

_____

_____

> **TIP**
> These could be linked to scripture or papal declarations.

Test the 4 mark question (b)

1 Explain **two** marks of the Church. **(4 marks)**

● **Explain one mark**	*The Church is one in the Father, Son, and Holy Spirit, according to the Catechism.* (1)
● Develop your explanation with more detail/an example/reference to a religious teaching	*This reflects the unity of the Trinity.* (1)
● **Explain a second mark**	*The Church is Holy, with Jesus as its source.* (1)
● Develop your explanation with more detail/an example/reference to a religious teaching	*Through teaching, prayer, and worship the Church is a visible sign of holiness.* (1)

2 Explain **two** functions of the magisterium. **(4 marks)**

● **Explain one function**	
● Develop your explanation with more detail/an example/reference to a religious teaching	
● **Explain a second function**	
● Develop your explanation with more detail/an example/reference to a religious teaching	

> **TIP**
> This question asks about the **function** of the magisterium, so make sure you write about this; don't just describe what the magisterium is.

3 Explain **two** reasons why the Church is called apostolic. **(4 marks)**

Exam Practice

Test the 5 mark question (c)

1. Explain **two** reasons why it is important for Catholics to understand Mary as a model of the Church. In your answer you must refer to a source of wisdom and authority. **(5 marks)**

• **Explain one reason**	One reason is that Mary's role is inseparable from Jesus. (1)
• Develop your explanation with more detail/an example	As Jesus' birth mother, she plays a unique and important role in literally giving birth to the Church. (1)
• **Either:** Add a reference to a source of wisdom and authority here	
• **Explain a second reason**	Another reason is that Mary accepted God's call to give birth to Jesus. (1)
• Develop your explanation with more detail/an example	This was a risk, showing her faith, which remains an inspiration to Catholics today. (1)
• **Or:** Add a reference to a source of wisdom and authority here.	This story is documented in the story of the annunciation in Luke 1. (1)

2. Explain **two** reasons why a Catholic might obey their conscience when making a personal decision. In your answer you must refer to a source of wisdom and authority. **(5 marks)**

• **Explain one reason**	
• Develop your explanation with more detail/an example	
• **Either:** Add a reference to a source of wisdom and authority here	
• **Explain a second reason**	
• Develop your explanation with more detail/an example	
• **Or:** Add a reference to a source of wisdom and authority here.	

> **TIP**
> 'Conscience' is not a vague term for Catholics – it must be informed by Church teaching and scripture.

3. Explain **two** ways Catholics can interpret the Bible. **(5 marks)**

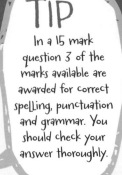

TIP

In a 15 mark question 3 of the marks available are awarded for correct spelling, punctuation and grammar. You should check your answer thoroughly.

Test the 15 mark question (d)

1 'The magisterium provides a vital function for today.' Evaluate this statement considering arguments for and against. In your response you should:

- refer to Catholic teachings
- reach a justified conclusion.

(15 marks)

ARGUMENTS IN SUPPORT OF THE STATEMENT ● **Explain why some people would agree with the statement.** ● Develop your explanation with more detail and examples. ● Refer to religious teaching. Use a quote or paraphrase of a religious authority. ● **Evaluate the arguments.** Is this a good argument? Explain why you think this. Use words such as convincing/strong/robust/weak/unpersuasive/unsuccessful within your reasoning.	*Catholics would agree that the magisterium does provide a vital function for today as part of the three key parts of the Church: scripture, tradition, and magisterium.* *As opposed to some Christians who believe the Bible on its own has the answers, Catholics believe that certain individuals are given the authority to teach, as Jesus appointed his apostles.* *The ordinary magisterium is the everyday teachings of the bishops and Pope, which is logical as they are leaders in the Church. It is useful for Catholics as it often covers issues not found in the Bible, such as abortion and IVF.* *On rare occasions the extraordinary magisterium is used by the Pope to make 'ex cathedra' teachings regarded as infallible (which means it cannot be wrong). This may be hard to accept, but it has only been used twice.*
ARGUMENTS SUPPORTING A DIFFERENT VIEW ● **Explain why some people would disagree with the statement.** ● Develop your explanation with more detail and examples. ● Refer to religious teaching. Use a quote or paraphrase of a religious authority. ● **Evaluate the arguments.** Is this a good argument? Explain why you think this. Use words such as convincing/strong/robust/weak/unpersuasive/unsuccessful within your reasoning.	*Many other Christians do not follow the Pope. They believe that the Bible contains all the answers, and they are free to interpret it more freely. This means, for example, that some Christians agree with issues such as abortion and euthanasia as they have come to their own decision and see them as an act of love. This allows greater freedom in what to believe, and some Christians feel this is more appropriate for modern living.*
CONCLUSION ● **Give a justified conclusion.** ● Include your own reasoning. ● Use words such as convincing/strong/robust/weak/unpersuasive/unsuccessful to weigh up the different arguments for and against. ● Do not just repeat arguments you have already used without explaining how they apply to your reasoned opinion/conclusion.	*In my opinion, the magisterium is useful in guiding Catholics through modern issues not covered in the Bible. Freedom to interpret is not always a good thing, because it can encourage disagreement and lack of unity.*

TIP

Other Christians may listen to the Pope, but may not see him as having the same the same level of authority as Catholics believe he has.

TIP

This answer clearly shows divergence within Christianity and links to a range of issues Christians face.

Exam Practice

TIP

There were 16 documents created by the Second Vatican Council in total – but you studied just four! You can give the Latin or English name.

2 'The Second Vatican Council changed life dramatically for Catholics today.' Evaluate this statement considering arguments for and against. In your response you should:

- refer to Catholic teachings
- reach a justified conclusion.

(15 marks)

ARGUMENTS IN SUPPORT OF THE STATEMENT	Some Christians/Catholics/people would agree with this statement because...
• **Explain why some people would agree with the statement.** • Develop your explanation with more detail and examples. • Refer to religious teaching. Use a quote or paraphrase of a religious authority. • **Evaluate the arguments.** Is this a good argument? Explain why you think this. Use words such as convincing/ strong/robust/weak/unpersuasive/ unsuccessful within your reasoning.	
ARGUMENTS SUPPORTING A DIFFERENT VIEW • **Explain why some people would disagree with the statement.** • Develop your explanation with more detail and examples. • Refer to religious teaching. Use a quote or paraphrase of a religious authority. • **Evaluate the arguments.** Is this a good argument? Explain why you think this. Use words such as convincing/ strong/robust/weak/unpersuasive/ unsuccessful within your reasoning.	On the other hand, some Christians/Catholics/people would hold a different point of view...
CONCLUSION • **Give a justified conclusion.** • Include your own reasoning. • Use words such as convincing/ strong/robust/weak/unpersuasive/ unsuccessful to weigh up the different arguments for and against. • Do not just repeat arguments you have already used without explaining how they apply to your reasoned opinion/conclusion.	Having considered both sides of the argument, I would say that...

TIP

Be careful of arguing against the statement in question unless you have studied this carefully. The Second Vatican Council was undeniably dramatic and there is much evidence to support this view.

3 'Christians must only obey the Bible.' Evaluate this statement considering arguments for and against. In your response you should:

- refer to Catholic teachings
- refer to different Christian points of view
- reach a justified conclusion.

(15 marks)

 **REVIEW**

- Check your answers to these exam questions on p.191, correct your answers with annotations, and note down any general areas for improvement.
- If you don't feel secure in the content of this chapter, you could reread the Recap sections.
- If you don't feel secure in your exam technique, you could revisit the exam support section on pp.7–14.

 **RECAP**

Essential information
- The word 'church' means the 'House of the Lord'.
- Church buildings are an important place for Catholics to pray and worship.
- Church building design often reflects symbolism in Catholicism.

The role of church buildings

The earliest church buildings were built around 233–256 CE. Before this, the word 'church' simply referred to the gathered people. Today there are churches and cathedrals all over the world.

> 66 **Church building design matters for worship:** it 'ought to be in good taste and a worthy place for prayer and sacred ceremonial' (*CCC 1181*)
>
> **The church building is an important symbol of God:** Church buildings 'make visible the Church living in this place' (*CCC 1180*)
>
> **Mass can still take place outside the church building:** 'worship … is not tied exclusively to any one place. The whole earth is sacred' 99 (*CCC 1179*)

How church design reflects belief

Feature	Belief
Many churches face east	The sun rises in the east, as Jesus rose on the day of the resurrection
Many churches are cruciform (shaped like a cross)	The cross is a symbol of the Church, a reminder of Jesus' death and sacrifice
Some churches are round (e.g. Church of the Holy Sepulchre in Jerusalem)	They represent the eternal nature of God
Some churches are octagonal (e.g. Church of the Nativity in Bethlehem)	They represent a star, bringing light into the world
High vaulted ceilings and spires	Connect to heaven and reach towards God
Stained-glass windows	Tell stories of the saints and from the Bible – useful when people couldn't read

How churches are used

Worship	• Mass • Other sacraments
Other uses	• Private prayer • Popular piety (see 2.5 Forms of popular piety)

 APPLY

TIP
Architecture of a building is not the same as interior features that can be updated and changed. Look carefully at the question.

AO1 The first point is made for you. Can you write a second point, and also add a reference to a source of wisdom and authority?

c. Explain **two** ways in which the church building reflects belief. In your answer you must refer to a source of wisdom and authority. (5)

> *Firstly, the high ceilings and spires try to connect the congregation with heaven. They are as high as possible to reach towards God, showing his importance in the lives of Catholics.*

AO2 The following planning table has been started. Can you finish it?

d. 'All Catholic church buildings should be the same.' Evaluate this statement considering arguments for and against. In your response you should:
- refer to Catholic teachings
- refer to different Christian points of view
- reach a justified conclusion. (12)

Agree	Disagree
• CCC 1180 – The church is a symbol of God, a sign of the living Church.	• Many UK churches have been built since 1829, so reflect modern architecture.

 REVIEW

Answers: Mark your answers using p.191 and note areas for improvement.
AO1: This question is testing your ability to answer an 'explain' question. For help with this skill, see p.12.
AO2: This question is testing your ability to plan a response. For help with this skill, see p.12.

 **RECAP**

Essential information

- The internal features of a Catholic church have clear and distinct purposes.
- These features help Catholics in their worship and prayer life.
- The lectern, altar, crucifix, and tabernacle particularly reflect Jesus' sacrifice, atonement, and reconciliation with God.

The different features and their purpose

Feature	Image	Meaning and significance
Lectern Book stand from which readings are proclaimed		• Liturgy of the Word is a key feature of the Mass • Homily and other prayers also read from here • Redemption is achieved through responding to the Word of God ❝The dignity of the Word of God requires the church to have a suitable place for announcing his message❞ *(CCC 1184)*
Altar The table that is a focal point inside a church		• Represents the table at the Last Supper • Links to the Temple, altar built by Moses, and message to Peter – 'on this rock I will build my church' *(Matthew 16:18)* • Redemption is made possible due to the sacrifice made by Jesus, prepared at the Last Supper ❝The altar is also the table of the Lord, to which the People of God are invited❞ *(CCC 1182)*
Crucifix A cross with an image of the crucified Jesus on		• Aid to prayer • Reminder of Jesus' suffering • Redemption is possible due to the sacrifice made by Jesus in his death on the cross
Tabernacle A box where consecrated host, or Eucharist, is kept		• 'Dwelling place' of Jesus, in a physical sense, in the church • Link to Tabernacle where Ten Commandments were kept by Moses • Physical reminder of the redemption made possible through Jesus' physical death and resurrection ❝The tabernacle is to be situated 'in churches in a most worthy place with the greatest honour'.❞ *(CCC 1183)*

Other key features

Baptismal font Holy water is used to wash away original sin and begin life in the Church. Baptism is the first sacrament of initiation. It may be found at the back (traditional) or at the front (most modern) of churches.

Confessional Small rooms or wooden constructions dedicated to private conversation for the sacrament of reconciliation.

Stations of the Cross Images from the story of the Passion of Christ (see 2.5).

Statues Usually at least one of Mary, visual aids to help prayer.

Water stoup Holy water at the entrance to make the sign of the cross.

 APPLY

 Write a paragraph either for or against the following statement.

AO1 One point has been made for you. Can you improve this answer from 1 mark to 3 marks?

a. Outline **three** key features of a Catholic church building. (3)

> The altar is the focal point of the church where the actions of the Liturgy of the Eucharist take place.

d. 'The altar is the most significant feature of the Catholic church.' Evaluate this statement considering arguments for and against. In your response you should:
- refer to Catholic teachings
- reach a justified conclusion. (12)

REVIEW

Answers: Mark your answers using p.191 and note areas for improvement.
AO1: This question is testing your ability to answer 'outline' questions. For help with this skill, see p.12.
AO2: This question is testing your ability to write a well-argued paragraph. For help with this skill, see p.12.

 **RECAP**

Essential information

- Sacred objects help Catholics to focus during worship.
- Sacred vessels are used by the priest during the Mass.
- Sarcophagi are still used today and help Catholics focus their prayers on an individual.
- Hunger cloths tell stories of God helping people in the Bible and are still used in developing countries.

What are sacred objects?

- Objects such as relics, rosary beads, candles, and holy water can be called sacred, and are called 'objects of devotion'.
- Devotional objects may be found in the church but also in the home.

Sacred vessels

- Sacred vessels are important in the celebration of the Eucharist.
- They are recognisable symbols as the congregation will know they contain the body and blood.

The Catechism states the following about the cross, images of Jesus, Mary, angels, and saints: ❝[they] are to be exhibited in the holy churches of God, on sacred vessels❞ *(CCC 1161)*

Ciborium (covered dish) for the rest of the hosts

Chalice (cup) for wine

Paten (plate) for the large host used by the priest

> **TIP**
> There are other items used in Mass, but these are not considered sacred vessels; for example, cloths, books, thurible, and vestments.

Sarcophagi

- A sarcophagus is a box-like container for a corpse.
- Earliest Christians were buried in large tombs or in underground tunnels.
- Later Christians began to be buried in sarcophagi with scenes from the Bible on the side.
- Sarcophagi are still sometimes used today. Many of the Popes buried in St Peter's Basilica are in sarcophagi.
- They are used as a physical reminder of the person buried, and a focus for prayer.

Hunger cloths

- Used in the Middle Ages to cover the altar during Lent. They were covered in images and stories from the Bible to help those who could not read.
- They are used in some developing countries today to remind people that God is with them and cares for their struggles.

 APPLY

AO1 **b.** Explain **two** ways hunger cloths are used by Catholics. (4)

This exam question could easily ask about sacred vessels, sarcophagi, or hunger cloths, so you should revise for all three.
Copy and complete this planning table with two points for each.
Then, develop each of your points to achieve 4 marks for each answer.

Sacred vessels	Sarcophagi	Hunger cloths
1. The ciborium is used to keep the Body of Christ in the tabernacle	1. Later Christians began using them	1. Used in developing countries today
2.	2.	2.

AO2 Now try answering this question on your own.

'Sacred objects help Catholics to focus on what is happening during worship.' Evaluate this statement considering arguments for and against. In your response you should:
- refer to Catholic teachings
- refer to different Christian points of view
- reach a justified conclusion. (12)

 **REVIEW**

Answers: Mark your answers using p.191–192 and note areas for improvement.
AO1: This question is testing your ability to answer a (b) question. For help with this skill, see p.12.
AO2: This question is testing your ability to answer a (d) question. For help with this skill, see p.12.

RECAP

Essential information

- Artwork (including paintings, frescos, mosaics, and drawings) can help Catholics learn and remember stories from the Bible.
- Artwork can also be used as a focus for prayer and meditation.
- Catholic art has played an important role in the development of Western art.

Meaning and significance

- Artwork is a visual expression of faith. It helps portray the teachings of the Church.
- Some capture a story from the Bible. Others express the artist's beliefs.
- Icons are usually images of Jesus, Mary, saints, and angels. Many were destroyed in the 8th and 9th centuries during the Iconoclasm and again during the Reformation. They remain popular features in many churches and homes.
- Renaissance art (1300–1700 CE) usually focused on religious themes or stories from the Bible.
- Artworks were originally important when many Catholics could not read or write, as they are relatable and understandable.

Example 1

The Sistine Chapel

Location: Sistine Chapel, the Vatican

Artist: Michelangelo

Date: 1508–1512

- The Sistine Chapel is the location of papal conclave.
- Michelangelo was deeply religious, although the majority of his artwork was sculpture.
- He tried to remain faithful to scripture in his depictions.
- Pope Julius II demanded layers of meaning that would serve as prompts for theological debate.
- 'The greatest work of art ever made' (YouGov 2014) – it is appreciated by Catholic and other visitors.

TIP

There are not specific works of art that you need to study – these are just two examples. Make sure you can be precise with whatever artwork you decide to write about.

Example 2

The Return of the Prodigal Son

Location: Hermitage Museum, St Petersburg, Russia

Artist: Rembrandt

Date: 1667

- Copies are often found in Catholic churches and schools as a reminder of the Prodigal Son (*Luke 15:11–32*).
- Rembrandt was moved by the parable, and he made a variety of drawings, etchings, and paintings over several decades.
- Henri Nouwen, a priest, suggested it helps explore meaning of the original parable:
  - the father's hands
  - the son's sandals
  - role of the older brother.

Divergent ways art is used in church and elsewhere

- Different types of artwork are acceptable in different churches, therefore some churches will have traditional artwork, while others will show more contemporary artwork.
- For Catholics, all church art must be:

> 66 evoking and glorifying, in faith and adoration, the transcendent mystery of God 99 (*CCC 2502*)

Bishops have a responsibility to remove anything that does not conform with this instruction.

- Orthodox Christians have a long history of iconography. Icons are used in Orthodox public liturgy and encouraged for use in private meditation.

TIP

Search for the section on the Sainsbury Wing on The National Gallery's website, which houses a wide collection of religious art. What is the story being told in a particular picture?

TIP

Knowledge of the use of icons in Orthodox liturgy is useful when considering different Christian points of view.

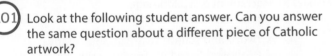

APPLY

AO1 Look at the following student answer. Can you answer the same question about a different piece of Catholic artwork?

b. Explain **two** features of a specific piece of Catholic artwork. (4)

> *Firstly, the Sistine Chapel is a piece of art, and painting is found on the ceilings and walls of the chapel, which makes it unusual and hard to paint. This location is significant as it is where the papal conclave takes place; this is the election of the new Pope by the cardinals.*
>
> *Secondly, as Michelangelo was a deeply religious man, he wanted to be faithful and accurate to scripture. As such, the majority of the artwork links directly to the accounts of the Bible, although it does have deep meaning that has promoted debate over the years.*

AO2 This essay has been started for you. Can you complete it?

d. 'Paintings help Christians understand their relationship to God.' Evaluate this statement considering arguments for and against. In your response you should:
- refer to Catholic teachings
- refer to different Christian points of view
- reach a justified conclusion. (12)

> *Many Catholics would agree with this statement. Most Catholic churches have Stations of the Cross, which give a visible form to the final hours of Jesus' life. They therefore help Catholics to have a clearer sense of Jesus' suffering, and this makes them more grateful for the sacrifice he made to atone for sins. In addition, paintings often portray images and stories from the Bible. They help worshippers understand their religion, especially these with weak literacy. Lastly, the Catechism of the Catholic Church encourages all sacred art that reflects the glory of God and draws the worshipper to adoration and prayer.*

REVIEW   **Answers:** Mark your answers using p.192 and note areas for improvement.
AO1: This question is testing your ability to answer an 'explain' question. For help with this skill, see p.12.
AO2: This question is testing your ability to write a well-argued paragraph. For help with this skill, see p.12.

4.5 Sculpture and statues

 **RECAP**

Essential information

- Statues and sculptures are a way of remembering individuals, stories, and teaching from the Bible and the saints.
- They are used by Catholics in the home and church as a focus of prayer and reminder of their faith in their daily lives.
- Most Catholic churches contain statues. They may have more than one altar or chapel dedicated to Mary or a saint, which would usually have a statue.

Meaning and significance

- Sculptures and statues reveal skills that are God-given:

> 66 Arising from talent given by the Creator and from man's own effort, art is a form of practical wisdom, uniting knowledge and skill. 99 (*CCC 2501*)

- They are used to recall the person or thing being depicted.
- They are used as a teaching tool, particularly in the early Church when many were unable to read.
- They are **not** worshipped by Catholics, but they are an aid to prayer and are treated as sacred objects.
- In the Old Testament there are occasions when God directed the construction of statues (e.g. *Exodus 25:18–20*).

Expressions of belief

	Expression of artist	Expression by audience
Statues	• Reflection of scripture, writings, or records • Attempt to produce a likeness	• Kneel before them • Touch or kiss them • Light a candle before them • Pray before them
Sculptures	• Expression of faith in an emotive way • Conveying message through an unconventional image	• Meditation • Reflection upon them

TIP

Always consider the the meaning and significance of the sculpture/ statue within Catholicism – what religious belief is the artist trying to express?

Use in church and other settings

- Most churches will have a number of statues.
- There is usually at least one of Mary in Catholic churches.
- It is common to have a set of statues to depict the Nativity; Catholics will often have a smaller version at home.
- On Good Friday, the cross is venerated and Catholics kiss the feet of Jesus.
- Catholics often have statues in their home as a reminder to keep spiritual values in their everyday lives.
- Some Catholics use statues during private prayer; these may be linked to a sacrament or a pilgrimage.

 **APPLY**

AO1 This student answer is worth 2 marks. Develop these simple points to gain 4 marks.

b. Explain **two** ways a sculpture or statue would be used in the Catholic Church. (4)

> There is usually a statue of Mary in a church.
> A Nativity set is brought out at Christmas when the Nativity scene is constructed.

AO2 It can be difficult to come up with arguments against a statement like the one below. See if you can write a paragraph against, using the starter sentences provided.

d. 'Artwork and sculpture are an important part of Catholic life today.' Evaluate this statement considering arguments for and against. In your response you should:
- refer to Catholic teachings
- refer to different Christian points of view
- reach a justified conclusion. (12)

> Though artwork and sculpture are important to many Catholics for the reasons already described, they are arguably not the most important part of Catholic life. More important would be...

 **REVIEW**

Answers: Mark your answers using p.192 and note areas for improvement.
AO1: This question is testing your ability to write a developed point. For help with this skill, see p.12.
AO2: This question is testing your ability to write a well-argued paragraph. For help with this skill, see p.12.

Symbolism and imagery in religious art

RECAP

Essential information

- Christians have used symbols from the beginning of their faith. At first it was to avoid detection.
- Many symbols including the cross, the fish, and those of the evangelists are found in the decoration of many churches.
- Christian symbols are used by Catholics today to express belief and faith.

How symbolism and imagery are used

Symbolism is using an object to mean something else. Early Christians used symbols to avoid detection in the Roman Empire when their religion was still illegal. Only other Christians would recognise them.

Symbol	Purpose	Use
The cross and crucifix	• Includes figure of Jesus • A reminder of his death and resurrection • His death led to the forgiveness of sin and possibility of redemption and salvation	• Cross used widely since the 4th century, crucifix since the 5th century • Found in all churches • Often found in Catholic homes • Focus of prayer • Sometimes worn as jewellery
The fish	• 'Ichthus' means fish in Greek, which stands for: Jesus Christ God Son Saviour • This also links to: 'I will make you fishers of men' (*Matthew 4:19*)	• Originally used by early Christians as a way of signalling to other Christians in secret • Now common on 'bumper stickers' or even business logos to indicate Christian owners
The chi rho	• The first two letters of the word 'Christ' in Greek: X (chi) and P (rho)	• The symbol used by the Romans when they adopted Christianity as the official religion of the Empire • Now often found on the altar and/or vestments of Catholic priests • Uncommon in non-Catholic churches
The dove	• Christian iconography traditionally uses a dove to suggest the Holy Spirit (*CCC 701*) • Also linked to peace for both Christians and non-Christians	• May be used in Christian artwork, or by Justice and Peace organisations • Sometimes found on the Tabernacle
The eagle	• Symbol of Jesus' divine nature (*Isaiah 40:31*) • Also a symbol of the evangelist John	• Commonly used in Protestant churches in the lectern design • Unusual to find such a lectern in a Catholic church
The Alpha and Omega	• Jesus says, 'I am the Alpha and the Omega' (*Revelation 22:13*) • Shows eternal nature of Jesus – from the first to the last – as these letters are the first and last of the Greek alphabet	• Found on the Paschal Candle, and other decoration such as the altar
The evangelists	• Most common ordering is that of St Jerome: Matthew: Human/Angel Mark: Lion Luke: Ox John: Eagle	• These may feature on decoration of stained-glass windows, lectern, around the altar, etc. • Common in baptisteries of Italian cathedrals

APPLY

AO1 This student answer is currently worth 1 mark. Can you improve it?

a. Outline **three** symbols that may be used in Church decoration. (3)

Alpha and Omega   Chi Rho   Crucifix

AO2 Which two symbols do you think are most important? Justify your views:

	Symbol	Reason
1		
2		

REVIEW

Answers: Mark your answers using p.191 and note areas for improvement.
AO1: This question is testing your ability to answer 'outline' questions. For help with this skill, see p.12.
AO2: This question is testing your ability to select appropriate information. For help with this skill, see p.12.

RECAP

Essential information

- Drama is used to bring stories from the Bible to life.
- Mystery plays helped people learn and remember Bible stories.
- Passion plays focused on the story of Jesus' death and resurrection.

Meaning and significance

- Drama is something that engages people.
- The Catechism describes the relationship between God and humanity as 'a covenant drama' that 'engages the heart' (*CCC 2567*).
- The Bible is full of dramatic stories that have been retold and acted out by Christians and non-Christians alike.

Mystery plays	Passion plays
• Earliest form of drama in medieval Europe • Performed Bible stories • Clergy were banned from being involved from 1210 • Guilds performed, travelling from town to town • Banned in England from 1534 as part of Reformation • Continued in Europe • Since 1950s have been revived	• Easter pageants • Story of Passion of Jesus • Popular in medieval times • Banned as part of Reformation • Now common again at Easter, particularly in public places like town centres on Good Friday • Also often ecumenical projects with different Christian churches working together

Expressing belief using drama

- Drama can help people to understand and remember Bible stories in a more powerful way than simply reading them.
- Those participating may feel it is a form of worship.
- Those observing may see it as a focus of prayer and devotion.
- Ecumenical performances may bring Christians together.

- Some dramas retell stories in contemporary settings, making them feel more relevant.

The use of drama in church and other settings

- Dramas do not take place within the church as a form of worship, but the church may be used as a performance space. More often, they take place in public areas involving other Christians and non-Christians.

TIP
Remember that many early Christians were illiterate – drama helped people learn and remember key stories.

APPLY

AO1 This answer shows no explanation, but does show some knowledge. How could you make this into a full mark answer?

b. Explain **two** ways drama is used to express belief. (4)

> *Mystery plays and Passion plays*

AO2 Plan three points for each side of this argument looking at why drama is useful and why it might not be. Remember, these plays were banned as part of the Reformation, and the Catholic Church banned clergy from being involved!

d. 'Drama is a useful way to express belief.' Evaluate this statement considering arguments for and against. In your response you should:
- refer to Catholic teachings
- refer to different Christian points of view
- reach a justified conclusion. (12)

Drama IS a useful way to express belief	Drama is NOT a useful way to express belief
•	•
What would your conclusion be?	

REVIEW

Answers: Mark your answers using p.191 and note areas for improvement.
AO1: This question is testing your ability to answer an 'explain' question. For help with this skill, see p.12.
AO2: This question is testing your ability to plan a response. For help with this skill, see p.12.

RECAP

Essential information

- Plainchant, hymns, psalms, and worship songs allow Catholics to join together and pray together through words and music.
- They help Catholics understand and remember Church teaching.
- They are used in the Mass and other services.

Traditional music in worship

- The Roman Gradual is the official source of music, like the Roman Missal for readings.
- Music connects parts of the liturgy, for example the Kyrie and Gloria.

Hymns	Plainchant	Psalms	Worship songs
• Religious songs for purpose of praise, adoration, or prayer • Earliest hymns are the Psalms • Often linked to the readings or Church season	• Singing without music • Gregorian Chant is sung in churches and monasteries	• Written by King David, King Solomon, and others • Found in Old Testament • Second reading is usually a responsorial psalm	• Referred to as contemporary music or 'Praise and Worship' • Often linked to charismatic or youth movements 

How music expresses belief

Music engages the heart in worship: 66 Make melody to the Lord with all your heart. 99 (*CCC 2641*)

Music increases the value of prayer: 66 The musical tradition of the universal Church is a treasure of inestimable value, greater even than that of any other art [...] He who sings prays twice. 99 (*CCC 1156*)

- Music helps Catholics understand and remember Church teaching.
- Hymns, plainchant, and psalms are traditional and have existed throughout Jewish and Christian history.

 APPLY

TIP

It may be appropriate to share your own view on which type of music you prefer, but make sure it is backed up with evidence.

(AO1) This answer is worth 1 mark. Can you make a further two points?

a. Outline **three** ways music is used in worship. (3)

> *Hymns are used to link parts of the liturgy.*

(AO2) Complete the planning table to help you answer this question.

d. 'Traditional music is preferable for Catholics to use during worship.' Evaluate this statement considering arguments for and against. In your response you should:
- refer to Catholic teachings
- refer to different Christian points of view
- reach a justified conclusion. (12)

Traditional music is preferable	• Roman Gradual sets out approved music that many believe should be followed. • •
Contemporary music is preferable	• Praise and worship music is preferable for many different Christians as it reflects more modern styles and they can therefore identify with it. • •

 **REVIEW**

Answers: Mark your answers using p.191 and note areas for improvement.
AO1: This question is testing your ability to answer 'outline' questions. For help with this skill, see p.12.
AO2: This question is testing your ability to plan a response. For help with this skill, see p.12.

Test the 3 mark question (a)

1 Outline **three** sacred objects. **(3 marks)**

Sacred vessels are objects used as part of the Mass. (1)

Sarcophagi are box-like containers for a corpse. (1)

Hunger cloths are covered in images from the Bible. (1)

2 Outline **three** types of artwork in Catholicism. **(3 marks)**

Frescoes are murals painted on fresh plaster. (1)

_____

_____

TIP
Remember you can use information from 4.4 Artwork in Catholicism and 4.5 Sculpture and statues.

3 Outline **three** features found inside a Catholic church. **(3 marks)**

_____

_____

_____

Test the 4 mark question (b)

1 Explain **two** architectural features of a Catholic Church that reflect belief. **(4 marks)**

● **Explain one feature.**	*Where possible, churches are built facing east. (1)*
● Develop your explanation with more detail/an example/reference to a religious teaching.	*This is a reminder of the belief that Jesus rose from the dead, just as the sun rises from the east. (1)*
● **Explain a second feature.**	*Many churches are cruciform. (1)*
● Develop your explanation with more detail/an example/reference to a religious teaching.	*This means shaped like a cross, which reflects the cross as a symbol of the Church. (1)*

2 Explain **two** reasons Catholics use statues and sculptures. **(4 marks)**

● **Explain one reason.**	
● Develop your explanation with more detail/an example/reference to a religious teaching.	
● **Explain a second reason.**	
● Develop your explanation with more detail/an example/reference to a religious teaching.	

3 Explain **two** ways sacred vessels are used by Catholics. **(4 marks)**

TIP
Make sure you know about specific sacred **vessels** rather than just any sacred **objects**.

Exam Practice

Test the 5 mark question (c)

1 Explain **two** ways music can make worship more relevant to the life of a Catholic. In your answer you must refer to a source of wisdom and authority. **(5 marks)**

● **Explain one way.**	*Christians are told to sing together in expectation of the Lord's return,* (1)
● Develop your explanation with more detail/an example.	*therefore singing and music are expressions of joy, hope and love of God* (1)
● **Either:** Add a reference to a source of wisdom and authority here.	*as detailed in CCC 2641, 'make melody to the Lord'.* (1)
● **Explain a second way.**	*Catholics are taught that music is a gift from God* (1)
● Develop your explanation with more detail/an example.	*and can be used to make liturgy more beautiful and so can lift the soul to higher things.* (1)
● **Or:** Add a reference to a source of wisdom and authority here.	*As it says in the CCC, 'He who sings prays twice'.*

TIP

Here, the student has referred to a second source of wisdom and authority. You are free to do this, though you are only required to refer to one.

2 Explain **two** reasons why artwork may be found within the church building. In your answer you must refer to a source of wisdom and authority. **(5 marks)**

● **Explain one reason.**	
● Develop your explanation with more detail/an example.	
● **Either:** Add a reference to a source of wisdom and authority here.	
● **Explain a second reason.**	
● Develop your explanation with more detail/an example.	
● **Or:** Add a reference to a source of wisdom and authority here.	

TIP

Remember that 'artwork' could be paintings, frescoes, statues or sculptures, for example.

3 Explain **two** significant features of a Catholic Church building. In your answer you must refer to a source of wisdom and authority. **(5 marks)**

Test the 12 mark question (d)

1. 'A church is designed as the best way to worship God.' Evaluate this statement considering arguments for and against. In your response you should:

- refer to Catholic teachings
- refer to different Christian points of view
- reach a justified conclusion.

(12 marks)

ARGUMENTS IN SUPPORT OF THE STATEMENT • **Explain why some people would agree with the statement.** • Develop your explanation with more detail and examples. • Refer to religious teaching. Use a quote or paraphrase of a religious authority. • **Evaluate the arguments.** Is this a good argument? Explain why you think this. Use words such as convincing/strong/robust/weak/unpersuasive/unsuccessful within your reasoning.	Many church buildings are built pointing east as a reminder of Jesus rising, as the sun rises from the east. Likewise, many are built in the shape of the cross. Inside, the altar is the focal point of the Mass, the table of the Lord, therefore it is central to worship in the Church. Most Catholic churches have Stations of the Cross, which give a visible form to the final hours of Jesus' life; a reminder of his suffering, which may aid prayer. The Catechism of the Catholic Church 1137 states church buildings 'signify and make visible the Church living in this place'. **TIP** This is a good answer as it explains the features rather than just listing them.
ARGUMENTS SUPPORTING A DIFFERENT VIEW • **Explain why some people would disagree with the statement.** • Develop your explanation with more detail and examples. • Refer to religious teaching. Use a quote or paraphrase of a religious authority. • **Evaluate the arguments.** Is this a good argument? Explain why you think this. Use words such as convincing/strong/robust/weak/unpersuasive/unsuccessful within your reasoning.	Worship can take place anywhere. The Catechism calls people to be the 'living stones', gathered to be 'built into a spiritual house' (CCC 1139). Some Christians feel that worship should be led by the Holy Spirit and not dictated by the physical building. Many church buildings have paintings and statues and some Christians believe these distract from worship. Some Christians meet in buildings that are not dedicated churches, such as halls. **TIP** The answer incorporates references to the Catechism. It is not necessary to include sources of wisdom and authority in 12 mark questions, but it can help to show your understanding of religious teachings.
CONCLUSION • **Give a justified conclusion.** • Include your own reasoning. • Use words such as convincing/strong/robust/weak/unpersuasive/unsuccessful to weigh up the different arguments for and against. • Do not just repeat arguments you have already used without explaining how they apply to your reasoned opinion/conclusion.	In conclusion, I feel it is clear that churches are well designed to worship God, decorated and built in very specific ways. Therefore it is important that Catholics worship in church buildings whenever possible as they are clearly the best way to worship God.

Exam Practice

2 'Symbols remain an important part of the Church today.' Evaluate this statement considering arguments for and against. In your response you should:

- refer to Catholic teachings
- refer to different Christian points of view
- reach a justified conclusion. **(12 marks)**

ARGUMENTS IN SUPPORT OF THE STATEMENT ● **Explain why some people would agree with the statement.** ● Develop your explanation with more detail and examples. ● Refer to religious teaching. Use a quote or paraphrase of a religious authority. ● **Evaluate the arguments.** Is this a good argument? Explain why you think this. Use words such as convincing/strong/robust/weak/unpersuasive/unsuccessful within your reasoning.	*Some Christians/Catholics/people would agree with this statement because...*
ARGUMENTS SUPPORTING A DIFFERENT VIEW ● **Explain why some people would disagree with the statement.** ● Develop your explanation with more detail and examples. ● Refer to religious teaching. Use a quote or paraphrase of a religious authority. ● **Evaluate the arguments.** Is this a good argument? Explain why you think this. Use words such as convincing/strong/robust/weak/unpersuasive/unsuccessful within your reasoning.	*On the other hand, some Christians/Catholics/people would hold a different point of view...*
CONCLUSION ● **Give a justified conclusion.** ● Include your own reasoning. ● Use words such as convincing/strong/robust/weak/unpersuasive/unsuccessful to weigh up the different arguments for and against. ● Do not just repeat arguments you have already used without explaining how they apply to your reasoned opinion/conclusion.	*Having considered both sides of the argument, I would say that...*

3 'Sculptures and statues help a Catholic understand their relationship to God.' Evaluate this statement considering arguments for and against. In your response you should:

- refer to Catholic teachings
- refer to different Christian points of view
- reach a justified conclusion. **(12 marks)**

 REVIEW

- Check your answers to these exam questions on p.192–193, correct your answers with annotations, and note down any general areas for improvement.
- If you don't feel secure in the content of this chapter, you could reread the Recap sections.
- If you don't feel secure in your exam technique, you could revisit the exam support section on pp.7–14

RECAP

Essential information

- Islam means many things including peace, obedience, and submission.
- The six Beliefs come from the **Qur'an** (holy book of Muslims) and the **hadith** (sayings of the Prophet Muhammad).
- Sunni and Shi'a Muslims are the two main groups in Islam. They share many of the same beliefs.

TIP

Sunni and Shi'a Muslims share many beliefs, but express them in different ways. Sunni tradition has formed the six Beliefs, and Shi'a the five roots of 'Usul ad-Din (see 5.2).

> ❝[Faith] is that you believe in God and His Angels and His Books and His Messengers and the Hereafter and the good and evil fate [ordained by your God]❞ (*Hadith – Sahih Muslim, Kitab al-iman 1:1–4*)

What are the six Beliefs?	What do they mean?	How are they expressed in Sunni and Shi'a communities?
Belief in the unity of Allah (**Tawhid**)	There is only one God, Allah, and he has no equal.	Muslims profess their faith using the Shahadah, declaring 'there is no God except Allah'.
Belief in the angels of Allah	Angels created by Allah to perform various tasks.	Muslims are taught to respect all the angels and say 'peace be upon them' when their names are mentioned.
Belief in the books of Allah	Books of Allah contain teachings Allah has given to humans.	Muslims regard all messages from God as holy, especially the Qur'an because it is Allah's final revelation. Many Muslims read the Qur'an daily.
Belief in the prophets of Allah	The prophets of Allah (also known as messengers) are sent by Allah to guide people.	Many Muslims are named after different prophets so that they can learn from their example.
Belief in the Day of Judgment and life after death (Hereafter)	The Day of Judgment refers to a time when the dead will be raised again and rewarded or punished for their actions on earth.	Muslims believe they are responsible for each and every one of their deeds.
Belief in Allah's decree and predestination (good and evil fate)	Allah's decree is about his power and will. Humans have freedom but many things are predetermined by Allah.	Muslims try their best to live good lives, and seek blessings on a special night called Laylat al-Qadr (Night of Power, see 6.4) during Ramadan.

The importance of these principles for Muslims today

- It is important to be obedient to Allah and have faith in him.
- The six Beliefs lead Muslims closer to Allah.
- The six Beliefs guide Muslims in worship and daily life as a community.

TIP

It can be challenging to argue against a statement like this. You could start by looking at the first Belief (Tawhid) and consider if the other five Beliefs would be possible without Tawhid.

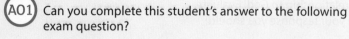
APPLY

AO1 Can you complete this student's answer to the following exam question?

b. Explain **two** ways that the six Beliefs are expressed in Muslim communities. (4)

> *One way that the six Beliefs are expressed in Muslim communities is through the profession of the Shahadah...*

AO2 Read the following exam question. Make a list of arguments for and against the statement.

d. 'The six Beliefs are all equally important.' Evaluate this statement considering arguments for and against. In your response you should:
- refer to Muslim teachings
- reach a justified conclusion. (15)

REVIEW

Answers: Mark your answers using p.193 and note areas for improvement.
AO1: This question is testing your ability to answer a (b) question. For help with this skill, see p.12.
AO2: This question is testing your ability to plan a response. For help with this skill, see p.12.

RECAP

Essential information

- The 'Usul ad-Din are the five main principles of faith for Shi'a Muslims.
- They are like the roots of a tree because they form the foundation of their belief.
- They guide Shi'a Muslims in worship and daily life.

In the core beliefs for Shi'a faith, as shown here, some roots are similar to Sunni six Beliefs, but not all.

- Means oneness of Allah
- There is none worthy of worship except Allah.

Tawhid

66 Say, He is God, the One, God the eternal 99 (Surah 112:1–2)

- Means divine justice
- Allah will judge people fairly for how they have lived.
- Human action is not predetermined by Allah – otherwise reward/ punishment would be unjust.

'Adl

Nubuwwah

- Means prophethood
- Messengers (from Adam to Prophet Muhammad) have been sent by Allah throughout history to guide human beings.

Imamah

Mi'ad

- Means Day of Judgment and Resurrection
- After death, each individual will be judged by Allah and rewarded or punished for their actions.

- Means successors to Prophet Muhammad
- After Muhammad, there are no more prophets. Instead, Allah appointed **Imams** (leaders) to guide human beings. These are all from the ahl al-bayt (family of Muhammad), the first being his son-in-law, Ali.

Seveners and Twelvers

- There is some debate among Shi'a traditions about how many Imams there have been after the Prophet Muhammad.
- The majority of Shi'a Muslims (called Twelvers) believe there have been 12 Imams, while others (such as Seveners) believe there have been fewer.

The importance of these principles for Shi'a Muslims today

- It is important to be obedient to Allah and have faith in him.
- The five roots lead Shi'a Muslims closer to Allah.
- Emphasising the justice of God places responsibility on humans for what they do.

TIP

Remember, 'Outline' means you have to write more than just a one-word answer (unlike a 'State' question). You should make three short points.

 **APPLY**

AO1 This student hasn't fully 'outlined' their points. Can you extend their answers?

a. Outline **three** of the five roots of 'Usul ad-Din. (3)

Oneness, Prophets, Justice

AO2 This student has started a paragraph in answer to the following exam question. Develop the point so that it includes a reference to a Muslim teaching, and a sentence evaluating that teaching.

d. 'Tawhid is the most important of the five roots of 'Usul ad-Din.' Evaluate this statement considering arguments for and against. In your response you should:
- refer to Muslim teachings
- refer to different Muslim points of view
- reach a justified conclusion. (15)

Shi'a Muslims may argue that belief in Tawhid is more important than the other roots of 'Usul ad-Din because belief in Allah and his oneness is the basis for all other beliefs.

 **REVIEW**

Answers: Mark your answers using p.193 and note areas for improvement.
AO1: This question is testing your ability to answer 'outline' questions. For help with this skill, see p.12.
AO2: This question is testing your ability to evaluate a statement. For help with this skill, see p.12.

RECAP

Essential information

- Muslims are **monotheists**, which means they believe in only one God named Allah.
- There are more than 130 characteristics of Allah mentioned in the Qur'an and the hadith.
- Each characteristic gives Muslims an understanding of what Allah is like.

The characteristics of Allah

- Allah revealed messages to the Prophet Muhammad. These messages are contained in the Qur'an.
- Chapters in the Qur'an start with the words 'In the name of God, the Lord of Mercy, the Giver of Mercy', which shows how important Allah's characteristic of Mercy is.

- Muslims believe it is impossible to visualise Allah because he is not a physical being. It is forbidden to try to draw him.
- Muslims believe that it is important for characteristics of Allah to be reflected in their own lives and behaviour. For example, as Allah is described as loving, Muslims should also be the same.

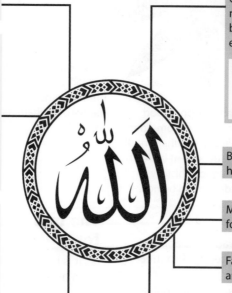

Immanence – Allah is present within the world. This does not mean as part of creation, for he is the creator.

Transcendence – Allah is beyond the physical world as the creator, all-knowing and all-powerful.

66 He is God, the One, God the eternal. He begot no one nor was He begotten. No one is comparable to Him. 99 (*Surah 112:1–4*)

Omnipotence – Allah has limitless and unimaginable power.

66 No vision can take Him in, but He takes in all vision. He is the All Subtle, the All Aware. 99 (*Surah 6:103*)

Tawhid – Allah is one: the unique and only God. This is the heart of Islamic belief, reflected in the Shahadah. Worshipping any being other than Allah is **shirk** (setting up equals to God), which is the worst sin.

66 Worship God and shun false gods. 99 (*Surah 16:36*)

Beneficence – Allah acts for the benefit of humanity.

Mercy – Allah shows compassion or forgiveness to those he could punish.

Fairness – Allah treats humans reasonably and with equality.

Justice/'Adl – Allah will punish and reward in a way that is right and fair.

TIP

It is a good idea to signpost your answer with a new line for the second point.

APPLY

(AO1) Read the start of the student answer to this question. What is wrong with it? Write an improved version.

c. Explain **two** Muslim beliefs about Allah. In your answer you must refer to a source of wisdom and authority. (5)

Muslims believe that Allah is part of the Trinity. The Qur'an teaches that 'The Word became flesh', showing that God became incarnate.

(AO2) Write down at least two points each both for and against the following statement.

'It's not possible to know what Allah is like.'

For	Against

REVIEW

Answers: Mark your answers using p.193 and note areas for improvement.
AO1: This question is testing your ability to explain beliefs correctly, using a source of wisdom and authority. For help with this skill, see p.12.
AO2: This question is testing your ability to evaluate a statement. For help with this skill, see p.12.

RECAP Essential information

- RiSalah is the channel of communication between Allah and people.
- This communication happens through prophets (also known as messengers) who are chosen by Allah to deliver his messages to humanity.
- Important prophets include Adam, Ibrahim, Isma'il, Musa, Dawud, Isa, and Muhammad.

The nature and importance of prophethood

- Muslims believe prophets are human beings appointed by Allah to guide people to truth.
- Twenty-five prophets are named in the Qur'an, but Muslim tradition says there have been approximately 124,000 prophets sent by Allah.
- The prophets received Allah's messages from the angel Jibril (Gabriel – see 5.6) but their words became ignored or distorted by people, and so Allah sent Muhammad with his final and perfect message.

- Prophets taught repentance and the need to obey Allah, and guided people to truth. Muslims follow their example in their own behaviour.

> 66 We believe in God and in what was sent down to us … and all the prophets by their Lord. We make no distinction between any of them 99 (*Surah 2:136*)

Key examples of the prophets

Adam: first prophet to receive a message from Allah. He was expelled from a beautiful garden after making a mistake, but Allah forgave him.

Ibrahim (Abraham): given the Sahifah Ibrahim sacred texts. He led many people away from idol worship and faced many tests of faith. He helped rebuild a sanctuary called the Ka'bah in Makkah, the centre of Muslim pilgrimage.

Dawud (David): became king of the Israelites after defeating Goliath. He was given the Zabur (the Psalms).

Muhammad: the perfect example for Muslims. He called for peace and social justice. The angel Jibril revealed Allah's last message, the Qur'an, to him. This is why Muhammad is called 'the Seal of the Prophets' (*Surah 33:40*).

1800–1700 BCE · 1250 BCE · 1000 BCE · 0 CE · 570 CE

Isma'il (Ishmael): son of Ibrahim willing to give his life to God when Ibrahim had a dream in which Isma'il was being sacrificed. Model of obedience for Muslims. Helped his father rebuild the Ka'bah.

Musa (Moses): main founder of Judaism who led the Jews out of slavery in Egypt into the Promised Land. The teachings given to him are in the Tawrat (Torah).

Isa (Jesus): born to Mary, without a biological father. He was given the Injil, which Muslims believe is the original Gospel. Muslims do not believe that he was divine or killed on the cross.

APPLY

AO1 This student answer has only two simple points. Can you develop them?

b. Explain **two** reasons why prophets are important in Islam. (4)

> *Guide people to truth.*
> *Good examples of how to live.*

AO2 The arguments for why prophets are important in Islam are usually quite clear. What would you include as a counter-argument in a question such as this? Use the sentence starter to write a full paragraph.

d. 'All of the prophets in Islam are as important as each other.' Evaluate this statement considering arguments for and against. In your response you should:
- refer to Muslim teachings
- reach a justified conclusion. (15)

> *However, some may argue that Muhammad was the most important prophet...*

REVIEW **Answers:** Mark your answers using p.193 and note areas for improvement.
AO1: This question is testing your ability to write a developed point. For help with this skill, see p.12.
AO2: This question is testing your ability to write a well-argued paragraph. For help with this skill, see p.12.

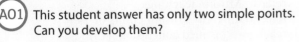

 **RECAP**

Essential information

- Allah's messages (also called revelations) to many different prophets have been recorded in holy books.
- Some holy books were only meant for a particular group of people living at a particular time.
- Many teachings were lost or changed and so became unreliable, so Allah revealed the Qur'an to be the final and perfect book.

The nature and history of Muslim holy books

Muslims believe that all revelations to prophets originally came from Allah. These include:

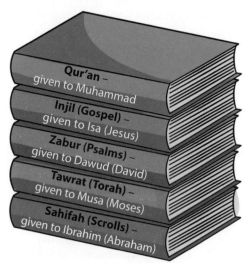

Qur'an – given to Muhammad

Injil (Gospel) – given to Isa (Jesus)

Zabur (Psalms) – given to Dawud (David)

Tawrat (Torah) – given to Musa (Moses)

Sahifah (Scrolls) – given to Ibrahim (Abraham)

- The final revelation from Allah is the Qur'an (which means 'recitation') given to the Prophet Muhammad.
- He received the Qur'an through the angel Jibril and the words were recorded by scribes before being compiled in a book. The third Khalifah (spiritual leader) after Muhammad, 'Uthman, had copies of the Qur'an made and sent to different cities.

> 66 The Qur'an is nothing less than a revelation that is sent to him [Muhammad]. It was taught to him by [an angel] with mighty powers and great strength 99 *(Surah 53:4–5)*

The holy books for Muslims today

- The Qur'an has supreme authority for Muslims and is the guidance for their life. The Qur'an is protected from corruption.
- For Muslims, all of the books are holy – this is why they are included in the six Beliefs, and some Muslims will study teachings in earlier scriptures in light of the Qur'an.
- Many Muslims try to memorise the whole Qur'an – those who succeed are given the title 'Hafiz' (guardian).

TIP

Remember, your conclusion must be justified, which means you must explain why you have reached your particular conclusion.

 APPLY

AO1 Read the first part of the student answer to this question, then write the second developed point so that it is complete.

b. Explain **two** Muslim attitudes to holy books. (4)

> *Muslims believe that all holy books are from Allah. Allah revealed messages to many different prophets which are still found in scriptures like the Tawrat and Qur'an. Therefore, a Muslim must respect all holy books.*
>
> *Secondly...*

AO2 Read the arguments for and against the statement, then write your own justified conclusion.

d. 'The Qur'an is the only book Muslims need to read.' Evaluate this statement considering arguments for and against. In your response you should:
- refer to Muslim teachings
- refer to different Muslim points of view
- reach of a justified conclusion. (15)

For	Against
• Holy books before the Qur'an are unreliable.	• Allah revealed many messages before the Qur'an.
• All other holy books paved the way for the Qur'an.	• Belief in holy books is one of the six Beliefs of Islam for Sunni Muslims.
• The Qur'an is the final and perfect book.	• Muslims must respect all holy books.

 **REVIEW**

Answers: Mark your answers using p.193 and note areas for improvement.
AO1: This question is testing your ability to write a developed point. For help with this skill, see p.12.
AO2: This question is testing your ability to write a justified conclusion. For help with this skill, see p.12.

RECAP

Essential information

- **Malaikah** is the Arabic word for the angels of Allah.
- Belief in angels is the second of the six Beliefs of Islam for Sunni Muslims.
- Angels perform various tasks for Allah.

What is the nature of angels?

> ❝if anyone is an enemy of God, His angels and His messengers, or Gabriel and Michael, then God is certainly the enemy of such disbelievers.❞ (*Surah 2:98*)

Diagram – Malaikah:
- Reveal Allah's message to humans through the prophets
- Immortal (will never die)
- Created by Allah out of light
- Free from sin
- Not physical beings, but can take a form if required
- No gender
- No free will

How are angels shown in the Qur'an?

Muslims believe Allah has created numerous angels. The ones considered the most important are called 'archangels'. These include:

Jibril (Gabriel)

- Angel of revelation: communicates Allah's messages to prophets including communicating the whole Qur'an to the Prophet Muhammad

> ❝Gabriel – who by God's leave brought down the Qur'an to your heart.❞ (*Surah 2:97*)

Mika'il (Michael)

- Angel of mercy: responsible for providing and maintaining life
- Brings the rain and wind and is in charge of the weather

Izra'il (Azrael)

- Called the 'Angel of Death' (*Surah 32:11*)
- Responsible for taking the last breath from humans and all living creatures when they die

Israfil (Rafael)

- Responsible for the Day of Judgment
- Will sound the Last Trumpet

There are other influential angels too:

- Al-kiraman al-katibin: honourable scribes who record every good and bad deed a person does for the book they receive on the Last Day
- Hafaza: keep watch day and night over every human being

Importance for Muslims today

- Angels obey every command of Allah – this teaches Muslims to do the same.
- Belief in angels is the second of the six Beliefs for Sunni Muslims, and is also important for Shi'a Muslims.
- Each angel holds an important role that directly affects the lives of Muslims.

APPLY

AO1 Complete the table below to help you answer this question.

a. Outline **three** important angels in Islam. (3)

Angel	Importance
Jibril	Communicates Allah's messages to prophets
Mika'il	
Izra'il	

AO2 What would you include as a counter-argument in a question such as this? Use the sentence starter to write a full paragraph.

d. 'Jibril is the most important angel in Islam.' Evaluate this statement considering arguments for and against. In your response you should:
- refer to Muslim teachings
- reach a justified conclusion. (15)

> *However, some Muslims would say that all angels are equally important. This is because...*

REVIEW

Answers: Mark your answers using p.193 and note areas for improvement.
AO1: This question is testing your ability to answer 'outline' questions. For help with this skill, see p.12.
AO2: This question is testing your ability to write a well-argued paragraph. For help with this skill, see p.12.

RECAP

Essential information

- **Al-Qadr** is the belief of predestination – that the universe follows the divine master plan of Allah.
- Allah is omnipotent (all-powerful) and omniscient (all-knowing) and has fixed many laws in the universe.
- Muslims believe Allah has also given humans free will to make many of their own choices.

What is predestination?

- Allah is the creator of the universe and knows everything. He has a plan for the world and the power to make it happen.
- However, this does not mean that a person is forced to do anything. Muslims believe everyone has the right and freedom to do and believe whatever they like.
- *Sahih Al-Bukhari 78:685* supports the idea that a person's destiny is set by Allah. It teaches Muslims that the choices people make may coincide with Allah's will.
- Allah knows what people will do before they do it, but humans have the free will to make the decision to do or not do what Allah wants.
- As humans are given free will, they need to be responsible for their choices and actions. This is why there is a **Day of Judgment** when Allah will decide if a person will go to **paradise** or hell.

66 The overall scheme belongs to God **99**
(Surah 13:42)

Divergent understandings of predestination

Sunni and Shi'a Muslims have different understandings about predestination.

Shi'a Muslims	Sunni Muslims
Shi'a Muslims believe *Surah 13:11* in the Qur'an allows the possibility that Allah can change a person's destiny according to the actions they decide to take. For instance, Allah may have destined for you to die at the age of 60, but if you are a good person and have a positive influence on others, Allah may grant you a longer life. This means that a person's actions can change their destiny.	Sunni Muslims believe that while a person has many choices in life, their destiny is set and known by Allah. This does not mean that their freedom is taken away, but that Allah already knows what choices they will make. For instance, a parent may already know their child will always choose a bar of chocolate over a piece of fruit, but it's still the child making the choice.

Muslims believe that we are always making choices, but the results are already known by Allah

The implications of al-Qadr for Muslims today

Belief in al-Qadr:

- helps guide Muslims to be better people
- can support faith during difficult times as a reminder that all things are part of Allah's plan
- makes Muslims accountable for how they have lived.

APPLY

AO1 This student answer has only two simple points. Can you develop them? Remember to include a source of wisdom and authority.

c. Explain **two** Muslim beliefs about al-Qadr. In your answer you must refer to a source of wisdom and authority. (5)

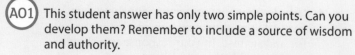

Allah is Omnipotent.
Humans have been given free will.

AO2 Write down at least two points each, both for and against this statement. Aim to include both Sunni and Shi'a Muslim beliefs.

'Everyone's destiny is decided.'

For	Against

REVIEW

Answers: Mark your answers using p.193 and note areas for improvement.
AO1: This question is testing your ability to explain beliefs correctly, using a source of wisdom and authority. For help with this skill, see p.12.
AO2: This question is testing your ability to break down the question and plan a response. For help with this skill, see p.12.

 **RECAP**

Essential information

- **Akhirah** is the belief in life after death. Muslims believe that our physical life will come to an end and we will be raised again in the next life.
- The Day of Judgment is when Allah will judge all people justly for how they lived their life and will send them to either paradise or hell.
- Paradise is described as a place of peace while hell is a place of punishment.

Muslims believe life is temporary and so it is important to live the best life they possibly can.

> ❝God created the heavens and earth for a true purpose: to reward each soul according to its deeds❞
> (*Surah 45:22*)

All of a person's thoughts, words, and actions are recorded and then judged by Allah on the Day of Judgment.

> ❝When we are turned to bones and dust, shall we really be raised up in a new act of creation?❞
> (*Surah 17:49*)

It is on this day that everyone learns whether they will go to paradise or hell. Before this happens, everyone goes through **Barzakh** (period between death and judgment), which is a foretaste of what is about to happen.

Judgment, paradise, and hell

Judgment	Paradise	Hell
<ul><li>Also known as resurrection</li><li>Heralded by the sound of a trumpet</li><li>Everyone learns about how they have lived</li></ul>	<ul><li>Also known as al-Jannah (the Garden)</li><li>A place of beauty and perfect happiness</li><li>Has a number of gates based on people's level of faith</li></ul>	<ul><li>Called Jahannam</li><li>A place of punishment for those who have done wrong</li><li>Has a number of gates based on people's level of sin</li></ul>

TIP

You don't need to put your conclusion at the end of an answer. You can begin an answer with a statement of conclusion, and then go on to justify it – ensuring you still evaluate both sides.

 APPLY

AO1 Read the first part of the student answer to this question, then write the second developed point so that it is complete.

b. Explain **two** reasons why Muslims believe in life after death. (4)

> *One reason why Muslims believe in life after death is because it is one of the six Beliefs. You cannot be a Muslim unless you believe in the Akhirah.*

AO2 Write a short statement of conclusion to start an answer to this question.

d. 'If there is no paradise, there is no need to be good.' Evaluate this statement considering arguments for and against. In your response you should:
- refer to Muslim teachings
- refer to different Muslim points of view
- reach a justified conclusion. (15)

 REVIEW

Answers: Mark your answers using p.193 and note areas for improvement.
AO1: This question is testing your ability to write a developed point. For help with this skill, see p.12.
AO2: This question is testing your ability to begin an essay with a strong line of argument. For help with this skill, see p.12.

RECAP

What is a compare and contrast question?

There are a few areas of the exam specification where you can be asked to compare and contrast two religions, or two groups within a religion. For example, you might get asked to compare Catholic Christianity with other Christian denominations, or you might be asked to compare two religions, for example Islam and Christianity.

In this paper, Paper 2, you will only be asked to compare Islam with Christianity (the 'main religious tradition of Great Britain'), and you will only be asked to compare them on two possible topics: eschatology and worship (see p.86). Here, you can revise for eschatology.

How is eschatology different for Christians and Muslims?

	Muslims	Christians
Heaven/ paradise, hell, and purgatory	• Muslims believe in both paradise (known as al-Jannah, or the Garden) and hell (called Jahannam). • Paradise is a place of beauty and perfect happiness, and has a number of gates based on people's level of faith. • Hell is a place of punishment for those who have done wrong, and similarly has a number of gates based on people's level of sin.	• Most Christians believe in heaven and hell. However, unlike the Muslim belief, hell does not have different gates. • Catholic Christians also believe in purgatory – a place of purification. • Some Christians would deny that an all-loving God would allow hell to exist, and so believe that everyone (not just Christians) will live together forever in heaven. This is called universalism.
Judgment	• Muslims believe the Day of Judgment will be sounded with a trumpet, blown by the angel Israfil. • Everyone will learn about how they have lived and their fate.	• Catholics believe in two kinds of judgment: Particular Judgment (which happens when you die) and Final Judgment (which happens at the end of time). • Some Christians place more emphasis on the Final Judgment, where they believe God will judge all people and give them the afterlife they deserve.
Resurrection	• There is a period between death and judgment called Barzakh. • Many Muslims believe in a physical resurrection while other Muslims believe souls will be given new bodies in the next life.	• Catholics believe physical resurrection happens after the Final Judgment; it is not just spiritual. • Some Christians believe in just a spiritual resurrection, not a physical one.

APPLY

You could be asked to compare and contrast in (b) questions (but being able to talk about different viewpoints within Islam is also a useful skill in (d) questions!). For example, here's a question you could be asked:

b. Describe **two** differences in beliefs about life after death between Islam and the main religious tradition of Great Britain. (4)

Here is an example of how you could structure an answer to this question:

● Give one belief in Islam.	The first difference is that Muslims believe when people die they will be sent either to paradise or to hell,
● Give a contrasting belief in Christianity.	whereas in Catholic Christianity there is a third place called purgatory where people go to be purified before going to heaven.
● Give a second belief in Islam.	Secondly, in Islam hell is a place of punishment for those who have done wrong.
● Give a contrasting belief in Christianity.	Yet for some universalist Christians, an all-loving God would not allow hell to exist, so all people will live together forever in heaven.

TIP

Remember, when the exam says 'the main religious tradition of Great Britain', it is referring to Christianity.

Now have a go at answering the same question yourself, using the grid below to help you. Try to choose **different** points from those given in the answer table above.

● Give one belief in Islam.	The first difference is that in Islam...
● Give a contrasting belief in Christianity.	Whereas in Christianity...
● Give a second belief in Islam.	Secondly, in Islam...
● Give a contrasting belief in Christianity.	Yet for Christians...

TIP

Words like 'whereas', 'yet', and 'however' will signal to the examiner that you're making a comparison.

Test the 3 mark question (a)

1 Outline **three** of the five roots of 'Usul ad-Din. **(3 marks)**

Three of the five roots of 'Usul ad-Din are belief in Tawhid (one God) (1), Nubuwwah (Prophethood) (1), and Mi'ad (Day of Judgment and Resurrection) (1).

2 Outline **three** Muslim beliefs about Allah. **(3 marks)**

Muslims believe that Allah is one (this is known as Tawhid). (1)

_____

_____

3 Outline **three** Muslim beliefs about angels. **(3 marks)**

_____

_____

_____

Test the 4 mark question (b)

1 Explain **two** reasons why Muhammad is an important prophet in Islam. **(4 marks)**

• **Explain one reason.**	*One reason why Muhammad is an important prophet in Islam is because he was given the final message from Allah.*
• Develop your explanation with more detail/an example/reference to a religious teaching or quotation.	*This is why he was called 'the Seal of the Prophets' (Surah 33:40).*
• **Explain a second reason.**	*A second reason why Muhammad is an important prophet in Islam is because he was the best example of how to live.*
• Develop your explanation with more detail/an example/reference to a religious teaching or quotation.	*Therefore, Muslims try their best to follow his example and preserve his legacy. In this way they hope that they will please Allah.*

TIP
It is not necessary to provide a source of wisdom and authority in this question, but doing so shows the examiner that you are confident giving evidence.

2 Explain **two** ways that a Muslim can show their commitment to their faith. **(4 marks)**

• **Explain one way.**	
• Develop your explanation with more detail/an example/reference to a religious teaching or quotation.	
• **Explain a second way.**	
• Develop your explanation with more detail/an example/reference to a religious teaching or quotation.	

TIP
Remember that although Muslims believe that the Qur'an is the most important of all holy books, they believe other holy books are also special and must still be respected.

3 Explain **two** reasons why the Qur'an is the most important holy book for Muslims. **(4 marks)**

Exam Practice

Test the 5 mark question (c)

1   Explain **two** Muslim beliefs about Allah. In your answer you must refer to
a source of wisdom and authority.

(5 marks)

● **Explain one belief.**	One Muslim belief about Allah is that he is one.
● Develop your explanation with more detail/an example.	This means that Muslims worship only Allah and not any other beings.
● **Either:** Add a reference to a source of wisdom and authority here.	They are taught in the Qur'an to 'shun false gods' (Surah 16:36).
● **Explain a second belief.**	Another Muslim belief about Allah is that he has more than 100 characteristics.
● Develop your explanation with more detail/an example.	These include belief in Allah as omnipotent, beneficent, merciful, and just.
● **Or:** Add a reference to a source of wisdom and authority here.	

> **TIP**
> Here is the reference to a source of wisdom and authority. You only need to make one reference to gain the fifth mark – you don't need evidence of a source of wisdom and authority to support both your points.

2   Explain **two** Muslim beliefs about al-Qadr. In your answer you must refer to a source of
wisdom and authority.

(5 marks)

● **Explain one belief.**	
● Develop your explanation with more detail/an example.	
● **Either:** Add a reference to a source of wisdom and authority here.	
● **Explain a second belief.**	
● Develop your explanation with more detail/an example.	
● **Or:** Add a reference to a source of wisdom and authority here.	

> **TIP**
> Giving a full reference for a source of wisdom and authority would really impress the examiner, but this is not essential. If you cannot remember the exact words then try paraphrasing (putting it into your own words), or if you can't give the correct reference then just naming the Muslim source it's from (e.g. Qur'an) is acceptable.

3   Explain **two** reasons why Jibril is important to Muslims. In your answer you must refer
to a source of wisdom and authority.

(5 marks)

Exam Practice

Test the 15 mark question (d)

1 'There are more similarities than differences between Sunni and Shi'a Muslims.'
Evaluate this statement. In your response you should:

- refer to Muslim teachings
- refer to different Muslim points of view
- reach a justified conclusion.

(15 marks)

ARGUMENTS IN SUPPORT OF THE STATEMENT ● **Explain why some people would agree with the statement.** ● Develop your explanation with more detail and examples. ● Refer to religious teaching. Use a quote or paraphrase of a religious authority. ● **Evaluate the arguments.** Is this a good argument? Explain why you think this. Use words such as convincing/strong/robust/weak/unpersuasive/unsuccessful within your reasoning.	Many Muslims would agree with this statement because the basic beliefs of Sunni and Shi'a Muslims are the same. This is because they have a shared history and both believe in the Qur'an and the prophethood of Muhammad, from where Muslim teachings come. Therefore, tenets such as Tawhid, Risalah, and Hajj unite Sunni and Shi'a Muslims, and feature in their main principles of belief, such as the six Beliefs and the five roots of 'Usul ad-Din. Sunni and Shi'a Muslims are often seen praying and going on pilgrimage together. This is in the spirit of teachings that promote unity: 'Hold fast to God's rope all together' (Surah 3: 103). This is a robust case in favour of the statement.

TIP
In a 15 mark question 3 of the marks available are awarded for correct spelling, punctuation and grammar. You should check your answer thoroughly.

ARGUMENTS SUPPORTING A DIFFERENT VIEW ● **Explain why some people would disagree with the statement.** ● Develop your explanation with more detail and examples. ● Refer to religious teaching. Use a quote or paraphrase of a religious authority. ● **Evaluate the arguments.** Is this a good argument? Explain why you think this. Use words such as convincing/strong/robust/weak/unpersuasive/unsuccessful within your reasoning.	However, other Muslims would disagree with the statement because Sunni and Shi'a Muslims do also differ on certain aspects, such as who should have led the Muslim community after the Prophet's death. Sunni Muslims believe in all four caliphs after the death of Muhammad, but Shi'a Muslims do not accept the first three, and consider Ali to have been the rightful leader of Muslims. As a result of this split, both groups have developed their own separate paths because of some fundamental disagreements – like the importance given to ahl al-bayt. Sunnis do not accept the authority of Shi'a imams, or vice versa. Sunni and Shi'a Muslims also have differences in the way they pray (for instance, Shi'as place a turbah on the ground) and how they conduct marriages and divorces. This affects unity within Islam, and has even led to violent clashes, such as in some parts of the Muslim world today. There are also further divisions within the two branches, like in Shi'a Islam where Twelvers and Seveners have separate lines of imams. Therefore, many would be unconvinced by the statement.
CONCLUSION ● **Give a justified conclusion.** ● Include your own reasoning. ● Use words such as convincing/strong/robust/weak/unpersuasive/unsuccessful to weigh up the different arguments for and against. ● Do not just repeat arguments you have already used without explaining how they apply to your reasoned opinion/conclusion.	In conclusion, I believe there are more convincing arguments in favour of there being more similarities between Sunnis and Shi'as. Yes there are key points of difference, notably about leadership, but the five pillars and six Beliefs of Sunnis are accepted by Shi'as too, and they are generally seen to be united rather than disunited. This makes a strong case for arguing that Sunnis and Shi'as have much more in common and this is why relations between the two groups are more harmonious than hostile.

TIP
Examiners like to see students making links between beliefs and the modern world, so try to include these where relevant.

Exam Practice

2 'Every person makes their own destiny.' Evaluate this statement. In your reponse you should:

- refer to Muslim teachings
- refer to different Muslim points of view
- reach a justified conclusion.

TIP

Remember, the examiner will also be assessing your Spelling, Punctuation, and Grammar on this question – so write carefully using your best written English.

(15 marks)

ARGUMENTS IN SUPPORT OF THE STATEMENT ● **Explain why some people would agree with the statement.** ● Develop your explanation with more detail and examples. ● Refer to religious teaching. Use a quote or paraphrase of a religious authority. ● **Evaluate the arguments.** Is this a good argument? Explain why you think this. Use words such as convincing/strong/robust/weak/unpersuasive/unsuccessful within your reasoning.	*Some Muslims/people would agree with this statement because...*
ARGUMENTS SUPPORTING A DIFFERENT VIEW ● **Explain why some people would disagree with the statement.** ● Develop your explanation with more detail and examples. ● Refer to religious teaching. Use a quote or paraphrase of a religious authority. ● **Evaluate the arguments.** Is this a good argument? Explain why you think this. Use words such as convincing/strong/robust/weak/unpersuasive/unsuccessful within your reasoning.	*On the other hand, some Muslims/people would hold a different point of view...*
CONCLUSION ● **Give a justified conclusion.** ● Include your own reasoning. ● Use words such as convincing/strong/robust/weak/unpersuasive/unsuccessful to weigh up the different arguments for and against. ● Do not just repeat arguments you have already used without explaining how they apply to your reasoned opinion/conclusion.	*Having considered both sides of the argument, I would say that...*

3 'Akhirah is the most important Muslim belief.' Evaluate this statement. In your response you should:

- refer to Muslim teachings
- refer to different Muslim points of view
- reach a justified conclusion.

(15 marks)

 **REVIEW**

Check your answers to these exam questions on p.194, correct your answers with annotations, and note down any general areas for improvement.
If you don't feel secure in the content of this chapter, you could reread the Recap sections.
If you don't feel secure in your exam technique, you could revisit the exam support section on pp.7–14.

RECAP

Essential information
- The Ten Obligatory Acts are the most important duties for Shi'a Muslims.
- Most of these acts are also shared by Sunni Muslims.
- They teach Shi'a Muslims that beliefs are not enough – actions are essential too.

For Shi'a Muslims, the Ten Obligatory Acts are like the branches of a tree that flourish and grow from strong roots (see 5.2). These acts enable Shi'a Muslims to connect with Allah, purify their hearts, ease the suffering of the poor, and promote a better society. Sunni Muslims also perform these acts, but officially recognise five acts (see 6.2–6.6).

> 66 The believers, both men and women, support each other; they order what is right and forbid what is wrong 99 *(Surah 9:71)*

Jihad
- Striving for Allah
- Includes greater and lesser jihad

Khums
- Payment of 20 per cent of an individual's surplus income

Zakah
- Payment of 2.5 per cent of a Muslim's wealth to the poor
- Its payment 'purifies' a Muslim's income

Hajj
Pilgrimage to Makkah, Saudi Arabia
Must undertake once in their lives if physically and financially possible

Sawm
- Fasting during the month of Ramadan
- Helps Muslims gain self-control, appreciate Allah's gifts, and understand the needs of the poor

Salah
- Praying five times a day
- Pray to Allah using set prayers and movements

Amr bil-Ma'ruf
- Encouraging others to do good

Nahy anil-Munkar
- Discouraging others from doing bad
- Amr bil-Ma'ruf and Nahy anil-Munkar will help a Muslim's progress towards paradise in the afterlife

Tawalla
- Expressing love for Allah or good
- Shi'as believe they should only associate with just and good people

Tabarra
- Expressing disdain for the enemies of Allah or evil

APPLY

AO1 Can you develop two basic points in this student's answer?

   b. Explain **two** reasons why the Ten Obligatory Acts are important for Shi'a Muslims. (4)

> It's how Shi'a Muslims live out their beliefs.
> It's how Shi'a Muslims become close to Allah.

AO2 Read the following exam question. Make a list of arguments for and against this statement.

   d. 'The Ten Obligatory Acts are as important as each other.' Evaluate this statement considering arguments for and against. In your response you should:
- refer to Muslim teachings
- refer to different Muslim points of view
- reach a justified conclusion. (12)

REVIEW

Answers: Mark your answers using p.194 and note areas for improvement.
AO1: This question is testing your ability to answer a (b) question. For help with this skill, see p.12.
AO2: This question is testing your ability to identify arguments for and against. For help with this skill, see p.12.

RECAP

Essential information

- **Shahadah** is the first of the **Five Pillars** of Islam.
- It is the declaration of faith for all Muslims, including Sunni and Shi'a.
- The Shahadah sums up the core beliefs in Islam.

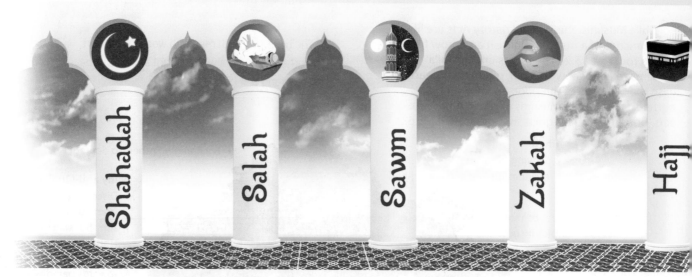

The Five Pillars

What is the Shahadah?

- The declaration of faith for all Muslims, based on this teaching:

> 66 God bears witness that there is no god but Him, as do the angels and those who have knowledge. 99 (*Surah 3:18*)

- The Shahadah has two parts that all Muslims recite:

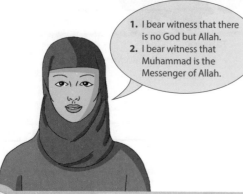

1. I bear witness that there is no God but Allah.
2. I bear witness that Muhammad is the Messenger of Allah.

- A number of Shi'a Muslims will also add a third phrase:

3. Ali is the Friend of God.

The importance of the Shahadah

- It sums up the core Muslim beliefs that are Tawhid (oneness of God) and RiSalah (prophethood).
- Fathers recite the words into the ears of newborn babies so that it is the first thing they hear.
- Anyone who wants to become a Muslim is required to repeat the words.
- They are also recited at the time of a person's burial.

APPLY

(AO1) Answer this question on your own!

a. Outline **three** of the Five Pillars of Islam. (3)

(AO2) This student has started a paragraph in answer to the following exam question. Develop the point so that it includes a reference to a Muslim teaching, and a sentence of evaluation.

TIP Remember, it is not enough to name three pillars. You should write a short sentence to explain each one.

d. 'Shahadah is the most important pillar of Islam.' Evaluate this statement considering arguments for and against. In your response you should:
- refer to Muslim teachings
- reach a justified conclusion. (12)

Many Muslims may argue that Shahadah is the most important pillar of Islam because it is the declaration of their core beliefs.

REVIEW

Answers: Mark your answers using p.194 and note areas for improvement.
AO1: This question is testing your ability to recall information. For help with this skill, see p.12.
AO2: This question is testing your ability to evaluate a statement. For help with this skill, see p.12.

 **RECAP**

Essential information
- **Salah** is the second Pillar of Islam for Sunni Muslims, and the first Obligatory Act for Shi'a Muslims.
- Salah means 'prayer' and connects Muslims to Allah.
- Muslims must pray five times a day, mainly in the mosque or at home.

What is Salah?
- A physical, spiritual, and mental act of worship following prescribed words and actions
- Offered at fixed times during the day (Sunni Muslims separate each of the five prayers, while Shi'a Muslims often combine a couple of them)
- Performed in the way the Prophet Muhammad did
- Aims to purify the mind and soul and develop closeness to Allah.

> 66 keep up the prayer: prayer restrains outrageous and unacceptable behaviour 99
> (*Surah 29:45*)

Features of Salah

Ablution (wudu'): It is important for Muslims to be clean before prayer, therefore they must wash or wipe various parts of the face and body including hands, mouth, elbows, and feet. Sunni Muslims wipe their whole head, while Shi'a Muslims only wipe the front of the head.

Timings: There are five daily prayers (Fajr, Zuhr, Asr, Maghrib, Isha). Sunni Muslims pray at these five set times, whereas Shi'a Muslims combine a couple of the prayers and pray three times a day.

Direction (qiblah): Muslims face Makkah, where the Ka'bah is located. This is for the purpose of unity.

Movements: Each Salah is made up of a sequence of actions and prayers known as rak'ah, such as standing, bowing, and prostrating.

Recitations: Words recited during Salah are taken mainly from the Qur'an and the hadith.

Where does Salah take place?
- Salah can be offered anywhere but Muslims aim to go to the mosque, which is built for the worship of Allah.
- Muslims can also offer Salah at home, where a clean space may be allocated to pray with relatives.
- The most important day of the week for Muslims is Friday. This is when the Jummah prayer takes place in mosques, the main part being a sermon by the Imam.

 APPLY

AO1 Write down a third point to complete the answer to this question.

a. Outline **three** features of Salah. (3)

> *It is one of the Pillars of Islam.*
> *There are five daily prayers.*

AO2 To practise the (d) question, write down at least one point each both for and against this statement.

'Salah is the best way for Muslims to become close to Allah.'

For	Against

 **REVIEW**

Answers: Mark your answers using p.194 and note areas for improvement.
AO1: This question is testing your ability to recall information. For help with this skill, see p.12.
AO2: This question is testing your ability to evaluate a statement. For help with this skill, see p.12.

RECAP

What is a compare and contrast question?

There are a few areas of the exam specification where you can be asked to compare and contrast two religions, or two groups within a religion. For example, you might be asked to compare Catholic Christianity with other Christian denominations, or you might be asked to compare two religions, for example Islam and Christianity.

In this paper, Paper 2, you will only be asked to compare Islam with Christianity (the 'main religious tradition of Great Britain'), and you will only be asked to compare them on two possible topics: eschatology and worship (see p.78). Here, you can revise for worship.

How is worship different for Christians and Muslims?

	Christians	Muslims
The nature of worship	• The Catholic Mass has a formal and structured order to the liturgy (liturgical). • For Catholics, the Eucharist is the 'source and summit' and 'sacrament of sacraments'. • Some Christians do not see one form of worship as superior to others; they believe there are equal ways to communicate with and praise God. • Some Christians do not celebrate the Eucharist and Protestants believe it to be symbolic.	• Prayer can take place in many different forms, both individually and collectively. • Salah is the main formal prayer to be offered five times a day at fixed times, mainly in the mosque or home. • Salah is a physical, spiritual, and mental act of worship, aiming to purify the mind and soul and develop closeness to Allah. • Muslims attend the Jummah prayer every Friday in mosques. The main part of this is a sermon given by the Imam.
Features of worship	• The priest, or other clergy, leads the Mass. • The Church of England has the Book of Common Prayer to guide worship. • Worshippers partake of the bread and wine, to receive the body and blood of Christ (transubstantiation in Catholicism). • Eucharistic adoration – where Catholics adore the presence of Jesus. • The Mass contains signs and symbols linking back to Apostolic Tradition and the teachings of the Bible and magisterium. • The Nicene Creed is sometimes recited by the people. • Some Christians feel that spontaneous involvement from the congregation, guided by the Bible and Holy Spirit, can help them connect to God.	• Sunni Muslims separate each of the five prayers while Shi'a Muslims often combine a couple of them. • Ablution (wudu') is performed prior to Salah so that Muslims are clean before prayer. They are required to wash or wipe various parts of the face and body including hands, mouth, elbows, and feet. Sunni Muslims wipe their whole head while Shi'a Muslims only wipe the front of the head. • Muslims face Makkah (qiblah) which is where the Ka'bah is located. This is for the purpose of unity. • Each Salah is made up of a sequence of actions and prayers known as rak'ah, such as standing, bowing, and prostrating. • Prescribed words, mainly taken from the Qur'an and hadith, are recited during Salah.

TIP
Remember, when the exam says 'the main religious tradition of Great Britain', it is referring to Christianity.

APPLY

You could be asked to compare and contrast in (b) questions (but being able to talk about different viewpoints within Islam is also a useful skill in (d) questions!).

For example, here's a question you could be asked:

b. Describe **two** differences between Islam and the main religious tradition of Great Britain. (4)

Here is an example of how you could structure an answer to this question:

Give one belief in Islam	The first difference is that Muslims worship five times a day at fixed times, mainly in the mosque or home,
Give a contrasting belief in Christianity	whereas in Christianity no specific number is given for how many times Christians should pray in a day, nor where worship needs to take place.
Give a second belief in Islam	Secondly, in Islam Muslims are required to perform ablution prior to Salah to prepare them both mentally and physically before standing in front of Allah.

Give a contrasting belief in Christianity	However, Christians attend church in order to become purified which is achieved through the partaking of the bread and wine which represent Jesus.

Now have a go at answering the same question yourself, using the grid below to help you.

Try to choose **different** points from those given in the answer table above.

Give one belief in Islam	The first difference is that in Islam...
Give a contrasting belief in Christianity	whereas in Christianity...
Give a second belief in Islam	Secondly, in Islam...
Give a contrasting belief in Christianity	However/Yet, Christians...

TIP
Words such as 'whereas', 'yet', and 'however' will signal to the examiner that you're making a comparison.

RECAP

Essential information
- **Sawm** is one of the Pillars of Islam (Sunni) and Obligatory Acts (Shi'a).
- It means 'to abstain' and is used in Islam for fasting, which is mainly observed during the holy month of Ramadan.
- The purpose of sawm is to be mindful of Allah.

What is sawm?

66 You who believe, fasting has been prescribed for you ... so that you may be mindful of God 99
(*Surah 2:183*)

The Prophet Muhammad taught that fasting is pointless if Muslims do not become better people

Fasting can happen at any time during the year, but is compulsory during the month of Ramadan

Only mature and healthy Muslims are required to fast

Enables Muslims to appreciate the suffering of the poor and be more grateful for what they have

Sawm

Starts from the first light of dawn and ends with sunset

Promotes physical and mental self-control

Muslims spend more time worshipping Allah

Why some Muslims don't fast

Some people are not required to fast, such as the very old, the sick, pregnant women, and young children. Apart from children, the others must either make up the missed days at another time, or pay money towards the feeding of poor families.

The Night of Power (or Laylat al-Qadr)

- Fasting has a special link to the **Night of Power**, which was when the Prophet Muhammad received his first revelation from Allah through the angel Jibril (see 5.5). This happened in 610 CE at the cave of Hira in Makkah.
- Muslims hope to experience their own Night of Power (a special feeling of being close to Allah) in the last days of Ramadan as a sign of Allah's acceptance of their prayers. During the final nights of Ramadan, Muslims hold extra prayers and vigils.
- The first revelation of the Qur'an took place during Ramadan, which is one of the reasons why it is the holiest month in Islam.

APPLY

AO1 This student answer has only two simple points. Can you develop them?

b. Explain **two** reasons why sawm is important in Islam. (4)

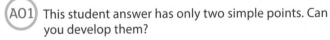
Develop spiritually.
Increases gratefulness.

AO2 The arguments for why sawm is important in Islam are usually quite clear. What would you include as a counter-argument in a question such as this? Use the sentence starter to write a full paragraph.

d. 'Sawm is necessary to become a better person.' Evaluate this statement considering arguments for and against. In your response you should:
- refer to Muslim teachings
- reach a justified conclusion. (12)

However, it could be argued that sawm is not the only way to become a better person. There are other actions that could improve a person's character more, for example...

REVIEW

Answers: Mark your answers using p.194 and note areas for improvement.
AO1: This question is testing your ability to write a developed point. For help with this skill, see p.12.
AO2: This question is testing your ability to write a well-argued paragraph. For help with this skill, see p.12.

Essential information

- **Zakah** is an act of charity that involves sharing one's wealth with the poor.
- It means 'purification' and is one of the Pillars of Islam (Sunni) and part of the Obligatory Acts (Shi'a).
- **Khums** is an additional tax paid by Shi'a Muslims to be spent by their leaders on various causes.

Zakah

> 66 Alms [food or money given to the poor] are meant only for the poor, the needy... to free slaves and help those in debt, for God's cause, and for travellers in need 99 (*Surah 9:60*)

Muslims believe that wealth is a gift from Allah, and so should be used for good things. In Islam spending in the way of Allah is one of the greatest deeds.

- 2.5% of the value of savings or wealth

- Only given by Muslims who have savings above a certain value

- Means 'purification', so is a way for Muslims to become purified from greed

- Goes to the less fortunate, helping widows, orphans, and other causes in the Muslim community

Khums

Shi'a Muslims also believe in khums, which means 'fifth'. It began as a contribution of 20 per cent of the value of 'battle gains' (*Surah 8:41*) given by Muslim armies to religious causes. Today Shi'a Muslims contribute 20 per cent of their wealth to the Imams (or their representatives) towards anything considered important for the community. This includes:

- the poor
- clergy (religious leaders)
- orphans
- mosques.
- schools

For Shi'a Muslims, khums is a way of showing faith and devotion to Allah.

Importance to Muslims

Zakah	Khums
- One of the Five Pillars (Sunni) - Prevents wealth staying only with the rich - Way of becoming closer to Allah	- One of the Ten Obligatory Acts (Shi'a) - Source of income for the clergy and community - Demonstrates devotion to Allah

TIP
Include 'linking' words such as 'therefore' and 'finally' in your chain of reasoning.

AO1 Read the first part of the student answer to this question, then write the second developed point so that it is complete.

b. Explain **two** purposes of Zakah. (4)

> *Muslims believe that one purpose of Zakah is to become less greedy. Zakah means 'purification' and so is a way of making sure that a person's money and possessions are kept pure.*
> *Secondly...*

AO2 Read the arguments for and against the statement, then write your own justified conclusion.

'It's the duty of governments, not individuals, to take care of the less fortunate.'

For	Against
- Governments are responsible for all citizens living in their country. - Money the government collects from tax should be given to support those who need it. - Individuals cannot give as much as governments can.	- Holy books like the Qur'an command believers to help the poor. - Not all governments believe they should care for the less fortunate. - Many charities started as small organisations set up by individuals and make a positive difference where governments do not.

Answers: Mark your answers using p.195 and note areas for improvement.
AO1: This question is testing your ability to write a developed point. For help with this skill, see p.12.
AO2: This question is testing your ability to write a justified conclusion. For help with this skill, see p.12.

RECAP

Essential information
- **Hajj** is the pilgrimage made by Muslims to Makkah in Saudi Arabia.
- It is one of the Pillars of Islam (Sunni) and Obligatory Acts (Shi'a).
- Muslims believe that by performing Hajj, all their sins can be forgiven.

What is Hajj and why is it important?
- The act of pilgrimage is commanded in the Qur'an: 'Proclaim the Pilgrimage to all people' (*Surah 22:27*).
- Muslims believe that Makkah is the holiest place on earth. The Ka'bah there is believed to be the first place in the world dedicated to the worship of one God, Allah. It was rebuilt by Ibrahim (Abraham) and Isma'il (Ishmael) around 4000 years ago.
- Since then, the Ka'bah was filled with statues of different gods that people used to worship. The Prophet Muhammad removed all these idols to 'purify' the Ka'bah and restored it.
- Hajj is important for Muslims because they are following in the footsteps of Ibrahim, Isma'il, and Muhammad.

> 66 We commanded Abraham and Ishmael: 'Purify My House for those who walk round it, those who stay there, and those who bow and prostrate themselves in worship' 99
> (*Surah 2:125*)

How Hajj is performed
There are a number of requirements for Hajj. To perform Hajj, Muslims must:

1. be physically able
2. be able to afford all the expenses
3. pass through a safe route.

Men wear ihram, which are two pieces of unstitched white cloth. Women dress in simple clothes that are also usually white to symbolise unity and equality.

There are also various rituals that take place during Hajj:

Ritual	Description and importance
Tawaf	Walking seven times anti-clockwise around the Ka'bah and trying to kiss or touch the black stone.
Sa'ya	Jogging or walking between two hills seven times in memory of Ibrahim's wife Hagar, who was left in the desert with their son Isma'il.
Wuquf	Day of repentance and prayer at Arafat, where Muhammad gave his final sermon.
Ramy al-Jamarat	Symbolic stoning of the devil by throwing stones at three wide walls, in memory of Ibrahim.
Sacrifice	Sacrifice of animals made in memory of Ibrahim's son Isma'il's readiness to give his life to God. The meat is distributed to the poor.
Halak	Men shave their heads to symbolise a new beginning. Women cut the ends of their hair.

Benefits and challenges of Hajj

Benefits	Challenges
• Makes relationship with Allah stronger	• Physically demanding
• Unites all Muslims	• Expensive especially if travelling from other countries
• Inspires pilgrims to become better people	• Fatalities have occurred due to volume of people

APPLY

AO1 The answer below does not include a reference to a source of wisdom and authority. What could be added to make sure it gets the additional mark?

c. Explain **two** reasons why Muslims perform Hajj. In your answer you must refer to a source of wisdom and authority. (5)

One reason why Muslims perform Hajj is because it is a commandment of Allah, and one of the Five Pillars. This means that it is compulsory for Muslims who meet the criteria.

AO2 The benefits of Hajj are usually quite clear. What would you include as a counter-argument in a question such as this? Use the sentence starter to write a full paragraph, developing the points mentioned.

d. 'The benefits of Hajj outweigh the challenges.' Evaluate this statement considering arguments for and against. In your response you should:
   - refer to Muslim teachings
   - reach a justified conclusion. (12)

However, Hajj may be seen to have more challenges than benefits. This is because...

REVIEW

Answers: Mark your answers using p.195 and note areas for improvement.
AO1: This question is testing your ability to explain beliefs correctly, using a source of wisdom and authority. For help with this skill, see p.12.
AO2: This question is testing your ability to write a well-argued paragraph. For help with this skill, see p.12.

 RECAP

Essential information

- **Jihad** means to strive or struggle, particularly against evil.
- Muslims believe there are two main types of jihad: greater (spiritual) and lesser (physical).
- The large majority of Muslims reject extremist interpretations of jihad.

What is jihad?

Muslims believe it is important to keep trying to be better people. Often this comes with difficulty, especially when it is trying to resist temptations or control emotions. In Islam, anything that involves striving and determination for the sake of Allah is known as jihad.

There are two main types of jihad:

Greater jihad	Lesser jihad
This is striving to overcome evil within oneself, to become a better person, and to make a positive contribution to society. Greater jihad can be categorised as follows: • Jihad of the heart: making their faith a force for good • Jihad of the tongue: speaking about their faith • Jihad of the hand: expressing their faith in good works. 66 Those who strove hard in God's way … it is they who will triumph 99 (*Surah 9:20*)	This is striving to respond to a physical threat, such as an attack from an enemy. It is known as jihad of the sword and is mainly to defend Islam and all oppressed people. Some conditions of lesser jihad are: • persecution (suffering because of your beliefs) must have reached an extreme level • must be declared by a recognised leader • no harming of innocent civilians, including women, children, and the elderly • crops and water supplies must not be attacked. 66 Fight in God's cause against those who fight you, but do not overstep the limits 99 (*Surah 2:190*) 66 Those who have been attacked are permitted to take up arms because they have been wronged 99 (*Surah 22:39*)

TIP
You can use either of these quotes to show that Muslims can only fight in self defence.

- Peace lies at the heart of Islam, therefore jihad is an important duty for every Muslim to perform to ensure the world is a more peaceful place to live.
- The Prophet Muhammad taught that greater jihad is more important than lesser jihad, so Muslims focus on self-improvement and the improvement of their community.
- However, it remains an important obligation for Muslims to defend their faith by force if under attack.
- The majority of Muslims do not agree with how extremist groups interpret lesser jihad.

 APPLY

AO1 This student answer has only two simple points. Can you develop them? Remember to include a source of wisdom and authority.

c. Explain **two** Muslim beliefs about jihad. In your answer you must refer to a source of wisdom and authority. (5)

> Become better people.
> Defend Islam.

AO2 Write down at least one point each both for and against this statement. Aim to include different Muslim beliefs.

'Muslims should only perform greater jihad.'

For	Against

REVIEW

Answers: Mark your answers using p.195 and note areas for improvement.
AO1: This question is testing your ability to explain beliefs correctly, using a source of wisdom and authority. For help with this skill, see p.12.
AO2: This question is testing your ability to evaluate a statement. For help with this skill, see p.12.

RECAP

Essential information

- All Muslims celebrate two main festivals – Id-ul-Adha and Id-ul-Fitr.
- Shi'a Muslims have two additional commemorations – Id-ul-Ghadeer and Ashura.
- Special occasions like these are a way for large sections of the ummah to unite, honour people and events in the past, and show their commitment to Allah.

> ❝Today I have perfected your religion for you, completed My blessing upon you❞ (*Surah 5:3*)

Celebration/ commemoration	Who is it important to?	Why is it important?	What happens?
Id-ul-Adha: festival of sacrifice that marks the annual completion of Hajj	Sunni and Shi'a	Commemorates the story of Ibrahim and Isma'il. Ibrahim had seen a dream that he was sacrificing Isma'il and interpreted this to mean that he needed to do this in real life, but God stopped him from carrying out the sacrifice. Both Ibrahim and Isma'il were praised for their dedication to God. The story reminds Muslims to show a similar level of devotion.	• Animals like sheep and cattle are sacrificed in memory of Ibrahim and Isma'il, as commanded in *Surah 37:77–111*. The meat is shared with the poor. • New clothes are worn. • Families go to the mosque to offer a special prayer and listen to the Imam's sermon. • The rest of the day is spent with families and friends, sharing food together.
Id-ul-Fitr: festival at the end of Ramadan	Sunni and Shi'a	Celebrates the end of Ramadan when Muslims express joy and gratitude for being able to pass through a month of fasting for the sake of Allah. By fasting, Muslims strengthen their relationship with Allah, improve themselves, and can appreciate the hunger and thirst of the less fortunate.	• New clothes are worn. • Gifts are exchanged. • Money is given to the poor so that they are not forgotten. • Families go to the mosque to offer a special prayer and listen to the Imam's sermon. • Families enjoy food and drink together.
Id-ul-Ghadeer: celebration of the appointment of Ali	Shi'a	Celebrates the day Shi'a Muslims believe the Prophet Muhammad appointed Ali ibn Abi Talib as his successor. This happened at a place called Ghadir Khumm during Muhammad's last Hajj. Shi'a Muslims consider this to be the fulfilment of *Surah 5:3*.	• Fasting is encouraged on this day. • Gatherings are held in mosques where poetry is recited and scholars give speeches.
Ashura: solemn day of remembrance	Shi'a	Commemorates the day Imam Husayn, Muhammad's grandson, was martyred (killed for having particular beliefs) along with his family and companions in Karbala, Iraq. This was after he refused to swear allegiance to the oppressive ruler Yazid who was going against the teachings of Islam. It is a reminder to Muslims to oppose injustice and for Shi'a Muslims to remain loyal to their Imams. The day of Ashura also coincides with the day Musa (Moses) and his followers were saved from Fir'awn (Pharaoh) in Egypt.	• Gatherings are held in Shi'a mosques. • Mosques are usually draped in black and Shi'a Muslims also wear black to symbolise mourning. • Millions of Shi'a Muslims make a pilgrimage to Karbala to visit Imam Husayn's shrine. • Some Shi'a Muslims will beat their chests and wail. • Many Sunni Muslims observe a two-day fast in memory of Musa's survival, as recommended by Muhammad.

APPLY

(AO1) Can you develop the student's answer to the following question?

b. Explain **two** reasons why commemorations are important for Muslims. (4)

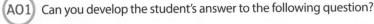
Commemorations are important for Muslims because it is a chance for them to remember sacrifices made in the past. For example...

(AO2) You don't need to put your conclusion at the end of an answer. You can begin an answer with a statement of conclusion, and then justify it – ensuring you still evaluate both sides. Write a short statement of conclusion to start an answer to this question.

d. 'All Muslims should celebrate the same commemorations.' Evaluate this statement considering arguments for and against. In your response you should:
- refer to Muslim teachings
- refer to different Muslim points of view
- reach a justified conclusion. (12)

REVIEW

Answers: Mark your answers using p.195 and note areas for improvement.
AO1: This question is testing your ability to write a developed point. For help with this skill, see p.12.
AO2: This question is testing your ability to write a justified conclusion. For help with this skill, see p.12.

Test the 3 mark question (a)

1   Outline **three** Muslim beliefs about jihad.   **(3 marks)**

> *Three Muslim beliefs are that the word jihad means striving (1), there are two types called greater and lesser (1), and that greater jihad is more important (1).*

2   Outline **three** Muslim features of Zakah.   **(3 marks)**

> *Zakah is one of the Five Pillars of Islam. (1)*

_____

_____

3   Outline **three** Obligatory Acts for Shi'a Muslims.   **(3 marks)**

_____

_____

_____

TIP

Make sure you are spending enough time on each question, but not more than necessary. The number of marks is a rough guide to how many minutes you should spend on that question.

Test the 4 mark question (b)

1   Explain **two** reasons why Shahadah is important to Muslims.   **(4 marks)**

● **Explain one reason.**	One reason why Shahadah is important to Muslims is because it is one of the Five Pillars of Islam.
● Develop your explanation with more detail/an example/reference to a religious teaching or quotation.	You cannot be a Muslim without following each of the Five Pillars, therefore belief in Shahadah is essential to be counted as one.
● **Explain a second reason.**	A second reason why Shahadah is important is because it is a commitment to believe in Tawhid.
● Develop your explanation with more detail/an example/reference to a religious teaching or quotation.	Muslims believe shirk is the worst sin in Islam. Therefore, saying the Shahadah makes them firm believers in one God, Allah.

2   Explain **two** reasons why Hajj is important for Muslims.   **(4 marks)**

● **Explain one reason.**	
● Develop your explanation with more detail/an example/reference to a religious teaching or quotation.	
● **Explain a second reason.**	
● Develop your explanation with more detail/an example/reference to a religious teaching or quotation.	

3   Explain **two** reasons why greater jihad is more relevant to most Muslims today than lesser jihad.   **(4 marks)**

Exam Practice

Test the 5 mark question (c)

1 Explain **two** Muslim beliefs about sawm. In your answer you must refer to a source of wisdom and authority. **(5 marks)**

● **Explain one belief.**	One Muslim belief about sawm is that it is a commandment of Allah.
● Develop your explanation with more detail/an example.	It is compulsory for all Muslims (exceptions can be made on occasion, for example, for the very old or sick).
● **Either:** Add a reference to a source of wisdom and authority here.	This is shown in the Qur'an where it states that 'fasting has been prescribed for you' (Surah 2:183).
● **Explain a second belief.**	Another belief about sawm is that it is a way for Muslims to experience what less fortunate members of society have to go through.
● Develop your explanation with more detail/an example.	Going without food and drink for a few hours every day during Ramadan is a reminder to Muslims to value what they have, and to support the poor through monetary donations.
● **Or:** Add a reference to a source of wisdom and authority here.	

TIP

Here is the reference to a source of wisdom/authority. You only need to make one reference to gain the fifth mark – you don't need evidence of a source of wisdom/authority to support both your points.

2 Explain **two** reasons why Muslims believe charitable giving is a central part of Islam. In your answer you must refer to a source of wisdom and authority. **(5 marks)**

● **Explain one reason.**	
● Develop your explanation with more detail/an example.	
● **Either:** Add a reference to a source of wisdom and authority here.	
● **Explain a second reason.**	
● Develop your explanation with more detail/an example.	
● **Or:** Add a reference to a source of wisdom and authority here.	

3 Explain **two** reasons why Muslims perform Hajj. In your answer you must refer to a source of wisdom and authority. **(5 marks)**

Exam Practice

1   'Laylat al-Qadr is the most important goal of a Muslim.' Evaluate this statement.
In your response you should:
- refer to Muslim teachings
- reach a justified conclusion.

(12 marks)

ARGUMENTS IN SUPPORT OF THE STATEMENT • **Explain why some people would agree with the statement.** • Develop your explanation with more detail and examples. • Refer to religious teaching. Use a quote or paraphrase of a religious authority. • **Evaluate the arguments.** Is this a good argument? Explain why you think this. Use words such as convincing/strong/robust/weak/ unpersuasive/unsuccessful within your reasoning.	Many Muslims would agree with this statement because the importance of the Night of Power is clearly stated in the Qur'an and hadith. The Qur'an describes it as "better than a thousand months" (Surah 97:3). The Prophet Muhammad said "only my ummah has been given Laylat al-Qadr" (Hadith – Al Durr Al Manthur) which points to its uniqueness and so it must be one of the main goals of a Muslim, as it is not experienced often. If anyone experiences it, they are extremely blessed, as the Prophet Muhammad himself experienced it at the start of Islam. It isn't every day that angels descend from heaven, as the Qur'an says occurs during Laylat al-Qadr. This is why some Muslims spend the last few days of Ramadan in a special retreat, called I'tikaf, when they focus purely on worship so that they might be able to achieve Laylat al-Qadr.If they do, it is like having all their prayers answered. Therefore there is a very strong case in favour of this statement.
ARGUMENTS SUPPORTING A DIFFERENT VIEW • **Explain why some people would disagree with the statement.** • Develop your explanation with more detail and examples. • Refer to religious teaching. Use a quote or paraphrase of a religious authority. • **Evaluate the arguments.** Is this a good argument? Explain why you think this. Use words such as convincing/strong/robust/weak/ unpersuasive/unsuccessful within your reasoning.	However, other Muslims would disagree with the statement because one of the first questions Allah will ask a Muslim on the Day of Judgment will be about Salah, not Laylat al-Qadr. Laylat al-Qadr is not one of the Five Pillars or the six Beliefs, nor does it feature in the 'Usul ad-Din for Shi'a Muslims, and so is not a central tenet of Islam. Muslims also try to experience it during one time of the year only – during the month of Ramadan, and even then it is in the last few days of it. Therefore, as something that makes up a small or brief part of a Muslim's life, Laylat al-Qadr is not viewed as the most important aim of a Muslim, and so the statement isn't convincing.
CONCLUSION • **Give a justified conclusion.** • Include your own reasoning. • Use words such as convincing/ strong/robust/weak/unpersuasive/ unsuccessful to weigh up the different arguments for and against. • Do not just repeat arguments you have already used without explaining how they apply to your reasoned opinion/conclusion.	In conclusion, I believe that there are persuasive arguments on both sides, but because Laylat al-Qadr is not one of the main tenets for either Sunni or Shi'a Muslims, it cannot be considered to be an important goal, let alone the most important, for any Muslim. If it was, the Qur'an and hadith would have stated it.

TIP

Providing a quote is an excellent way of supporting your points and shows the examiner that you have made an effort to remember them.

2 'All Muslims should celebrate the same commemorations.' Evaluate this statement considering arguments for and against. In your response you should:

- refer to Muslim teachings
- refer to different Muslim points of view
- reach a justified conclusion.

(12 marks)

ARGUMENTS IN SUPPORT OF THE STATEMENT	
● **Explain why some people would agree with the statement.** ● Develop your explanation with more detail and examples. ● Refer to religious teaching. Use a quote or paraphrase of a religious authority. ● **Evaluate the arguments.** Is this a good argument? Explain why you think this. Use words such as convincing/strong/robust/weak/unpersuasive/ unsuccessful within your reasoning.	*Some Muslims/people would agree with this statement because...*
ARGUMENTS SUPPORTING A DIFFERENT VIEW	
● **Explain why some people would disagree with the statement.** ● Develop your explanation with more detail and examples. ● Refer to religious teaching. Use a quote or paraphrase of a religious authority. ● **Evaluate the arguments.** Is this a good argument? Explain why you think this. Use words such as convincing/strong/robust/weak/unpersuasive/ unsuccessful within your reasoning.	*On the other hand, some Muslims/people would hold a different point of view...*
CONCLUSION	
● **Give a justified conclusion.** ● Include your own reasoning. ● Use words such as convincing/strong/robust/weak/ unpersuasive/unsuccessful to weigh up the different arguments for and against. ● Do not just repeat arguments you have already used without explaining how they apply to your reasoned opinion/conclusion.	*Having considered both sides of the argument, I would say that...*

3 'The benefits of Hajj outweigh the challenges.' Evaluate this statement considering arguments for and against. In your response you should:

- refer to Muslim teachings
- reach a justified conclusion.

(12 marks)

 **REVIEW**

Check your answers to these exam questions on p.195, correct your answers with annotations, and note down any general areas for improvement.

If you don't feel secure in the content of this chapter, you could reread the Recap sections.

If you don't feel secure in your exam technique, you could revisit the exam support section on pp.7–14.

RECAP

Essential information
- Judaism is a monotheistic religion: a religion with one God.
- God ('the Almighty') is One, Creator, Lawgiver, and Judge.
- God's different characteristics and names help Jews understand something of the nature of God.

Different groups in Judaism

The different groups within Judaism take a different approach to their faith, though they may share many of the same beliefs and practices.

Orthodox	Liberal and Reform (Progressive)	Secular
• Believe the Torah is the literal Word of God. • Believe tradition and following the commands of the Torah are important. • Ultra-Orthodox are the most strict.	• Believe the Torah is the inspired Word of God and should be interpreted in light of modern life and issues.	• Do not affiliate with a religious group, but view themselves as Jewish because of cultural or ethnic heritage.

The nature of the Almighty

- God, the Almighty, is non-physical, so Jews believe it is difficult to describe him fully.
- They believe that the name of God is so holy it should not be spoken aloud or written, and never erased.
- He has different names (found in the Tenakh and Talmud – see 8.2) that describe some of his characteristics.

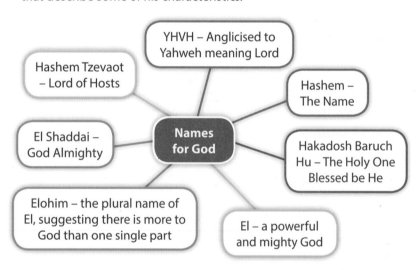

Names for God:
- YHVH – Anglicised to Yahweh meaning Lord
- Hashem Tzevaot – Lord of Hosts
- El Shaddai – God Almighty
- Hashem – The Name
- Hakadosh Baruch Hu – The Holy One Blessed be He
- Elohim – the plural name of El, suggesting there is more to God than one single part
- El – a powerful and mighty God

Jews believe that God is just

How the characteristics of the Almighty are shown in the Torah

One	Creator
66 Hashem is the one and only 99 (The Shema (see 8.4), *Deuteronomy 6:4–9*)	66 And Hashem formed the man of dust from the ground 99 (*Genesis 2:7*)
• Impossible to divide God into parts, or describe him by physical attributes. • God is the only being to whom Jews should offer praise and prayer.	• As there is just one God, everything in the universe is created by God. • Many Orthodox Jews interpret the Creation story more literally, while Reform and Liberal Jews see it as a metaphor.

Lawgiver	Judge
66 Hashem is our Judge, Hashem is our Lawgiver 99 (*Isaiah 33:22*)	
• The Law, the Torah, is a gift from God to Moses – guidance so that Jews can live good lives. • Jews believe they are children of God; he is father-like to them. • Judaism is based upon Law, and God's justice, but he is also merciful. These qualities are balanced. • When Moses accepted the Law, he and the Jewish people entered into a covenant to keep it. God judges how well they keep the laws.	

Importance for Jewish life today

- The names of God help bring Jews closer to him even if they do not fully understand his greatness.
- The different names show God's complexity, yet he remains One.
- Reciting the Shema twice a day reinforces the importance of God as One.
- Understanding God as a Creator, Lawgiver, and Judge helps Jews to act 'in the image of God' with justice and mercy.

 APPLY

TIP
Remember that 'outline' questions are assessing your ability to recall knowledge of religion and belief.

 Can you improve the following student answer? Remember, 'outline' requires more than just one-word answers. You should provide three short sentences.

a. Outline **three** characteristics of the Almighty. (3)

> *Creator, Lawgiver, and Judge.*

 Can you complete this planning table to evaluate the following statement?

d. 'Oneness is the most important characteristic of the Almighty.' Evaluate this statement considering arguments for and against. In your response you should:
  - refer to Jewish teachings
  - reach a justified conclusion. (15)

Oneness is the most important	Something else is the most important
	Creator
	Lawgiver
	Judge

Conclusion: Oneness is the most important because…
OR _____ is the most important because…
OR They are all equally important because…

 REVIEW

Answers: Mark your answers using p.196 and note areas for improvement.
AO1: This question is testing your ability to answer 'outline' questions. For help with this skill, see p.12.
AO2: This question is testing your ability to identify arguments for and against a statement. For help with this skill, see p.12.

RECAP

Essential information

- God created the world and continues to work in the world.
- The Shekhinah is the divine presence of God within the created world.
- Jewish people can connect with the Shekhinah through study of the Torah, in prayer, and during worship.

The divine presence

- The Shekhinah is not a teaching explicitly contained within the Torah, but there are references in the Talmud (the oral law – see 8.2).
- The divine presence of God is felt in different ways by Jews, including through:
  - the study of the Tenakh and the Talmud
  - the Tabernacle, prayer, and worship today.

Study	Worship	Prayer

Study

- Study of the Tenakh and the Talmud is an important part of being Jewish.
- To study is regarded as an act of worship, and as such the Shekhinah is also present.
- Jewish people can study at any time. Sometimes they may attend a Jewish school called a **yeshiva**.
- The Talmud evolved from **Rabbis** studying and discussing the Torah.

Divergence

- At some Orthodox yeshiva schools, Torah study is the primary focus. Other subjects like English and Maths take second place.
- Some Hassidic Jews (Ultra-Orthodox) reject secular study and focus purely on the Torah.

Worship

- God instructed Moses to build the Tabernacle, a portable temple where God would dwell as they travelled in search of the Promised Land.
- The Tabernacle maintained the Jewish people's connection with God.
- This continues today in the synagogue. A light burns in front of the Ark as a reminder of God's presence.

Prayer

- Jews can pray alone or as part of a **minyan** (group of 10 adults over the age of 13 – men only in Orthodox tradition).
- When Jews pray as a community they believe God is present.
- Some prayers such as the **Kaddish** (praise) and Barachu (call to prayer) can only be said with a minyan.
- In 2 Chronicles Solomon dedicates the newly built Temple, and he and the Jewish people are overcome with God's power:

> 66 the glory of Hashem filled the Temple 99 (*2 Chronicles 7:1*)

APPLY

TIP
You can 'signpost' your answer by beginning each point with 'Firstly . . .' or 'Secondly . . .', for example.

AO1 Can you finish off this student's answer?

b. Explain **two** reasons why Jewish people believe in the Shekhinah. (4)

Firstly, despite few direct references in the Torah, understanding of the Shekhinah developed through the Talmud and it continues to be understood today.

Secondly...

AO2 'Worship is the best way for Jewish people to connect with the Shekhinah.' Can you think of three points to finish this table and expand on the points already made?

Agree	Disagree
•	• Study is an important part of Jewish worship
•	• Prayer can be an individual activity
•	• Tabernacle in time of Moses was not directly part of worship

REVIEW

Answers: Mark your answers using p.196 and note areas for improvement.
AO1: This question is testing your ability to answer 'outline' questions. For help with this skill, see p.12.
AO2: This question is testing your ability to identify arguments for a statement. For help with this skill, see p.12.

RECAP

Essential information

- The idea of the **Messiah** is an ancient one in Judaism and is based around a great leader.
- The Messianic Age means the time when the Messiah will rule.
- Many Jews live in expectation of the Messiah or Messianic Age and live their lives accordingly.

The nature and purpose of the Messiah

- Messiah means 'anointed one', and anointed means 'marked for greatness'.
- The Messiah is the one who will be anointed King of Israel in the End of Days (Messianic Age).
- It is not detailed in the Torah, but mentioned frequently by the Jewish prophets (**Nevi'im**).
- It is an ancient idea – the Jews had been forced into exile and the prophets reassured them a great leader would come to restore society.

> 66 A king will reign and prosper and he will administer justice and righteousness in the land. 99
> (*Jeremiah 23:5–6*)

How messiahship is shown in the scriptures

Here are some things that Jews believe about the Messiah, based on the Nevi'im and other scriptures:

Jewish responsibility

Many Jews are motivated to bring about a better world (**Tikkun Olam**) by being active partners in hastening the Messianic Age. This may be through involvement in social, political, and environmental improvements.

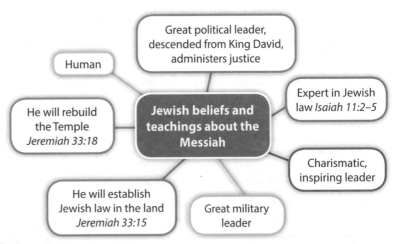

Divergent understandings of Messiah

Some people believed Jesus was the Messiah and the start of the Christian religion. Jews reject this idea as Jesus did not fulfil their expectations for a Messiah.

What is the Messianic Age?
• For Orthodox Jews, the Messianic Age means the time when the Messiah has come and is ruling the world. • The emphasis for Reform and Liberal Jews is not on the Messiah (indeed some reject the idea of a personal Messiah). Instead their focus is the Messianic Age as a time of peace and harmony.

When will the Messiah come?
• Some Jews believe there is the possibility of the Messiah in every generation. • Some believe God has set a date. • Some believe the Messiah will come when most needed, or most deserved.

APPLY

AO1 This question requires a source of wisdom and authority. In this topic, the Nevi'im is the most useful source. How would you use the quotation from *Jeremiah* (above) in a developed point?

c. Explain **two** reasons why Jewish people live in expectation of the Messiah. In your answer you must refer to a source of wisdom and authority. (5)

TIP It may be worth highlighting the strongest reason from each box to help you write your conclusion.

AO2 Make a list of points that agree and another of points that disagree with the statement below. Then write a justified conclusion.

d. 'It is the responsibility of Jews today to bring about the Messianic Age.' Evaluate this statement considering arguments for and against. In your response you should:
- refer to Jewish teachings
- refer to different Jewish points of view
- reach a justified conclusion. (15)

REVIEW

Answers: Mark your answers using p.196 and note areas for improvement.
AO1: This question is testing your ability to write a developed point. For help with this skill, see p.12.
AO2: This question is testing your ability to break down the question and plan a response. For help with this skill, see p.12.

 **RECAP**

Essential information

- A covenant is an everlasting agreement between two parties. For Jews this is God and man.
- The Jewish people entered into a covenant with God after Moses led them out of slavery in Egypt to the Promised Land.
- Moses received the Torah, or Law, which continues to play an important role in Judaism.

A covenant

- A covenant is formed in love, and creates an important relationship.
- Brit olam means 'everlasting covenant', which shows Jews believe that God will not break the covenant. However, they recognise that from time to time they do not fulfil their obligations and break the Law.

The covenant at Sinai

- Before the covenant at Sinai other covenants had been made with the three main patriarchs: Abraham, Isaac, and Jacob (Israel).
- Moses was chosen to lead their descendants to freedom.

The nature and history of the covenant

Moses grew up in Pharaoh's household, but after discovering he was actually a Jew, he fled.

↓

God spoke to him at the burning bush and then sent ten plagues upon Egypt.

↓

Pharaoh surrendered and let Moses lead the Hebrews out of Egypt.

↓

Pharaoh chased Moses as he crossed the **Reed Sea** (some scholars believe a mistranslation led to it being called the 'Red Sea') and eventually to Mount Sinai.

↓

At Mount Sinai a new covenant was given.
- It made it clear those who didn't follow it would be punished.
- It identified Jews as chosen people of God – 'chosen for responsibility'.
- The Ten Commandments (the Decalogue) were given.

↓

Moses was then given the rest of the Torah, and was also given the Oral Torah, later written as the Talmud. Jews believe every Jewish soul was present at Sinai and agreed to the terms of the covenant.

TIP

This story helps us understand why the Law is so important to Jews. It was given to Moses by God.

Why it is important for Jews today

- The Law of the Torah is still followed today – it is still the most important part of the Tenakh.
- The Torah is read in the synagogue every Sabbath from the scroll kept in the Ark.
- Study of the Torah is an important part of Jewish life.
- The gift of the Torah is celebrated every year at the festival of Shavuot, which commemorates the day God gave the Torah to those at Sinai.
- As made clear to Moses, obedience will be blessed, disobedience punished.

The Ten Commandments

> Today, they are read three times a year: during the reading of Exodus and Deuteronomy, and during Shavuot.

> The first ten of 613 commandments, all of which, Rabbis remind Jews, are important.

The Ten Commandments

TIP
You will need to learn at least three of the Ten Commandments for your exam.

> During early times, they were recited daily but this stopped because some Jews saw them as more important than other Mitzvot, the commandments that guide Jews.

> They are in *Exodus 20:1–17* and *Deuteronomy 5:4–21*.

TIP
You can attempt this question in full on page 112.

APPLY

AO1 Read the student's answer to the question below, which is only worth 4 marks, and add an appropriate source of wisdom or authority to gain the last mark.

c. Explain **two** Jewish teachings about the covenant with Moses. In your answer you must refer to a source of wisdom and authority. (5)

> *It is the covenant where the Almighty gives the Law to Moses, which has remained important to Jews today as they continue to follow the Law.*
>
> *This covenant made clear that the Jews were a people chosen by the Almighty, but that failure to follow the Law would mean punishment.*

AO2 You need to know the two main covenants – Moses and Abraham. You could get a question such as:

d. 'The covenant with Moses is the most important covenant for Jewish people.' Evaluate this statement considering arguments for and against. In your answer you should:
  - refer to Jewish teachings
  - refer to different Jewish points of view
  - reach a justified conclusion. (15)

To prepare to answer this, list the reasons why the covenant with Moses is the most important.

TIP
It is a good idea to signpost your answer with a new line for the second point.

REVIEW
Answers: Mark your answers using p.196 and note areas for improvement.
AO1: This question is testing your ability to explain beliefs correctly, using source of wisdom or authority. For help with this skill, see p.12.
AO2: This question is testing your ability to plan a response. For help with this skill, see p.12.

RECAP

Essential information

- God and Abraham entered into a covenant that promised many descendants, a Promised Land and a blessed nation.
- God showed that he would keep his promises; this remains important to Jews today.
- Israel is the Promised Land that Abraham and Sarah settled in.

Why is Abraham important?

The three patriarchs of Judaism are:

- Abraham (grandfather)
- Isaac (father)
- Jacob (son).
- Abraham (born Abram) was the founder of Judaism. He came to believe that the universe was the work of a single creator. This was unusual as most early religions were polytheistic – they believed in many gods.

The nature and history of the Abrahamic covenant

- God called Abraham to leave his home and family. He was promised the reward of land and many descendants.
- Abraham sealed the covenant by circumcising himself (removing the foreskin of the penis) and all the males in his family.
- There were ten tests for Abraham; the first was leaving his home.
- The final test was to sacrifice his son Isaac; an angel stopped the sacrifice because Abraham and Isaac showed they were obedient.
- Abraham was promised a 'great nation' but he and his wife, Sarah, were very old and had no children.

> 66 I will ratify My covenant [...] as an everlasting covenant, to be a God to you and to your offspring after you 99 (*Genesis 17:7*)

- Abraham had a son called Ishmael with his wife's maidservant.
- God blessed Abraham and Sarah with a child called Isaac.
- Isaac's son Jacob fathered 12 sons who established the 12 tribes of Israel.

How the covenant affects Jews today

- The covenant is fundamental to all Jews.
- The covenant has not yet been fulfilled. Jews hope to live as a great nation in the Promised Land (Israel), blessed and redeemed by God.
- The covenant with Moses at Sinai gave them Laws to live by, but by obeying these, they will also fulfil the Abrahamic covenant.
- Jews are still circumcised today (see 8.5 Ritual and ceremony).
- The birth of Isaac showed that God always keeps his promises and intervenes when needed.

TIP Remember, this covenant came first chronologically!

The Promised Land: how this affects Jewish life today

- The land of Israel remains central to Judaism and many Laws link to the idea of a Promised Land.
- Prayers for a return to Israel are included in Sabbath prayers and festivals.
- Living outside of Israel is viewed as a form of exile by some Jews.

TIP The (d) question requires you to analyse different views. You have already analysed the covenant with Moses in the (d) question on page 101.

APPLY

AO1 The answer given to the question below is only worth half the available marks. Can you add a second developed point to gain full marks?

b. Explain **two ways** the concept of the Promised Land affects Jewish life today. (4)

> *Firstly, many Jews do not live in Israel and so it is impossible to follow all Laws, as many are tied to living in Israel. Secondly...*

AO2 To prepare to answer this question, list the reasons why the covenant with **Abraham** is the most important. Can you also write a conclusion?

d. 'The covenant with Moses is the most important covenant for Jewish people.' Evaluate this statement considering arguments for and against. In your response you should:
  - refer to Jewish teachings
  - reach a justified conclusion. (15)

REVIEW

Answers: Mark your answers using p.196 and note areas for improvement.
AO1: This question is testing your ability to write a developed point. For help with this skill, see p.12.
AO2: This question is testing your ability to plan a response. For help with this skill, see p.12.

 **RECAP**

Essential information

- The story of Creation makes it clear that God is the giver of life, so life is sacred.
- Most Jewish laws can be broken in order to save a person's life. This is called Pikuach Nefesh.
- Pikuach Nefesh influences how Jews approach moral and ethical decisions.

The nature and sanctity of human life

- Life is given by God and as such is sacred.
- The Talmud says all people are descended from a single person. To take a life is like destroying the world.

66 So God created Man in his image 99 (*Genesis 1:27*)

Pikuach Nefesh

Principle	Implication	Example
• Jewish law states that the preservation of human life overrides virtually any other law. • When a person's life is in danger, almost any Mitzvah can be broken. • Exceptions: murder, idolatry, incest, and adultery.	• Jews should live by the Torah, not die because of it. • If Jews break Shabbat rules to save a life they should be praised.	Actions that otherwise would be work on Shabbat: • rescuing a drowning child • breaking down a door to prevent it trapping a child • moving rubble from a collapsed wall to save a child • extinguishing a fire to save a life (*Talmud Yoma 83–84*).

Human life in the Torah

Leviticus 24:17 states that anyone who kills should be put to death. However, there is little evidence Jews took this literally. Traditionally there would have been fair financial compensation. Perpetrators should beg for forgiveness and do **Teshuva** – return to God or repentance.

Pikuach Nefesh today and divergent understandings of it

- Doctors may answer emergency calls on Shabbat.
- Abortions to save the mother's life are mandatory – the unborn child is not considered equal to the mother.
- Euthanasia, suicide, and assisted suicide are strictly forbidden.
- It may be permissible to switch off life support machines, or end treatment that artificially prolongs life.
- Generally, Orthodox Jews take a stricter view on what Pikuach Nefesh permits, but it should not be assumed, for example, that Reform Jews would take a more liberal approach.

	Orthodox	Reform/Liberal
Abortion	Should only happen to save the mother's life.	May allow for wider circumstances, such as social and non-life threatening medical issues, to be considered.
Organ donation	Very controversial. Allow it if: • from a living person with no danger to health • from a dead body, to save a life. • But question whether transplant stops heart beating and causes death.	Usually permitted in most circumstances.

 TIP
Ensure you are familiar with the meaning of important concepts such as euthanasia and abortion.

 APPLY

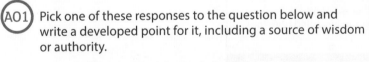

(AO1) Pick one of these responses to the question below and write a developed point for it, including a source of wisdom or authority.

- Man is created in God's image.
- The Torah outlines explicit punishments for those who take away life.

c. Explain **two** reasons why protecting human life is important for Jews. In your answer you must refer to a source of wisdom and authority. (5)

(AO2) Create a planning table for this question, outlining 'for' and 'against'.

d. 'Pikuach Nefesh should be applied in all situations.' Evaluate this statement considering arguments for and against. In your response you should:
- refer to Jewish teachings
- reach a justified conclusion. (15)

 **REVIEW**

Answers: Mark your answers using p.196 and note areas for improvement.
AO1: This question is testing your ability to write a developed point. For help with this skill, see p.12.
AO2: This question is testing your ability to plan a response. For help with this skill, see p.12.

RECAP

Essential information

- The **Mitzvot** are commandments that guide actions: the 613 laws in the Torah; a Mitzvah is also a good deed.
- The **Halakhah** is the list of Mitzvot that guide Jewish life. Jews believe they have free will and a choice in following the Mitzvot.
- The Mitzvot are a way of deepening a relationship with God.

The nature and importance of the Mitzvot

> **❝**I present before you today a blessing and a curse**❞** (*Deuteronomy 11:26*)

- Halakhah teaches Jews how to perform or fulfil the Mitzvot.
- Maimonides (1135–1204 CE) compiled the Mishneh Torah, a compilation of all the Mitzvot.
- Jews believe the Mitzvot were given by God to Moses. They follow the Mitzvot as they form part of the covenant between the Jewish people and God and there is punishment for not following the Mitzvot.
- Orthodox Jews believe the Halakhah was given orally on Sinai and written in the Torah. Reform Jews believe it evolves through the generations. They try to keep as many Mitzvot as possible.
- Reform Jews believe the Torah is divinely inspired rather than the literal Word of God. They consider how the Mitzvot may have been influenced by culture, so may no longer be relevant or ethical.

The Mitzvot and free will

> God seems to predetermine fate, for example telling Abraham his descendants would be enslaved, freed, and return to Canaan. However, Jews believe they have free will.

> Some philosophers thought God knew what would happen rather than determining what would happen. This was a sign of God's **omniscience** – knowledge of all human actions, past, present, and future.

The Mitzvot

Between humans and the Almighty
Jews obey because the Mitzvot come from God.
• Some Jews see them as a gift from God.
• Observing Mitzvot shows gratitude to God.
• They show the best way to live, which deepens the relationship with God.
• Religious significance is given to everyday actions such as eating, by giving blessings for food

Between humans
• The Mitzvot include rules on how humans should behave towards each other.
• Mitzvah used informally to mean 'good deed'. Such as:
○ visiting the sick
○ comforting mourners
○ feeding the hungry
○ helping the poor

The importance for Jews today

The Mitzvot continue to be studied and analysed.

Some decisions are controversial, and not all Jews will agree with all Rabbis and their decisions.

Moral principles and the Mitzvot

Judaism is a living religion that considers modern issues in light of tradition and scripture.

The Talmud is the starting point for modern questions, such as organ donation or abortion.

Many laws are no longer practised, such as animal sacrifice.

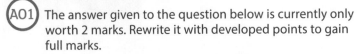

TIP

Remember that debate continues today about interpretations of the Mitzvot and how to apply it to modern living.

 APPLY

AO1 The answer given to the question below is currently only worth 2 marks. Rewrite it with developed points to gain full marks.

b. Explain **two** reasons why Jews follow the Mitzvot. (4)

> *The Mitzvot are from the Almighty.*
> *Obeying the Mitzvot is the best way for a Jewish person to live.*

AO2 Complete the planning table for the question below. You must refer to **at least two** different Jewish groups.

d. 'It is important for Jews to follow the Mitzvot.' Evaluate this statement considering arguments for and against. In your response you should:
- refer to Jewish teachings
- refer to different Jewish points of view
- reach a justified conclusion. (15)

For	Against
• Given to Jews from God via Moses	• Some no longer appropriate such as sacrificing animals
• _____	• _____
• _____	• _____
• This would be view of most _____ Jews.	• This would be view of most _____ Jews.

 **REVIEW**

Answers: Mark your answers using p.196 and note areas for improvement.
AO1: This question is testing your ability to write a developed point. For help with this skill, see p.12.
AO2: This question is testing your ability to identify arguments for and against a statement. For help with this skill, see p.12.

RECAP

Essential information

- Jews do not agree on the nature of life after death, but are generally convinced death is not the end.
- There is little scripture on life after death.
- Most teachings come from ancient Rabbis such as Maimonides.

Life after death

- There are different Jewish opinions about the possibility of life after death, but there is a general agreement that death is not the end.
- Some Jews believe in The World to Come (**Olam Ha-Ba**, a spiritual afterlife following the physical death), that there will be a heaven (**Gan Eden**, not the place where Adam and Eve lived), and a place of purification of the soul (**Gehinnom**).
- Both resurrection and reincarnation are traditional Jewish beliefs.
- Most Jews do not believe in eternal punishment.

Jewish teachings about life after death

> 66 Thus the dust returns to the ground, as it was, and the spirit returns to God Who gave it 99 (*Ecclesiastes 12:7*)

This is one of the few Torah verses about life after death and suggests the soul returns to God. This could be an afterlife with God, or simply being part of him again. Most Jewish beliefs formed through the teachings of Rabbis and scholars such as Maimonides.

> 66 I believe with perfect faith that there will be a revival of the dead at the time when it shall please the Creator. 99 (*Maimonides, Thirteen Principles of Faith*)

Reunited

- The Torah suggests those who die are reunited with their family.
- Jacob was 'gathered with his people' when he died (*Genesis 49:33*).

Reward and punishment

- Those who break the Mitzvot will be punished in the afterlife: 'that soul shall be cut off' (*Exodus 31:14*).
- 'Many of those who sleep in the dusty earth will awaken: these for everlasting life and these for shame, for everlasting abhorrence' (*Daniel 12:2*)

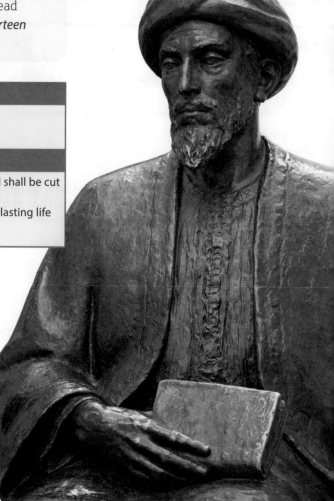

Maimonides

The nature of resurrection and judgment

- Orthodox Jews believe the promised Messiah will come to lead a Messianic Age when the righteous will be resurrected and live in a restored Israel.
- Reform Jews share some beliefs in this age to come, but reject the idea of an individual Messiah.

Gan Eden

- The place for the righteous.
- Unclear whether souls will go there immediately after death, or in the Messianic Age.
- Maimonides taught that righteous gentiles (who have followed the Seven Laws of Noah) will also be rewarded.

Gehinnom

- Place of punishment for the unrighteous – those who neglected the Torah.
- Souls go there to be cleansed.
- Rabbis taught that, once cleansed, these souls move to Gan Eden

TIP
Maimonides is one of the most well known and admired Jewish thinkers. Remember that quotes from Rabbis such as Maimonides count as sources of wisdom and authority.

 **APPLY**

AO1 Read the start of this student's answer, which lacks a reference to a source of wisdom and authority. What could be added to make sure they get the additional mark?

c. Explain **two** Jewish beliefs about life after death. In your answer you must refer to a source of wisdom and authority. (5)

> *Firstly, Judaism is far more focused on the life here and now, rather than an afterlife. There is not much in the Torah, but there is a general consensus that death is not the end.*
>
> *However, there is a suggestion that the soul returns to the Almighty. This could be an afterlife, or simply a being part of the Almighty again.*

AO2 Fill in the planning table for the question below, adding arguments in support of the statement.

d. 'Living a righteous life is the most important duty for Jews.' Evaluate this statement considering arguments for and against.
In your response you should:
- refer to Jewish teachings
- reach a justified conclusion. (15)

For	Against
• Most Jews believe there will be an afterlife, and therefore it is a consideration for Jews. • The Torah makes clear that those who do not follow the Mitzvot will be punished (*Exodus 31:14*). • Although all souls eventually reach Gan Eden, they do not want the punishment and cleansing of Gehinnom.	• _____ • _____ • _____

 **REVIEW**

Answers: Mark your answers using p.196–197 and note areas for improvement.
AO1: This question is testing your ability to explain beliefs correctly, using a source of wisdom and authority. For help with this skill, see p.12.
AO2: This question is testing your ability to identify divergent views. For help with this skill, see p.12.

 **RECAP**

What is a compare and contrast question?

There are a few areas of the exam specification where you can be asked to compare and contrast two religions, or two groups within a religion. For example, you might get asked to compare Catholic Christianity with other Christian denominations, or you might be asked to compare Christianity with a second religion, such as Judaism or Islam.

In this paper, Paper 2, you will only be asked to compare Judaism with Christianity (the 'main religious tradition of Great Britain'), and you will only be asked to compare them on two possible topics: eschatology and worship (see p.118). Here, you can revise for eschatology.

How are beliefs about the afterlife and their significance different for Jews and Christians?

	Judaism	Christianity
Teaching on life after death	• Little in the Torah about life after death. • Lots of different interpretations including resurrection and reincarnation.	• Extensive teachings in the Gospels about Kingdom of God. • Universal belief that death is not the end, and possibility of life with God in heaven.
Nature of resurrection and judgment	• Gan Eden is a place for the righteous, but unclear as to whether this is at death, in the Messianic Age, or the end of time. • Gehinnom is a place of punishment for the unrighteous souls. Souls are cleansed in Gehinnom, then they can enter Gan Eden.	• Heaven is a place with God. Jesus implied the Kingdom of God was both present and future. • Only some Christians, such as Catholics, believe in purgatory, which is a place of purification. Many dismiss the idea as not biblical. • Hell is a place of eternal punishment for the unrighteous.

TIP
Remember, when the exam says 'the main religious tradition of Great Britain', it is referring to Christianity.

APPLY

You could be asked to compare and contrast in (b) questions (but being able to talk about different viewpoints within Judaism is also a useful skill in (d) questions!).. For example, here is a question you could be asked:

b. Describe **two** differences in beliefs about life after death in Judaism and the main religious tradition of Great Britain. (4)

Here is an example of how you could structure an answer to this question:

● Give one belief in life after death from Judaism.	*The first difference is that in Judaism there is very little in the Torah about life after death.*
● Give a contrasting belief from Christianity.	*However, for Christians, one of Jesus' main missions, as documented in the Gospels, is to introduce the concept of the Kingdom of God.*
● Give a second belief from Judaism.	*Secondly, in Judaism ancient Rabbis spoke about a place called Gan Eden for the righteous, but they were unsure when souls would enter.*
● Give a contrasting belief from Christianity.	*Yet for Christians, Jesus made clear that the Kingdom of God was something the disciples should try to make present.*

Now have a go at answering the same question yourself, using the grid below to help you. Try to choose **different** points from those given in the answer table to the left.

● Give one belief in life after death from Judaism.	*The first difference is that in Judaism...*
● Give a contrasting belief elsewhere from Christianity.	*Whereas in Christian tradition...*
● Give a second belief from Judaism.	*Secondly, in Judaism...*
● Give a contrasting belief from Christianity.	*Yet for Christians...*

TIP
Words like 'whereas', 'yet', and 'however' will signal to the examiner that you're making a comparison.

Test the 3 mark question (a)

1   Outline **three** reasons Moses is important to Jews.   **(3 marks)**

Moses was chosen by God to lead the Hebrews to safety from Egypt. (1)

God made a covenant with Moses on Mount Sinai. (1)

Moses led the Hebrew people to the Promised Land. (1)

2   Outline **three** expectations of the Messiah for Jews.   **(3 marks)**

A great political leader descended from King David. (1)

_____

_____

3   Outline **three** good deeds to humans that some Jews would consider a Mitzvah.   **(3 marks)**

_____

_____

_____

> **TIP**
> Ensure you know the difference between Mitzvot and Mitzvah.

Test the 4 mark question (b)

1   Explain **two** reasons why the covenant at Sinai is important for Jews today.   **(4 marks)**

● **Explain one reason.**	*Firstly, Moses received the Torah.*
● Develop your explanation with more detail/an example/reference to a religious teaching.	*This Law is still used today by Jewish people to guide their lives.*
● **Explain a second reason.**	*Secondly, it sealed a covenant.*
● Develop your explanation with more detail/an example/reference to a religious teaching.	*According to Jewish tradition, every soul that would ever be born was present and agreed to be bound by this covenant.*

2   Explain **two** reasons why human life is regarded as holy by Jews.   **(4 marks)**

● **Explain one reason.**	
● Develop your explanation with more detail/an example/reference to a religious teaching.	
● **Explain a second reason.**	
● Develop your explanation with more detail/an example/reference to a religious teaching.	

> **TIP**
> Ensure you use vocabulary that is specific to Judaism in your answer.

3   Explain **two** reasons why Jewish people believe in the Shekhinah.   **(4 marks)**

Exam Practice

Test the 5 mark question (c)

1   Explain **two** ways the Torah is an important part of Jewish life.   **(5 marks)**

● **Explain one way.**	Firstly, the Torah is important because it contains the Mitzvot, including the Ten Commandments.
● Develop your explanation with more detail/an example.	These remain relevant to Jewish people today,
● **Either:** Add a reference to a source of wisdom and authority here.	for example 'Do not kill' (Exodus).
● **Explain a second way.**	Secondly, the Torah is still used for worship by Jews today.
● Develop your explanation with more detail/an example.	Jews read from a Torah scroll during synagogue services.
● **Or:** Add a reference to a source of wisdom and authority here.	

TIP

Remember, you don't need the chapter and verse when quoting a source of wisdom and authority, as long as it is accurate, specific, and clearly recognisable.

2   Explain **two** Jewish teachings about the covenant with Abraham.   **(5 marks)**

● **Explain one teaching.**	
● Develop your explanation with more detail/an example.	
● **Either:** Add a reference to a source of wisdom and authority here.	
● **Explain a second teaching.**	
● Develop your explanation with more detail/an example.	
● **Or:** Add a reference to a source of wisdom and authority here.	

TIP

Be clear which covenant is which – be careful not to muddle them!

3   Explain **two** characteristics of the Almighty.   **(5 marks)**

Exam Practice

Test the 15 mark question (d)

1 'Jewish laws can be broken in order to save a person's life.' Evaluate this statement considering arguments for and against. In your response you should:
- refer to Jewish teachings
- reach a justified conclusion.

(15 marks)

ARGUMENTS IN SUPPORT OF THE STATEMENT • **Explain why some people would agree with the statement.** • Develop your explanation with more detail and examples. • Refer to religious teaching. Use a quote or paraphrase of a religious authority. • **Evaluate the arguments.** Is this a good argument? Explain why you think this. Use words such as convincing/strong/robust/weak/unpersuasive/unsuccessful within your reasoning.	Many Jews would agree with this statement because when the life of a specific person is in danger, almost any Mitzvah lo ta'aseh (command to not do an action) of the Torah can be broken. Pikuach Nefesh is a principle of Jewish law that says that the preservation of human life overrides almost all other laws. In Jewish scripture it says that you should keep God's rules; but not cause death by following them. For example, saving a life by organ donation can override the law against damaging a body (Talmud Yoma 83–84). There are several instances in Rabbinic teaching where the laws of the Sabbath are to be broken to save the life of another; these occasions include rescuing a child from the sea, breaking apart a wall that has collapsed on a child and extinguishing a fire.
ARGUMENTS SUPPORTING A DIFFERENT VIEW • **Explain why some people would disagree with the statement.** • Develop your explanation with more detail and examples. • Refer to religious teaching. Use a quote or paraphrase of a religious authority. • **Evaluate the arguments.** Is this a good argument? Explain why you think this. Use words such as convincing/strong/robust/weak/unpersuasive/unsuccessful within your reasoning.	There are still some Mitzvah that cannot be disregarded when life is in danger, for example idolatry, which includes worshipping any other god, saying God's name in vain, or pretending God does not exist in order to avoid persecution. People are not allowed to murder someone (deliberately killing someone) or to create a dangerous situation which may put more lives at risk (speeding to reach a hospital and killing an innocent motorist) or commit adultery; it is clear to see why this is the case. While one is not permitted to automatically give up one's life in order to save the life of another (an act of suicide, forbidden in Jewish law), one may risk one's life to save the life of another. It is, however, forbidden to place one's own life at more risk than the other person is already in. This is clearly reckless behaviour.
CONCLUSION • **Give a justified conclusion.** • Include your own reasoning. • Use words such as convincing/strong/robust/weak/unpersuasive/unsuccessful to weigh up the different arguments for and against. • Do not just repeat arguments you have already used without explaining how they apply to your reasoned opinion/conclusion.	In conclusion, I think that many Jews would say that it is clear that most Jewish laws can be broken, just not those most serious ones. This is all based on the fact that Jews believe life is sacred, and must be saved at all costs.

TIP
It is important that you know exactly what is allowed and what is not allowed under Jewish laws. This answer details them well.

TIP
In a 15 mark question 3 of the marks available are awarded for correct spelling, punctuation and grammar. You should check your answer thoroughly.

2 'The covenant with Moses is the most significant covenant for Jewish people.' Evaluate this statement considering arguments for and against. In your response you should:

- refer to Jewish teachings
- refer to different Jewish points of view
- reach a justified conclusion.

(15 marks)

ARGUMENTS IN SUPPORT OF THE STATEMENT ● **Explain why some people would agree with the statement.** ● Develop your explanation with more detail and examples. ● Refer to religious teaching. Use a quote or paraphrase of a religious authority. ● **Evaluate the arguments.** Is this a good argument? Explain why you think this. Use words such as convincing/strong/robust/weak/unpersuasive/unsuccessful within your reasoning.	*Some Jews/people would agree with this statement because...*
ARGUMENTS SUPPORTING A DIFFERENT VIEW ● **Explain why some people would disagree with the statement.** ● Develop your explanation with more detail and examples. ● Refer to religious teaching. Use a quote or paraphrase of a religious authority. ● **Evaluate the arguments.** Is this a good argument? Explain why you think this. Use words such as convincing/strong/robust/weak/unpersuasive/unsuccessful within your reasoning.	*On the other hand, some Jews/people would hold a different point of view...*
CONCLUSION ● **Give a justified conclusion.** ● Include your own reasoning. ● Use words such as convincing/strong/robust/weak/unpersuasive/unsuccessful to weigh up the different arguments for and against. ● Do not just repeat arguments you have already used without explaining how they apply to your reasoned opinion/conclusion.	*Having considered both sides of the argument, I would say that...*

3 'The Almighty is the only one who can judge.' Evaluate this statement considering arguments for and against. In your response you should:

- refer to Jewish teachings
- reach a justified conclusion.

(15 marks)

REVIEW

Check your answers to these exam questions on p.197, correct your answers with annotations, and note down any general areas for improvement.

If you don't feel secure in the content of this chapter, you could reread the Recap sections.

If you don't feel secure in your exam technique, you could revisit the exam support section on pp.7–14.

RECAP

Essential information

- Prayer is the most important part of Jewish worship: synagogues play a key role in this.
- Shabbat, festivals, and daily prayers are the most important services that take place in the synagogue.
- These unite the community while providing time for the individual to offer their own prayers.

The nature, features, and purpose of public worship

- Avodat Hashem means 'worship of God'.
- After the Temple was destroyed in 586 BCE and again in 70 CE, the synagogue became the main place of worship.
- Jews continue to worship in the synagogue today. It is a reminder that they are part of a community.

> 66My vows to Hashem I will pay, in the presence, now, of His entire people [...] in the courtyards of the House of Hashem 99 *(Psalm 116:14–19)*

- This quotation highlights the value of public worship.
- Prayer in the synagogue became more important after the destruction of the Temple.

Synagogue services

Shabbat	Daily prayers
• Shabbat services take place on Friday evening and Saturday morning. • Reform and Liberal Jews usually focus on these services rather than daily prayers. • The Amidah (adjusted for Shabbat; see 8.4) and Aleinu (see 8.6) are expressed. • There is a longer reading of the Torah than usual and a sermon by the Rabbi. • The whole family is encouraged to attend.	• Jews can pray anywhere, but if a minyan is present they can say the Kaddish, kedusha (the third section of all Amidah recitations), or other prayers linked to the Torah. • Jews are expected to pray three times daily – morning, afternoon, and evening. • Orthodox synagogues say prayers in Hebrew; Reform synagogues use the local language. • The Siddur (literally meaning 'order') is the book of daily prayers Jews follow.

The importance of synagogue services

- Synagogue services unite the local community.
- They are a reminder of the global community that Jews are part of.
- Jews pray towards the site of the Holy Temple in Jerusalem, Israel.
- Private prayers usually involve thanksgiving, praise, and requests for something.
- A sermon will be given by a Rabbi, which may affect the way Jews then live their lives.

> **TIP**
> For information on festivals see 8.7; for more on Shabbat see 8.6.

 APPLY

> **TIP**
> Remember, in this question you could use Shabbat, daily prayers, or festivals – try to be as specific as possible.

AO1 Try this one on your own!

a. Outline **three** occasions that Jews may attend the synagogue for public acts of worship. (3)

AO2 Consider the arguments for and against the statement provided below. Which is the most convincing? Write a justified conclusion to an essay on this topic.

d. 'It is important Jews take part in public acts of worship.'

For	Against
• Used to take place in the Temple, but the synagogue now replaces this. • Made clear in Psalms: 'My vows to Hashem I will pay [...] in the [...] House of Hashem.' • Unites local and global community.	• Jews can pray anywhere. • Patriarchs such as Abraham and Moses did not take part in such acts. • Teaching of Rabbis is available elsewhere, not just in the synagogue service.

 **REVIEW**

Answers: Mark your answers using p.197 and note areas for improvement.
AO1: This question is testing your ability to answer 'outline' questions. For help with this skill, see p.12.
AO2: This question is testing your ability to write a justified conclusion. For help with this skill, see p.12.

 **RECAP**

Essential information

- The Torah is the most important and holy book for Jewish people. It contains the Law of Moses and forms part of the Tenakh, the Hebrew Bible.
- The Talmud is the Oral Law and contains information on how the Torah's laws should be interpreted. It is widely studied by Jews.
- Some Jews observe the food laws (kashrut); others do not observe them as strictly.

The nature and purpose of the Tenakh and the Talmud

The Tenakh	The Talmud
• The Torah is the most sacred object in Judaism, kept in the Ark in the synagogue. • The rest of the Tenakh shows how Jewish people lived and tried to keep on the right path. • Orthodox Jews believe it is the literal Word of God and cannot be changed. • Reform Jews think it is a human creation, inspired by God.	• Oral tradition – literally 'instruction or learning'. • Orthodox tradition says it is the Oral Torah, also given to Moses on Sinai and written down 1000 years later. • Reform Jews believe it is a human creation, reflecting the wisdom of many generations of Jewish people. • It is made up of the Mishnah (core text) and Gemara (Rabbinical analysis). • It contains the teachings and opinions of thousands of early Rabbis on topics such as law, ethics, philosophy, customs, and history, and is the source of Jewish legal teaching and decision.

The importance of their use in daily life and worship

The different views of Jews have led to the separation of Orthodox and Reform Jews in worship and practice. However, the Torah remains central to all Jews.

- The Torah is used and read four times a week in Orthodox synagogues, once a week in Reform synagogues.
- Jews are encouraged to study the Talmud. Perkei Avot or 'Ethics of the Fathers' is a set of ethical teachings in the Mishnah. Chapter 2 commends study:

> ❝If [a man] has acquired words of the Torah, he has attained afterlife❞ (*Perkei Avot 2:8*)

- Regular study and lectures are held in synagogues, while Daf Yomi ('a page a day') is an international programme where Jews study in unison.

The nature and purpose of kashrut, Jewish food laws

Acceptable food is called kosher, meaning 'fit' and 'correct'; non-kosher food is called treifah, meaning 'torn'.

Deuteronomy 14:3–10 lists some of the foods that are allowed and forbidden.

Kashrut

It is an opportunity to bring kedusha, or holiness, into everyday life.

Some suggest the laws had health benefits at the time they were made – seafood would have travelled long distances without refrigeration, pigs carried disease, etc.

Jews believe these laws come from God, which is why they keep them.

The application of kashrut today

- Orthodox Jews feel they are still important to keep, while some Reform and Liberal Jews may not observe all laws.
- Most Jews refrain from eating pork.
- There are other kosher requirements that can create challenges for Jews today especially if eating out:

Meat and dairy should not be mixed – including during preparation.

Meat must be slaughtered in the correct way.

TIP
Remember that study is an important part of life for Jews. The Shekhinah (see 7.2) is present during study.

 APPLY

 AO1 The first point has been done for you, so develop the second, ensuring you link to Jews today.

b. Explain **two** ways that the food laws (kashrut) affect the lives of Jews today. (4)

Firstly, Jews do not eat pork. However, they can eat other meat, as long as it is slaughtered in an appropriate way. Secondly...

AO2 Answer the questions in the table to plan a response to this question.

d. 'It is important that all Jews study the Talmud.' Evaluate this statement considering arguments for and against. In your response you should:
- refer to Jewish teachings
- refer to different Jewish points of view
- reach a justified conclusion. (12)

For	Against
Why is it important?	What is the **most** important book?
Why do Orthodox Jews agree? (Source of wisdom and authority)	Why may Reform and Liberal Jews disagree?
What practical provision is made for Jews?	What practical issues might there be?

 REVIEW **Answers:** Mark your answers using p.197 and note areas for improvement.
AO1: This question is testing your ability to write a developed point. For help with this skill, see p.12.
AO2: This question is testing your ability to plan a response. For help with this skill, see p.12.

RECAP

Essential information
- Jews are encouraged to carry out the daily prayers at home if they cannot attend synagogue.
- Formal, personal, and constant prayers are important to the everyday lives of Jews.
- Different types of prayer bring Jews closer to God, their families, and the Jewish community.

The nature of prayer in the home and of private prayer
- Most Jews cannot attend the synagogue daily.
- Jews will often pray at home, individually, or as a family.
- They are encouraged to clear their mind and then 'reflect in your heart' (*Psalm 4:4*), meaning to look inward and connect with God from the heart.

Shabbat prayer	Prayer three times a day
• Meal prepared and candles lit • Prayers recited before the meal • **Kiddush** (prayer of sanctification) recited – celebrates creation and freedom of slaves from Egypt • Connection of family, friends, and global community considered of great value (see 8.6)	• Directly instructed to do so by God: 66 Evening, morning, and noon, I supplicate and moan; and He has heard my voice 99 (*Psalm 55:17*) • Orthodox Jews pray three times a day. For Reform Jews, however, it is a matter of personal choice. • Keeps God at the forefront of a Jew's thoughts • Shema often said at night • **Modeh ani** prayer is recited upon waking to thank God for gift of life

Jews often pray before and after eating.

Jews pray for a wide variety of reasons.

Private prayer

Prayer in a group unites the community.

Jews praise God, make requests and give thanks.

TIP Consider whether you think private prayer might be more important than public prayer.

TIP Remember that private prayer might coincide with Shabbat prayer in the home but it can also happen in other moments when alone.

When prayer might be used and why
Different types of prayer allow Jews to connect with God in different ways:

| Daily prayer: connecting in faith as a family | Individual prayer: personal time with God | Constant prayer: keeps God in a Jew's heart and mind | Shabbat prayer: brings together family and friends |

APPLY

AO1 Have a go at this question on your own.

c. Explain **two** reasons why a Jew may pray daily. In your answer you must refer to a source of wisdom and authority. (5)

AO2 Write down at least two points each both for and against the following statement, followed by a justified conclusion.

d. 'Praying three times a day is the responsibility of all Jews.' Evaluate this statement considering arguments for and against. In your response you should:
- refer to Jewish teachings
- refer to different Jewish points of view
- reach a justified conclusion. (12)

For	Against
Conclusion:	

REVIEW
Answers: Mark your answers using p.197 and note areas for improvement.
AO1: This question is testing your ability to answer a (c) question. For help with this skill, see p.12.
AO2: This question is testing your ability to answer a (d) question. For help with this skill, see p.12.

RECAP

Essential information

- Daily prayer is an important part of Jewish life; it may be used in the synagogue or privately.
- The Shema is the most important Jewish prayer and describes the core beliefs about God.
- The Amidah consists of three sections: praise, request, and thanks. It is a core part of Jewish prayer services and contains a number of blessings from God.

Examples of the different types of prayer

	Nature	Importance
The Shema	• Most important prayer in Judaism • Recited twice a day in morning and evening services • Found in *Deuteronomy 6:4–9, 11:13–21*, and *Numbers 15:37–41*	• Declares most fundamental principle of Jewish faith: the belief in one God • Contains many important beliefs about God
The Amidah	• HaTefillah or 'the prayer' • Known as 'standing prayer'	• Core part of every Jewish service • Features three parts that are central to a relationship to God: praise, requests, thanks

66 Hear O Israel, Hashem is our God, Hashem is the One and Only 99 *(Deuteronomy 6:4)*

Tallit	Tefillin	Mezuzah
• Prayer shawl • Reminder of the Mitzvot in the Torah 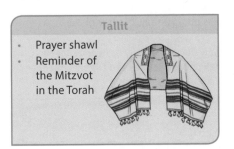	• Black boxes with leather straps • Connects heart and mind to God *(Deuteronomy 6:8)* 	• Container attached to doorposts in Jewish homes, containing Shema • Reminder of God's presence 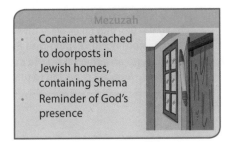

Importance of having different forms of prayer

Prayers were originally unstructured – individual Rabbis picked words of the Amidah blessings and selected parts of the Torah to read. Over time the format and themes were formalised and standard versions of prayers agreed.

Morning	Afternoon	Evening
• Thanks for the use of the body • Psalms and sections of Tenakh chosen to focus the mind on God • Shema and Amidah recited	• *Psalm 145* ('Praise' by David) read • Followed by the Amidah and Aleinu (see 8.6)	• Shema, Amidah, and Aleinu recited

Other prayers

- The Kaddish – prayer of praise; used after Rabbi's teaching or longer version called Mourner's Kaddish at a funeral
- Barkhu – the call to prayer at the start of a synagogue service by the prayer leader.

These different prayers allow Jews to connect with God in different ways.

APPLY

TIP
Remember that the alternative argument might not be that a prayer is unimportant, but why another prayer is **more** important.

AO1 Answer the question below; the first example is done for you.

a. Outline **three** Jewish prayers. (3)

The Shema is the prayer that makes it clear there is just one God.

AO2 Can you think of a reason why a Jewish person may say each of the following prayers is the 'most important'?
- The Shema
- The Amidah
- The Aleinu
- The Kaddish
- Barkhu

REVIEW

Answers: Mark your answers using p.197 and note areas for improvement.
AO1: This question is testing your ability to recall information. For help with this skill, see p.12.
AO2: This question is testing your ability to identify divergent views. For help with this skill, see p.12.

Compare and Contrast:
8.4 The Shema and the Amidah

 **RECAP**

What is a compare and contrast question?

There are a few areas of the exam specification where you can be asked to compare and contrast two religions, or two groups within a religion. For example, you might get asked to compare Catholic Christianity with other Christian denominations, or you might be asked to compare Christianity with a second religion, such as Judaism or Islam.

In this paper, Paper 2, you will only be asked to compare Judaism with Christianity (the 'main religious tradition of Great Britain'), and you will only be asked to compare them on two possible topics: eschatology (see p.108) and worship. Here, you can revise for worship.

How is the practice of worship different for Christians and Jews?

Judaism	Christianity
• Prayer aids such as the tallit (prayer shawl) and tefillin (small black boxes with leather strap) are used during formal worship. • The Shema is the most important prayer in Judaism and is usually recited twice a day. • Synagogue worship takes place on a Friday night and Saturday morning, in keeping with Shabbat. • Daily prayers can either take place in private or in the synagogue; Jews are expected to pray three times daily.	• Rosary beads may be used by Catholics for prayer, but these are not part of formal worship. • The Lord's Prayer or Our Father is the universal Christian prayer, which Jesus gave to the disciples. • The Christian Sabbath is on a Sunday, the day of the Resurrection. • Christians may pray daily either formally or informally, for examples Catholics may choose to pray the Divine Office, but this is not compulsory.

TIP Look back to 8.1 – this topic will help you to think about the Shema and the Amidah as acts of worship or elements within a worship service. Remember that this compare and contrast question focuses on the Shema and Amidah, not other acts of worship in Judaism.

TIP Remember, when the exam says 'the main religious tradition of Great Britain', it is referring to Christianity.

 **APPLY**

You could be asked to compare and contrast in (b) questions (but being able to talk about different viewpoints within Judaism is also a useful skill in (d) questions!). For example, here is a question you could be asked:

b. Describe **two** differences in worship in Judaism and the main religious tradition of Great Britain. (4)

Here is an example of how you could structure an answer to this question:

● Give one feature of worship in Judaism.	The first difference is that in Judaism prayer aids such as the tallit are used in every morning service.
● Give a contrasting feature of worship from Christianity.	However, for Christians, aids to prayer such as rosary beads are only used by Catholics, and usually in private prayer.
● Give a second feature from Judaism.	Secondly, in Judaism the Shema is seen as the most important prayer, and as such, is recited twice daily.
● Give a contrasting feature from Christianity.	Yet for Christians, the Our Father or Lord's Prayer is the most important, but there is no teaching that people should pray daily.

Now have a go at answering the same question yourself, using the grid below to help you. Try to choose **different** points from those given in the answer table above.

● Give one feature of worship in Judaism.	The first difference is that in Judaism...
● Give a feature of worship from Christianity.	Whereas in Christian tradition...
● Give a second feature from Judaism.	Secondly, in Judaism...
● Give a contrasting feature from Christianity.	Yet for Christians...

TIP Words like 'whereas', 'yet', and 'however' will signal to the examiner that you're making a comparison.

RECAP

Essential information

- Rituals are an important part of Jewish life representing the significant moments of both religious and daily life.
- Birth, coming of age, marriage, and death all have rituals associated with them for Jews.
- Most rituals are followed by all Jews, but sometimes with slight differences.

The importance of ritual for Jews today

- Rituals are grounded in Jewish law.
- Observance shows gratitude to God, a sense of Jewish identity, and brings the Almighty into everyday life.
- Important moments are marked by customs that go back to biblical times.

Birth

- Life begins as a baby emerges halfway from the mother's womb; it is pure and free from sin.
- *Leviticus 12:4–5* outlines the Temple rituals for purification of the mother after birth.
  She could not enter or touch anything sacred for:
  - Boy: 7 days plus 33 days
  - Girl: 14 days plus 66 days
  The recovery time was doubled for a girl to reflect the extra work the mother has done to create another creator.
- Offerings would then have been made at the Temple to 'become purified' (*Leviticus 12:8*)
- Today the mother attends **mikvah** (ritual bath of purification) once she has stopped bleeding –
  but not before 7 days for a boy or 14 days for a girl.
- Children are always given a Hebrew name, and often an English name.
  - A girl's name is given in the synagogue.
  - A boy's name is given during the Brit Milah (circumcision).

> 66[the mother] may not touch anything sacred and she may not enter the Sanctuary 99
> (*Leviticus 12:4*)

Brit Milah

- Circumcision is one of the most universally observed Mitzvot. It is an outward sign of the everlasting covenant with the Almighty.
- Abraham circumcised himself and his descendants, starting with Isaac.
- Circumcision is performed by a religiously trained person known as a mohel.
- Orthodox Jews still perform Pidyon ha-ben (Redemption of the Son – tradition that the first-born male serves the Temple) and give a small amount of money to a kohein priest to be saved from Temple service.

> 66Abraham circumcised his son Isaac at the age of eight days as God had commanded him 99
> (*Genesis 21:4*)

Bar and Bat Mitzvah ceremonies

Young people are seen as 'coming of age' and become responsible at this point.

Bar Mitzvah (boys)	Bat Mitzvah (girls)
• Happens at age of 13 • Can lead synagogue service after this • Need to learn enough Hebrew to read from the Torah	• Happens at age of 12 (13 in Reform/Liberal synagogues) • Ceremony only about 100 years old • Will be taught to cook **challah** (plaited bread for Shabbat) and other important preparations in the home
• Both expected to study and prepare carefully • Reform/Liberal communities may allow boys and girls to read from the Torah	

Marriage

- There are very few teachings on marriage in the Torah.
- The Talmud explains how to find a partner, the form of the ceremony, and the nature of marital relationships.
- Jews must first go through a ritual engagement or Kiddushin.
- Full marriage is called Nisuin.

Mourning ceremonies

- These help the bereaved to return to normal life after the loss of a loved one.
- Orthodox Jews will often tear their clothes when they lose a loved one, as Jacob did (*Genesis 37:34*).
- Reform Jews may wear a torn black ribbon.

Five periods of avelut (mourning)

	1. Aninut	2. Shiva	3. Sheloshim	4. Yud-bet chodesh	5. Yahrzeit
When?	From death to burial	First seven days after burial	First 30 days (including Shiva) to complete mourning	Additional 'year of mourning' for the loss of a parent	Anniversary of the date of death
What happens?	Usually 24 hours	Stay at home praying, no work done	Normal life, but no parties		On anniversary a yahrzeit candle is lit

The funeral

- Jews are usually buried rather than cremated, ideally within 24 hours of death.
- Candles are lit and the body is never left alone.
  - It is wrapped in a linen shroud.
  - Men are wrapped in a tallit too.
  - Plain coffins are used.
- The funeral takes place entirely at the cemetery as the synagogue is considered a place for the living.
- Hands are washed outside the ceremony to signify leaving death behind.

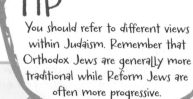

TIP

You should refer to different views within Judaism. Remember that Orthodox Jews are generally more traditional while Reform Jews are often more progressive.

 APPLY

 AO1 This answer has been started; can you finish it off? Make sure you add a source of wisdom or authority.

a. Explain **two** important features of Jewish birth ceremonies. In your answer you must refer to a source of wisdom and authority. (5)

The first feature is that after giving birth, at the time of the Temple, the woman was unable to touch anything sacred or attend the Sanctuary. Today, she will attend mikvah once she has stopped bleeding.

The second feature...

- refer to Jewish teachings
- refer to different Jewish points of view
- reach a justified conclusion. (12)

Agree	Disagree
• Circumcision is the most observed Mitzvah, even by secular Jews. • All Jews have a 'coming of age' for boys and girls – Bar and Bat Mitzvah – that may have some differences, but are largely similar. • Mourning is a key ritual for Jews, even if it is slightly different for different groups of Jews.	

 AO2 Arguments in support of the statement have been given. Complete the other side of the argument in the table.

d. 'All Jews celebrate the same rites and rituals.' Evaluate this statement considering arguments for and against. In your response you should:

 **REVIEW**

Answers: Mark your answers using p.197–198 and note areas for improvement.
AO1: This question is testing your ability to answer a (c) question. For help with this skill, see p.12.
AO2: This question is testing your ability to identify divergent views. For help with this skill, see p.12.

RECAP

Essential information

- Shabbat is observed from Friday evening to Saturday evening.
- It is celebrated at home on Friday with a special meal and in the synagogue on either Friday evening or Saturday morning.
- Modern life can make strict observance of Shabbat challenging for Jews.

The nature, features, history, and purpose of celebrating Shabbat

It is a time to relax, with family and community, as well as worship in the synagogue.

Some Reform communities observe Shabbat from 6pm on Friday to 6pm on Saturday to ease conflict with modern work commitments.

Shabbat

Jews believe that the Almighty instructed them to observe the Sabbath.

This is the end of the week for Jews.

It begins Friday evening at dusk and ends when three stars appear in the sky on Saturday.

How it is celebrated

❝on the seventh day He rested and was refreshed❞ (*Exodus 31:17*)

The home	The synagogue

• House cleaned and tidied in preparation
• Candles lit before Shabbat begins
• Friday evening meal
• Common to sing Shabbat hymns
• Havdalah blessing over wine and lighting of a candle to mark the end of Shabbat on Saturday evening
	• Main Shabbat service can last two hours
	• Outline of service:
	  ◦ Amidah – facing Jerusalem
	  ◦ Torah removed from Ark as Shema recited
	  ◦ Torah reading
	  ◦ Rabbi's sermon
	  ◦ Aleinu prayer
	  ◦ Kaddish prayer
	  ◦ Adon Olam 'Master of the World' hymn

No work takes place on Shabbat (there are 39 categories of activities that are considered work).

Food needs careful preparation in advance.

Jews do not always agree – mobile phone usage would be considered work by some Jews as the electrical connection would be seen as an 'ignition'; other Jews would find it acceptable.

Shabbat's importance today

- Observance of Shabbat is a core part of the Jewish faith – it is one of the Ten Commandments.
- It can be a challenge to observe it with modern living because life has changed dramatically since the time of Moses.
- There are many new issues to address for Jews, and there is not always agreement. For example:
  ◦ What should you do if driving a car is considered work, due to its ignition, but you cannot walk to the synagogue? Orthodox Jews will try to live near a synagogue, but Reform Jews will often compromise and drive as they feel it is more important to get to the synagogue.
- It remains a day of enjoyment and a time to connect to family.
- Many Jews attend the synagogue and may join Torah study groups.
- Youth groups often meet on Shabbat afternoons for discussion and social interaction.
- By observing Shabbat, Jews are following God's commandment of resting and keeping the day holy.

TIP
You can't always predict what different branches of Judaism will decide about particular actions, however, generally, Orthodox Jews will follow the Mitzvot more strictly.

 APPLY

AO1 The following answer is only worth 2 marks. How can you develop the points to ensure full marks?

c. Explain **two** reasons why Jews consider Shabbat to be important. (4)

> It is an instruction from the Almighty.
> It allows a connection to a Jew's family.

AO2 There is some divergence among Jews about what is rest. For the two examples below, explain why Orthodox Jews would consider them work, and why Reform Jews might not. Can you think of any other examples?

	Orthodox	Reform
Using a mobile phone		
Driving a car to the synagogue		

 **REVIEW**   **Answers:** Mark your answers using p.198 and note areas for improvement.
AO1: This question is testing your ability to write a developed point. For help with this skill, see p.12.
AO2: This question is testing your ability to identify divergent views. For help with this skill, see p.12.

**RECAP**

Essential information

- Festivals are an important part of Jewish life and are used to remember key events in Jewish history.
- They are a time for families and wider Jewish communities to unite and celebrate their faith.
- Rosh Hashanah and Yom Kippur are seen as the most important festivals: Jews' observance of other festivals varies depending on whether they are Reform, Liberal, or Orthodox, and where they live in the world.

The nature, origins, and purpose of festivals, and their importance for Jews today

- Festivals occur at a set time in the Jewish calendar, with some variation in dates as it is a lunar calendar.
- Most festivals are linked to the history of the Jewish people, connecting Jews today with the history of the faith.
- Joyful events are remembered as God's intervention.
- Festivals are often celebrated both at home and in the synagogue, as opportunities for families and synagogue communities to come together and share their common past.
- Tradition is an important part of Jewish life.
- Orthodox Jews try to continue as the forefathers did, while Reform Jews may adapt festivals to give relevance and meaning for their communities today.

Rosh Hashanah	Yom Kippur
• 'Head of the year' – first day of Jewish year • Remembers story of creation • First of the 'Days of Awe' • Orthodox Jews celebrate over two days, Reform Jews usually one day • The Mishnah says God writes down the deeds of a person, judges them, and makes decisions for the year to come • A time to reflect on behaviour and make peace before judgment is finalised on Yom Kippur • After visiting the synagogue Jews wish each other 'L'shanah tovah' (a good year) • Jews attend the synagogue the following morning and the shofar (ram's horn) is blown 100 times 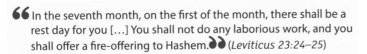 ❝In the seventh month, on the first of the month, there shall be a rest day for you […] You shall not do any laborious work, and you shall offer a fire-offering to Hashem.❞ (*Leviticus 23:24–25*)	• Day of Atonement • Second of the 'Days of Awe' • Holiest day of the year • Jews seek forgiveness from others for any wrong they have done them • Jews then ask God for forgiveness • God finalises his judgment about each Jew's behaviour and decides their fate • Many Jews fast for 25 hours (*Leviticus 16:29–31*) • Festival is a joyful experience, repairing their relationship with God • Evening service where Jews cancel any promises they cannot keep • White is often worn as a symbol of purity 

The first pilgrim festival: Pesach

- The pilgrim festivals were originally a time to visit the Temple.
- They were linked to history and agriculture.
- Pesach is also called Passover after the night that God 'passed over' Egypt killing first-born males, but not those of the Jewish people.
- It is a reminder of God's love for the Jews.
- To celebrate, all chametz, food containing wheat (leaven, or 'risen'), is removed from the house and the house is thoroughly cleaned.
- It lasts for eight days for Orthodox Jews and seven days for Reform Jews.
- The seder meal is the most important event.
- Every part of the seder meal is symbolic and follows an order set out in the Jewish book of Pesach rituals, the Haggadah.
- At the end, Jews wish they will celebrate the meal together in Jerusalem next year.

The second pilgrim festival: Shavuot

- Shavuot celebrates the giving of Law on Mount Sinai as well as the wheat harvest.
- Jews traditionally took wheat to the Temple.
- It marks 49 days between Passover and Shavuot.
- Jews may do extra Torah study.
- Often Jews eat dairy food and decorate the synagogue with greenery.

The third pilgrim festival: Sukkot

- Sukkot happens four days after Yom Kippur.
- It marks the end of summer and the start of the autumn fruit harvest.
- It is also called the Feast of the Tabernacles.
- Sukkot is a reminder of the dwelling places where Jews lived during the wilderness years.
- It's celebrated for eight days – it is a holiday period where Jews offer hospitality to others.

> **TIP**
> It is important that you can differentiate between the different festivals. Students can often get them mixed up.

APPLY

AO1 In this question the names of the festivals are not enough! The names have been given to you, but you need to expand them to ensure you have fully outlined them.

a. Outline **three** Jewish festivals. (3)

Rosh Hashanah.

Yom Kippur.

Shabbat.

AO2 Complete the planning table for the question below. What would your conclusion be? Try to link to different groups within Judaism.

d. 'Festivals are important events for Jews to observe.' Evaluate this statement considering arguments for and against. In your response you should:
- refer to Jewish teachings
- refer to different Jewish points of view
- reach a justified conclusion. (12)

For	Against
• Rosh Hashanah is specified in the Tenakh, Leviticus 23	• May not be possible to celebrate all Jewish festivals, as it would require too much time off work or school
• Link to history of the Jewish people, for example…	• Most festivals are not specified in the Torah, so are later parts of the Jewish faith
• _____	• _____

REVIEW

Answers: Mark your answers using p.198 and note areas for improvement.
AO1: This question is testing your ability to answer 'outline' questions. For help with this skill, see p.12.
AO2: This question is testing your ability to write a justified conclusion. For help with this skill, see p.12.

8.8 Features of the synagogue

RECAP

Essential information

- The synagogue is the Jewish place of worship.
- The synagogue has features that remind Jews of the Temple in Jerusalem.
- Orthodox, Reform, and Liberal synagogues share many similarities such as the Ark and the bimah, but can vary in layout.

The nature and history of the synagogue

- Synagogue means 'bringing together'; as shown in *Proverbs 14:28*, the more people, the better.
- It facilitates worship, focusing on the bimah where the Torah is read.
- It is sometimes called the shul (school) as it is a centre for education too.
- Synagogues are often recognisable due to a Star of David or menorah on the outside.
- It is a place for the community. Activities may include: Hebrew classes, adult education classes, youth clubs, charity events.

> 66 A multitude of people is a king's glory 99 (*Proverbs 14:28*)

Synagogue design and practice

Orthodox	Reform/Liberal
• Seating on three sides facing the bimah • Ark on fourth side • Men and women sit separately. Often a balcony for women • Women cover their heads for modesty • No music (considered work on Shabbat) • Men lead services and read	• May be the same as Orthodox • Or bimah may be at front with seating facing Ark • Men and women may sit together • Women may wear a tallit, or kippah • Musical instruments may be used • Women may take active role in services
• Face Jerusalem; in UK this is east • If that is not possible, Jews will face Jerusalem while they pray	

Objects of devotion

	Ark	Ner tamid	Menorah	Bimah	Yad
What is it?	Area to store Torah scrolls	'Eternal light' above the Ark	Seven-branched candlestick	Reading platform	Reading stick
How is it used?	Door or curtain opened when scrolls are in use	Light burns at all times as reminder of God's eternal nature	Used in the Temple as the eternal light	Rabbi leads service from here; Torah read from here	As a pointer while reading from the Torah
Why is it used?	Reminder of the Holy of Holies in the Temple; to keep scrolls safe	Requirement in *Exodus 27:20–21*	Requirement in *Exodus 25:31–40*	Represents Temple altar; makes Torah main focus	So as not to touch the sacred Torah

APPLY

AO1 Use the planning table below to ensure you produce two developed points.

b. Explain **two** features of a synagogue. (4)

First feature	
Development	
Second feature	
Development	

AO2 Fill in the table with reasons for and against the statement.

d. 'Synagogues should all be designed the same way.' Evaluate this statement considering arguments for and against. In your response you should:
- refer to Jewish teachings
- refer to different Jewish points of view
- reach a justified conclusion. (12)

For	Against

REVIEW

Answers: Mark your answers using p.198 and note areas for improvement.
AO1: This question is testing your ability to write developed points. For help with this skill, see p.12.
AO2: This question is testing your ability to plan a response. For help with this skill, see p.12.

Exam Practice

Test the 3 mark question (a)

1 Outline **three** features of the synagogue. **(3 marks)**

> The Ark is the place where the Torah scroll is kept. (1)
> The bimah is the reading platform. (1)
> The building will face Jerusalem if possible. (1)

TIP
Remember to briefly explain each feature.

2 Outline **three** Jewish rituals. **(3 marks)**

> Brit Milah is when the boy is circumcised as a baby. (1)
> _____
> _____

3 Outline **three** ways Shavuot is celebrated. **(3 marks)**

> _____
> _____
> _____

Test the 4 mark question (b)

1 Describe **two** differences between Orthodox and Reform synagogues. **(4 marks)**

● Describe a point from one religious tradition.	Firstly, an Orthodox synagogue will usually have men and women sitting separately, with women in a balcony.
● Provide a contrasting description from the other religious tradition.	In a Reform synagogue, they will usually sit together, on one level.
● Describe a second point from one religious tradition.	Secondly, Orthdox synagogues will usually have the bimah in the centre of the synagogue, with the Ark taking up a whole side of the synagogue.
● Provide a contrasting description from the other religious tradition.	However, in many Reform synagogues the bimah will be in front of the Ark, yet could be in the middle too.

TIP
For 'Describe' questions you will need to show that you understand and can contrast the differences between religious traditions.

2 Explain **two** reasons why dietary laws are important for Jews. **(4 marks)**

● **Explain one reason.**	
● Develop your explanation with more detail/an example/reference to a religious teaching.	
● **Explain a second reason.**	
● Develop your explanation with more detail/an example/reference to a religious teaching.	

TIP
Questions such as this demonstrate the importance of being familiar with key terms such as 'kashrut'.

3 Explain **two** reasons why Jews celebrate Pesach. **(4 marks)**

Exam Practice

Test the 5 mark question (c)

1   Explain **two** reasons why Brit Milah is important for Jews. In your answer you must refer to a source of wisdom and authority.   **(5 marks)**

● **Explain one reason.**	*The first reason is that it is a tradition within Judaism that contributes to Jewish identity.*
● Develop your explanation with more detail/an example.	*It links back to Abraham and the covenant with the Almighty,*
● **Either:** Add a reference to a source of wisdom and authority here.	*as 'when his son Isaac was eight days old, Abraham circumcised him, as God commanded him' (Genesis 21:4).*
● **Explain a second reason.**	*Secondly, it marks the entry into the Jewish community.*
● Develop your explanation with more detail/an example.	*Such rituals are important because partaking in them is keeping tradition.*
● **Or:** Add a reference to a source of wisdom and authority here.	*This is seen in Genesis 17:14. 'Any uncircumcised male, who has not been circumcised in the flesh, will be cut off from his people; he has broken my covenant.'*

> **TIP**
> Here, the student has referred to a second source of wisdom and authority. You are free to do this, though you are only required to refer to one. This might help you gain full marks if the other source is inaccurate.

2   Explain **two** reasons why celebrating Shabbat is important for Jews. In your answer you must refer to a source of wisdom and authority.   **(5 marks)**

● **Explain one reason.**	
● Develop your explanation with more detail/an example.	
● **Either:** Add a reference to a source of wisdom and authority here.	
● **Explain a second reason.**	
● Develop your explanation with more detail/an example.	
● **Or:** Add a reference to a source of wisdom and authority here.	

> **TIP**
> You should focus in explaining why Shabbat is important not on explaining what it is.

3   Explain **two** reasons why private prayer is important for Jews. In your answer you must refer to a source of wisdom and authority.   **(5 marks)**

Exam Practice

Test the 12 mark question (d)

1 'The Amidah is the most important part of worship.' Evaluate this statement considering arguments for and against. In your response you should:

- refer to Jewish teachings
- reach a justified conclusion.

(12 marks)

ARGUMENTS IN SUPPORT OF THE STATEMENT • **Explain why some people would agree with the statement.** • Develop your explanation with more detail and examples. • Refer to religious teaching. Use a quote or paraphrase of a religious authority. • **Evaluate the arguments.** Is this a good argument? Explain why you think this. Use words such as convincing/strong/robust/weak/unpersuasive/unsuccessful within your reasoning.	Many Jews consider the Amidah as the most important prayer as it is where an individual comes before the Almighty with thanksgiving. Therefore, there is a convincing argument that it is the core of worship for Jews as all worship is focused around glorifying the Almighty and showing that he is the most important (Deuteronomy 13:3–13). Additionally, some would consider it the most important aspect of worship as the individual asks the Almighty for something during the Amidah, which can be seen to be the central purpose of prayer and worship. Finally, it is the central act of worship as it involves praise to the Almighty, so it reminds humanity of their standing before him, which is the whole design of worship.
ARGUMENTS SUPPORTING A DIFFERENT VIEW • **Explain why some people would disagree with the statement.** • Develop your explanation with more detail and examples. • Refer to religious teaching. Use a quote or paraphrase of a religious authority. • **Evaluate the arguments.** Is this a good argument? Explain why you think this. Use words such as convincing/strong/robust/weak/unpersuasive/unsuccessful within your reasoning.	On the other hand, full and proper concentration is the most important part of prayer, therefore it can be argued that the actual form of words, such as in the Amidah, is unimportant when compared to the intention and thoughts behind it. Secondly, the Ark and Torah scrolls could be seen as more important as they are divinely revealed, whereas the Amidah has only been codified by Rabbis, suggesting it is only important because of this. Lastly, private prayer is more important as people should remain connected to God at all times. The Amidah is a very formal prayer, which may not reflect a person's true thoughts. **TIP** This answer shows clear chains of reasoning by starting paragraphs with words such as 'additionally', 'on the other hand', and 'lastly'.
CONCLUSION • **Give a justified conclusion.** • Include your own reasoning. • Use words such as convincing/strong/robust/weak/unpersuasive/unsuccessful to weigh up the different arguments for and against. • Do not just repeat arguments you have already used without explaining how they apply to your reasoned opinion/conclusion.	In conclusion, the Amidah is commonly regarded by Jews as being HaTefillah or 'the prayer' as it is the more central prayer in worship, therefore it would be considered the most important too.

2 'Observing Shabbat is important for Jews.' Evaluate this statement considering arguments for and against. In your response you should:

- refer to Jewish teachings
- reach a justified conclusion.

(12 marks)

ARGUMENTS IN SUPPORT OF THE STATEMENT ● **Explain why some people would agree with the statement.** ● Develop your explanation with more detail and examples. ● Refer to religious teaching. Use a quote or paraphrase of a religious authority. ● **Evaluate the arguments.** Is this a good argument? Explain why you think this. Use words such as convincing/strong/robust/weak/unpersuasive/unsuccessful within your reasoning.	Some Jews/people would agree with this statement because... **TIP** Ensure that you include more than just resting on Shabbat. Remember that there are prayers in the synagogue and the home.
ARGUMENTS SUPPORTING A DIFFERENT VIEW ● **Explain why some people would disagree with the statement.** ● Develop your explanation with more detail and examples. ● Refer to religious teaching. Use a quote or paraphrase of a religious authority. ● **Evaluate the arguments.** Is this a good argument? Explain why you think this. Use words such as convincing/strong/robust/weak/unpersuasive/unsuccessful within your reasoning.	On the other hand, some Jews/people would hold a different point of view...
CONCLUSION ● **Give a justified conclusion.** ● Include your own reasoning. ● Use words such as convincing/strong/robust/weak/unpersuasive/unsuccessful to weigh up the different arguments for and against. ● Do not just repeat arguments you have already used without explaining how they apply to your reasoned opinion/conclusion.	Having considered both sides of the argument, I would say that...

3 'It is important that Jews regularly attend synagogue services.' Evaluate this statement considering arguments for and against. In your response you should:

- refer to Jewish teachings
- reach a justified conclusion.

(12 marks)

 **REVIEW**

Check your answers to these exam questions on p.198, correct your answers with annotations, and note down any general areas for improvement.

If you don't feel secure in the content of this chapter, you could reread the Recap sections.

If you don't feel secure in your exam technique, you could revisit the exam support section on pp.7–14.

RECAP

Essential information
- **Revelation** is God revealing or showing something of himself.
- Jesus is the complete and final revelation of God.
- The Bible is the most important source of revelation and helps lead Catholics to God.

The nature of revelation and revelation as proof of God

- To reveal is to uncover something that was previously hidden.
- Catholics use revelation to mean the ways in which God has made himself known to humans.
- God is *not* trying to prove he exists! He is communicating and teaching.
- However, Christians may believe revelation is proof of his existence.

Jesus Christ as the culmination of God's revelation

- God first revealed himself to the people of Israel.
- For example, God spoke to Moses from a burning bush and revealed his name:

> ❝I am who I am ❞ *(Exodus 3:14)*

- Catholics believe that Jesus is the **final revelation** of God – that God no longer spoke at a distance, but came down to earth in human form.

> ❝in these last days he has spoken to us by a Son, whom he appointed the heir of all things❞ *(Hebrews 1:2)*

- Jesus is clear proof for Christians of the existence of God:

> ❝He reflects the glory of God and bears the very stamp of his nature❞ *(Hebrews 1:3)*

- This revelation was first given to the apostles, then passed on to the community now called the Church.
- This revelation is authoritatively recorded in the Bible – it is guaranteed by the Church as being a faithful record of God's revelation.
- Catholics believe that today, through the Church and the Bible, people can encounter Jesus, and therefore God.

What the revelation of Jesus shows about God

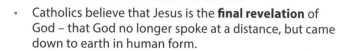

Sending Jesus was a sacrifice for God

God sent Jesus out of love for humans

John's Gospel

God sent Jesus to save humans and lead them back to faith

TIP
Revelation can come via visions (9.2), miracles (9.3), or religious experiences (9.4). Try to make links between these topics.

APPLY

AO1 A key Catholic belief is that Jesus is the **final** revelation. Use this point, and one other, to answer the following question.

  b. Explain **two** key beliefs about revelation held by Catholics. (4)

AO2 Can you write the counter-argument for the statement below?

  d. 'Revelation contained in the Bible proves that God exists.' Evaluate this statement considering arguments for and against. In your response you should:
- refer to Catholic teachings
- reach a justified conclusion. (15)

For	Against
• Jesus was God's final revelation, and therefore for Christians, this is proof that God exists.	•
• The Old Testament contains God's revelation to the people of Israel. People such as Moses did great things as they believed God existed and this inspires Christians today.	•
• For Christians, the Bible is a true and accurate record of God's revelation, therefore God must exist.	•

REVIEW

Answers: Mark your answers using p.199 and note areas for improvement.
AO1: This question is testing your ability to write a developed point. For help with this skill, see p.12.
AO2: This question is testing your ability to identify divergent views. For help with this skill, see p.12.

RECAP

Essential information

- A vision is a visual appearance, usually of Jesus, Mary, an angel, or another saint.
- Visions have been reported since Old Testament times and many Catholics believe visions are God showing Christians his loving and mysterious nature.
- Non-religious groups suggest that a lack of evidence means visions do not prove God exists.

The nature and importance of visions

- A vision may be seen as private revelation. However, Catholics will only accept one if it does not contradict anything taught by the Church.
- The Church has officially recognised some visions (e.g. St Bernadette and St Joan of Arc), which gives Catholics permission to believe in their truth.
- Visions take many forms:
  - Corporeal visions: physically seeing something
  - Imaginative visions: seeing something in dreams.

Biblical and non-biblical examples of visions

Old Testament	New Testament
• Abraham is visited by God with a promise of protection and reward: 66 Fear not, Abram, I am your shield; your reward shall be very great. 99 *(Genesis 15:1)*	• During the transfiguration of Jesus, Moses and Elias (also known as Elijah) appeared to Jesus, Peter, James, and John. • The voice of God spoke: 66 This is my beloved Son, with whom I am well pleased; listen to him. 99 *(Matthew 17:5)*

Non-biblical

- In 1424, a peasant called Joan (later St Joan of Arc) had visions of Saints Michael, Catherine, and Margaret.
- She was instructed to force the English from her French homeland.
- After convincing the French military leaders, she helped them to victory.
- She was captured by the English and burnt at the stake as a heretic, aged 19.

Reasons why visions might lead people to believe in God	Arguments against visions as proof that God exists
• Visions can be powerful, personal experiences, giving great strength and faith. • Examples from the Bible and history allow people to interpret their own visions in a religious way. • Private revelations are rare, but may help prove the existence of God.	• There is often no lasting or physical proof of the visions. • They could be hallucinations, misunderstandings, or just made up. • Even if the vision is genuine, it is not certain proof of God. • Dreams could be subconscious wish fulfilment.

> **TIP**
> Remember: Catholics only accept visions that do not contradict existing Church teaching.

APPLY

AO1 Can you finish the two simple points for the question below?

c. Explain **two** reasons that visions are important to Catholics. In your answer you must refer to a source of wisdom and authority. (5)

> *Firstly, visions are important as they may lead to a stronger belief in God...*
>
> *Secondly, there are many examples of visions in the Bible...*

AO2 What would your conclusion be in your answer to this question? Try to write two possible conclusions; you may need to plan first.

d. 'Visions are an important source of revelation.' Evaluate this statement considering arguments for and against. In your response you should:
- refer to Catholic teachings
- refer to non-religious points of view
- reach a justified conclusion. (15)

REVIEW

Answers: Mark your answers using p.199 and note areas for improvement.
AO1: This question is testing your ability to write developed points. For help with this skill, see p.12.
AO2: This question is testing your ability to write a justified conclusion. For help with this skill, see p.12.

9.3 Miracles

 **RECAP**

Essential information

- A miracle is something that appears to break the law of nature.
- Catholics and other Christians may claim God is the only explanation.
- Non-religious groups argue that miracles are not proof that God exists; there may be another explanation, even if people don't yet know it.

The nature and importance of miracles

- Miracles have been recorded throughout history, and claims are still made today.
- They involve a religious experience of some kind.
- Experiencing such an event may lead to faith or a strengthening of faith.

- Jesus' miracles are seen as clear signs of his divine nature:
  - Healing
  - Natural
  - **Exorcisms** (removal of evil spirits that have possessed a person).

TIP Try to learn some examples of Jesus' miracles, such as feeding the five thousand with five loaves and two fish (see Mark 11:3–4, and 11.3 in this Guide).

Biblical examples of miracles	Non-biblical examples of miracles
• Moses parting and crossing the Red Sea (*Exodus 14:21–22*) • Jesus turning the water into wine at the wedding in Cana (*John 2:6–9*) • Jesus healing a blind man at Beth-sa'ida by placing his hands on the man's eyes (*Mark 8:22–25*) • Jesus healing the official's son who was not present (*John 4:46–54*)	• The Virgin Mary appeared to Juan Diego in Mexico City in 1531. Her image hasn't faded as would be expected and has avoided fire and bomb damage. • The Virgin Mary appeared to Bernadette Soubirous in 1858 in Lourdes, France. She pointed to a spring, which is now visited by over 5 million people a year. Around 70 verified healing miracles have happened there.

Reasons why miracles might lead people to believe in the existence of God	Arguments against miracles as proof that God exists
• No natural scientific explanation means God is the only possible explanation. • Those who experienced or witnessed a miracle feel like they have had direct contact with God. • Natural laws have been broken, and only God is able to do such a thing?	• Coincidences or unusual/uncommon events do occur. • Scientific and medical knowledge is still continuing to develop – explanation may occur in the future. • Inexplicable things do not necessarily mean the answer is God.

Catholic responses

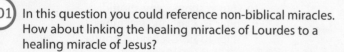

- Reveal God's omnipotent nature
- Necessary for people to believe in God: 'Unless you see signs and wonders you will not believe' (John 4:48)
- Jesus' miracles often demanded faith, a quality that cannot be explained or justified
- Since there are miracles in the Bible, it is not unreasonable for them to happen today
- **Miracles**
- Catholics usually accept that God cannot grant every request and denial may be part of a bigger plan (see 9.7, 9.8, and 2.4)
- A way God communicates with people
- Healing miracles show God's love for humans

 **APPLY**

AO1 In this question you could reference non-biblical miracles. How about linking the healing miracles of Lourdes to a healing miracle of Jesus?

c. Explain **two** reasons why some Catholics see miracles as good evidence for God's existence. In your answer you must refer to a source of wisdom and authority. (5)

AO2 Use the second table above to plan a response to this question. What would your conclusion be?

d. 'Miracles are clear proof of God's existence.' Evaluate this statement considering arguments for and against. In your response you should:
- refer to Catholic teachings
- refer to non-religious points of view
- reach a justified conclusion. (15)

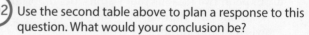 **REVIEW**

Answers: Mark your answers using p.199 and note areas for improvement.
AO1: This question is testing your ability to answer a (c) question. For help with this skill, see p.12.
AO2: This question is testing your ability to write a justified conclusion. For help with this skill, see p.12.

Essential information

- A religious experience is a feeling of the presence of God.
- Catholics believe religious experiences are confirmation of God's role in the world.
- There is often a lack of credible evidence for religious experiences.

The nature of religious experiences

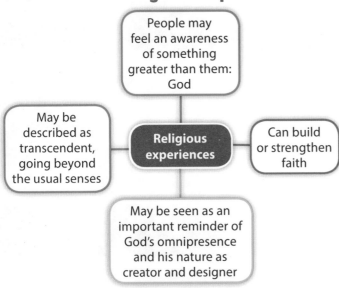

Religious experience and revelation

- Catholics believe Jesus was **the final and complete revelation**. The Catechism (*CCC 66–67*) suggests that the revelation of Jesus can be further explained, and some private revelations have been recognised by the Church.
- Any private revelations are seen as secondary to the revelation of Jesus and will contain no new information.
- They are only able to provide insight into what has already been revealed.

Philosophical arguments

Richard Swinburne (a Christian) suggested it is reasonable to believe the world is probably how we experience it – the Principle of Credulity. Therefore:

- unless we have a specific reason to question a religious experience, it is possible that it is evidence for God
- religious experiences increase the probability of God, even if they do not prove God exists.

Why religious experiences may not be proof that God exists

Laws of nature	Lack of evidence	Use of stimulants	Hallucinations	Wish fulfilment
David Hume argued every human can observe the laws of nature; this is more persuasive than a few having religious experiences.	There is no testable evidence to prove religious experiences. Often the event is brief and personal.	Drugs can relax and make the user more open to religious experiences. Some drugs can also cause hallucinations.	These can be caused by many things: anxiety, stress, grief, migraine, epilepsy, etc. Hallucinations could easily be mistaken for visions.	Sigmund Freud believed this was the case. He claimed adults still have childlike feelings and great delusions.

Catholic responses to the question of proof

- God, an omnipotent being, is not bound by the laws of nature, so it is expected that religious experiences can and do break them.
- Just because there is no evidence, it does not mean something didn't happen. Faith does not require proof.
- Catholics do not disagree about stimulants, hallucinations, and wish fulfilment, which is why the Church conducts detailed investigations into some claims before it recognises them as authentic.

 APPLY

- refer to Catholic teachings
- refer to non-religious points of view
- refer to relevant philosophical arguments
- reach a justified conclusion. (15)

 (AO1) One reason has been given below. Can you think of two others?

   a. Outline **three** reasons an atheist would reject religious experiences as proof of God's existence. (3)

> *There is a lack of evidence; there is no reasonable proof the event has happened.*

 (AO2) Fill in the arguments against the statement.

   d. 'The Church should recognise more religious experiences.' Evaluate this statement considering arguments for and against. In your response you should:

For	Against
• They have a big impact on believers, for example 5 million people visit Lourdes each year. • They lead to people of no faith converting to religion. This shows their power. • They are in keeping with God's nature, so they are to be expected and should be recognised.	• • •

**Answers:** Mark your answers using p.199 and note areas for improvement.
AO1: This question is testing your ability to answer 'outline' questions. For help with this skill, see p.12.
AO2: This question is testing your ability to plan a response. For help with this skill, see p.12.

 **RECAP**

Essential information
- The design argument suggests that as there appears to be design in the world, there must be a designer and this is God.
- It is strong because it is based on human experience and gives a sense of meaning and purpose.
- However, evolution is an adequate explanation for some; there also appear to be examples of bad design, such as suffering.

The classical design argument
- The design argument is sometimes called the **teleological** argument (teleology is the study of a thing's purpose or design).
- It originates with ancient Greek and Roman thinkers.
- It was one of St Thomas Aquinas' 'Five Ways' to prove God.
- William Paley used a watch analogy – if you found a watch in a field, you would not assume it had come together by chance; it would be clear it had a designer. He believed the universe is the same; it appears to have design, therefore it has a designer.

66 Ever since the creation of the world his invisible nature, namely, his eternal power and deity, has been clearly perceived in the things that have been made 99 *(Romans 1:20)*

The strengths of the argument

It is based on our own experience of design – many things in nature are perceived to have purpose, order, and design.	**It complements a Christian view of the nature of God** – an omnipotent and omniscient God is able to create the universe.	**It encourages scientific examination of the universe** – the underlying rules of nature lead to the conclusion of a designer.

Evidence against the design argument	Catholic responses
The uniqueness of the universe – David Hume said it was impossible to use an analogy to explain the universe.	Just because it is unique, it does not mean we cannot attempt to explain it.
The existence of evil and suffering – either God is a poor designer, or there is no designer – surely the universe should be perfect?	Humans can learn from the suffering and evil in the world; some is the result of free will.
There is no order, just the appearance of order – Richard Dawkins suggested people see the world with 'purpose-coloured spectacles'.	Science and evidence support the concept of order.
Evolution as an explanation of order and purpose – evolutionary theory suggests that complex organisms have developed through genetic mutation and natural selection.	Specific evolution must have been directed by a designer God to get where we are today.

 APPLY

 **TIP** Ensure you know some good examples of design – Paley used the human eye.

AO1 The key source of wisdom and authority to include in this answer is *Romans 1:20* (above). What developed point would you write around this particular quote?

c. Explain **two** ways that the design argument complements Catholic beliefs about God. In your answer you must refer to a source of wisdom and authority. (5)

AO2 What do you feel is the strongest argument for and the strongest argument against the statement? This would be central to your response. For each point you pick, justify it.

d. 'The design argument is a strong argument for God's existence.' Evaluate this statement considering arguments for and against. In your response you should:
- refer to Catholic teachings
- refer to non-religious points of view
- refer to relevant philosophical arguments
- reach a justified conclusion. (15)

 REVIEW

Answers: Mark your answers using p.199 and note areas for improvement.
AO1: This question is testing your ability to explain beliefs correctly, using a source of wisdom and authority. For help with this skill, see p.12.
AO2: This question is testing your ability to plan a response. For help with this skill, see p.12.

RECAP

Essential information

- The **cosmological** argument follows the universal law of cause and effect.
- St Thomas Aquinas proposed that God was the first cause of the universe.
- **Atheists** argue that the world does not necessarily need a first cause, and there is also no proof that the first cause is God.

The nature of the argument

- Ancient Greek thinkers Plato and Aristotle called the first cause of all other moving things the **prime mover**.
- The first three of St Thomas Aquinas' Five Ways connect to the cosmological argument.
- The argument proposes that cause and effect are key features of our world.

The strengths of the cosmological argument

| **It is based on experience** – hard to deny chains of cause and effect. | **It is more logical than the alternative** – an infinite chain of cause and effect seems impossible. | **It is compatible with scientific evidence** – most scientists agree on the beginning of the universe (the Big Bang), which is in keeping with the cosmological argument. |

What the cosmological argument reveals about God's nature

Catholics believe the argument shows the omnipotent nature of God. God has the power to do all things – to create a universe from nothing. Therefore his power is limitless.

Evidence against the cosmological argument	Catholic responses
The impossibility of a total explanation – Bertrand Russell argued that a total explanation was impossible, humans should just accept the universe's existence as fact.	A rejection of infinite chains of cause and effect means a total explanation *is* possible.
The universe as a whole does not need a cause – Russell also said that just because everything in the universe needs a cause, it does not mean the universe as a whole does.	All things in the universe can have their cause investigated, so why not the universe itself?
The first cause doesn't have to be God – some scientists accept the Big Bang as the start of the universe.	Everything starts somewhere, and only an omnipotent God could be the absolute beginning.

APPLY

AO1 The first point has been done for you, add a second point.

b. Explain **two** weaknesses of the cosmological arguments. (4)

> *Firstly, the universe as a whole does not need a cause. Everything within the universe needs a cause, but this does not mean that the universe as a whole needs a cause.*
> *Secondly...*

AO2 The table in the Recap section would be a good outline of the content for a response on this question. What would your conclusion be? Remember, it must be justified.

d. 'Catholics believe the cosmological argument is evidence for the existence of God.' Evaluate this statement considering arguments for and against. In your response you should:
- refer to Catholic teachings
- refer to non-religious points of view
- refer to relevant philosophical arguments
- reach a justified conclusion. (15)

TIP

Some d questions will be worth 12 marks and some worth 15. The difference is that in 15 mark questions, 3 marks will be awarded for your spelling and grammar.

REVIEW

Answers: Mark your answers using p.199 and note areas for improvement.
AO1: This question is testing your ability to write a developed point. For help with this skill, see p.12.
AO2: This question is testing your ability to answer a (d) question. For help with this skill, see p.12.

 RECAP

Essential information

- Evil in the world suggests there cannot be an omnipotent, omniscient, and omnibenevolent God.
- Catholics believe that suffering can be a consequence of free will.
- Some Catholics believe suffering provides an opportunity for people to do good, to learn and to grow.

The issue of suffering for Catholics

Catholics, like most other **theists** (people who believe in the existence of God(s)), believe that God is:

Omnipotent – has unlimited power	**Omniscient** – has complete knowledge of all human actions, past, present, and future	**Omnibenevolent** – has unlimited goodness and love.

This leads to the 'problem of evil':

- If God is omnipotent, surely he has the power to stop suffering.
- If God is omniscient, surely he is aware of the suffering.
- If God is omnibenevolent, he would surely want to stop suffering.

Isaiah 45 seems to suggest that God will reward the good and punish rebels. Therefore, some Catholics would believe that if the good suffer, they should keep faith as there is a purpose that only God understands.

Examining or rejecting belief in God

- David Hume says suffering is one of the weaknesses of the design argument (see 9.5); he calls it 'the rock of atheism'.
- J. L. Mackie produced an inconsistent triad: the combination of any two positions means the third is logically impossible – either God does not exist, or he is not worthy of worship:

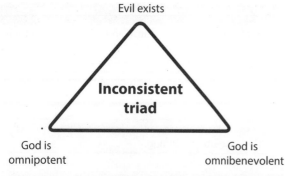

Evil exists

Inconsistent triad

God is omnipotent

God is omnibenevolent

TIP

It's a good idea to memorise some examples of natural and moral evil to use in your answers.

Natural evil	Moral evil
• Evil from **natural events** that humans cannot control. • Examples include: natural disasters such as tsunamis and earthquakes; illness, disease. • Seems like unjust punishment for victims. • Catholics may see them as a test of faith. • Opportunity to do good.	• Evil from actions of **humans**. • Examples include: murder, theft, assault, terrorism. • Catholics believe humans have free will; suffering is the price people pay for freedom. • God gave humans a conscience and encourages them to act in the right way.

 APPLY

 Write two sentences in answer to this question: 'Which form of evil is the most significant for Christians?'

This is useful preparation for a (d) question on this topic.

> Some Christians would say moral evil because...
> Some Christians would say natural evil because...

(AO1) Here are three suggestions to help you answer this question. Can you develop them into full points?

a. Outline **three** reasons the existence of suffering might lead some people to reject belief in God. (3)
   - Design
   - Logic
   - Natural disasters

 REVIEW

Answers: Mark your answers using p.199 and note areas for improvement.
AO1: This question is testing your ability to answer 'outline' questions. For help with this skill, see p.12.
AO2: This question is testing your ability to plan a response. For help with this skill, see p.12.

RECAP

Essential information

- The Bible tells of individuals who suffered greatly but remained faithful.
- St Irenaeus and St Augustine tried to provide solutions to the problem of evil and suffering in their **theodicies**.
- Catholics believe God is creator of all, and all of creation is good.
- Charity and prayer can be practical solutions for many Catholics.

Biblical responses

Job	Psalms	New Testament
• God allows Job to be tested and tormented by Satan. • Faith gives strength to those who are suffering. • It helps them understand suffering may be something not understood by humans.	• 119 teaches Christians they can learn from their previous suffering. • God's omnipotence (*135*), omniscience (*147*), and omnibenevolence (*100*) are also made clear.	• A God who suffered through Jesus is revealed. • Any problem of evil has Christ at the heart of the answer. • There must be a higher purpose, incomprehensible to humans.

Theoretical responses

St Augustine	St Irenaeus
• Some Catholics do not believe that evil is a thing in itself, but an absence of good – just as darkness is absence of light. • Evil exists due to the abuse of free will. • Free will must be used to choose good, and the reward will be entry into heaven.	• It's the best way for humans to develop and grow. • People learn to make the correct moral choices. • People are created in God's image, but incomplete, so they must try to be like him.

Practical responses

Prayer	Charity
	Donations
• Suffering can be shared in prayer. • Prayers of intercession are part of the Mass. • This can sometimes be the only meaningful response for the individual Catholic.	• Helping others is the same as helping Christ (Parable of the Sheep and Goats – *Matthew 25:31–46*). • Those who help others in need will gain salvation (see 2.7 and 2.8).

Success of the solutions

- The Bible is a reminder of the suffering of both Jesus and the people of God in the Old Testament.
- Some find the theoretical solutions useful, while others turn to practical responses.
- For many, suffering remains a mystery.
- Statistics suggest suffering is a problem that many Christians can overcome.
- It may still be a key factor in some Christians deciding to stop practising their faith.

 **TIP**
For examples of Catholic charitable organisations, see 2.7 and 3.8.

 **APPLY**

AO1 There is no source of wisdom and authority in the first point given below, so write a second point that includes one.

c. Explain **two** ways Catholics might respond to the problem of suffering. In your answer you must refer to a source of wisdom and authority. (5)

> *Firstly, Catholics may find it useful to respond practically to the problem of suffering with their prayers, but also their actions. For example, they may give to or even volunteer with charities helping those in need.*

AO2 Complete the plan for the question below.

d. 'Christians are able to successfully respond to the problem of suffering.' Evaluate this statement considering arguments for and against. In your response you should:
- refer to Catholic teachings
- reach a justified conclusion. (15)

For	Against

REVIEW **Answers:** Mark your answers using p.199 and note areas for improvement.
AO1: This question is testing your ability to explain beliefs correctly, using a source of wisdom and authority. For help with this skill, see p.12.
AO2: This question is testing your ability to plan a response. For help with this skill, see p.12.

Test the 3 mark question (a)

1 | Outline **three** reasons Catholics might give for the existence of suffering in the world. **(3 marks)**

The Bible (Isaiah 45) suggests that God will punish rebels.

God tested Job, and may be testing Catholics today.

God gave the gift of free will, which some misuse.

2 | Outline **three** things the design argument shows about the nature of God for Catholics. **(3 marks)**

God is the designer of the universe. (1)

_____

_____

3 | Outline **three** types of miracles. **(3 marks)**

_____

_____

_____

Test the 4 mark question (b)

1 | Explain **two** ways Catholics respond to the problem of suffering. **(4 marks)**

● **Explain one way.**	*Firstly, humans have been given the opportunity to pray,*
● Develop your explanation with more detail/an example/reference to a religious teaching or quotation.	*and this may bring a sense of relief and comfort knowing they can talk to God about their suffering.*
● **Explain a second way.**	*Secondly, Catholics will follow the example of Jesus during his mortal life*
● Develop your explanation with more detail/an example/reference to a religious teaching or quotation.	*by helping people who are suffering.*

2 | Explain **two** ways a Catholic could argue that the world appears designed. **(4 marks)**

● **Explain one way.**	
● Develop your explanation with more detail/an example/reference to a religious teaching or quotation.	
● **Explain a second way.**	
● Develop your explanation with more detail/an example/reference to a religious teaching or quotation.	

3 | Explain **two** ways miracles might lead people to believe in God. **(4 marks)**

TIP

Ensure you are clear on each term – don't confuse revelation, visions, miracles, and religious experiences.

Exam Practice

Test the 5 mark question (c)

1 Explain **two** features the revelation of Jesus shows about the nature of God.
In your answer you must refer to a source of wisdom and authority.   **(5 marks)**

● **Explain one feature.**	Firstly, Catholics believe that Jesus is the full and final revelation of God.
● Develop your explanation with more detail/an example.	As such, he was sent to save humans and lead them back to faith.
● **Either:** Add a reference to a source of wisdom and authority here.	This is made clear in Hebrews 1:2 where it says, 'He has spoken to us by a Son, whom he appointed the heir of all things.'
● **Explain a second feature.**	Secondly, it shows the loving nature of God.
● Develop your explanation with more detail/an example.	Jesus was sent as a great sacrifice as God loved humans so much.
● **Or:** Add a reference to a source of wisdom and authority here.	

2 Explain **two** Catholic beliefs about religious experiences. In your answer you must refer to a source of wisdom and authority.   **(5 marks)**

● **Explain one belief.**	
● Develop your explanation with more detail/an example.	
● **Either:** Add a reference to a source of wisdom and authority here.	
● **Explain a second belief.**	
● Develop your explanation with more detail/an example.	
● **Or:** Add a reference to a source of wisdom and authority here.	

TIP

Ensure you explain beliefs which are specifically Catholic, not beliefs about religious experience in general.

3 Explain **two** reasons why miracles are important for Catholics. In your answer you must refer to a source of wisdom and authority.   **(5 marks)**

Exam Practice

Test the 15 mark question (d)

1. 'Visions prove the existence of God.' Evaluate this statement considering arguments for and against. In your response you should:

   - refer to Catholic teachings
   - refer to non-religious points of view
   - reach a justified conclusion.

TIP

In a 15 mark question 3 of the marks available are awarded for correct spelling, punctuation and grammar. You should check your answer thoroughly.

(15 marks)

ARGUMENTS IN SUPPORT OF THE STATEMENT ● **Explain why some people would agree with the statement.** ● Develop your explanation with more detail and examples. ● Refer to religious teaching. Use a quote or paraphrase of a religious authority. ● **Evaluate the arguments.** Is this a good argument? Explain why you think this. Use words such as convincing/strong/robust/weak/unpersuasive/unsuccessful within your reasoning.	*Abraham had a vision from God about the future of his nation recorded in Genesis 15; this experience confirmed Abraham's faith in God's presence so that he was then able to continue his life of faith and obedience to God.* *St Paul encountered God on the road to Damascus; this experience was powerful enough to bring about his conversion to Christianity; would-be converts to Christianity were inspired by the faith this vision gave him to believe and seek baptism.* *Peter, James, and John saw Jesus transfigured (Matthew 17) and heard a voice affirming Jesus as the Son of God. This gave the disciples assurance about the divinity of Christ and enabled them to witness to others.*
ARGUMENTS SUPPORTING A DIFFERENT VIEW ● **Explain why some people would disagree with the statement.** ● Develop your explanation with more detail and examples. ● Refer to religious teaching. Use a quote or paraphrase of a religious authority. ● **Evaluate the arguments.** Is this a good argument? Explain why you think this. Use words such as convincing/strong/robust/weak/unpersuasive/unsuccessful within your reasoning.	*Many non-believers argue that visions are similar to psychological illness; they say it is impossible to prove that the experience of God is real. They therefore conclude that no vision can count as proof of the existence of God.* *Most visions are personal; some Christians argue that such an experience could cause a conversion or increase in faith for that person. However, the experience of others is not sufficient to convert those who only hear accounts of the vision.* *Many religious and non-religious people believe that visions do not happen today and are purely hallucinations; as such they have no grounds in reality and so cannot prove the existence of God.*
CONCLUSION ● **Give a justified conclusion.** ● Include your own reasoning. ● Use words such as convincing/strong/robust/weak/unpersuasive/unsuccessful to weigh up the different arguments for and against. ● Do not just repeat arguments you have already used without explaining how they apply to your reasoned opinion/conclusion.	*In conclusion, I believe that despite the powerful effect on an individual as a result of a vision, it is impossible to conclude God's existence purely from the evidence of visions. This is because there is rarely any physical evidence to be tested.*

TIP

It is important you clearly focus your answer on visions, as this student does. Try not to confuse visions with other religious experiences.

2 'Religious experiences prove the existence of God.' Evaluate this statement considering arguments for and against. In your response you should:

- refer to Catholic teachings
- refer to non-religious points of view
- refer to relevant philosophical arguments
- reach a justified conclusion.

(15 marks)

ARGUMENTS IN SUPPORT OF THE STATEMENT ● **Explain why some people would agree with the statement.** ● Develop your explanation with more detail and examples. ● Refer to religious teaching. Use a quote or paraphrase of a religious authority. ● **Evaluate the arguments.** Is this a good argument? Explain why you think this. Use words such as convincing/strong/robust/weak/unpersuasive/unsuccessful within your reasoning.	*Some Catholics/people would agree with this statement because...*
ARGUMENTS SUPPORTING A DIFFERENT VIEW ● **Explain why some people would disagree with the statement.** ● Develop your explanation with more detail and examples. ● Refer to religious teaching. Use a quote or paraphrase of a religious authority. ● **Evaluate the arguments.** Is this a good argument? Explain why you think this. Use words such as convincing/strong/robust/weak/unpersuasive/unsuccessful within your reasoning.	*On the other hand, some people would hold a different point of view...*
CONCLUSION ● **Give a justified conclusion.** ● Include your own reasoning. ● Use words such as convincing/strong/robust/weak/unpersuasive/unsuccessful to weigh up the different arguments for and against. ● Do not just repeat arguments you have already used without explaining how they apply to your reasoned opinion/conclusion.	*Having considered both sides of the argument, I would say that...*

3 'The cosmological argument proves the existence of God.' Evaluate this statement considering arguments for and against. In your response you should:

- refer to Catholic teachings
- refer to non-religious points of view
- refer to relevant philosophical arguments
- reach a justified conclusion.

TIP

Remember that the cosmological argument is the 'first cause' argument.

(15 marks)

 **REVIEW**

- Check your answers to these exam questions on p.199–200, correct your answers with annotations, and note down any general areas for improvement.

- If you don't feel secure in the content of this chapter, you could reread the Recap sections.

- If you don't feel secure in your exam technique, you could revisit the exam support section on pp.7–14.

RECAP

Essential information

- For Catholics, marriage is established in the Creation story in Genesis.
- The Church sees marriage as uniting a couple and as the best environment in which to bring up children.
- Marriage is important in society as it provides legal rights and responsibilities for the couple.

The importance and purpose of marriage

- The Bible teaches that marriage is not just a human institution or legal arrangement, but something established by God from the beginning of the world.
- St Paul says marriage bears witness to the everlasting love of Christ for his Church. Husbands should love their wives as Jesus loved the Church (*Ephesians 5:25–26*).

Marriage as a sacrament

For Catholics, marriage is a sacrament called holy matrimony. This includes the marks, or external signs, of marriage. Catholics make promises (vows) to one another in the ceremony to commit to these marks of marriage.

TIP

It is important that you are able to make the distinction between the features of a Catholic marriage (matrimony) and the legal process.

Loving: a relationship of love and faithfulness		**Lifelong:** lifelong support and comfort	
Exclusive: commitment to just one partner		**Fruitful:** being open to the possibility of children. Infertile couples 'can radiate a fruitfulness of charity, of hospitality and of sacrifice' (*CCC 1654*).	

Catholic teachings about marriage

- Catholics believe marriage is a gift from God with these main elements:

Unites a couple in faithful and mutual love	Opens a couple to the giving of new life
A way to respond to God's call to holiness	Calls the couple to be a sign of Christ's love in the world.

- The vows are the sacrament and the couple enters into a covenant, while the signing of the register at the end of the service is the legal marriage. The legal contract can be ended, but the covenant cannot.
- The Catholic Church teaches the sacrament of marriage can only be between a man and woman. This is based upon *Genesis 2:24*, which shows that man and woman were created for one another.
- Pope Francis wrote a book called *Not Just Good, But Beautiful* after an interfaith conference in 2014. It celebrates the benefits of marriage and reminds Catholics that marriage is a cornerstone of healthy families, communities, and societies.

Marriage in society

- A legal marriage establishes rights and obligations between the couple, and with their children.
- Other Christians may consider marriage a religious ceremony and conduct it in a church, but may not see it as a sacrament.
- **Humanists** campaign for Humanist weddings to be recognised as legal. Currently couples must also have a civil ceremony.
- Civil marriages are considered important events by many as they make a public declaration of
two people's love and commitment.

Different views of marriage

- Same-sex couples can marry in England, Wales, and Scotland since 2014. Before this, they were only allowed a civil partnership.
- The Catholic Church does not permit same-sex marriages, but other Christian Churches may grant permission if they choose.
- Not all couples wish to marry. Some same-sex couples may choose a civil partnership, or to cohabit. However, legal rights of cohabiting couples are not the same as those in a civil partnership or marriage.
- Cohabiting couples are the fastest growing family type in the UK. Some suggest this shows the diminishing value of marriage in society. The Catholic Church sees cohabitation as a temptation to have premarital sex.

 APPLY

 Think of arguments for and against the statement. What would your conclusion be?

AO1 Here is a developed point addressing the question below. Can you add a second developed point?

b. Explain **two** significant features of marriage for Catholics. (4)

> *Firstly, Catholic matrimony is intended to be fruitful.*
> *This means that the couple need to be open to having children. However, the Catechism makes it clear that infertile couples are not excluded from the sacrament.*

d. 'Marriage should always happen in a church.' Evaluate this statement considering arguments for and against. In your response you should:
- refer to Catholic teachings
- refer to different Christian points of view
- refer to non-religious points of view
- reach a justified conclusion. (12)

 REVIEW

Answers: Mark your answers using p.200 and note areas for improvement.
AO1: This question is testing your ability to answer a (b) question. For help with this skill, see p.12.
AO2: This question is testing your ability to write a justified conclusion. For help with this skill, see p.12.

RECAP

Essential information

- The Church teaches that sexual relationships bring together a man and a woman who are married to each other for the purpose of having children.
- The Church teaches that sex connects married couples in a spiritual and loving way.
- Non-religious groups such as Humanists often believe consensual sex before marriage is acceptable.

Marital, unitive, and procreative

Sex is a 'joy and pleasure' (*CCC 2362*), and a sign of 'spiritual communion' (*CCC 2360*).

Relationships outside marriage

The Catholic Church teaches that sex should only happen within marriage. Therefore sex outside marriage is wrong:

- **Premarital:** sex before marriage
- **Cohabitation:** living together before marriage; most couples are also in a sexual relationship
- **Same-sex:** homosexuality is not a sin, but homosexual relationships are
- **Extramarital sex:** adultery, or having an affair

Different attitudes towards relationships

- Family life has changed in the UK since the 1960s. Previously people were expected to wait until marriage to have sex, be married in a church by the age of 25, live as a nuclear family, and not get divorced.
- Many people in the UK do not wait until marriage to have sex – around 50 per cent of 17 year olds have had sex (Unicef, 2001).
- 47.5 per cent of babies in the UK are born to unmarried parents (ONS, 2013), indicating how many couples cohabit.
- Same-sex marriage has been legal in England, Wales, and Scotland since 2014.

The 20-year switch

How sexual activity has changed

Average number of partners of opposite sex over the lifetime (people aged 16–44)

1990–91 survey

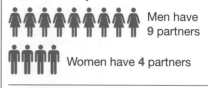
Men have 9 partners
Women have 4 partners

2010–12 survey

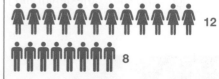
12
8

Views of non-religious groups	Catholic responses
- Non-religious groups generally believe that people should behave morally, but should have freedom within the limits of morality. - Sexual relationships between two consenting adults are acceptable, whatever their form. This involves careful consideration about marriage, contraception, being faithful, etc.	- Catholics would not agree sex before marriage was acceptable. - The Church teaches all forms of artificial contraception are wrong. - Catholics agree couples should be faithful. - The Church does not recognise same-sex marriages.

Catholics and many Humanists would agree with the principle of treating others as you want to be treated (*Luke 6:31*).

APPLY

TIP

Highlighting the most significant point from each side from a list of possible agree/disagree arguments such as this may help you write a conclusion.

AO1 Three points have been started for you. Can you finish them?

a. Outline **three** relationships outside of marriage according to Catholic belief. (3)
- Premarital… • Same-sex… • Cohabitation…

AO2 Arguments in support of the statement have been given below. Fill in the arguments against it.

d. 'Sex should only take place within marriage.' Evaluate this statement considering arguments for and against.
In your response you should:
- refer to Catholic teachings
- refer to different Christian points of view
- refer to Catholic teachings
- reach a justified conclusion. (12)

Agree – Catholic view	Disagree – Other views
- Unitive: seals the bond of a couple and ensures they have a unique relationship	-
- Procreative: an openness to children is a requirement for Catholic marriage and marriage is the appropriate place for their upbringing	-
- Sex is something to be enjoyed, a source of 'joy and pleasure' (*CCC 2362*), but as a sign of 'spiritual communion' (*CCC 2360*)	-

REVIEW

Answers: Mark your answers using p.200 and note areas for improvement.
AO1: This question is testing your ability to answer 'outline' questions. For help with this skill, see p.12.
AO2: This question is testing your ability to plan a response. For help with this skill, see p.12.

RECAP

Essential information

- Catholics believe that the family was created by God and should be a faithful place to bring up children.
- Religious and non-religious groups share some ideas about the purpose of the family.
- There is a great variety of family structures in the UK.

Procreation, security, and education

What do Catholics believe?	What influences Church teaching?

• The family was created by God.
 • It is the basic unit of society.
 • It is the place where children should be brought up.
 • It is the principal place for the education of morals.
 • It is the place where children learn the faith and pray.
 • Pope Benedict XVI called it 'a communion of love'.
 • It is also called the 'domestic church' (*CCC 1666*).
	• The Holy Family – Mary, Joseph, and Jesus – provide a model to follow: faithful, obedient, protective, and dedicated.
	 • Family life is seen as a vocation of the Church.
	 • The purposes of family are similar to the purposes of marriage:
	   ○ lifelong relationships of love and faithfulness
	   ○ support, comfort
	   ○ procreate (have children)
	   ○ faithful family who receive the sacraments
	   ○ a sign of Christ's love in the world.

The purpose of family

- There are many types of family in society, but the main purpose is shared by Catholics and non-religious people:
  - 'A family is any unit committed to sharing resources and to mutual support and the welfare of children' (*A Humanist Discussion of Family Matters*).
- However, Catholic beliefs come from the teachings of the Church.

Different types of family

The Church recognises that different types of family exist, but believes the nuclear family is the best way to raise a faithful Catholic family.

In the *Familiaris Consortio* 36–85 the nuclear family is affirmed and upholding the role of the family is highlighted as a key part of the Church's mission. *Familiaris Consortio* goes on to address struggles of 21st-century families and the need to support them.

Recent guidance from the Church
Amoris Laetitia (The Joy of Love) (2016) by Pope Francis recognised some of the struggles of modern families. Some bishops have interpreted this document as allowing the Eucharist to divorced and remarried individuals.

Nuclear: two parents and their children

Blended: a couple where one or both has children from previous relationships

Family types

Single parent

Same-sex parents

Extended: including grandparents, aunts, uncles, etc. living together

APPLY

(A01) Try this question on your own.

  c. Explain **two** beliefs about the family for Catholics. In your answer you must refer to a source of wisom or authority. (5)

TIP
Remember to include a source of wisdom or authority which can include the Bible, the CCC and documents from the Pope.

REVIEW

Answers: Mark your answers using p.200 and note areas for improvement.
AO1: This question is testing your ability to answer a (c) question.
For help with this skill, see p.12.

Essential information

- Families are a core part of the larger Church family.
- Supporting families is an important role of the parish.
- Parishes may offer classes, groups for children, and counselling for the community, which help families to overcome their problems.

Supporting families

Families are important to parish life. Catholic parents are often full members of the Church, and their children grow up to become active members, living out the sacraments too.

The Church provides both practical and spiritual support via the parish. Catholic families are not immune from the pressures, struggles, and difficulties that all families face. These may include debt, domestic violence, separation, or infidelity.

Family worship	Groups for children
• Attendance at Mass is a time to be together. • Family Masses can encourage those with younger children to attend.	• Mother and toddler groups, youth clubs, Guides, and Scouts give children time to socialise with Catholics. • Children's liturgy during Mass gives children time to grow in their faith.
Classes for parents	**Counselling**
• Catechesis for baptism or First Holy Communion helps parents better understand the sacraments. • Classes exist to train parents in how to be a good Catholic parent. • Marriage preparation classes teach family planning.	• Most parish priests are trained counsellors, and are supported by parish or diocese volunteer teams. • Organisations such as Marriage Care provide free counselling.
Family Group Movement	**Other help**
• Parish friendship groups, open to all, encourage parishioners to support one another. • They often partake in low-cost activities.	• Charities such as St Vincent de Paul might help with donations of furniture for a struggling family, for example.

> ❝Parents have the mission of teaching their children to pray and to discover their vocation as children of God❞
> (*CCC 2226*)

AO1 The first point has been done for you; add two more.

a. Outline **three** parish-based sources of help for families. (3)

> *They may have children's liturgy to help children understand the readings of the Mass.*

AO2 Use the table to think of arguments for and against the statement.

d. 'Support for the family is one of the most important things a parish does.' Evaluate this statement considering arguments for and against. In your response you should:
- refer to Catholic teachings
- reach a justified conclusion. (12)

Agree	Disagree

Answers: Mark your answers using p.200 and note areas for improvement.
AO1: This question is testing your ability to answer 'outline' questions. For help with this skill, see p.12.
AO2: This question is testing your ability to plan a response. For help with this skill, see p.12.

RECAP

Essential information

- The Catholic Church believes any form of contraception, apart from natural family planning is wrong.
- Many other Christians, such as Church of England, do not regard contraception as a sin.
- Many atheists believe individuals should make their own choices about family planning.

Catholic teaching

The Church believes contraception undermines sexual relations as being unitive **and** procreative – these two things should not be separated.

Artificial

Natural

Papal teaching	Sanctity of life
• *Humanae Vitae* (*On Human Life*), 1968, by Pope Paul VI confirmed the Church's position on family planning. • Pope Paul VI said that preventing pregnancy 'contradicts the will of the Author of life'. • Couples should not be forced to have children, but can space them out using natural methods. • Contraception can encourage sex outside marriage.	• Abortion is expressly forbidden by *Humanae Vitae*. • Pro-life is the term for religious and **secular** campaigns for the rights of the unborn. • In the UK, abortion is legal under certain circumstances. • Some Catholic countries, such as Ireland, only allow abortion to save a mother's life.

Divergent attitudes to family planning

- Many Humanists and atheists argue that contraception helps couples to be responsible and regulate births.
- Most non-religious people believe individuals should make decisions for themselves on issues such as contraception, family planning, and abortion.

> ❝If contraception results in every child being a wanted child, and in better, healthier lives for women, it must be a good thing.❞
> (*A Humanist Discussion of Family Matters*)

Other Christian attitudes

- Most other Christians allow non-abortive contraception methods – preventing pregnancy rather than terminating it. This means allowing condoms, but not the morning-after pill, for example.
- The Church of England says, 'Contraception is not regarded as a sin or going against God's purpose.'
- Individual Christians may believe in **situation ethics** – that they need to decide what is right or wrong depending on the circumstances.
- The Catholic Church does not agree. It believes:
  ○ humans do not have the power to contradict the will of God regarding life
  ○ sex outside of marriage is wrong
  ○ life begins at conception, and the unborn child is created in the image of God.

TIP
It may be useful to be aware of types of contraception – both artificial and natural.

APPLY

AO1 A good way to approach this question would be to give a reason why natural family planning is a good idea, and then a reason why artificial contraception goes against Catholic belief.

b. Explain **two** reasons why the Catholic Church promotes natural family planning. (4)

AO2 The arguments for the statement have been done for you. Can you write the main arguments against it?

d. 'Catholics should only use natural family planning.' Evaluate this statement considering arguments for and against. In your response you should:
- refer to Catholic teachings
- refer to different Christian points of view
- refer to non-religious points of view
- refer to ethical points of view
- reach a justified conclusion. (12)

For	Against
• It allows Catholics to take responsibility over how many children they have. • This is what Church teaching says. *Humanae Vitae* (1968) outlined the reasons why artificial contraception should not be used. • It is a way of allowing God's will, through the menstrual cycle, without resorting to artificial means that stop the procreative process or can be abortive.	• • •

REVIEW

Answers: Mark your answers using p.201 and note areas for improvement.
AO1: This question is testing your ability to write developed points. For help with this skill, see p.12.
AO2: This question is testing your ability to identify divergent views. For help with this skill, see p.12.

RECAP

Essential information

- The Catholic Church does not believe divorce from sacramental marriage is possible and annulment can only take place under strict circumstances.
- Other Christians do not encourage it but allow divorce and remarriage.
- Non-religious groups usually allow divorce and remarriage but encourage people to act in the family's best interests.

The meaning of divorce, annulment, and remarriage

	Meaning	Can you get remarried?
Divorce	Ending of a legal marriage by a court of law	Not in the Catholic Church, but other Christian Churches allow it
Annulment	A declaration that the marriage was never valid – they are rare	Allowed in the Catholic Church as long as a legal divorce is also obtained
Remarriage	One or both people getting married have been married before	Catholic Church states marriage only ends when one of the partners dies. A Catholic can get remarried at this point if they wish.

Church teaching

- *Matthew 19:8* says God does not want divorce and the only reason it was allowed was people refusing to obey God.
- A covenant is made during the sacrament of marriage that cannot be broken by any earthly power.
- Three key points from the Catechism of the Catholic Church:
  - *2382*: God has joined man and woman together, it can never be dissolved
  - *2383*: legal separation or divorce allowed for the safety or health of the couple or children, for example if a parent is abusive
  - *2384*: but they remain married in the eyes of God so cannot get remarried.

> 66 I hate divorce, says the Lord the God of Israel 99 (*Malachi 2:16*)

Different attitudes to divorce

Other Christian attitudes	Non-religious attitudes
Many other Christians allow divorce and remarriage. This is because: - some suggest Jesus allowed divorce for adultery (*Matthew 5:32*) - Christianity is based on forgiveness; it offers people who repent another chance - some suggest it is the 'lesser of two evils'.	- Marriage is not considered sacred, so most support liberal divorce laws. - Most non-religious people do not object to remarriage. - Some believe in situation ethics – that the decision depends on individual cases.

Catholic responses

- Matrimony is a sacrament.
- The Church offers support to couples to try to help with any marital problems.
- The needs of the family and children come above the needs of the individual.
- The effects of a bad marriage can be significant to the couple and children, so sometimes it is necessary to end the legal marriage.

APPLY

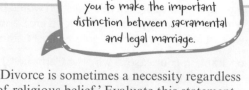

TIP

This question would require you to make the important distinction between sacramental and legal marriage.

AO1 Finish the two points to answer this question.

b. Explain **two** reasons why Catholics cannot end the sacrament of matrimony. (4)

> *Firstly, a sacrament represents a covenant with God. This means...*
> *Secondly, God does not permit divorce. This is made clear...*

d. 'Divorce is sometimes a necessity regardless of religious belief.' Evaluate this statement considering arguments for and against. In your response you should:
- refer to Catholic teachings
- refer to different Christian points of view
- refer to non-religious points of view
- refer to ethical points of view
- reach a justified conclusion. (12)

AO2 Make a list of the key arguments for and against the statement.

REVIEW

Answers: Mark your answers using p.201 and note areas for improvement.
AO1: This question is testing your ability to write developed points. For help with this skill, see p.12.
AO2: This question is testing your ability to plan a response. For help with this skill, see p.12.

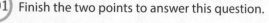

RECAP

Essential information

- The Catholic Church teaches that men and women should have equal roles in life and equal rights in society.
- Genesis shows the equality of, and differences between, men and women.
- Many other Christian Churches also believe in equality between men and women within the family.

Equality in Catholicism

- The Church teaches that men and women should have equal roles and rights.
- Both men and women can teach catechesis, distribute the Eucharist, and perform many other jobs and lay roles within the Church.
- Women cannot be ordained.

Attitudes in the Bible

The story of Adam and Eve can be interpreted differently to emphasise either similarities or differences between men and women:

Similarities

- Both were created in the image of God (*Genesis 1:27*).
- Both disobeyed God.
- Both are cursed for their disobedience.

Differences

- Eve was created from Adam's rib (*Genesis 2:22*) so they would complement and fulfil each other's needs (neither is superior).
- They are cursed for their disobedience in different ways (*Genesis 3:16–17*).

The role of men and women in the family

> 66 The family [...] is the natural society in which husband and wife are called to give themselves in love and in the gift of life 99 (*CCC 2207*)

- The equality of men and women is emphasised in the Catechism (*CCC 2207*).
- Both husbands and wives are called to 'give themselves' in commitment.
- The Catechism refers to 'fraternity within society', which means friendship.

Dignity of work in the home

- The Church recognises the value of domestic work – whoever does it, it is not less important than work to generate income.
- The Church teaches that a man or woman who dedicates their life to work in the home should not be judged by society or financially penalised ('Letter to the Bishops of the Catholic Church on the Collaboration of Men and Women in the Church and the World').

Divergent Christian views

- Other Christian Churches, such as the Church of England and Methodists, have female clergy or ministers.
- Many Christians agree women should be supported as they juggle home and careers. Some would also argue men should be equally supported in balancing their work and home lives.
- The importance of the family is agreed upon by all Christian Churches. Equality is increasingly accepted and promoted by most mainstream Christian groups, reflecting the views of many non-religious people and society in general.

APPLY

(AO1) Have a go at answering this question on your own.

b. Explain **two** different Christian views about equality. (4)

TIP

Catholic views about women's roles in church life will help here.

REVIEW

Answers: Mark your answers using p.201 and note areas for improvement.
AO1: This question is testing your ability to answer a (b) question. For help with this skill, see p.12.

 **RECAP**

Essential information

- Some Bible passages can be interpreted to suggest gender inequality, but others suggest men and women should support each other.
- Jesus did not discriminate against women, and set an example for Catholics to follow.
- Christian denominations vary in the roles they allow women within their churches.

Gender prejudice:	Discrimination:
believing people of one gender are inferior or superior on the basis of their sex.	treating people less favourably because of their gender, ethnicity, colour, sexuality, age, class, etc.

Catholic opposition to prejudice and discrimination

Source of wisdom and authority	Explanation
66 There is neither male nor female; for you are all one in Christ Jesus 99 (*Galatians 3:28*)	God has no preferences between people.
66 Wives, be subject to your husbands [...] For the husband is the head of the wife as Christ is the head of the church 99 (*Ephesians 5:22–23*) 66 Husbands, love your wives, as Christ loved the church and gave himself up for her 99 (*Ephesians 5:25*)	*Ephesians 5:21–33* made it clear that everyone should be submissive to God and wives likewise should submit to their husbands.
66 Women should keep silence in the churches 99 (*1 Corinthians 14:34*)	Scholars believe Paul was trying to reduce chaos in the early Church. Earlier in *1 Corinthians 14*, he speaks positively about women praying.

Jesus' example

Many Christians think Jesus actively combatted prejudice and discrimination.

He treated everyone with respect and as individuals (see 12.7). Examples are:

- the Samaritan woman at the well (*John 4:4–26*)
- the woman caught in adultery (*John 7:53–8:11*)
- the Greek woman (*Matthew 15:21–28, Mark 7:24–30*).

> 66 Excessive economic and social disparity between individuals and people of the one human race [...] militates against social justice, equity, human dignity 99 (*CCC 1938*)

Divergent Christian attitudes

- Catholic, Orthodox, and some Evangelical Churches oppose women's ordination.
  - Jesus was male and did not have female disciples.
  - Some believe *Ephesians 5:23* suggests women should not be ordained.
- Women still play an active role in the Church (see 10.7).
- Some Baptist and Pentecostal Churches have been ordaining women for nearly 100 years.
- The Church of England ordained its first women priests in 1994, and had its first woman bishop in 2014.

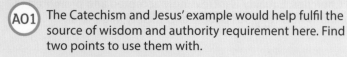 **APPLY**

AO1 The Catechism and Jesus' example would help fulfil the source of wisdom and authority requirement here. Find two points to use them with.

c. Explain **two** reasons why Catholics challenge gender prejudice and discrimination. In your answer you must refer to a source of wisdom and authority. (5)

AO2 Complete the table with arguments for and against the statement.

d. 'Women should be ordained in all Christian churches.' Evaluate this statement considering arguments for and against. In your response you should:
- refer to Catholic teachings
- refer to different Christian points of view
- reach a justified conclusion. (12)

For	Against
Some Baptist and Pentecostal Churches have been ordaining women with great success for over 100 years.	Division was caused by the Church of England ordaining women – some priests left and joined the Catholic Church.

 **REVIEW**

Answers: Mark your answers using p.201 and note areas for improvement.
AO1: This question is testing your ability to write developed points. For help with this skill, see p.12.
AO2: This question is testing your ability to plan a response. For help with this skill, see p.12.

Test the 3 mark question (a)

1 Outline **three** purposes of the family for Catholics. **(3 marks)**

> The family is the place where children are taught the Catholic faith. (1)
>
> It provides a secure economic and religious unit in which everyone is supported including children, the sick, and the elderly. (1)
>
> Catholics accept that the family is the basis of society. (1)

2 Outline **three** features of marriage for Catholics. **(3 marks)**

> It is a sacrament joining one man and one woman. (1)
>
> _____
>
> _____

TIP
Read the question carefully. This one asks about the features of marriage itself, **not** the ceremony.

3 Outline **three** reasons the Catholic Church does not permit artificial contraception. **(3 marks)**

_____

_____

_____

Test the 4 mark question (b)

1 Explain **two** Christian views on divorce. **(4 marks)**

● **Explain one view.**	At a Catholic wedding, couples make a promise to keep the marriage permanent.
● Develop your explanation with more detail/an example/reference to a religious teaching.	As the promises are a sacrament, they cannot be broken.
● **Explain a second view.**	Other Christians also teach that marriage is for life but accept that there may be circumstances when the vows cannot be kept.
● Develop your explanation with more detail/an example/reference to a religious teaching.	They see it as better to divorce and then seek forgiveness.

2 Explain **two** reasons why the Catholic Church teaches that sexual relationships should only exist within marriage. **(4 marks)**

● **Explain one reason.**	
● Develop your explanation with more detail/an example/reference to a religious teaching.	
● **Explain a second reason.**	
● Develop your explanation with more detail/an example/reference to a religious teaching.	

3 Explain **two** ways the Catholic Church supports the family. **(4 marks)**

TIP
Make sure you give **specific examples** of the ways in which the Church supports the family – avoid giving vague answers.

Exam Practice

Test the 5 mark question (c)

1 Explain **two** teachings about why marriage may be important for Catholics.
In your answer you must refer to a source of wisdom and authority.   **(5 marks)**

● **Explain one teaching.**	The Catholic Church teaches the importance of marriage as the intimate union and equal partnership of a man and a woman.
● Develop your explanation with more detail/an example.	This comes to us from a belief that God created male and female so that they might become one body.
● **Either:** Add a reference to a source of wisdom and authority here.	
● **Explain a second teaching.**	Catholic marriage is held to be permanent.
● Develop your explanation with more detail/an example.	This means that Catholic couples will promise that the marriage will last for ever and that they will not divorce,
● **Or:** Add a reference to a source of wisdom and authority here.	which is shown in the Sacramental vow 'till death us do part'.

2 Explain **two** reasons why the family is so important to the Catholic Church.
In your answer you must refer to a source of wisdom and authority.   **(5 marks)**

● **Explain one reason.**	
● Develop your explanation with more detail/an example.	
● **Either:** Add a reference to a source of wisdom and authority here.	
● **Explain a second reason.**	
● Develop your explanation with more detail/an example.	
● **Or:** Add a reference to a source of wisdom and authority here.	

TIP
This could mean that you include a source of wisdom and authority as a development and another, different one for the actual 'source of wisdom and authority' mark.

3 Explain **two** Catholic beliefs about gender prejudice and discrimination.
In your answer you must refer to a source of wisdom and authority.   **(5 marks)**

Exam Practice

Test the 12 mark question (d)

1. 'The purpose of sex is to have children.' Evaluate this statement considering arguments for and against. In your response you should:
   - refer to Catholic teachings
   - refer to different Christian points of view
   - refer to non-religious points of view
   - reach a justified conclusion.

TIP

In 12 mark questions you will not be marked for your spelling and grammar, but it is still a good idea to take care with your writing.

(12 marks)

ARGUMENTS IN SUPPORT OF THE STATEMENT • **Explain why some people would agree with the statement.** • Develop your explanation with more detail and examples. • Refer to religious teaching. Use a quote or paraphrase of a religious authority. • **Evaluate the arguments.** Is this a good argument? Explain why you think this. Use words such as convincing/strong/robust/weak/ unpersuasive/unsuccessful within your reasoning.	The Catholic Church teaches that one of the natural functions of sex is to reproduce; this means that sexual activity not open to the possibility of reproduction is against natural law. Consequently the use of artificial contraceptives is forbidden to Catholics. To have sex simply for pleasure is viewed by some Christians as sinful; it demeans the sanctity of humanity. This means that sexual relations must always be both unitive and procreative. During the Catholic marriage ceremony, the couple are asked about their commitment to having children. This suggests that children are the primary purpose of marriage and sex; by having children Catholics are fulfilling their marriage vows to accept children lovingly from God.
ARGUMENTS SUPPORTING A DIFFERENT VIEW • **Explain why some people would disagree with the statement.** • Develop your explanation with more detail and examples. • Refer to religious teaching. Use a quote or paraphrase of a religious authority. • **Evaluate the arguments.** Is this a good argument? Explain why you think this. Use words such as convincing/strong/robust/weak/ unpersuasive/unsuccessful within your reasoning.	Some people, including non-religious people, could suggest that there is no reason why sex should not be for pleasure; it would provide an experience unique to the married couple. Also with this purpose in mind, sex can still be unitive in developing a loving bond between sexual partners. Some Christians argue that not all acts of sex need to be open to life, for valid reasons. They may apply situation ethics in recognising that a couple may want to space out their children using a legitimate birth control method. This means they can control the size of their family and perhaps look after their children more effectively. Married couples who are not able to conceive children are still allowed to have sexual relations. This is sex that is knowingly not procreative. Consequently the rules about having sex need to be adapted to the real life situations of couples.
CONCLUSION • **Give a justified conclusion.** • Include your own reasoning. • Use words such as convincing/ strong/robust/weak/unpersuasive/ unsuccessful to weigh up the different arguments for and against. • Do not just repeat arguments you have already used without explaining how they apply to your reasoned opinion/conclusion.	In conclusion, sex has a dual purpose: it is unitive and procreative. In a loving relationship, it is sometimes not possible to have children, but sex can unite a couple and valid for that reason alone. The Catholic Church may allow natural family planning, so the purpose of sex is not just to have children.

TIP

Ensure you have an accurate knowledge of what the Church teaches about sexual activity. It is also useful to know the rationale behind the teaching.

2 'Marriage is a lifelong commitment that needs careful preparation.' Evaluate this statement considering arguments for and against. In your response you should:

- refer to Catholic teachings
- refer to different Christian points of view
- refer to non-religious points of view
- reach a justified conclusion.

(12 marks)

ARGUMENTS IN SUPPORT OF THE STATEMENT	*Some Catholics/Christians/people would agree with this statement because...*
● **Explain why some people would agree with the statement.** ● Develop your explanation with more detail and examples. ● Refer to religious teaching. Use a quote or paraphrase of a religious authority. ● **Evaluate the arguments.** Is this a good argument? Explain why you think this. Use words such as convincing/strong/robust/weak/unpersuasive/unsuccessful within your reasoning.	
ARGUMENTS SUPPORTING A DIFFERENT VIEW	*On the other hand, some Catholics/Christians/people would hold a different point of view...*
● **Explain why some people would disagree with the statement.** ● Develop your explanation with more detail and examples. ● Refer to religious teaching. Use a quote or paraphrase of a religious authority. ● **Evaluate the arguments.** Is this a good argument? Explain why you think this. Use words such as convincing/strong/robust/weak/unpersuasive/unsuccessful within your reasoning.	
CONCLUSION	*Having considered both sides of the argument, I would say that...*
● **Give a justified conclusion.** ● Include your own reasoning. ● Use words such as convincing/strong/robust/weak/unpersuasive/unsuccessful to weigh up the different arguments for and against. ● Do not just repeat arguments you have already used without explaining how they apply to your reasoned opinion/conclusion.	

> **TIP**
> Make sure you are able to clearly distinguish between the Catholic sacrament (matrimony) and the legal process.

3 'Christians should only use natural family planning.' Evaluate this statement considering arguments for and against. In your response you should:

- refer to Catholic teachings
- refer to different Christian points of view
- refer to non-religious points of view
- refer to ethical points of view
- reach a justified conclusion.

(12 marks)

 **REVIEW**

- Check your answers to these exam questions on p.201–202, correct your answers with annotations, and note down any general areas for improvement.
- If you don't feel secure in the content of this chapter, you could reread the Recap sections.
- If you don't feel secure in your exam technique, you could revisit the exam support section on pp.7–14.

 **RECAP**

Essential information

- Messiah is Hebrew for 'anointed one': a person who is set aside for a specific mission. Christ is the Greek word for Messiah.
- Christians believe Jesus was the Messiah, sent by God to save them.
- 'Son of Man' was one of the titles Jesus used about himself; it can be a way of talking about a special being sent from and connected to God.

What were the expectations of the Messiah?

- Jews believed the Messiah would fulfil the prophecies of the Old Testament.
- Jewish people looked forward to a warrior king who would free them from Roman rule.
- The Messiah would also be a religious leader.

What does the use of the title Messiah show about Jesus?

- Jesus most likely knew the title would be treated with suspicion (see 11.5). Some Jews would find it difficult to believe the Messiah had finally arrived.
- Jesus finally accepted the title when questioned by the high priest (*Mark 14:62*).
- As a Jew himself, Jesus' idea of the Messiah would have been influenced by Jewish scriptures.
  - Isaiah spoke of a suffering servant (*Isaiah 52*) and gentle leader.
  - *Isaiah 53:5* refers to the nature and suffering of a rejected Messiah who carried the 'transgressions' (wrongdoing) of humanity and, by doing so, saved them.

Who is the Son of Man?

- The **Son of Man** is a title connected with the Messiah. It is used in the Gospels in relation to Jesus.
- The title is also used in the Old Testament. In Ezekiel and *Psalm 8* it refers to how ordinary humans are in comparison with God. In the Book of Daniel, however, the Son of Man is a special being sent by and connected to God:

> 66 and behold, with the clouds of heaven there came one like a son of man [...] his dominion is an everlasting dominion. 99 (*Daniel 7:13–14*)

- There are two main interpretations of what it suggests:
  - The ordinary humanity of Jesus
  - The cosmic divinity of Jesus.
- Jesus uses the title himself; it is not just Mark who calls him this.
- Many suggest the title was used both to conceal and to reveal he was the Messiah.
- Using this title in the Gospel, Jesus reveals himself as human, but also divine.

Significance for Christians today

- The title Son of Man suggests the idea of God's rule – Jesus remains a mighty ruler sent from God for Christians today.
- The cross has become a symbol of the sacrifice Jesus made.
- Christians today should understand that Jesus was a divine leader sent with the mission of salvation.

TIP

Ensure you are familiar with key terms such as 'Messiah' and 'Son of Man' and at least one Old Testament reference for Son of Man such as *Daniel 7:13*.

 APPLY

AO1 Complete this student's answer.

a. Outline **three** beliefs about the Messiah. (3)

> The Jewish people believed he would be a religious leader.

AO2 List arguments for and against the following statement. Two examples have been provided. Then, write a justified conclusion.

d. 'Jesus used the title 'the Son of Man' to indicate his divine nature.' Evaluate this statement considering arguments for and against. In your response you should:
- refer to St Mark's Gospel
- reach a justified conclusion. (15)

For	Against
In Daniel, the Son of Man is a supernatural figure, with cosmic authority.	In Ezekiel, 'Son of Man' means ordinary human.

 **REVIEW**

Answers: Mark your answers using p.202 and note areas for improvement.
AO1: This question is testing your ability to answer 'outline' questions. For help with this skill, see p.12.
AO2: This question is testing your ability to identify arguments for and against a statement. For help with this skill, see p.12.

 RECAP

Essential information

- According to Mark's Gospel, Jesus was baptised by John the Baptist in the River Jordan.
- The baptism of Jesus also involved the Holy Spirit and God the Father.
- Mark's Gospel suggests the voice from heaven showed that Jesus was sent from God.

Who was John the Baptist?

- A preacher who was related to Jesus and began his public ministry before him. He called people to repentance, offering baptism for forgiveness of sins.
- John refers to the prophet Isaiah, who predicted a forerunner to the Messiah:

> 66 Prepare the way of the Lord, make his paths straight 99 (*Mark 1:3*)

- He made clear there was someone greater than him to come:

> 66 I have baptised you with water; but he will baptise you with the Holy Spirit 99 (*Mark 1:8*)

Jesus' baptism

> 66 he saw the heavens opened and the Spirit descending upon him like a dove; and a voice came from heaven, 'Thou art my beloved Son; with thee I am well pleased' 99 (*Mark 1:10–11*)

In this quotation Mark gives two important details:
1. The Holy Spirit descended like a dove.
2. The voice is God the Father, using the words of *Psalm 2:7*, written by David to celebrate his coronation as king.

Many scholars therefore see the baptism as being like a coronation, and the start of Jesus' ministry.

The significance of the baptism for Christians today

It shows Jesus' divine origin and divine command – Jesus is the 'beloved Son' (*Mark 1:11*).	**It is one of only a few passages in the New Testament where there is reference to the Trinity** – Father, Son, and Holy Spirit. Jews had clear beliefs of one God, they experienced Jesus in person, and were then inspired by the Holy Spirit; the Trinity was a 'lived' experience for them.
It gives an example for Christians to follow – baptism is an important beginning to the Christian life.	**It is an indication of Jesus' willingness to take on the sins of humanity** – due to the Immaculate Conception of Mary, Jesus was sinless, therefore his baptism was an act of solidarity with the rest of humanity.

 **APPLY**

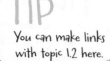 **TIP**
You can make links with topic 1.2 here.

AO1 Answer the following exam question, which requires two developed points. The first point has been made for you.

b. Explain **two** reasons Jesus' baptism is an important event for Christians today. (4)

> *Firstly, it was one of the first passages in the New Testament where God the Father, Son, and Holy Spirit are present. This is important as the doctrine of the Trinity grew out of the lived experience of the early Church, and remains important today.*

AO2 Read the arguments against this statement. Can you write some arguments in support of the statement? This will help you prepare for a (d) question.

'Jesus' baptism is important to understanding the rest of Jesus' ministry.'

Against
• Jesus' ministry is best understood in light of his death and resurrection.
• There were other occasions where God affirmed Jesus, such as the transfiguration (see 11.6).
• Jesus' miracles and teachings spoke for themselves.

 REVIEW

Answers: Mark your answers using p.202 and note areas for improvement.
AO1: This question is testing your ability to develop points. For help with this skill, see p.12.
AO2: This question is testing your ability to plan a response. For help with this skill, see p.12.

RECAP

Essential information

- **Nature miracles** are where the natural order of life is surpassed by the activity of God.
- Christians believe that miracles Jesus performs are evidence that he was sent from God.
- Nature miracles encourage Christians to keep faith and trust in God in all situations.

Examples of nature miracles in Mark's Gospel

	Calming of the Storm (*Mark 4:35–41*)	The Feeding of the Five Thousand (*Mark 6:32–44*)	Walking on the Water (*Mark 6:45–52*)
What happened?	• Jesus was asleep on a boat on Lake Galilee. • Jesus was awakened by the disciples and rebuked the storm, which obeyed. • The disciples were amazed.	• 5000 fed with five loaves and two fish. • He arranged them into groups of 50s and 100s. • 12 baskets were left over – a link to the tribes of Israel.	• Jesus walks over the Sea of Galilee to his disciples who are caught in a storm. • The disciples thought he was a ghost, but he reassured them.
Key quote	'Who then is this, that even wind and sea obey him?' (*Mark 4:41*)	'He looked up to heaven, and blessed, and broke the loaves […] they all ate and were satisfied' (*Mark 6:41–42*)	'Take heart, it is I; have no fear' (*Mark 6:50*)
Significance	• Jesus was human and got tired. • Sign of being God, as he could control nature. • Scholars suggest this is a message of comfort to persecuted Christians in Rome.	• The actions of breaking and blessing bread are repeated at the Last Supper (*Mark 14:22*). • Leftovers suggests God will provide what people need, just like he did for Moses in the wilderness. • Food can be a metaphor for the Word of God – more than enough for everyone.	• Shows Jesus' power over nature. • Link to Creation: 'the Spirit of God was moving over the face of the waters' (*Genesis 1:2*). • Disciples' amazement and struggle to understand what they are witnessing.

The meaning of these miracles for Christians today

Some Christians may take these accounts literally, while other Christians may not. However, all three show why Christians can proclaim Jesus as God, Creator, and Lord of nature. They show Jesus is both human and divine. Miracles show the Kingdom of God is present, as well as a future event.

Christian responses to non-religious arguments

- Non-religious arguments (e.g. atheist and Humanist views) sometimes suggest miracles have natural explanations (see 9.3) and can be scientifically explained.
- Atheists would insist that even if there is no scientific explanation it does not follow that Jesus is capable of performing miracles.
- Coincidence and chance could play a part in any miraculous event, or accounts could be exaggerated or made up.
- Christians believe Jesus' divinity is reasonable given the number and variety of miracles he performed.

APPLY

TIP
Writing about the disciples' amazement may be a useful way to illustrate Jesus' divine nature.

AO1 Answer the following exam question.

  c. Explain **two** reasons that nature miracles could act as proof of Jesus' divine nature. In your answer you must refer to a source of wisdom and authority. (5)

AO2 Read the following arguments for and against the statement. Then, write a justified conclusion.

  'The nature miracles clearly show the divine nature of Jesus.'

For	Against
• Power over wind and sea in Calming of the Storm and Walking on Water. • Only a miracle could provide food for 5000 from five loaves and two fish. • Genuine amazement of the disciples indicates that miracles and not coincidences took place.	• Shows a human side, i.e. being tired – does this take away from his divine nature? • Could have been exaggerated tales from the disciples – can the stories be trusted? • A non-religious person could argue the Calming of the Storm was just a coincidence.

REVIEW

Answers: Mark your answers using p.202 and note areas for improvement.
AO1: This question is testing your ability to explain beliefs correctly, using a source of wisdom and authority. For help with this skill, see p.12.
AO2: This question is testing your ability to write a justified conclusion. For help with this skill, see p.12.

RECAP

Essential information

- **Healing miracles** are acts of God that return people to full physical, mental, and spiritual health.
- Christians believe that healing miracles show Jesus' divine power.
- Mark's Gospel suggests that miracles can only occur when faith is also present.

Examples of healing miracles in Mark's Gospel

	The healing of Legion (Mark 5:1–20)	**The raising of Jairus' daughter** (Mark 5:21–43)
	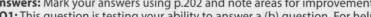	
What happened?	 • A man is violently possessed by demons of Legion. • Jesus orders Legion out. • The demon recognised Jesus for who he was. • The demons were driven into a herd of pigs who then drowned themselves. • It took place in an area where gentiles lived.	Two miracles: • Synagogue leader Jairus asked Jesus to heal his daughter. • On the way, Jesus encounters a woman who had bled for 12 years. • She touches his cloak and is healed. • At Jairus' house, Jesus is told the girl has died, but he raises her from the dead.
Key quotes	'And when he saw Jesus from afar […] he said, "What have you to do with me, Jesus, Son of the Most High God?"' (Mark 5:6–7) 'Go home to your friends, and tell them how much the Lord has done for you, and how he has had mercy on you' (Mark 5:19)	'Daughter, your faith has made you well' (Mark 5:34) 'Do not fear, only believe' (Mark 5:36)
What it shows about Jesus	• The demon recognised Jesus even though the disciples did not. • Pigs were considered unclean, all is cleansed by Jesus. • Jesus has power to remove evil, which can only come from God. • The 'unworthy' ones are the ones who recognise God – it was the demon. • Jesus brings people out of darkness into the light of faith.	• Scholars believe it was menstrual bleeding – indicating the woman would have been considered unclean, which is why she only touches Jesus' cloak. Jesus overturns purity laws. • Outcasts who show faith are of the most significance. • Jairus' daughter: Jesus has power over death. • Preparation for Jesus' own resurrection.

The meaning of these miracles today

For Christians, these show:

- Jesus has the power to defeat evil and death
- Jesus' power is bound to the faith of the individual
- the Kingdom of God is present in Jesus

- no matter how desperate things may appear (12 years' bleeding, even death), faith in Jesus can lead to healing and renewal.

Some Christians believe their prayers will be answered and they will literally be healed. On the other hand, other Christians believe they will receive comfort and spiritual strengths rather than the physical healing of the Gospel stories.

> **TIP**
> You could either write about specific healing miracles in Mark, or you could write about their wider significance for Christians.

 APPLY

AO1 Try this one on your own!

b. Explain **two** things that healing miracles show about Jesus. (4)

AO2 Write a detailed essay plan for the following exam question.

d. 'Healing miracles are important for showing Jesus' power and authority.' Evaluate this statement, considering arguments for and against. In your response you should:
- refer to St Mark's Gospel
- reach a justified conclusion. (15)

 REVIEW

Answers: Mark your answers using p.202 and note areas for improvement.
AO1: This question is testing your ability to answer a (b) question. For help with this skill, see p.12.
AO2: This question is testing your ability to plan a response. For help with this skill, see p.12.

 RECAP

Essential information

* Peter's confession in *Mark 8* is that Jesus is 'the Christ' (Messiah).
* Peter's confession prompts Jesus to reveal the end of his life to his disciples.
* The **Messianic secret** is the idea of keeping Jesus' identity as the Messiah a secret.

'Who do men say that I am?'

At Caesarea Philippi, outside Galilee, Jesus asked his disciples who the people thought he was. They answered:

* John the Baptist
* Elias (also known as Elijah)
* one of the prophets.

He then asked who the disciples thought he was:

> 66 Peter answered him, 'You are the Christ' 99 (*Mark 8:29*)

* This story shows there was mystery around Jesus. While some thought he was Elias, who would be reincarnated to reveal the identity of the Messiah, only Peter gave the right answer. This is the first time the disciples used the term Messiah.
* For Catholics, Peter's confession of faith suggests that he is the most important leader of the early Church.

Jesus and his purpose

* Peter's confession was a prompt for Jesus to begin teaching that the Son of Man had to suffer and die, but that he would rise again on the third day.
* This would have been the opposite of what the disciples expected – a warrior king who would free the Jews from oppression.

* Peter tried to rebuke Jesus for saying this and Jesus replied:

> 66 Get behind me, Satan! 99 (*Mark 8:33*)

* Jesus was revealing his ultimate purpose: sacrifice as salvation for humanity.

The Messianic secret

* Jesus repeatedly told his followers to keep his status as the Messiah secret:
  * After raising Jairus' daughter, he tells the parents not to tell anyone (*Mark 5:43*).
  * After Peter's confession, Jesus warned the disciples to tell no one (*Mark 8:30*).
* When exorcising demons, Jesus would not permit the demons to speak, because they knew him (*Mark 1:34*).
* Commentators say Jesus is reluctant to accept the title due to the misunderstanding that would come with it (see 11.1). They argue that his vision of being a suffering servant rather than a warrior king needed to be revealed gradually.
* The Romans would have understood enough about the Messianic prophecy to arrest Jesus as a threat to the empire.

 APPLY

AO1 Can you develop this simple point, and then add a second developed point?

  b. Explain **two** features of the Messianic secret. (4)

> *Firstly, Jesus instructed others to keep his messiahship a secret on several occasions.*

AO2 **d.** 'Jesus was right to keep his messiahship a secret.' Evaluate this statement, considering arguments for and against. In your response you should:
* refer to St Mark's Gospel
* reach a justified conclusion. (15)

Using this table, write a conclusion:

For	Against
• Allowed people to work out for themselves the kind of Messiah that Jesus was – suffering servant. • Reduced the threat of Jesus being arrested too early. The Romans would have been on the lookout for the prophesied warrior king. • Jesus had a clear plan and needed to ensure all the necessary teaching had taken place.	• As Jesus was a miracle worker, he could easily have convinced his followers early on that he was the Messiah. • Many people realised anyway. Many people would have been unable to keep the secret. • The Romans would have realised that Jesus was not building an army to overthrow them, so would not have arrested him straight away.

 REVIEW

Answers: Mark your answers using p.202 and note areas for improvement.
AO1: This question is testing your ability to write a developed point. For help with this skill, see p.12.
AO2: This question is testing your ability to write a justified conclusion. For help with this skill, see p.12.

 RECAP

Essential information

- The **transfiguration** was a glimpse of the kingdom Jesus would bring as the Messiah.
- Christians believe that the voice from heaven is God the Father, who calls Jesus his son.
- Christians believe the presence of Moses and Elias (Elijah) shows that Jesus is the fulfilment of the Old Testament hopes for a Messiah.

The transfiguration

When: Six days after Peter's confession (see 11.5).
Who: Peter, James, and John (the inner group of disciples).
Where: A high mountain.

- Whiteness demonstrated the divine purity of Jesus.
- This was a glorified state.

- Revelation of the **❝**kingdom of God come with power**❞** (*Mark 9:1*).

❝He was transfigured before them, and his garments became glistening, intensely white **❞** (*Mark 9:2–3*)

The Law and the prophets show their support for Jesus

Two people from Israel's past appeared. Their message was that Jesus was the fulfilment of God's purpose.

Moses	Elias
• Represented the Law • Reminder of the rescue from slavery in Egypt.	• Greatest of the prophets • Challenged kings who were not true to religion of Israel • His return was a sign of the coming Messiah.

A confused Peter responded:

❝let us make three booths, one for you and one for Moses and one for Eli'jah [Elias]. **❞** (*Mark 9:5*).
This may be a reference to the Feast of the Tabernacles (Sukkot – see 8.7), a Jewish feast day. A cloud appeared and a voice said:

❝This is my beloved Son; listen to him. **❞** (*Mark 9:7*) Christians believe this voice was God. Jesus told them:

❝to tell no one what they had seen, until the Son of Man should have risen from the dead **❞** (*Mark 9:9*).
This confused the disciples, because death and resurrection did not fit with their view of the Messiah.

The significance of the transfiguration

- For Christians today, it shows Jesus is not a break from the Old Testament – he fulfils it. He is uniquely from God and has authority to speak for God the Father as he is God the Son.
- Non-religious arguments suggest that visions such as this provide no proof that Jesus is of a divine nature (see 9.2).
- Christians may respond that there were multiple witnesses, and as it presented a challenge to the disciples' faith, it is unlikely to be wish fulfilment.

 APPLY

(AO1) Can you complete this student's answer?

b. Explain **two** key features of the transfiguration. (4)

> *Firstly, Moses and Elias were present. This is relevant as it linked to the Old Testament with Moses representing the Law, and Elias the prophecy about the Messiah.*
> *Secondly...*

(AO2) Create a table with arguments for and against the following statement.

'The transfiguration is proof that Jesus was the Son of God.'

TIP
When you have finished your table think about your conclusion. Is the transfiguration proof or not?

 **REVIEW**

Answers: Mark your answers using p.202 and note areas for improvement.
AO1: This question is testing your ability to answer an 'explain' question. For help with this skill, see p.12.
AO2: This question is testing your ability to identify arguments for and against a statement. For help with this skill, see p.12.

RECAP

Essential information

- Christians believe that Jesus challenged the religion of his day.
- Mark's Gospel shows that this brought him into conflict with powerful Jewish groups over issues like the Sabbath and the Temple.

Healing the paralysed man

- In Capernaum, a man was lowered through a roof to Jesus, because his friends couldn't get to Jesus through the crowd.

> 66 And when Jesus saw their faith, he said to the paralytic, 'My Son, your sins are forgiven' 99 (*Mark 2:5*)

TIP
Illness and sin were seen as connected in Jesus' time.

- Jewish teachers of the law felt this was blasphemy as only God could forgive sins.
- Jesus challenged them about what difference it made which words he used:

> 66 Which is easier, to say to the paralytic, 'Your sins are forgiven,' or to say, 'Rise, take up your pallet and walk'? 99 (*Mark 2:9*)

- Jesus said the Son of Man had the authority to forgive sins and he would prove it.
- This story shows Jesus' authority but also his conflict with the authorities.

Observing the Sabbath

- The Sabbath was a holy day that God had decreed should be kept free of work.
- The disciples picked grain to eat on the Sabbath, and the Pharisees (an influential group within the Jewish community) said this was unlawful (*Mark 2:23–3:6*).
- Jesus pointed out that King David ate sacred bread in the Temple. He also said:

> 66 The Sabbath was made for man, not man for the Sabbath; so the Son of Man is lord even of the Sabbath. 99 (*Mark 2:27–28*)

- Jesus was making clear that he is one with God who had created the Sabbath.

Jesus the controversialist

- The Temple was the holiest place for Jews.
- Jesus visited the week he was crucified *(Mark 11:15–18)*.
- He drove out those changing money – they made profit as people had to change their Roman money to Jewish money to buy Temple sacrifices.
- As he overturned tables, Jesus said:

> ❝Is it not written, 'My house shall be called a house of prayer for all the nations'? But you have made it a den of robbers. ❞ *(Mark 11:17)*

- This prompted the chief priests and scribes to find a way to 'destroy him' *(Mark 11:18)* because 'all nations' challenges the Jewish belief of a chosen people.

The significance of these conflicts

Jesus was unafraid to challenge those in power who were failing to live up to high standards.

He did not avoid conflict.

The conflicts of Jesus

He found the narrow keeping of laws unacceptable when people were in need.

Jesus tried to demonstrate serving God and others in love.

The narrative of Mark's Gospel

Mark focused on Jesus' adult life.

First half	Second half
• Jesus' miracles and preaching	• Peter's confession
	• Moving towards the end of his life and inevitable suffering
	• Challenging Jewish authorities brings Jesus closer to his arrest.

 **APPLY**

> **TIP**
> You need to know why some events in Jesus' life caused conflict.

AO1 Answer the following question. One point has been made for you.

a. Outline **three** ways that Jesus challenged the Jewish authorities. (3)

Jesus did not challenge his disciples for picking corn on the Sabbath.

AO2 Can you complete this table with arguments in support of the statement?

'Jesus was right to create conflict with the authorities.'

For	Against
	• This led to him being labelled as a troublemaker, and singled him out to be punished. Eventually he was crucified as a result.
	• The Jewish authorities did not like to be publicly embarrassed, as they were at the Temple. This is why they plotted to 'destroy him' *(Mark 11:18)*.
	• Jesus was indirectly claiming to be God, by forgiving sins. This was considered blasphemy, as Jesus knew.

 **REVIEW**

Answers: Mark your answers using p.202–203 and note areas for improvement.
AO1: This question is testing your ability to answer 'outline' questions. For help with this skill, see p.12.
AO2: This question is testing your ability to plan a response. For help with this skill, see p.12.

 **RECAP**

Essential information

- Christians believe Jesus' death on the cross brought salvation to the world and established the Kingdom of God.
- Christians believe the resurrection is proof that Jesus was God and defeated death.
- At the Last Supper, Jesus began the sacrament of the Eucharist with his blood and body.

Event	What happened	Other Gospel accounts
The Last Supper	<ul><li>Jesus' meeting with his disciples to celebrate Passover.</li><li>The bread and wine was the institution of the Eucharist: ❝this is my body […] This is my blood❞ (*Mark 14:22–24*).</li><li>His blood was a sign of the covenant to establish the Kingdom of God and was: ❝poured out for many❞ (*Mark 14:24*).</li><li>Jesus revealed one disciple would betray him (Judas) and that Peter would deny him three times.</li></ul>	John's Gospel mentions the washing of feet, which was seen as a great act of love.
The prayers in Gethsemane	<ul><li>Jesus took his inner group (Peter, James, and John) to pray: ❝Abba, Father, all things are possible to thee; remove this cup from me.❞ (*Mark 14:36*).</li><li>He asked his disciples to stay awake: ❝Watch and pray that you may not enter into temptation❞ (*Mark 14:38*) – but they fell asleep.</li></ul>	John's account is less detailed than others'.
Betrayal and arrest of Jesus	<ul><li>After being betrayed by Judas' kiss, Jesus was abandoned by his disciples. It was a solitary path as Messiah.</li><li>The chief priests and scribes wanted to arrest him by stealth, indicating that not everyone would agree with their actions.</li><li>Different groups probably wished for Jesus' death for different reasons:<ul><li>Sadducees: saw Jesus' attack on the Temple as a threat to their authority and wealth</li><li>Herodians: felt Jesus' popularity could be politically destabilising</li><li>Pharisees: saw Jesus' lawbreaking as an offence to God.</li></ul></li></ul>	All accounts are identical.
The trials of Jesus	**First trial before the High Priest**<ul><li>When asked if he was the Messiah, Jesus replied: 'I am' (*Mark 14:62*). 'I am' was the Old Testament name of God.</li><li>This infuriated the council, which sent him to the Romans for a death sentence.</li></ul>**Second trial before Pilate**<ul><li>Pilate was told Jesus said he was a king (ie. a threat to Caesar).</li><li>Pilate tried to free Jesus but the crowd chose a murderer, Barabbas, to be freed instead.</li></ul>	Mark is the only Gospel where Jesus admitted he was the Messiah.
The Passion and crucifixion	<ul><li>The Passion is the suffering of Jesus.</li><li>Mark *15:21–39* and *16:1–8* describe Jesus being taken to Golgotha, being crucified, dying, then rising from the dead.</li><li>Jesus was crucified at Golgotha between two criminals. A sign above him read: ❝The King of the Jews❞ (*Mark 15:26*).</li><li>At his moment of death, the curtain in the Temple that separated ordinary Jews from the holiest part tore in two. This was a sign of the invitation to enter into God's presence.</li><li>A centurion was the first person to recognise Jesus for who he was: ❝Truly this man was the Son of God!❞ (*Mark 15:39*).</li><li>Women followers watched and arranged his burial, while Joseph of Arimathea lent his family tomb.</li></ul>	Other Gospel accounts are similar, but John does not include the Temple curtain tearing.
Resurrection	<ul><li>On Sunday morning Mary Magdalene, Mary (James' mother), and Salome went to anoint Jesus' body. They found the stone had been rolled away from the entrance.</li><li>A young man was standing there who said Jesus was raised from the dead.</li><li>They fled from the tomb trembling and astonished.</li></ul>	Matthew's Gospel agrees there was one angel, but John and Luke report two. Matthew, Luke, and John detail the women going to tell the disciples. Only in Luke and John does a disciple go to the tomb.

The purpose of Jesus' mortal life

- The institution of the Eucharist at the Last Supper allowed a continued physical relationship with Jesus.
- The prayers in Gethsemane demonstrated Jesus' human fear and the value of prayer and a close relationship with God.
- The betrayal shows Jesus' acceptance of the persecution that was to come for Christians – he became a model of behaviour.
- Jesus' endurance of suffering during the Passion and crucifixion brought redemption for the world.
- The resurrection demonstrated the physical nature of resurrection through being a follower of Christ.

God incarnate, in human form, allowed a close relationship with humanity. It restored the relationship damaged through the Fall of Adam and Eve. It demonstrated the promise of eternal life through Jesus.

The significance of the events for Christians today

- Jesus' death and resurrection are the central events of Christianity – not his birth. These events revealed:
  - Jesus was Messiah
  - what Jesus had said was true
  - Jesus' path was the right path to follow.
- Christians believe they will be saved from sin by the grace of God if they accept the offer of salvation. Commitment is shown by following Jesus' example.

Important symbols from the last days of Jesus' life

	**Bread and wine** • Core part of communion and Catholic Eucharist • Act of thanksgiving and communion
	**The cross** • Core symbol of Christianity • Place where salvation was achieved
	**Reality of Jesus' death** • God was made flesh, bringing God and man closer
	Empty tomb • Death is not the end
	**Core message of Jesus was love** • Acts of sacrifice are demonstration of Christian love

> **TIP**
> Remember to signpost to the examiner with two different, short paragraphs that begin with 'Firstly... Secondly...' (or similar).

 APPLY

AO1 Try this one on your own!

   c. Explain **two** ways the last days of Jesus' life are still important for Christians today. In your answer you must refer to a source of wisdom and authority. (5)

AO2 Consider carefully how someone might argue against the following. Write three different developed points disagreeing with it.

   d. 'The crucifixion of Jesus was the most important event of his last days.'
Evaluate this statement considering arguments for and against. In your response you should:
- refer to Mark's Gospel
- reach a justified conclusion. (15)

 REVIEW

Answers: Mark your answers using p.203 and note areas for improvement.
AO1: This question is testing your ability to answer an 'explain' question. For help with this skill, see p.12.
AO2: This question is testing your ability to write a well-argued paragraph. For help with this skill, see p.12.

Exam Practice

Test the 3 mark question (a)

1 Outline **three** events of Jesus' trial before the High Priest in St Mark's Gospel. **(3 marks)**

Jesus was tried before the Sanhedrin. (1)

Jesus referred to himself as the Son of Man. (1)

The High Priest accused him of blasphemy. (1)

2 Outline **three** events of the transfiguration in St Mark's Gospel. **(3 marks)**

Peter, James, and John were taken up a high mountain. (1)

_____

_____

> **TIP**
> Remember to make three clearly separate points.

3 Outline **three** things Jesus' baptism revealed to Christians. **(3 marks)**

_____

_____

_____

Test the 4 mark question (b)

1 Explain **two** meanings of the title the Son of Man. **(4 marks)**

● **Explain one meaning.**	*Firstly, the Son of Man was used by the prophet Ezekiel to refer to the ordinariness of humans before God.*
● Develop your explanation with more detail/an example/reference to a religious teaching or quotation.	*This clearly indicates Jesus' nature as a human being, while also reducing the risk of his arrest by the Romans.*
● **Explain a second meaning.**	*Secondly, a very different idea is presented in the Book of Daniel – a supernatural figure with cosmic authority.*
● Develop your explanation with more detail/an example/reference to a religious teaching or quotation.	*This is more like the image of the Messiah the Jews expected, a warrior king.*

2 Explain **two** reasons why the healing of the paralysed man caused conflict. **(4 marks)**

● **Explain one reason.**	
● Develop your explanation with more detail/an example/reference to a religious teaching or quotation.	
● **Explain a second reason.**	
● Develop your explanation with more detail/an example/reference to a religious teaching or quotation.	

3 Explain **two** reasons why the Messianic secret is significant for Christians. **(4 marks)**

> **TIP**
> You need to fully understand the concept of the Messiah (11.1) to understand the secret.

Exam Practice

Test the 5 mark question (c)

1 Explain **two** reasons why the nature miracles in St Mark's Gospel have meaning for Christians today. In your answer you must refer to a source of wisdom and authority.

(5 marks)

● **Explain one reason.**	*Firstly, they give a reason for Christians to proclaim Jesus as God.*
● Develop your explanation with more detail/an example.	*This God is clearly creator, with power over nature, and this is also true of Jesus.*
● **Either:** Add a reference to a source of wisdom and authority here.	*For example, he walks on water to his disciples (Mark 6:45–52).*
● **Explain a second reason.**	*Secondly, Christians understand the stories metaphorically, and keep faith during difficult times.*
● Develop your explanation with more detail/an example.	*An example of this is when Jesus calms the storm by saying 'Peace! Be still!' (Mark 4:39).*
● **Or:** Add a reference to a source of wisdom and authority here.	

TIP
Here the student does well to include a clear, precise and specific reference to a source of wisdom and authority.

2 Explain **two** events in St Mark's Gospel in which Jesus engaged in conflict. In your answer you must refer to a source of wisdom and authority.

(5 marks)

● **Explain one event.**	
● Develop your explanation with more detail/an example.	
● **Either:** Add a reference to a source of wisdom and authority here.	
● **Explain a second event.**	
● Develop your explanation with more detail/an example.	
● **Or:** Add a reference to a source of wisdom and authority here.	

TIP
You must focus on the Calming of the Storm miracle. Be precise! However, don't just retell the story.

3 Explain **two** ways the Calming of the Storm proves Jesus is God. In your answer you must refer to a source of wisdom and authority.

(5 marks)

Exam Practice

Test the 15 mark question (d)

1 'Jesus was not the Messiah people were waiting for.'
Evaluate this statement, considering arguments for and against.
In your response you should:
- refer to St Mark's Gospel
- reach a justified conclusion.

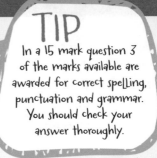

TIP
In a 15 mark question 3 of the marks available are awarded for correct spelling, punctuation and grammar. You should check your answer thoroughly.

(15 marks)

ARGUMENTS IN SUPPORT OF THE STATEMENT • **Explain why some people would agree with the statement.** • Develop your explanation with more detail and examples. • Refer to religious teaching. Use a quote or paraphrase of a religious authority. • **Evaluate the arguments.** Is this a good argument? Explain why you think this. Use words such as convincing/strong/robust/weak/unpersuasive/unsuccessful within your reasoning.	*Some Christians accept that the people were waiting for someone to save them from the Romans. They knew that he would be the one to govern the people of Israel but they did not understand that his kingship was not of this world.* *Some would argue that Jesus did not fulfil the messianic Old Testament prophecies of kingship, and that true salvation needs to include political freedom.* *Jesus did not use the title Messiah about himself before his trial, which could suggest that Christians should view him solely as a moral teacher.*
ARGUMENTS SUPPORTING A DIFFERENT VIEW • **Explain why some people would disagree with the statement.** • Develop your explanation with more detail and examples. • Refer to religious teaching. Use a quote or paraphrase of a religious authority. • **Evaluate the arguments.** Is this a good argument? Explain why you think this. Use words such as convincing/strong/robust/weak/unpersuasive/unsuccessful within your reasoning.	*Some Christians accept that many Jewish people of the time recognised Jesus as the Messiah. Jesus fulfilled the messianic Old Testament prophecies of the suffering servant through his life, miracles, and death, which many consider characteristic of the true Messiah. St Mark's Gospel says the people greeted Jesus with the words 'Blessed is the kingdom of our father David that is coming', indicating that many contemporaries recognised Jesus' life and teaching as messianic.* *Jesus healed people – a lot of Jews in this period would have recognised that the Old Testament scriptures talk about healing in the end of days and would have thought that that was a sign that the end of days was on its way. Therefore, this is a strong reason.*
CONCLUSION • **Give a justified conclusion.** • Include your own reasoning. • Use words such as convincing/strong/robust/weak/unpersuasive/unsuccessful to weigh up the different arguments for and against. • Do not just repeat arguments you have already used without explaining how they apply to your reasoned opinion/conclusion.	*In conclusion, it was clear Jesus was a very different type of Messiah to the one people were waiting for. However, once people realised who he was, they often followed him. This is evident by the rapid growth of early Christianity.*

TIP
This is a good answer as the student clearly knows about Jesus as Messiah, as well as the Old Testament prophecy and expectations. This is vital for success in this question.

Exam Practice

2   'The Resurrection is the most significant moment in the last days of Jesus' life.' Evaluate this statement considering arguments for and against. In your response you should:

- refer to St Mark's Gospel
- reach a justified conclusion.

                                                                           (15 marks)

ARGUMENTS IN SUPPORT OF THE STATEMENT	*Some Christians/people would agree with this statement because...*
• **Explain why some people would agree with the statement.** • Develop your explanation with more detail and examples. • Refer to religious teaching. Use a quote or paraphrase of a religious authority. • **Evaluate the arguments.** Is this a good argument? Explain why you think this. Use words such as convincing/strong/robust/weak/unpersuasive/unsuccessful within your reasoning.	
ARGUMENTS SUPPORTING A DIFFERENT VIEW • **Explain why some people would disagree with the statement.** • Develop your explanation with more detail and examples. • Refer to religious teaching. Use a quote or paraphrase of a religious authority. • **Evaluate the arguments.** Is this a good argument? Explain why you think this. Use words such as convincing/strong/robust/weak/unpersuasive/unsuccessful within your reasoning.	*On the other hand, some Christians/people would hold a different point of view...*
CONCLUSION • **Give a justified conclusion.** • Include your own reasoning. • Use words such as convincing/strong/robust/weak/unpersuasive/unsuccessful to weigh up the different arguments for and against. • Do not just repeat arguments you have already used without explaining how they apply to your reasoned opinion/conclusion.	*Having considered both sides of the argument, I would say that...* **TIP** In this question you could argue that another event is the most significant, such as Jesus' death. Alternatively, you could argue that one event alone can't be singled out as the most significant as many are dependent on others.

3   'A good leader should not engage in conflict.' Evaluate this statement, considering arguments for and against. In your response you should:

- refer to St Mark's Gospel
- reach a justified conclusion.

                                                                           (15 marks)

 **REVIEW**

- Check your answers to these exam questions on p.203, correct your answers with annotations, and note down any general areas for improvement.
- If you don't feel secure in the content of this chapter, you could reread the Recap sections.
- If you don't feel secure in your exam technique, you could revisit the exam support section on pp.7–14.

RECAP

Essential information

- The nature of discipleship (following the teaching and example of Jesus) is to answer Jesus' call without hesitation.
- Jesus chose a wide variety of people to be disciples, not always people who would seem to be naturally good.
- Being a disciple involves sacrifice and hardship.

The call

Mark 1:14–20	Mark 2:13–17

• After John the Baptist is imprisoned, Jesus starts to gather his disciples.
• Galilee was full of ordinary working people.
• He first called two fishermen, Simon and his brother Andrew:
 	
   ❝Follow me and I will make you become fishers of men.❞ *(Mark 1:17)*
 	
• Two more brothers, James and John, also fishermen, answered without hesitation too.
Key theme: disciples did not always grasp what was happening, but were unhesitating in response, leaving livelihoods and families behind.
	• Jesus called on a tax collector named Levi to follow him.
	• Tax collectors were unpopular, as they collaborated with the Romans, and mixed with gentiles, making them unclean in Jewish law.
	• Religious leaders were appalled when they saw Jesus eating with him. Jesus replied:
	
	   ❝Those who are well have no need of a physician, but those who are sick; I came not to call the righteous, but sinners.❞ *(Mark 2:17)*
	
	Key theme: Jesus preached an inclusive message; the Kingdom of God was open to all.

Relevance today

- Christians today can learn from the disciples' unhesitating response.
- They may also need to give up things to follow Jesus.
- Those who are rejected can find a place with Jesus, and be transformed.
- Everyone is called, however ordinary, and no one will be discriminated against.

TIP

It is important that you consider the ongoing impact that these stories and events had. How do they relate to Christians today, despite being set 2000 years ago?

Sending out of the Twelve
(Mark 6:7–13)

- Jesus sent the **twelve disciples** in pairs to announce that the Kingdom of God had arrived.
- They were entrusted to call people to repent, heal the sick, and to cast out demons *(Mark 6:7)*.

This would have encouraged people to put donations in it.

They needed to show their trust and faith in God, not wealth.

They should have a simple lifestyle, committed to enduring physical hardship for the Gospel.

> **❝** He charged them to take nothing for their journey except a staff; no bread, **no bag, no money in their belts**; but to **wear sandals and not put on two tunics**. And he said to them, '**Where you enter a house, stay there until you leave the place**. And if any place will not receive you and they refuse to hear you, when you leave, **shake off the dust that is on your feet for a testimony against them**.' **❞** (*Mark 6:8–10*)

Disciples should accept hospitality.

Washing the dirt of any place that didn't welcome disciples or their message off their feet was a way of saying that rejecting Jesus and his message would bring judgment.

The meaning of this for different Christians today

- Jesus was sharing the responsibility and authority of announcing the Kingdom of God, and Christians today can share in the authority to heal and confront evil.
- The work of the Church today is to keep communicating that message:

The Catholic Church believes it should tell others of the good news of the Gospel and how it can transform lives.

Evangelical Christians also believe that public witness to faith is important in sharing the message of Jesus.

Other Christians may prefer to be disciples in their everyday lives by serving others (see 12.5).

TIP

You should draw on your wider understanding of Catholic Christianity to plan your points; see 2.8 for more about evangelism in the Catholic Church.

 APPLY

AO1 This student answer has one developed point. Can you write a second one, including a source of wisdom and authority?

c. Explain **two** reasons Jesus sent out the twelve disciples. In your answer you must refer to a source of wisdom and authority. (5)

Firstly, he wanted them to spread the Gospel message. This was the good news of the Kingdom of God that he announced.

AO2 Create a table with arguments for and against this statement.

'Christians today should continue the work of the disciples sent out by Jesus.'

 **REVIEW**

Answers: Mark your answers using p.203 and note areas for improvement.
AO1: This question is testing your ability to answer an 'explain' question. For help with this skill, see p.12.
AO2: This question is testing your ability to identify arguments for and against a statement. For help with this skill, see p.12.

Essential information

- **Parables** are short stories used by Jesus to explain the idea of the Kingdom of God.
- Jesus told the Parable of the Tenants to religious leaders in Jerusalem, and the Parable of the Sower to his followers.
- Mark's Gospel says the parables are designed to confuse as well as explain, in order to reveal the truly faithful (*Mark 4:10–13*).

Two parables

The Parable of the Tenants (*Mark 12:1–12*)

- A man rents his vineyard to tenants.
- He sends servants to collect a share of the harvest, but they are all attacked or murdered by the tenants.
- Finally the man's son is sent and killed.
- Jesus asked:

> 66 What will the owner of the vineyard do? He will come and destroy the tenants, and give the vineyard to others. 99 (*Mark 12:9*)

Meaning
The servants represented the prophets.
The owner represented God.
The son was Jesus.
The tenants were the religious leaders of Israel.

- In this parable, Jesus was warning that the religious leaders should submit to God.
- Jesus is saying that the kingdom that is offered to and rejected by Israel will be taken from them and offered to the gentiles.

- Mark makes it clear the leaders understood the message (*Mark 12:12*).

The cost of discipleship
- Jesus was dangerous to associate with because he spoke out against the religious leaders and challenged their authority.
- It was a risk to follow him.
- For Christians today this means they should accept his message and stand up for their belief even when persecuted.

The Parable of the Sower (*Mark 4:1–20*)

- A man sows seed in a field.
- As he scatters it, it falls in different places and grows with differing amounts of success:

1.
> 66 some seed fell along the path, and the birds came and devoured it 99 (*Mark 4:4*)

3.
> 66 Other seed fell among thorns and the thorns grew up and choked it 99 (*Mark 4:7*)

2.
> 66 Other seed fell on rocky ground [...] since it had no root it withered away 99 (*Mark 4:5–6*)

4.
> 66 other seeds fell into good soil and brought forth grain 99 (*Mark 4:8*)

Meaning
The seed represents God's message, and each area represents a different response to the message:
1. Path/birds: people who hear but do not listen in their hearts
2. Rocky ground: people who listen and respond at first, but their response has no depth
3. Thorns: people who listen and respond at first, but worldly distractions choke their faith
4. Good soil: people who hear and respond to the Gospel.

The Kingdom of God
- Agriculture references would have appealed to the audience of the time.
- However, this parable was not easy to understand, as Jesus had to explain it – he refers to them being given 'the secret of the kingdom of God' (*Mark 4:11*).
- This began to divide people – those who understood the message and those who didn't.
- Jesus is the sower, the seed is offered to everyone, but its conditions determine growth.

The meaning of the parables and the Kingdom of God for Christians today

The Kingdom of God

> **Realised:** The idea that Jesus was bringing about the Kingdom of God in the present for his followers.

> **In the future:** The idea that Jesus was building the Kingdom of God for a future point; the Final Judgement.

Different Christians interpret parables like these to justify both viewpoints about the Kingdom of God.

- Some scholars argue that the Kingdom of God is not a place – it is life lived with God's love. That starts now, but will be completed in an age to come.
- Parables show there are difficulties to face, but if the message of God is taken seriously, it will transform lives, and enable people to begin living as part of the Kingdom of God.

TIP

Parables are some of the most memorable of Jesus' teachings. If you learn them, they should be useful sources of wisdom and authority to use when discussing other topics.

TIP

This kind of question allows for a variety of answers. You could write about what happens, the audience, the language, the meaning and purpose, etc.

 APPLY

AO1 Try this one on your own!

a. Outline **three** features of the Parable of the Tenants. (3)

AO2 Complete this table with some more arguments for and against the statement.

d. 'The Kingdom of God is a future event.'
Evaluate this statement considering arguments for and against. In your response you should:
- refer to St Mark's Gospel
- reach a justified conclusion. (12)

For	Against
• • It is clearly not present now – there is much pain and suffering, even for Christians. Therefore it must be a time to come. •	• People were, and still are, following the word of God and therefore are living as part of the Kingdom of God. • • The struggles for the kingdom began from the time of Jesus' ministry, likewise the rewards of the kingdom must have, too.

 REVIEW

Answers: Mark your answers using p.203 and note areas for improvement.
AO1: This question is testing your ability to answer 'outline' questions. For help with this skill, see p.12.
AO2: This question is testing your ability to identify arguments for and against a statement. For help with this skill, see p.12.

 **RECAP**

Essential information

- In *Mark 10*, Jesus challenged a rich man to think about the power of money.
- Jesus told his disciples that trusting in riches will prevent their entering the Kingdom of God.
- Christians believe they should not presume they are righteous, but concentrate on doing good and following Jesus.

The story of the rich man (*Mark 10:17–31*)

The story	The meaning
• A rich man asks Jesus: ❝Good Teacher, what must I do to inherit eternal life?❞ (*Mark 10:17*) • Jesus listed the commandments, which the man said he had lived by. • Jesus then added: ❝Go, sell what you have, and give to the poor, and you will have treasure in heaven; and come, follow me.❞ (*Mark 10:21*)  • The man left feeling sad, as he was very rich.	• Jesus has to explain this to his disciples as they were confused by it (*Mark 10:23–26*). • They were amazed that it will be hard for rich people to enter the Kingdom of God. Most people were poor, and aspired to be rich – wealth was also seen as a sign of God's favour. • They thought, if the rich can't get in, what chance for the poor? • Jesus said: ❝With men it [salvation] is impossible, but not with God; for all things are possible with God.❞ (*Mark 10:27*)  **TIP** Remember that Jesus is not teaching that is necessarily bad to be wealthy. Be careful how your phrase your answers when discussing this story. • The rich young man was clearly righteous and just, but this was not enough. There was tension between Jewish law and the Gospel. • Jesus had to reassure the disciples their sacrifice would be recognised (*Mark 10:28*) – they would receive a 'hundredfold' what they had given up (*Mark 10:29–30*).

❝Many that are first will be last, and the last first❞ (*Mark 10:31*)

This is a teaching against complacency.	Peter and his disciples were poor and lowly (last) in this world, but they were far closer to Jesus and the Kingdom of God than any religious leaders or those in high society (first).	In the Kingdom of God there would be a reversal of positions.

The meaning of this story for Christians today

- Some scholars point out Jesus was talking to a specific individual, not a crowd – it was *this* man's barrier.
- Others (like Mother Teresa) believe they must give up comforts in order to help the poor.
- Disciples did make great sacrifice to follow Jesus, and this would be necessary to join Jesus in the Kingdom of God – the same would be true of Christians today, but the sacrifice may be different.
- Christians believe they should not assume they are righteous as the rich man did, but instead focus on doing good through actions.
- Many suggest wealth on its own is not a problem, provided that it is used for good.

The world is still divided into rich and poor

 APPLY

AO1 The two key ideas here are sacrifice, and making assumptions about righteousness. Can you develop this into a full mark answer?

   b. Explain **two** things that Jesus' command to the rich man teaches Christians today. (4)

AO2 Read the points in the table below. What would your justified conclusion be?

'The story of the rich man means that Christians today should give all their money to the poor.'

> **TIP**
> This has been a point of discussion for many Christians. However, few would argue they should give up everything and instead lead simpler lives.

For	Against
• Jesus told the rich man to 'sell what you have, and give to the poor' (*Mark 10:21*). • He also said: 'It is easier for a camel to go through the eye of a needle than for a rich man to enter the kingdom of God' (*Mark 10:25*). • The wealth of the religious authorities was seen as a sign of God's favour, but Jesus challenged this.	• The instruction was given to a specific individual, not a large crowd. As such, perhaps wealth was an issue for this man, but not for everyone. • It is possible to have a balance by being charitable while also having a comfortable life. • It is impossible to live in the way the disciples did, relying on the hospitality of strangers.

 REVIEW

Answers: Mark your answers using p.204 and note areas for improvement.
AO1: This question is testing your ability to answer an 'explain' question. For help with this skill, see p.12.
AO2: This question is testing your ability to write a justified conclusion. For help with this skill, see p.12.

 **RECAP**

Essential information

- This story demonstrates that Jesus has the authority to cast out evil spirits.
- He granted this authority to the disciples but they could not use it without faith.
- Jesus shows that faith is one of the necessary qualities to bring about miracles.

The spirit cast out of the boy
(*Mark 9:14–29*)

- This happened just after the transfiguration (see 11.6).
- A crowd mobbed Jesus and a man said:

> 66 Teacher, I brought my son to you, for he has a dumb spirit [...] I asked your disciples to cast it out, and they were not able. 99 (*Mark 9:17–18*)

- Jesus replied:

> 66 O faithless generation, how long am I to be with you? How long am I to bear with you? Bring him to me. 99 (*Mark 9:19*)

- When the father confessed doubt, Jesus said:

> 66 All things are possible to him who believes. 99 (*Mark 9:23*)

The father then cries out:

> 66 I believe; help my unbelief!. 99 (*Mark 9:24*)

- Jesus casts the spirit out of the boy.

Problem of discipleship

- The disciples asked Jesus why they were not able to perform this miracle.
- Jesus replied that it could only be driven out by 'prayer and fasting' (*Mark 9:29*), implying they were not faithful enough.
- When the disciples were sent out, they had the authority to cast out spirits, but here their faith was not strong enough.
- Mark's Gospel frequently shows the disciples as weak in faith, or unable to grasp the complete truth.

The meaning of this story for Christians today

- The lack of faith and prayer the disciples and others showed was rebuked by Jesus.
- He taught that faith, fasting, and prayer are necessary to experience miracles.
- Christians gain hope today from the belief that there is no force so powerful or evil that Jesus cannot defeat it.
- Some Christians use the line 'Lord, I believe; help my unbelief' (*Mark 9:24*) as a prayer to help them to grow in faith.

> **TIP**
> Don't forget to refer to a source of wisdom and authority. There are some useful lines in this story that are easy to memorise; for example:
> - 'ALL things are possible to him who believes.'
> - 'This kind cannot be driven out by anything but prayer and fasting.'

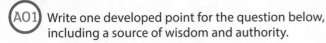 **APPLY**

(AO1) Write one developed point for the question below, including a source of wisdom and authority.

  c. Explain **two** key teachings from the story of the spirit cast out of the boy. In your answer you must refer to a source of wisdom and authority. (5)

(AO2) Read the arguments against the statement in the table, then write down some arguments for, and a conclusion.

  d. 'Christians today can learn much from the story of Jesus casting the spirit out of the boy.' Evaluate this statement considering arguments for and against. In your response you should:
  - refer to St Mark's Gospel
  - reach a justified conclusion. (12)

For	Against
	• Few people are considered to be possessed by evil spirits today, therefore this story is less relevant today.
	• Some see the story as a criticism of the disciples, who had been given a specific task by Jesus, but not a criticism of ordinary people.
	• Christians may relate better to other healing stories, which they feel are more connected to their everyday lives.

 **REVIEW**

Answers: Mark your answers using p.204 and note areas for improvement.
AO1: This question is testing your ability to answer an 'explain' question. For help with this skill, see p.12.
AO2: This question is testing your ability to answer a (d) question. For help with this skill, see p.12.

 **RECAP**

Essential information

- Jesus taught his followers that discipleship involves sacrifice.
- James and John asked for a reward when the Kingdom of God came, but Jesus said they must be willing to endure the same hardships as him.
- *Mark 10:41–45* shows that part of sacrifice is service to others.

The command to serve

The call to serve Jesus came with costs:

- Peter and Andrew (fishermen) and Levi (tax collector) gave up their jobs.
- Disciples left family and friends.
- Followers had to give up money and possessions (see 12.3).
- Jesus promised rewards, but told followers they would be persecuted and suffer.

The price of service

66 Grant us to sit, one at your right hand and one at your left, in your glory. 99 (*Mark 10:37*)

- James and John wanted a reward when the Kingdom of God came.
- They thought the Kingdom of God would be earthly, not spiritual.
- They were ambitious, seduced by power.
- They hadn't grasped the idea of Jesus as a servant rather than a leader. Jewish ideas of messiahship still influenced them (see 11.1).
- Jesus warned them they didn't know what they were asking for, and asked if they would be able to deal with the suffering that was to come. They said they were (*Mark 10:38–39*). This foretold their suffering: James was the first to be martyred (*Acts 12:2*) and John was exiled.
- Jesus pointed out God alone has the authority to choose who rules in his kingdom (*Mark 10:40*).

Serving, not being served

- The other disciples were angry at James and John. Jesus realised and said:

> 66 whoever would be first among you must be slave of all. For the Son of man also came not to be served but to serve. 99 (*Mark 10:44–45*)

- The Son of Man was characterised by selflessness and service, and so should his disciples be.

The meaning of this discipleship for Christians today

- Christians today believe everyone can serve.
- Christians should give service to the poor or oppressed.
- This may also involve giving money or possessions to help others.
- Serving others shows love to God.

> **TIP**
> Service is a key feature of Catholic Social Teaching (see 2.7).

 APPLY

AO1 Can you write two more points to complete the following answer?

  a. Outline **three** of Jesus' teachings on service. (3)

  Service would be costly in terms of jobs and relationships.

AO2 Try answering this question on your own.

  d. 'For Christians today, service to others must be a priority in their lives.' Evaluate this statement considering arguments for and against. In your response you should:
  - refer to St Mark's Gospel
  - reach a justified conclusion. (12)

 REVIEW

Answers: Mark your answers using p.204 and note areas for improvement.
AO1: This question is testing your ability to answer 'outline' questions. For help with this skill, see p.12.
AO2: This question is testing your ability to answer a (d) question. For help with this skill, see p.12.

 **RECAP**

Essential information

- Mark's Gospel shows Peter failed Jesus by denying him.
- The guilt that Peter feels at this failure can be understood by Christians today, who should repent and seek forgiveness for their own sins.
- Non-religious groups often see discipleship as unnecessary but Christians would say it is an active, positive path towards being a better person.

Peter's denial

The denial	Challenges and forgiveness
• Jesus foretold Peter's denial (*Mark 14:30*). • Peter was in the courtyard outside where Jesus was on trial. • 1st denial: a serving girl said he was with Jesus, but Peter denied it (*Mark 14:67–68*). • 2nd denial: the girl told others, but again he denied it (*Mark 14:70*).	It was not easy to be a disciple. Peter's denial highlights the faults of human beings: • **Pride:** he assures Jesus he will not betray him (*Mark 14:29*). • **Inattention:** he cannot stay awake in Gethsemane (*Mark 14:38*). • **Fear:** when he betrays Jesus by denying him. There was forgiveness for Peter: • Peter is not excluded from news about the resurrection (*Mark 16:10*). • Commentators suggest Peter was one of the sources of Mark's Gospel – people are often more critical of themselves than others are. • It is not recorded how Peter was forgiven, but clearly he was redeemed as he led the early Church.

I do not know this man

- 3rd denial: bystanders continued to quiz him, but Peter said:

> **"**I do not know this man of whom you speak.**"**
> (*Mark 14:71*)

- A cock crowed for a second time, and Peter remembered Jesus had predicted this (*Mark 14:72*). He broke down and wept.

The meaning of Peter's denial for Christians today

- This may have offered hope to early persecuted Christians.

- Peter failed Jesus badly – that someone who failed so badly could still lead the Church gives great hope to Christians today.

- Commentators believe Peter told the authors this story to serve as an example.

Peter's denial

- Peter shows remorse, and Christians believe they too can repent and be forgiven. This is why Catholics go to confession.

- This experience helped Peter to become the leader of the Church – he was released to serve.

Non-religious attitudes to discipleship

- Non-religious people, such as atheists and Humanists, may look to their own conscience for guidance on how to be the best person they can (see 3.8).
- Christians do not see discipleship as passive submission to an individual, but a positive path to being a better Christian. They believe Jesus is the supreme example to follow, because as the Son of God and the Son of Man he shows Christians how to be truly human.

TIP

Atheism and Humanism are both non-religious views but atheism rejects God more firmly. The atheist by definition excludes God from any explanation of a miracle, whilst a humanist emphasises the importance of human reason for working out the evidence.

After Jesus' ascension, Peter became a dynamic leader

TIP

There are different ways to ensure a developed point, such as the Point, Evidence, Explanation (PEE) method, or ensuing you use connectives such as 'therefore', 'because', 'as a result'.

 APPLY

 AO1 Can you develop these two basic points, and add a reference to a source of wisdom and authority?

- refer to St Mark's Gospel
- refer to non-religious points of view
- reach a justified conclusion. (12)

   c. Explain **two** challenges that Peter's denial presents. In your answer you must refer to a source of wisdom and authority. (5)

> *Firstly, Peter shows pride, a fault in many human beings.*
> *Secondly, he shows fear and weakness by denying Jesus.*

 AO2 Can you complete the following planning table for this exam question?

   d. 'Religious observance such as discipleship is necessary to live a good life.' Evaluate this statement, considering arguments for and against. In your response you should:

For	Against
•	• Non-religious people may see discipleship as passive submission.
•	• Non-religious people may understand that letting your friends down, like Peter did, is damaging to a relationship, but not more so because it was Jesus.
•	• Religious observances include all kinds of behaviour and activities would be seen as pointless if you didn't believe in God; prayer, worship, festivals, etc.

 **REVIEW**

Answers: Mark your answers using p.204 and note areas for improvement.
AO1: This question is testing your ability to answer an 'explain' question. For help with this skill, see p.12.
AO2: This question is testing your ability to answer a (d) question. For help with this skill, see p.12.

Essential information
- Mark's Gospel shows women were important followers of Jesus.
- Women demonstrated faith, love, and strength through their connection with Jesus.
- Women were the first witnesses to news of the resurrection of Jesus and communicated that news to the disciples.

The Greek woman (*Mark 7:25–30*)

A Greek gentile woman approached Jesus and asked him to help her possessed daughter. Jesus said:

> 66 Let the children first be fed, for it is not right to take the children's bread and throw it to the dogs 99 (*Mark 7:27*).

- By children, Jesus means the Jews; the dogs represent the gentiles; and the bread his message and salvation.
- Scholars debate Jesus' intended meaning: is he saying he needs to help the Jews first, or is he simply testing her faith?
- Her response demonstrated faith:

> 66 Yes, Lord; yet even the dogs under the table eat the children's crumbs. 99 (*Mark 7:28*)

She continues the analogy, without being offended, suggesting she could still share in the faith.
- Jesus is impressed by her faith, and heals her daughter.

The anointing at Bethany (*Mark 14:3–9*)

- At Simon's house a woman poured ointment over Jesus' head:

> 66 an alabaster jar of ointment of pure nard, very costly 99 (*Mark 14:3*)

- Some people got angry at the waste – the money used to buy the ointment could have gone to the poor.

- Jesus said they will always have the poor, but they would not always have him. He added:

> 66 she has anointed my body beforehand for burying. 99 (*Mark 14:8*)

- She is in fact anointing Jesus as Messiah, an act of love and prophetic compassion.
- Jesus said she will be remembered for her kindness (*Mark 14:9*).

Witnesses to the cross and the resurrection

DIVISERVNT MILITES VESTIMĒTA EIVS SORTEM MICTENTES. M. XXVI. C.
RESVREXI ET ADHVC TECVM SVM. PS. CXXXVIII.

IHESVM QVERITIS NAZZARENVM SVRREXIT NON E HIC. M. VI.

Women at the resurrection of Jesus

The cross	The resurrection
• Mary Magdalene, Mary mother of James, Salome, and many other women witnessed Jesus' death on the cross. • Both Marys accompanied the body to the tomb. • Only one man took part in the burial – Joseph of Arimathea.	• The women returned to the tomb on Sunday to anoint Jesus. • They met a 66 young man […] in a white robe 99 (*Mark 16:5*) and received instruction from him: 66 He has risen. 99 (*Mark 16:6*) • They were authorised to share the good news themselves.

The significance for Christians today

These stories show the faith, love, and strength of women.

> The Greek woman is a person who shows great faith and trust in God. This is an example to Christians today.

> The anointing at Bethany shows a woman who displays an act of great love and compassion for Jesus, which Christians should try to do in worship.

> The women at the cross and resurrection show strength and devotion in a moment of great challenge. Christians today should try to be as courageous.

- Some Christians use these examples as justification for women in roles of ministry in the Church, as women clearly played an important role during the life of Jesus.

- However other Christians, for example, Catholics, see women as having an important and equal role in ministry, but not in the ordained priesthood.

> **TIP**
> Remember that women were treated as second-class citizens at the time of Jesus. Knowing this is vital to understanding how important these interactions are.

> **TIP**
> The two key interactions are the woman at Bethany and the Greek woman – how does Jesus react to them?

APPLY

AO1 Can you develop these two basic points?

b. Explain **two** ways in which Jesus shows compassion towards women in Mark's Gospel. (4)

> The first way is to the Greek woman who asks for her daughter to be healed...
>
> The second way is to the woman who anoints him at Bethany...

AO2 Plan an answer in response to this question.

d. 'Jesus ensured women had a key part to play in his ministry.' Evaluate this statement considering arguments for and against. In your response you should:
- refer to St Mark's Gospel
- reach a justified conclusion. (12)

For	Against
Conclusion:	

REVIEW

Answers: Mark your answers using p.204 and note areas for improvement.
AO1: This question is testing your ability to answer an 'explain' question. For help with this skill, see p.12.
AO2: This question is testing your ability to plan a response. For help with this skill, see p.12.

 **RECAP**

Essential information

- Dietrich Bonhoeffer demonstrated that there was a cost to being a disciple.
- Mother Teresa reflected the call to 'deny self' to live out a life for others.
  She also showed that faith was not always easy.
- The Bible teaches that disciples of Jesus should have a special concern for the poor.
- It remains a challenge to follow Jesus in a world where people follow other religions,
  or no religion at all.
- There is sometimes hostility to faith, often related to the extremism of some groups.

Dietrich Bonhoeffer (1906–45)

- He was a Lutheran Christian writer who spoke out against Adolf Hitler and the Nazi regime.
- He refused to take an oath to support Hitler and refused to put Hitler's book, *Mein Kampf*, next to the Bible in his church.
- In his book *The Cost of Discipleship* he said: 'When Christ calls a man, he bids him come and die.'
- Bonhoeffer was part of the German resistance and was imprisoned for helping Jews.
- He was linked to a plot to kill Hitler and was executed as a result.

Mother Teresa (1910–97)

- She was an Albanian nun who cared for the poor and oppressed in India.
- In 1946, she started a charity called the Missionaries of Charity.
- The sisters would go out into the street to feed and care for the poor and dying.
- She said they should treat every person as if they were Jesus himself.
- Mother Teresa struggled with her beliefs, but never doubted God.
- She showed total devotion to God, and a life of positive action.

> **TIP**
> If you are able to give more than one example of a modern disciple in *d* questions, it may help you to produce a better answer.

> ❝I was to give up all and follow Jesus into the slums❞
> (Mother Teresa, *A Simple Path*)

Being a disciple today

- Mark's Gospel calls for self-sacrifice in the name of discipleship:

> 66 Let him deny himself and take up his cross and follow me. 99 *(Mark 8:34)*

- There are still many challenges for Christians today:

| living a simple lifestyle | not obsessing over money and possessions | the Christian message of love and forgiveness is rejected by a world where hatred and revenge are glorified in entertainment. |

- Christians continue to be persecuted in some countries including North Korea, Iraq, and Afghanistan.
- Standing up for the oppressed remains important in all areas of the world.
- Modern Christians should believe they can overcome any obstacle.

Christians in Pakistan protest after suicide bombers killed 80 people attending Mass

Discipleship is clearly lived out in different ways by Christians. Some see it as the full focus of their lives; this may be reflected in their choice of profession and they may even become an ordained priest, for example.

However other Christians see it as the foundation of their attitudes, values and morals. This means treating people fairly, and acting justly in all that they do, but not necessarily devoting every aspect of their life to discipleship.

 APPLY

 AO1 Can you write two more points to complete this student's answer?

a. Outline **three** challenges Christian disciples face in the modern world. (3)

> *Some Christians are persecuted because of their beliefs.*

 AO2 Plan an answer in response to this question by filling in the table. Then, write a justified conclusion.

d. 'A good disciple should lay down their life for the poor and oppressed.' Evaluate this statement considering arguments for and against. In your response you should:
- refer to St Mark's Gospel
- reach a justified conclusion. (12)

For	Against

 **REVIEW** **Answers:** Mark your answers using p.204 and note areas for improvement.
AO1: This question is testing your ability to answer 'outline' questions. For help with this skill, see p.12.
AO2: This question is testing your ability to plan a response. For help with this skill, see p.12.

Test the 3 mark question (a)

1 Outline **three** beliefs about discipleship that are shown in the call of the first disciples. **(3 marks)**

Anyone can be called to follow Jesus as the first disciples were fishermen and a tax collector.

Disciples are 'fishers of men' spreading the good news.

The first disciples showed total commitment to Jesus by giving up their jobs and family.

2 Outline **three** ways Christians can be disciples today. **(3 marks)**

By following Jesus' teachings.

_____

_____

TIP

Remind yourself of the examples of modern-day disciples (12.8), such as Mother Teresa, to help you outline your ideas.

3 Outline **three** features of the story of the spirit cast out of the boy. **(3 marks)**

_____

_____

_____

Test the 4 mark question (b)

1 Explain **two** features of the calling of the twelve disciples. **(4 marks)**

● **Explain one feature.**	*Firstly, Jesus says he will make the disciples 'fishers of men'.*
● Develop your explanation with more detail/an example/reference to a religious teaching or quotation.	*This phrase is used because they were fishermen, but means they would be bringing people to the Kingdom of God instead.*
● **Explain a second feature.**	*Secondly, when calling Levi and people criticised him, Jesus said 'I came not to call the righteous, but sinners'.*
● Develop your explanation with more detail/an example/reference to a religious teaching or quotation.	*This was clear evidence he was coming to change people, to turn them to the Kingdom of God.*

2 Explain **two** messages included in the Parable of the Sower. **(4 marks)**

● **Explain one message.**	
● Develop your explanation with more detail/an example/reference to a religious teaching or quotation.	
● **Explain a second message.**	
● Develop your explanation with more detail/an example/reference to a religious teaching or quotation.	

3 Explain **two** reasons why Jesus told the Parable of the Tenants. **(4 marks)**

TIP

Remember: don't just retell the stories!

Exam Practice

Test the 5 mark question (c)

1. Explain **two** reasons why the teachings of Jesus about service are important today.
In your answer you must refer to a source of wisdom and authority.

(5 marks)

● **Explain one reason.**	The need for Christians to serve others is a central message of the Gospel.
● Develop your explanation with more detail/an example.	The teaching indicates that one of the costs of being a disciple today involves service to others; as such this can involve self-sacrifice,
● **Either:** Add a reference to a source of wisdom and authority here.	as shown in: 'Whoever would be great among you must be your servant, and whoever would be first among you must be slave of all' (Mark 10:43–44).
● **Explain a second reason.**	Another reason is that Jesus himself was a servant.
● Develop your explanation with more detail/an example.	He was not interested in wealth and status, he was selfless towards others, which is an approach that Christians today can participate in.
● **Or:** Add a reference to a source of wisdom and authority here.	

TIP

Here is the reference to a source of wisdom and authority. You only need to make one reference to gain the mark – you don't need evidence of a source of wisdom and authority to support both your points.

2. Explain **two** challenges for Christians in the story of the rich man. In your answer you must refer to a source of wisdom and authority.

(5 marks)

● **Explain one challenge.**	
● Develop your explanation with more detail/an example.	
● **Either:** Add a reference to a source of wisdom and authority here.	
● **Explain a second challenge.**	
● Develop your explanation with more detail/an example.	
● **Or:** Add a reference to a source of wisdom and authority here.	

3. Explain **two** of Jesus' teachings on service. In your answer you must refer to a source of wisdom and authority.

(5 marks)

Test the 12 mark question (d)

1. 'Parables were a good way of teaching about the Kingdom of God.' Evaluate this statement considering arguments for and against. In your response you should:
   - refer to St Mark's Gospel
   - reach a justified conclusion.

(12 marks)

ARGUMENTS IN SUPPORT OF THE STATEMENT ● **Explain why some people would agree with the statement.** ● Develop your explanation with more detail and examples. ● Refer to religious teaching. Use a quote or paraphrase of a religious authority. ● **Evaluate the arguments.** Is this a good argument? Explain why you think this. Use words such as convincing/strong/robust/weak/unpersuasive/unsuccessful within your reasoning.	Many people would agree with this statement as parables were a common method of teaching at the time of Jesus. His audience would have been familiar with this style, so it would have been a good way of communicating a difficult idea. Parables were linked to agricultural living, for example the Parable of the Tenants and the Parable of the Sower. This is also the kind of life that the Jews lived so this was a good way of communicating ideas to them. Christians today can appreciate the parables and still learn from them. It was clear they worked by the number of people who became Christians as a result of Jesus' teaching, which contained many parables. This is a strong argument in favour of the statement. If people did not understand, Jesus explained the stories, as with the Parable of the Sower.
ARGUMENTS SUPPORTING A DIFFERENT VIEW ● **Explain why some people would disagree with the statement.** ● Develop your explanation with more detail and examples. ● Refer to religious teaching. Use a quote or paraphrase of a religious authority. ● **Evaluate the arguments.** Is this a good argument? Explain why you think this. Use words such as convincing/strong/robust/weak/unpersuasive/unsuccessful within your reasoning.	However, other people might disagree about the effectiveness of parables, as, although Jesus wanted people to work out the message for themselves, it could be confusing. Jesus felt the religious leaders understood the Parable of the Tenants (Mark 12:12), but it is not clear if everyone did. Some of the parables required an explanation, such as the Parable of the Sower. This shows their complexity and potential ambiguity. Only some stayed behind to get the meaning from Jesus, while others may have been too confused and just left. It is unclear how many people didn't get the message about the Kingdom of God as a result of the use of parables. Some did, but many more could have done with more direct teaching.
CONCLUSION ● **Give a justified conclusion.** ● Include your own reasoning. ● Use words such as convincing/strong/robust/weak/unpersuasive/unsuccessful to weigh up the different arguments for and against. ● Do not just repeat arguments you have already used without explaining how they apply to your reasoned opinion/conclusion.	In conclusion, parables were commonplace, and deliberately memorable. Jesus was seen as a good teacher, or rabbi, and able to gauge his audience. He decided when extra explanation was needed, presumably understanding when his audience 'got it' themselves. Therefore, I believe they were a good way to teach about the Kingdom of God.

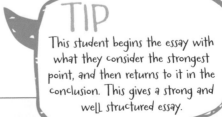

TIP
This student begins the essay with what they consider the strongest point, and then returns to it in the conclusion. This gives a strong and well structured essay.

2 'The woman at Bethany was right to anoint Jesus.' Evaluate this statement considering arguments for and against. In your response you should:

- refer to St Mark's Gospel
- reach a justified conclusion.

(12 marks)

ARGUMENTS IN SUPPORT OF THE STATEMENT ● **Explain why some people would agree with the statement.** ● Develop your explanation with more detail and examples. ● Refer to religious teaching. Use a quote or paraphrase of a religious authority. ● **Evaluate the arguments.** Is this a good argument? Explain why you think this. Use words such as convincing/ strong/robust/weak/unpersuasive/ unsuccessful within your reasoning.	*Some Christians/Catholics/people would agree with this statement because...*
ARGUMENTS SUPPORTING A DIFFERENT VIEW ● **Explain why some people would disagree with the statement.** ● Develop your explanation with more detail and examples. ● Refer to religious teaching. Use a quote or paraphrase of a religious authority. ● **Evaluate the arguments.** Is this a good argument? Explain why you think this. Use words such as convincing/ strong/robust/weak/unpersuasive/ unsuccessful within your reasoning.	*On the other hand, some Christians/Catholics/people would hold a different point of view...*
CONCLUSION ● **Give a justified conclusion.** ● Include your own reasoning. ● Use words such as convincing/ strong/robust/weak/unpersuasive/ unsuccessful to weigh up the different arguments for and against. ● Do not just repeat arguments you have already used without explaining how they apply to your reasoned opinion/conclusion.	*Having considered both sides of the argument, I would say that...*

3 'To be a good disciple today you must be willing to give up everything.' Evaluate this statement considering arguments for and against. In your response you should:

- refer to St Mark's Gospel
- reach a justified conclusion.

(12 marks)

 **REVIEW**

- Check your answers to these exam questions on p.204–205, correct your answers with annotations, and note down any general areas for improvement.

- If you don't feel secure in the content of this chapter, you could reread the Recap sections.

- If you don't feel secure in your exam technique, you could revisit the exam support section on p.7–14.

Activity Answers Guidance

1.1 The Trinity

AO1: Award 2 marks for a developed point. Here is an example of a second developed point: When Jesus was baptised, there are clear references to God the Father (the voice from heaven), God the Son (Jesus himself) and the Holy Spirit (descending like a dove). **(1)** This again makes the oneness of God clear, due to all three being present and one at the same time. **(1)**

1.2 The Trinity in the Bible

AO1: Here is a suggestion for how these two points could be developed: One source was the decisions made at the Council of Nicaea **(1)**, which clarified the Church's belief in the oneness of God and Jesus after there had been disagreement about Jesus' nature. **(1)** Another source was the Apostolic Tradition **(1)**, which reflected the lived experiences of early Christians who had experienced revelation of God through Jesus and were given the power of the Holy Spirit. **(1)**

AO2: Suggested arguments include:

The Trinity **is** the most essential belief about God.	The Trinity **is not** the most essential belief about God.
The Trinity is revealed at Jesus' baptism, therefore Catholics believe all three persons are active in their lives.	The most essential belief is actually the Paschal Mystery as this is what saved humanity from sin and enables them to spend eternity with God.
The Trinity is the main theme of the Nicene Creed, emphasising that it is a core Christian belief.	The Trinity is a 'mystery' and it isn't possible to fully understand it in this life – therefore it is more important that a Christian follows God's teachings on earth.
The Trinity confirms that Jesus is divine, and therefore his teachings have divine authority.	It might be more important for some people to focus on each person of the Trinity individually, rather than focusing on the nature of God as Trinity, which can be difficult to comprehend.

1.3 Creation

AO1: Here are some suggested answers, but any other key features from the account are also worth credit. Any two of the following would complete the answer for three marks: On the second day, God created the sky. **(1)** On the third day, God created dry land apart from the sea including plant life. **(1)** On the fourth day, God created the stars and the planets. **(1)** On the fifth day he created the animals that lived in the sea. **(1)** On the sixth day he created the animals, followed by human beings. **(1)**

AO2: Suggested arguments include:

For	Against
Clearly symbolic: Given its date (contested but perhaps 600BCE), scientific knowledge was limited.	**An exact retelling:** Strong point as any interpretation comes from humans and therefore could be wrong.
How and why the universe was created are two different questions: Genesis focused on the why, modern science can answer the how – a strong point as it is hard to argue against modern science.	**Other parts of the Bible are taken literally:** Such as Jesus' miracles – what would happen if Christians decided those were simply metaphorical?
'Generally accurate': The ordering of Creation is quite similar to the way in which scientists believe the world came into existence.	**Bible as word of God:** If the Bible is the Word of God then it is important to take those words literally as Christians believe God is likely to know more than we do.
Conclusion: Here you need to have identified the strongest argument and explain why it convinces you to either agree or disagree with the statement.	

1.4 Creation and the nature of humanity

AO1: Here is a suggestion for how these two points could be developed: Humans have free will which means they have the ability to choose right and wrong. **(1)** Humans can give and receive love, which allows them to experience true happiness in community with others. **(1)**

AO2: Suggested points include: However, there is a minority of Christians who focus more on dominion. This idea suggests that God gave human beings the authority to rule. This is a [strong/weak] argument because… [give a reason]. **OR:** However, some Christians would argue that sometimes you do need to prioritise care of other humans over the environment. For example, it is acceptable to overfarm or overfish to help people suffering from food shortages. This is a [strong/weak] argument because… [give a reason].

1.5 The Incarnation

AO1: Here is a suggestion for how these two points could be organised and signposted effectively: One reason is that Mary was Jesus' mother. **(1)** He was born to a human being, which means he is also fully human. **(1)** The second reason is that John's Gospel says 'the Word became flesh' **(1)**, which means that Jesus became flesh, God in human form. **(1)**

AO2: A suggested paragraph: Jesus was clearly fully God and fully human because he was born to a human, but his birth had been a miracle as Mary was a virgin. Despite his miraculous birth, there were few signs of him being fully God until he began performing miracles as an adult. This is a strong indication that he was both fully human and fully God.

1.6 The Paschal Mystery

AO1: Remember, you could choose any two events to write about. Here is one possible full mark answer: The Passion of Jesus is significant for Catholics today as it teaches them to act with restraint when experiencing suffering. **(1)** Jesus responded with forgiveness. **(1)** The resurrection of Jesus is the centre of Christian belief; **(1)** it is a significant reminder to Catholics that death is not the end. **(1)** Matthew's Gospel explains it is a present event, 'I am with you always', highlighting the significance for Catholics today. **(1)**

AO2: An example order, with explanations:

1. The Resurrection: This proves Jesus was truly the Son of God. I think this is most important because it is vital to Christianity and understanding the Trinity.
2. The Ascension: This shows Christians that there is a path to heaven for them too, which encourages them to follow the teachings of Jesus.
3. The Death: This is important as it provided redemption and saving from sin. Without this, salvation would not be possible.
4. The Passion: This gives a practical example of how to behave in moments of suffering. This is an important example, but not as important as the other examples Jesus gave.

1.7 The significance of the Paschal Mystery

AO1: Here is a suggested answer: The sacraments are sources for experiencing God's grace through the Holy Spirit. **(1)** Catholics act with charity as they are inspired by the Holy Spirit. **(1)** The Holy Spirit is called Counsellor as it guides the Church with wisdom. **(1)**

AO2: Your thesis could be for or against the statement. Two examples include: **For:** The Holy Spirit was clearly needed to bring about salvation as it was sent by Jesus after his ascension. **Against:** The Holy Spirit was not needed to bring about salvation as Jesus completed this through the Paschal Mystery.

1.8 Eschatology

AO1: Here is a suggested answer: One Catholic belief is purgatory. **(1)** This means that there is a place where a person's soul is prepared or purified for heaven. **(1)** A second Catholic belief is that Catholics will be resurrected like Jesus was. **(1)** This means that their soul will be reunited with their glorified body. **(1)**

AO2: Your answer could include some of the following arguments:

For	Against
Stage of purification, recognising that most people will die without all their sins forgiven.	Not a belief held by all Christians as it is not specifically mentioned in the Bible.
Enables people to reach the holiness required to get into heaven (CCC 1030).	Not a belief held by all Christians as it is not specifically mentioned in the Bible.
Revelation says, 'nothing unclean shall enter [heaven]' (21:27).	Some Christians might say that Jesus' atonement on the cross was sufficient and Christians do not need to suffer further.

A possible conclusion could be: In conclusion, I feel it is clear why Catholics see belief in purgatory as important. They believe that most people will not die fully prepared for heaven, and purgatory allows them to be purified. It is impossible to go to purgatory and then not enter heaven.

Compare and Contrast: 1.8 Eschatology

See the completed table in the Apply section of this Compare and Contrast topic for a sample answer.

Chapter 1 Exam Practice

3 mark question

2. Answers include any three from: Human beings are rational and can find their way to God. **(1)** Human beings have free will and conscience. **(1)** Human beings can relate to God and have a relationship with him. **(1)** Human beings are answerable to God. **(1)**

3. Answers include any three from: Jesus' arrest in the Garden of Gethsemane. **(1)** Jesus' two trials. **(1)** Jesus' suffering at the hands of the Romans. **(1)** Jesus' death on the cross. **(1)** Jesus' resurrection. **(1)** Jesus' ascension into heaven. **(1)**

4 mark question

2. A possible response for the second reason: The second reason is that Jesus was human **(1)** and was able to fully understand the difficulties and temptations that humans face. **(1)**

3. A possible response: In baptism, **(1)** which is performed in the name of the Father, Son and Holy Spirit. **(1)** In the Eucharist, **(1)** which begins with the sign of the cross and is referred to in the Eucharistic Prayer. **(1)**

*Remember, for most questions it does say in the mark scheme: **Accept any other valid responses**. These are not the only possible answers!*

5 mark question

1. A possible source of wisdom and authority for this question is: These help Catholics to understand God's presence on earth. Jesus' baptism in Matthew 3:13 shows the three persons clearly identified.

2. A response: The first way is that the creation accounts in Genesis 1–2 **(1)** teach that God brought the universe into existence. **(1)** Catholics believe the world can help them understand the nature of God, and so get closer to him. **(1)**

The second way is that only an all-powerful God could create the universe. **(1)** This means that Catholics understand the omnipotent nature of God. **(1)** God as the almighty creator is referred to in the Nicene Creed. **(1)**

This indicates where 6 marks could be given, but the maximum available is 5. If you can include a source of wisdom and authority for both ways, that should ensure you get the fifth mark.

3. A possible answer with six ways of achieving 5 marks: Firstly, the death of Jesus on the cross took away the sins of the world. **(1)** God showed his grace in this act of love **(1)** and through Jesus' mercy: 'Forgive them, for they know not what they do.' (*Luke 23:34*) **(1)**

Secondly, the Holy Spirit sent at Pentecost was an expression of God's grace **(1)** as it helped the apostles to better understand the full Paschal Mystery, **(1)** as made clear in Acts 2. **(1)**

15 mark question

2. Some arguments for the statement: Some Catholics would argue that if God is all forgiving, there is no one whose sins cannot be forgiven, therefore, no one should be condemned to hell; this would even apply to a serious sinner who repents at the end of their life like the thief crucified with Jesus. Catholics believe in post-death purification; this is considered a place of temporal punishment known as purgatory, and this purification and punishment will allow sinners access to heaven eventually. God is believed to be endlessly loving; people do not need to worry about hell as nothing in either life nor after death can separate people from the love of God, so some Christians believe that this means that people do not need to be concerned should they occasionally fall into sin.

You don't have to have three reasons – you can do with fewer as long as you can fully develop them!

Some arguments against the statement: All Christians are encouraged to avoid occasions of sin; belief in the existence of hell encourages Catholics to go to confession regularly; in this way they will always be in a sinless state whenever death comes. The existence of hell is required for ultimate justice; God is referred to as a just judge who will reward and punish; this makes sense of the moral life that the good will be rewarded and the bad punished (*2 Corinthians 5:1–10*). Many Protestant Christians believe that entry to heaven is not based on how a life is lived but only in believing in salvation through the death of Jesus; so these Christians will try to convert others in order to save them from hell as they believe there is no second chance after death.

A possible conclusion: In conclusion, it is clear that a belief in hell is important as it affects the way Christians live their lives. They want to get to heaven, and as such they try to avoid sin.

3. Some arguments for the statement: For some Catholics, Jesus' incarnation is the most important belief because it is what enables Catholics to fully share in the life of Christ. They believe that God made flesh to enable humans to have a relationship with Jesus on earth, responding to his teachings. Through Jesus' death and resurrection, death is overcome and heaven is made possible.

Some arguments against the statement: Other Christians would argue that the persons of the Trinity are one and work together in perfect unity and therefore the doctrine of the Trinity is more important than the incarnation. The Paschal mystery, though made possible by Jesus' incarnation, is what ultimately saves humans from separation from God and is therefore arguably most important. All of these core doctrines cannot be separated as they are all part of God's wider work – therefore no one belief is most important.

A possible conclusion: In conclusion, the Incarnation is inseparable from the other core doctrines such as the Trinity. Therefore, it does not make sense to call it the most important; they are all important.

2.1 The sacramental nature of reality

AO1: Here is a suggested answer for the sacrament of reconciliation: A person speaks to a priest to show genuine repentance for their sins. **(1)** The priest takes away the sins on God's behalf. **(1)** The penitent is given an act of penance to perform and doing these acts of penance shows willingness to change. **(1)**

AO2: Example answers could include:

1. Catholics and Orthodox.
2. Because they believe the sacraments were instituted by Jesus, which is described in the Bible and Church teaching.
3. CCC 1210, for example.
4. Many Protestants only recognise baptism and the Eucharist; some Protestants do not recognise any.
5. Protestants do not believe these sacraments to have been instituted by Christ as Catholics/Orthodox Christians do, though they might still perform them as acts of faith or commitment.

2.2 Liturgical worship

AO1: Developed points might be: Firstly, the CCC, which is a source of guidance for Catholics, **(1)** makes it very clear that Eucharist is the most important **(1)** when it says that it is 'the source and summit'. **(1)**

Secondly, the Paschal Mystery is a key to salvation for Catholics **(1)** and the Last Supper is part of this. **(1)** Jesus said 'Do this in remembrance of me.' (*1 Corinthians 11:24*), highlighting the importance of the sacrament today. **(1)**

AO2: Suggested completed sentences: The Catholic Church believes that the Liturgy is something God does, and that humans take part in. **Therefore** it has a formalised structure. The Catholic belief is based upon the words and actions of Jesus at the Last Supper alongside the traditions, words, and actions of the earliest apostles. It is based on the Church, rather than decisions of individuals. **However**, in other Christian Churches worship may be far less structured and guided by members of the congregations. This is appealing to Christians who believe worship can be tailored to different people's needs and want flexibility to add their own interpretations and personality.

Additionally, the Mass unites Catholics around the world as it follows the same formal structure, even if it is in different languages. This creates a sense of unity. **Finally**, in scripture we only read about the Last Supper and not much about worship and liturgy in the Early Church so it is unknown how exactly this took place.

Compare and Contrast: 2.2 Liturgical worship

See the completed table in the Apply section of this Compare and Contrast topic for a sample answer.

2.3 The funeral rite

AO1: Two reasons could include: Firstly, it is important as it shows the communion of the whole community. **(1)** This means the people at the funeral are connected as the Body of Christ. **(1)**

Secondly, it is a reminder to people that they share in eternal life **(1)** and that death is not the end, but simply a passage from this world to life with God. **(1)**

AO2: Some arguments for the statement: The people gathered are reminded that they are still connected to the deceased in the Church, the Body of Christ. It is a reminder that death is not the end, and that they can live in future hope of eternal life. Comfort is provided during time of grief both from the community and through prayer.

Some arguments against the statement: Prayer is for the benefit of the deceased to aid their journey into the next life. The focus is on prayers for the deceased, not the family or wider community. Reminders that death is not the end are arguably of most significance to the deceased not the community.

A possible conclusion: In conclusion, it is clear that for Catholics, the funeral rite is incredibly important for the living. Many people fear death, but the service reminds Catholics that they can live in hope of eternal life.

2.4 Prayer

AO1: Three types might include: Adoration is a prayer recognising God as God. **(1)** Thanksgiving is a prayer thanking God and expressing love and gratitude. **(1)** Repentance is a prayer recognising sin and asking for forgiveness. **(1)**

AO2 Here are two completed points: For Catholics, daily prayer is naturally an essential part of life. This is because prayer is the 'raising of hearts and minds to God' (*CCC 2559*), which is something that must be part of daily life. It is impossible to do this only on occasions. Some may claim that attending Mass on a Sunday is more important. However, the final command at Mass is 'Go in peace to love and serve the Lord', indicating that it is not enough to just attend Mass on a Sunday.

2.5 Forms of popular piety

AO1: This is an answer with two clear points: Firstly, the stations of the cross are used as a reminder of Jesus' suffering and death. **(1)** They help Catholics reflect on these events, helping in their time of need. **(1)** The four Gospel accounts of Jesus' suffering and pain, particularly his journey carrying the cross, can be powerful aids to prayer. **(1)**

Secondly, the Blessed Sacrament might be exposed to pray in front of. **(1)** Adoration is beneficial as Catholics pray in front of the physical body of Christ. **(1)**

AO2:

	The Rosary	Stations of the Cross	Eucharistic adoration
Catholics	Gives honour to Mary	Key feature of church building, reminder of Passion story	Actual body of Christ
Other Christians' view	Do not share same view on Mary and do not elevate her	Features of building not as important as what goes on inside	If Eucharist is just symbolic, action does not have meaning

2.6 Pilgrimage

AO1: Here are improved answers: To get closer to God and leave the world behind. **(1)** They are ill and want God to heal them. **(1)** It's not the journey but the action of being a pilgrim, giving time to God. **(1)**

AO2: Here are two possible conclusions: I believe that for many Catholics today pilgrimage is vitally important as it can deepen and strengthen their faith. They spend time in prayer in holy places. Even though it isn't as significant for some Christians, pilgrimage can still be very rewarding for all. **Or:** I believe that while pilgrimage is valuable for some people, it is not vitally important for all Christians. There are many other ways for Christians to strengthen their faith, such as personal prayer within your own church or community, and it is right that these Christians decide for themselves how they will demonstrate devotion to God.

2.7 Catholic Social Teaching

AO1: Three ways might include: CAFOD helps those in need after a natural disaster with short-term aid. **(1)** It provides resources so that people can help themselves to improve their future. **(1)** It raises awareness in England and Wales about issues such as fair trade, HIV and clean water. **(1)**

AO2: Here is a possible answer: Acting in a loving way, as Jesus instructed, is clearly part of Catholic teaching. In the Parable of the Sheep and the Goats, Jesus said, 'Whatever you did for one of the least of these brothers and sisters of mine, you did for me.' However, it may be questioned as to how far this is an individual responsibility.

Many Catholics will try to act in ways that bring about justice, peace, and reconciliation. They recognise the struggles of others and try to bring about change. On an individual level, they may try to follow the guidance provided in the lists of seven spiritual and seven corporal acts of mercy.

Other Catholics may feel that the best way to bring about change is not on an individual level, but by supporting organisations such as CAFOD that can bring about change through collective power and that this is more effective.

I believe that both approaches are valid, and that actually it would make sense for Catholics to do both – work individually, as well as with organisations. Jesus made it clear that it was a personal call to change the lives of those around you.

2.8 Catholic mission and evangelism

AO1: More detailed answers would be: Parish life shares the Gospel through the Sacraments, social events, and so on. **(1)** The Bishops' Conference holds national events and initiatives. **(1)** The Pope uses Instagram and Twitter to spread the Gospel through social media. **(1)**

AO2:

Individual Catholics are better placed	The Church is better placed
Personal touch to those they meet	Huge reach via social and traditional media
National or international events would not happen without individual Catholics taking part	Bigger resources to organise large events which can reach thousands, even millions of people

Chapter 2 Exam Practice

3 mark question

2. Two further features could be: The penitent makes an act of contrition. **(1)** The priest offers advice to the penitent. **(1)**

3. Three reasons could include: Catholics say the Lord's Prayer because it was taught to them by Jesus. **(1)** Catholics use petitionary prayers for their needs and the needs of others. **(1)** Some Catholics say prayers of thanksgiving to express gratitude for their life. **(1)**

4 mark question

2. A possible response: Firstly, CAFOD ensures the 'dignity of work and the rights of workers' **(1)** by setting up Fairtrade partnerships around the world. **(1)** Secondly, CAFOD works for 'solidarity with all people as one global family' **(1)** by helping all those of all faiths who are in need internationally – not just Catholics. **(1)**

3. Two reasons could include: Firstly, it is important because it is the re-presentation of the events of the Last Supper, **(1)** where Jesus gave himself in the form of the Eucharist. **(1)**
Secondly, it is important because it enables all Catholics to become part of the Body of Christ. **(1)** The whole Church community regularly celebrates the Mass. **(1)**

5 mark question

2. A possible response: Firstly, the sacraments use natural things to help Catholics recognise God's grace. **(1)** Therefore, anything found in creation, such as water, bread, wine, and so on, can be used by God. **(1)** This is clear in the Catechism when it makes the link between the natural life and spiritual life (CCC 1210). **(1)**
Secondly, God's grace and presence continue throughout life. **(1)** The sacraments become reminders of this in a real way for Catholics as they continue their sacramental journey. **(1)**

3. Two reasons could be: Firstly, Jesus gave a clear instruction to his apostles to 'make disciples of all nations' (*Matthew 28:19–20*), **(1)** which meant they should travel and spread the Gospel. **(1)** Many Christians have taken this literally as missionaries. **(1)**
Secondly, modern Popes have realised this evangelisation is needed in the West. **(1)** This is called the New Evangelisation and they have used social media and large events to interest people in the Gospel. **(1)**

12 mark question

2. Some arguments for the statement: Some Christians would agree with this statement because Jesus sent the apostles into the world on a mission to 'make disciples of all nations' (*Matthew 28:19–20*). This means they were to share and live out the Gospels. As made clear in *Lumen Gentium*, even the laity are called to the 'priesthood of the faithful'.
Christians could also point convincingly to the long history of mission work including St Benedict bringing the Gospel to Western Europe in the fifth century. It could be argued that the mission is a personal one from Jesus, empowered by the Holy Spirit to share and build the Kingdom of God in love.

Some arguments against the statement: On the other hand, some people would argue that Jesus' instructions to the apostles are meant more for the bishops and priests of today, and not ordinary people. Many people in the West are not religious, and society is increasingly secular. As such religion has become more private and some people do not appreciate evangelism. Some Christians would maintain that a prayerful life, with the sacraments and following the commandments, is more important as you can ensure your own life is filled with holiness.

A possible conclusion: In conclusion, the idea of mission is more applicable to the clergy, as they more directly carry out the instructions of Jesus eg. preaching and healing. For lay Catholics, a faithful life filled with prayer is clearly more important.

3. Possible arguments for the statement: Many Catholics would state that prayer is the primary way in which Catholics communicate with God. This allows them to develop a fuller relationship with God, which gives them the grace to live devoted Catholic lives. Some forms of prayer express concern for others; they believe this helps Catholics to be constantly aware of the teaching of Jesus to love others; they then follow his example to serve others in their daily lives. Regularly following a prayer such as the Lord's Prayer (Matthew 6:9–14) helps Catholics to focus on God as well as obey the instructions for prayer laid down by Jesus.

Possible arguments against the statement: An alternative view among some Catholics might be that daily prayer may become stale and routine. As a consequence, it could lack proper devotion and conviction, which could damage their spiritual lives.

Some Catholics could argue that as God is all-knowing, he knows what we need before we ask him. If he judged something needed to be done he would have done it, so Christians should focus on doing what they can, rather than asking God for help.

A possible conclusion: On balance, while people in the modern world lead busy lives, I think that lay peoples' time could be better used in other ways, such as raising their families; whereas some Christians would conclude that prayer helps them cope with these modern pressures.

3.1 The Bible

AO1: Two other features could include: Law: the 613 commandments revealed to Moses. **(1)** Prophets: messages from God, which are often warnings and calls for repentance. **(1)**

AO2: Here is a possible answer: As well as different translations of the Bible, Catholics often use a version of the Bible that has an additional section called the Vulgate. These books cover the period between the Old and New Testaments and were affirmed by the Council of Trent in 1545. The Church sees them as useful, and this is a strong argument for Catholics to have them included in their Bibles. It is believed they were used by the early Church.

However, the Catechism makes clear that 'The Gospels are the heart of all the Scriptures' (125) and therefore this is the most important thing even if other parts of the Bible are different. Also, the additional books of the Vulgate are rarely used by Catholics, or even known by some. Most copies of the Bible do not include them, which demonstrates that most Christians do not see them as important.

In conclusion, it would be a good thing if all Christians used the same version of the Bible, but there is already variation with denominations and so it is unsurprising that there are different versions.

3.2 Interpretation of the Bible

AO1: Two reasons might be: Firstly, some Christians see the Bible as the literal Word of God **(1)** because God revealed himself to the writers and they were guided by the Holy Spirit. **(1)**

Secondly, other Christians see the Bible as the Word of God, but take into consideration the human authors and the context in which they were writing. **(1)** They believe the Bible is true because it was inspired by God. **(1)** This is made clear in 2 Timothy: 'All scripture is inspired by God' (3:16) **(1)**

AO2: This is a possible justified conclusion: In conclusion, despite the advantages of taking the Bible literally, for example there is less disagreement over modern issues, it is clear that many Christians decide to take a different approach because they accept scientific theories such as the Big Bang.

3.3 The magisterium

AO1: A second point might be: Secondly, it gives ex cathedra teaching on certain issues, **(1)** which helps Catholics understand their faith better; for example, the idea of the Immaculate Conception. **(1)**

AO2: Some possible arguments for the statement: Guidance is needed on modern issues such as abortion, IVF etc. as they are not discussed in the Bible. Individual Catholics need informed consciences to make decisions, and the teaching of the magisterium helps to inform them. It is part of the three-way nature of the Church: scripture, Apostolic Tradition, Magisterium.

Some possible arguments against the statement: The issues that the magisterium addresses are small in number, compared to key principles such as the moral teaching of Jesus. The magisterium is entrusted to interpret the Bible, therefore scripture is still at the heart of any decisions, and most important (CCC 100). Ex Cathedra declarations have only been made twice, therefore other teaching could still have errors.

3.4 The Second Vatican Council

AO1: This expanded answer would gain the extra marks: Firstly, the Mass can now be said in the local language rather than Latin. This helps the congregation understand what is happening. **(1)**

Secondly, the Eucharist can be received under both forms. Some people feel this means they are more fully involved in the Mass, not just the priest. **(1)**

AO2: Here is an example table:

Why is it the most important?	· Focused on key beliefs of Church · Opened salvation to more than just Catholics · Emphasis on role of laity · Priesthood of the faithful
Why might other documents be more important?	SC: Changes to Mass to enable all to participate
	DV: Important to realise Church is not just based on Bible alone
	GeS: Focus on social justice and relationship with other humans in modern world
Conclusion	*Here you should decide which side is the strongest and explain why.* _____ is the strongest argument in this debate because _____, and therefore I conclude _____

3.5 The Church as the Body of Christ

AO1: An improved answer: Firstly, it helps Catholics show love to God. **(1)** Under the guidance of the Pope and other clergy, Catholics are guided towards salvation. **(1)**

Secondly, the vocation that a Catholic lives out, whether as part of the laity, clergy or religious, can help them be part of the Body of Christ. **(1)** In this way members of the Body can perform different functions and contribute. **(1)**

AO2: Here is an example table:

Agree – how is the Church unified?	Disagree – how is the Church not unified?
· 1 Corinthians 12:13: reminder that we are all baptised into one body by the 'Spirit' · Romans 12:5: all members do not have the same function but are still 'one body in Christ' · Some ecumenical movements try to unify the Christian Church. Vatican II encouraged ecumenism	· Only Catholics regard Pope as Head of the Church · Catholics mean only the Catholic Church when referring to the Body of Christ · Several thousand denominations worldwide highlights division within the Christian Church

3.6 The four marks of the Church

AO1: Firstly, 'One' is important for Catholics, as it means working towards unity. **(1)** This is important because Catholics are encouraged to work for ecumenism among the many different denominations. **(1)**

Secondly, 'Apostolic' is important as it provides a way for Catholics to be guided by the magisterium on today's issues, **(1)** for example abortion, IVF, and contraception. **(1)**

AO2: An example table might be:

	One	Holy	Catholic	Apostolic
Agree	· Irreconcilable differences between Christian denominations	· Some Christians feel the call to holiness only applies to those who are, or want to become, priests	· The Church is no longer 'universal' due to its divisions and denominations	· Modern issues provide such difficult ethical dilemmas that advice from the Church presents a challenge to the faithful
Disagree	· Heals division amongst Christians	· Universal call to holiness through prayer and sacraments	· Gives strength to the Church through its history and tradition	· Provides continued guidance on modern issues in face of modernisation and secularism
Conclusion	In conclusion, the marks of the church remain relevant as they connect the Church to its history and other Christians around the world today. Persecution and division remains, and the marks are a reminder of the unity of the Church.			

3.7 Mary as a model of the Church

AO1: Full sentences could include: The Rosary is a devotion that honours Mary and includes ten sets of the Hail Mary. **(1)** Celebrating the Feast of the Immaculate Conception remembers how Mary was born without sin. **(1)** Pilgrimage to Lourdes in France, as Mary appeared there 18 times in 1851. **(1)**

AO2: Two possible justified conclusions might be: For Catholics, Mary is clearly important and as such should be given a significant role. This is because she is the Mother of Jesus, so the Church literally came from Mary. **OR** Other Catholics may feel that actually Jesus remains the most important role model. There is much that Jesus said and did, while very little is known about Mary.

3.8 Personal and ethical decision-making

AO1: An example table:

Firstly…	The Church believes that Natural Law is discoverable, never changes, and applies to all human beings.
DEVELOPMENT	It is designed to help human beings flourish, and as such is important to Catholics.
Secondly…	It comes from St Thomas Aquinas.
DEVELOPMENT	He is a Doctor of the Church and considered an authority on moral teaching for the Church.

AO2: A completed table might look like this:

An informed conscience DOES enable clear decisions	• It is a sacred obligation – this means it is something Catholics are obliged to do, it is not an option. • Conscience is informed by apostolic tradition and the magisterium – they investigate, study, and pray about issues in the modern world to help guide Catholics. • If Catholics are making decisions to the best of their knowledge, knowing Christ and the Gospels, they are doing the right thing.
An informed conscience DOES NOT enable clear decisions	• Other Christians do not see 'informed' as meaning following Apostolic Tradition and the magisterium. • The Bible can appear contradictory in places. • The Bible does not cover many of the modern issues (abortion, IVF, etc.) that Christians may struggle with. • There isn't agreement between other Christians on certain moral and ethical issues.

Chapter 3 Exam Practice

3 mark question

2. Two other principles could include: Conscience, but for Catholics this must be fully informed. **(1)** Following the teaching of the magisterium as the authority of the Church. **(1)**

3. Three beliefs could include: Mary is joined with Jesus in the work of salvation. **(1)** She is a model of discipleship, accepting the will of God. **(1)** She is a model of faith and charity, risking everything for God. **(1)**

4 mark question

2. A possible response: It can look at issues that did not exist in the time of Jesus; **(1)** for example, infertility treatment. **(1)** It also shows Catholics how to achieve salvation **(1)** and as it is guided by the Holy Spirit, its teachings must be holy and right. **(1)**

3. Two reasons might be: It means that the Church developed from the mission of the apostles. **(1)** They were sent out by Jesus to spread the Gospel, which is continued today. It also means that the teaching of the Church follows the tradition of the apostles **(1)** and it is therefore faithful to Jesus' teaching. **(1)**

5 mark question

2. A possible response: The Catholic Church teaches that the conscience must be informed **(1)** because a well-formed conscience will never contradict the objective moral law, as taught by Christ in Matthew 5:17-24 **(1)** and his Church, which teaches that humans must obey judgements of their conscience. **(1)** Conscience is a natural faculty of a person's reason that helps them to do good and avoid evil. **(1)** It also allows them to judge the good or evil of what they have done. **(1)** Jesus said we should not judge others until we have judged ourselves. **(1)**

3. Two ways might include: Catholics believe that the Bible is the inspired word of God, **(1)** which means that it had human writers, but that God is the primary author. **(1)** This is made clear in *2 Timothy 3:16*: 'All scripture is inspired by God.' **(1)** Some Catholics do take a literal view of the Bible, **(1)** which means everything in the Bible is true and without error. **(1)**

15 mark question

2. Some arguments for the statement: Since Mass was celebrated in the local language instead of Latin after the Second Vatican Council, many Catholics would say that this was hugely significant. They could receive both forms of Eucharist and

the laity were far more involved. These two changes were outlined in *Sacrosanctum Concilium* (The Constitution on the Sacred Liturgy). All were called to the priesthood of the faithful, which was a reminder about participating in the sacraments and living out a Catholic life in *Lumen Gentium* (Dogmatic Constitution on the Church).

Some arguments against the statement: Some Catholics would disagree with the statement, because theological documents about salvation for non-theists, as found in *Lumen Gentium*, focused on beliefs rather than everyday lives of Catholics. It should also be noted that Mass is still celebrated in the Latin Rite for those who want to attend in certain parishes.

A possible conclusion: I would say that the Second Vatican Council was one of the most dramatic events in the last four hundred years of Church history. Every aspect of Church life was opened up to change. Being able to celebrate Mass in the vernacular (local language) made it more accessible to Catholics, for example. There is no doubt that the experience was dramatically different for Catholics.

3. Some arguments for the statement: There is a strong argument in favour of this statement, as Christians believe that the Bible is the Word of God and is the guidance and teaching they need to live their lives (2 Timothy 3:16) so they must obey it to gain salvation. The Bible contains the Ten Commandments; these are at the heart of the covenant between God and Chosen People led by Moses. Many Christians today believe they are the heirs to that covenant and are bound by it. The Catechism of the Catholic Church 105–108 teaches that the Bible was inspired by the Holy Spirit; this means that it contains truthful teachings; Catholics who live by the Bible can therefore be sure they are living good lives.

Some arguments against the statement: On the other hand, some Christians point out that the Bible does not always reflect modern science; an example would be the account of the creation of the world in six days: they therefore conclude that the Bible cannot be accepted word for word. A further argument against the statement is that the Catholic Church accepts a relationship between Scripture and Tradition; the magisterium, as successors of the apostles, need to interpret the Bible in the light of apostolic tradition; this means that Catholics must obey the teachings of the Church. Furthermore, Christians believe that their conscience is the voice of God; it is therefore a personal communication between God and each individual human being. Thus, some Christians would conclude that they must obey that voice as God's will for them.

A possible conclusion: In conclusion, even though it is the Word of God, the Bible alone is not sufficient for dealing with many modern issues. Therefore, it is important for Catholics that they have the bishops to interpret the Bible for today's world.

4.1 Catholic church architecture

AO1: Here is a possible full answer: Firstly, the high ceilings and spires try to connect the congregation with heaven. **(1)** They are as high as possible to reach towards God, showing his importance in the lives of Catholics. **(1)** This is because the Catechism says that the church building should be a 'worthy place for prayer'. **(1)**

Secondly, many churches have stained glass windows, which tell the stories from the Bible, as well as the saints. **(1)** These were particularly useful in days when people could not read or write. **(1)**

AO2: A sample table:

Agree	Disagree
• CCC 1180 – The church is a symbol of God, a sign of the living Church. • CCC 1181 – The church is a worthy place for prayer and sacred ceremonial. • Many features are the same.	• Many UK churches have been built since 1829, so reflect modern architecture. • It is not even necessary for Mass to take place in a church. • There are lots of different ways to fulfil the requirements of the Catechism.

4.2 Catholic church features

AO1: Two other features could include: The lectern is where the Bible readings take place during the Liturgy of the Word. **(1)** The tabernacle is where the Eucharist is stored as a reminder of Jesus' physical presence in the church. **(1)**

AO2: A possible argument for the statement: The altar is the most significant feature of Catholic churches because the Liturgy of the Eucharist takes place here. As it resembles a table it is a link to the Last Supper. As such it provides a focal point of the church, which everyone can see clearly, reminding them of Jesus' sacrifice.

A possible argument against the statement: While the altar is at the heart of a Catholic church, some Catholics would argue that the lectern is equally significant. This is where the Liturgy of the Word is read to the congregation, and the Word of God is vital to Catholics. The baptismal font is also more important to many Catholics as without it, people could not be baptised, and therefore not receive any other sacraments. Finally, the crucifix could be seen as most important, as it is a reminder of Jesus' sacrifice.

4.3 Sacred objects

AO1:

Sacred vessels	Sarcophagi	Hunger cloths
1. The ciborium is used to keep the Body of Christ in the tabernacle. Most churches will always keep this presence and hence people genuflect when entering the building. 2. The chalice is used in Mass to hold the blood. The congregation drinks from the cup of blood just as Jesus' disciples did.	1. Later Christians began using them for burial of the dead. Originally bodies would have just been laid in caves. 2. Still used today for Popes in St Peter's. These create dramatic places to pray and remember the Popes.	1. Used in developing countries today. Literacy may still be an issue for some congregations. 2. Used in Middle Ages to help those who could not read. This would have been the majority of the congregation. Also Mass was in Latin so hard to remember.

AO2: Some arguments for the statement: Rosary beads are used to help pray the Rosary, which is a prayer to Mary; each bead is a reminder of which prayer to say, which helps with focus. A candle can draw attention to the altar, which may be where adoration or liturgical worship is taking place. Objects such as sacred vessels are used to hold the body and blood of Christ; they are recognisable to Catholics and help them focus on the contents.

Some arguments against the statement: The Lord's Prayer, as given by Jesus, does not require any aids or sacred objects. Focus can be gained through silent contemplation. Hands are often put together to avoid distraction, rather than using an object; use of objects could disrupt focus.

A possible conclusion: For most Catholics, sacred objects do help focus prayer, as they are a focus, and part of, the liturgy. As such they are important, but clearly not always needed.

4.4 Artwork in Catholicism

AO1: Here is another possible response: Firstly, Rembrandt's *The Return of the Prodigal Son* was the result of many years' work on the Parable of the Prodigal Son (1), a story that helps explain reconciliation and forgiveness for Catholics. (1)

Secondly, priest Henri Nouwen suggested there are lots of details for Catholics to meditate upon. (1) For example, the father's hands, the son's sandals, and the role of the other brother. (1)

AO2: Some arguments against the statement: In most religious images God is depicted as male; this can reinforce gender stereotypes in religion. Some Christian women could find that undermines their commitment to the Gospel. Many paintings represent an image of God: some Christians believe that to represent God is to lessen his greatness; a Christian's sense of awe before God could be lessened as a consequence. Some of the images represented in paintings may seem traditional and alien to modern society; some people may struggle to connect with the concept of God portrayed; they may therefore confuse a person's faith rather than enhance it.

A possible conclusion: In conclusion, it is clear that paintings have helped Christians develop and understand their relationships with God for hundreds of years. They are a key feature of most churches and are used as a focus of prayer.

4.5 Sculpture and statues

AO1: Here is a more developed answer: Firstly, there is usually a statue of Mary in a church as she is seen as having a unique and special role. (1) There may even be a separate altar or chapel where this statue is kept. (1)

Secondly, a Nativity set is brought out at Christmas when the Nativity scene is constructed. This is a reminder of the important event of the incarnation. (1) Families will often have a set in the home too. (1)

AO2: A possible argument against the statement: Though artwork and sculpture are important to many Catholics for the reasons already described, they are arguably not the most important part of Catholic life. More important would be the sacraments including receiving the Eucharist. Some Christians would say that prayer and the reading of scripture are not dependent on artwork. Some Catholics might feel that they could be distracted or have their perceptions challenged by artwork, which does not help deepen their relationship with God. Catholics are not encouraged to worship statues; they are only there as a reminder and devotional aid.

4.6 Symbolism and imagery in religious art

AO1: Here is an improved answer: Alpha and Omega remind Catholics of Jesus' eternal nature. (1) Chi Rho are the first two letters of the word Christ in Greek. (1) The crucifix is found above or behind the altar in Catholic churches. (1)

AO2: You can argue any symbol is the most important. An example could be: The crucifix is the most important symbol for Catholics because it is a visible reminder of Jesus' death and sacrifice which offers the possibility of salvation. Its prominent position in Catholic churches demonstrates its importance.

Another example is: The fish is the most important symbol as it dates back to the earliest of Christian times. It has multiple meanings; it is a reminder of Jesus as the Christ; it also reflects Jesus telling his disciples that they would be fishers of men and the miracle of the Feeding of the Five Thousand.

4.7 Drama

AO1: A possible full answer: Firstly, mystery plays are used to tell stories from the Bible. (1) They were popular in medieval times, but have become more popular again in England. (1)

Secondly, passion plays retell the story of Jesus' trial, suffering, and death. (1) They are popular at Easter. (1)

AO2:

Drama IS a useful way to express belief	Drama is NOT a useful way to express belief
• Mystery plays help to remember and bring alive Bible stories. • Passion plays can bring together people from different Christian Churches, expressing belief in the same things. • They can put the Bible into a contemporary context, which can help Christians.	• Acting something out could mean that details are added to the story that weren't in the Bible. • The Reformation banned both mystery and Passion plays. • They are not a form of worship and so time would be better spent in conventional prayer and worship.

4.8 Music in worship

AO1: Two further points could include: Plainchant is unaccompanied singing, compiled by Pope Gregory. (1) Psalms from the Old Testament can be set to music and used as part of the readings. (1)

AO2:

Traditional music is preferable	• Roman Gradual sets out approved music that many believe should be followed. • It unifies congregations and Catholics from around the world. • It has a history linking back to even pre-Christian times with Psalms.
Contemporary music is preferable	• Praise and worship music is preferable for many different Christians as it reflects more modern styles and they can therefore identify with it. • It appeals to some young people who find it engaging and expresses their faith. • The charismatic movement has used this as it is informal and familiar in its lyrical style.

Chapter 4 Exam Practice

3 mark question

2. Two further examples: Paintings were popular during the Renaissance period. (1) Statues are artworks, and found in most churches. (1)

3. Three features could include: The font is used to perform baptism. (1) The altar is used as the focal point. (1) The tabernacle is where the host is preserved. (1)

4 mark question

2. A possible response: Firstly, they may be used as a focus for prayer. (1) For example, in a church someone may pray in front of a statue and light a candle. (1) Secondly, at Christmas a Nativity set is used to help tell the Christmas story. (1) Many Christians will also have one in the home; they are useful for young children to learn the story of the Nativity. (1)

3. Two reasons could include: Firstly, the chalice is used to hold the wine. (1) The congregation cannot see the wine, which becomes the blood, but they know it is there as they recognise the cup. (1)
Secondly, the ciborium, which is a covered dish, is used to carefully store the consecrated hosts. (1) This is put in the tabernacle, so there is always a real presence of the Body of Christ in church. (1)

5 mark question

2. A possible response: Firstly, church buildings are supposed to be a place of beauty, (1) and artwork that has been approved by the bishop can be displayed. (1) The Catechism states: 'Sacred art is true and beautiful' (*CCC 2502*). (1)

Secondly, it may be used to help focus prayer. **(1)** This is similar to other artwork such as statues or sculptures. **(1)**

3. Two features could be: Firstly, the altar is the main focus of the church; **(1)** this is where the Eucharist is consecrated, so the congregation needs to see it. **(1)** The Catechism reminds Catholics of the link to the Temple in Jerusalem (*CCC 1182*). **(1)** Secondly, there is always a cross with the crucified Jesus near the altar. **(1)** This is a powerful reminder of his sacrifice. **(1)**

12 mark question

2. Arguments for the statement could include: Despite Christians no longer being persecuted there is a strong tradition of using these symbols. For many Catholics, it helps to create a connection to these early Christians and ensures their sacrifice is remembered. The symbols also include a depth of meaning; for example, the dove links to both the story of Noah in Genesis 8:11 and Jesus' baptism in Luke 3:22. This can help Catholics better understand connections between the Old and New Testament. Some symbols such as Alpha and Omega link to the Greek heritage of the New Testament, but are also the words of Jesus himself in Revelation 22:13, so it makes sense to keep these as symbols.

Arguments against the statement could include: The fish and Chi Rho were originally used when Christians were in hiding. As this is no longer the case, some Catholics may feel there is no need to use confusing and cryptic symbols. Different symbols are attributed to the Gospel writers by different people, so as there is no single universally accepted set, it seems confusing for Catholics today. The cross is a universally recognised symbol of Christianity around the world, therefore it could be argued that it is not necessary to have any further symbols.

A possible conclusion: In conclusion, the symbols are important as they link to the history of the Church as well as act as a reminder of key features of the Bible. They have evolved over time and are part of the story of the faith.

3. Some arguments for the statement: There is a strong argument that sculptures and statues can help Catholics understand and remember Bible stories and those of the saints. They also help worshippers understand God's dealings with humanity, and through them they come to understand more clearly the history of salvation. The Catechism of the Catholic Church encourages all sacred art that reflects the glory of God and draws the worshipper to adoration and prayer; sculptures and statues are part of this tradition. The Church confirmed at the Council of Trent (1545–1653) that statues were not idol worship and they simply showed honour for the individuals represented.

Some arguments against the statement: Some Christians do not have statues or sculptures in their churches. They either believe it is like idol worship or a distraction to the congregation. Some Christians make the convincing point that many of the statues are meaningless as they depict people who lived before we had ways of recording their image, so we do not know what they looked like. Some Christians feel that it is better to focus on the Bible, and do not accept the idea of saints. Therefore they argue that the statues would have little meaning.

A possible conclusion: In conclusion, sculptures and statues can often aid help Christians focus their prayer. This in turn helps develop their relationship with God and better understand him as a result.

5.1 The six Beliefs of Islam

AO1: Here is a possible completed response: One way that the six Beliefs are expressed in Muslim communities is through the profession of the Shahadah, the Muslim declaration of faith. **(1)** This acknowledges that there is one God, Allah, and that he has no equal. **(1)**

Another way is at funerals, when Muslims remember and pray for the deceased. **(1)** This also reminds Muslims that their time on earth is limited and they will need to answer to Allah for how they lived. **(1)**

AO2:

For	Against
• The six Beliefs are mentioned in the Qur'an and hadith, which shows their collective importance. • Muslims must believe in each of them to make their faith complete. • They bring the ummah together and unite Muslims as one body.	• All Beliefs depend on Tawhid, therefore this can be seen as the most important. • This world is temporary while the Hereafter is eternal, so belief in life after death has special significance. • Without prophets and holy books, Muslims would not know how to live.

5.2 The five roots of 'Usul ad-Din

AO1: Possible extended answers: Tawhid, the belief in the oneness of Allah. **(1)** Nubuwwah, the belief that Allah has sent prophets throughout history. **(1)** 'Adl, the belief that Allah is fair and just. **(1)**

AO2: Here is a possible developed point: Shi'a Muslims may argue that belief in Tawhid is more important than the other roots of 'Usul ad-Din because belief in Allah and his oneness is the basis for all other beliefs. The Qur'an teaches: 'Say, He is God, the One, God the eternal' (Surah 112: 1–2). Unless Tawhid came first, the other roots would be meaningless. While all roots help make the foundations of a Shi'a Muslim's faith firm, the strongest root is Tawhid.

5.3 The nature of Allah

AO1: Here is an improved answer: Muslims believe that Allah is the one and only God. **(1)** This belief is reflected in the Shahadah. **(1)** The Qur'an teaches Muslims to 'shun false Gods' (Surah 16:36) **(1)** as they have no power, **(1)** and nothing can compare with Allah. **(1)**

AO2:

For	Against
• As Allah is transcendent (above and beyond his creation), and our minds are limited, we can never understand him fully. • It is forbidden to draw Allah, as it is impossible to visualise him.	• The Qur'an contains many examples of how Allah acts, such as showing mercy to humanity. Therefore we know Allah is merciful. • There are many characteristics of Allah, which gives us an idea of his nature.

5.4 RiSalah

AO1: Here are two developed points: Prophets are important in Islam because they are chosen by Allah to guide people to truth and the right path. **(1)** This usually comes at a time when people have become very sinful and forgotten God. **(1)**

Prophets also set an example of how to live a good life. **(1)** Everything they did and said serves as a model for how everyone should live their life so that Allah will be pleased with them. This includes how people should treat others. **(1)**

AO2: Here are some possible 'against' arguments: However, some people may argue that Muhammad was the most important prophet because he was the only prophet with a message for the whole world. Muslims are required to follow the Sunnah, which is to try to live their life like Muhammad. In addition, Muhammad received Allah's final message and has been called 'the Seal of the Prophets' (Surah 33:40).

5.5 Muslim holy books

AO1: A possible second developed point: Secondly, Muslims believe the Qur'an has authority over other holy books because it is the last revelation from Allah. **(1)** The Qur'an does not contain errors found in previous scriptures, which is why most Muslims use only the Qur'an for guidance. **(1)**

AO2: A good evaluation answer shows you have considered different points of view and have been able to give at least one detailed reason why you believe one argument is more convincing than another, or why both arguments are equally strong.

5.6 Malaikah

AO1:

Angel	Importance
Jibril	Communicates Allah's messages to prophets
Mika'il	Provides and maintains life
Izra'il	Takes the last breath of living creatures

AO2: A possible counter-argument: However, some Muslims would say that all angels are equally important. This is because in the six Beliefs, no individual angel is singled out, with each angel having a specific role to fulfil. The Qur'an mentions all angels together and says that anyone who is an enemy of Allah's angels will become the enemy of Allah (Surah 2:98).

5.7 Al-Qadr

AO1: Two possible developed points: One belief Muslims have about al-Qadr is that Allah is omnipotent. **(1)** This means that he has control over the universe and the power to do whatever he wills, as part of his plan. The Qur'an says: 'The overall scheme belongs to God' (Surah 13:42). **(1)**

Another belief is that humans have been given free will. **(1)** Allah does not force anyone to do anything, as they have the freedom to do and believe whatever they like. **(1)** This is why there is a Day of Judgment when everyone will have to answer for the choices they made. **(1)**

For	Against
• Allah has a plan. • Many laws in the universe are fixed. • Sunni Muslims believe Allah already knows everyone's destiny.	• Humans have freedom. • People's choices will be rewarded or punished in the next life. • Shi'a Muslims believe a person's destiny can change depending on how they live.

5.8 Akhirah

AO1: Another possible developed point: A second reason Muslims believe in life after death is because they hope for a reward for how they have lived on earth. **(1)** Allah is just and omniscient, which gives them assurance that he will not let their lives go to waste. **(1)**

AO2: Here are some possible statements of conclusion: **a.** I believe that paradise is the main incentive for doing good deeds, therefore it would seem pointless to be honest and give to charity, for example, unless there was a reward in the next life. **b.** I believe that there is no need to be religious to be a good person. Many atheists make a positive difference without believing in a paradise after death. **c.** The only motivation for doing good deeds is to live selflessly purely to please Allah. **d.** Some Muslims perform good deeds only because they want to get to paradise, while other Muslims do so to create a better society and to make Allah happy.

Compare and Contrast: 5.8 Akhirah

See the completed table in the Apply section of this Compare and Contrast topic for a sample answer.

Chapter 5 Exam Practice

3 mark question

2. Answers could include: Muslims believe that Allah is one (this is known as Tawhid). **(1)** They also believe that Allah is beneficent (kind) **(1)** and omnipotent (all-powerful). **(1)**

3. Possible answers: Muslims believe that angels are created out of light. **(1)** They provide a link between Allah and the prophets. **(1)** Finally, Muslims believe that angels have no free will. **(1)**

4 mark question

2. A possible response: One way Muslims can show commitment to their faith is by reciting and understanding the Qu'ran. **(1)** It is the holiest book for Muslims as it is Allah's final revelation and is free from any distortion. **(1)**

A second way Muslims can show commitment to their faith is by naming their children after prophets. **(1)** This is because, by doing this, the children are encouraged to try to develop similar qualities to the prophet they have been named after. **(1)**

3. Two reasons could include: One reason why the Qur'an is the most important holy book for Muslims is because they believe it contains the actual words of Allah. **(1)** The angel Jibril brought the revelation directly from Allah to the Prophet Muhammad, who was the final messenger to receive a scripture. **(1)**

Another reason is because the Qu'ran has never been corrupted. **(1)** Unlike other religions whose books were changed or are no longer reliable, Muslims believe that the Qur'an is perfect. Therefore it offers the most accurate guidance on how to live a life that is pleasing to Allah. **(1)**

5 mark question

2. A possible response: One belief Muslims have about al-Qadr is that Allah is omnipotent. **(1)** This means that he has control over the universe and the power to do whatever he wills, as part of his plan. **(1)** The Qur'an says: 'The overall scheme belongs to God' (Surah 13:42). **(1)**

A second belief is that humans have been given free will. **(1)** Allah does not force anyone to do anything, as they have the freedom to do and believe whatever they like. This is why there is a Day of Judgment when everyone will have to answer for the choices they made. **(1)**

3. Two possible reasons: One reason why Jibril is important to Muslims is because, like other angels, he is greatly valued by Allah. **(1)** The Qur'an says: 'If anyone is an enemy […] of Gabriel and Michael, then God is certainly the enemy of such disbelievers' (Surah 2:98). **(1)** This emphasises the importance for Muslims to believe in Jibril and all the angels. **(1)**

A second reason is because Jibril is the angel of revelation who communicates Allah's messages to prophets. **(1)** This includes communicating the whole Qur'an to the Prophet Muhammad who received Allah's final message to humanity. **(1)**

12 mark question

2. An argument for the statement: Many Muslims would agree with this statement because they believe in free will. They believe life on earth is preparation for the Akhirah and their actions will determine whether they will be punished or rewarded, so because of this they control their destiny. Shi'a Muslims believe Surah 13:11 in the Qur'an allows the possibility that Allah can change a person's destiny according to the actions they decide to take. For instance, Allah may have destined for you to die at aged 60, but if you are a good person and have a positive influence on others, Allah may grant you a longer life. This is a convincing argument in favour of the belief that a person's actions can change their destiny.

An argument against the statement: However, Muslims also believe in al-Qadr, that the universe follows the divine master plan of Allah who is omnipotent, omniscient, and has a plan for the world. Therefore, it could be argued that their destiny is already known, and some Muslims believe this plan is written by Allah in Al-Lawh al-Mahfuz (The Preserved Tablet). This is closer to the view of Sunni Muslims who believe that human choices are already known by Allah before they make them. For instance, a parent may already know their child will always choose a bar of chocolate over a piece of fruit, but it's still the child making the choice.

A possible conclusion: In conclusion, I believe that there is a strong case to argue that Islam teaches that every person does make their own destiny. Although Muslims believe Allah is omnipotent and omniscient, and some may argue that their destiny is already set, they have to make their choices without knowing their ultimate destiny. As humans are given free will, they need to be responsible for their choices and actions. This is why there is a Day of Judgment when Allah will decide if a person will go to paradise or hell. Therefore every person controls their destiny.

3. An argument for the statement: Some Muslims would agree with this statement. This is because for Sunni Muslims Akhirah is one of the six Beliefs, and for Shi'a Muslims Mi'ad (the Day of Judgment and the Resurrection) is one of the five roots of 'Usul ad-Din. The Qur'an teaches: 'all praise belongs to Him in this world and the next: His is the Judgement; and to Him you shall be returned' (Surah 28:70). This teaching shows that there is a link between the next life and meeting Allah, who will then decide whether a person goes to paradise or hell. This has an enormous influence on how believers live on earth.

Some arguments against the statement: Other Muslims would say that other beliefs are either equally or more important, such as Tawhid, which forms the basis of all other beliefs. The first Pillar of Islam for Sunnis and the first of the five roots of 'Usul ad-Din for Shi'a Muslims are about the oneness of Allah, which highlights how important this is. Many Muslims would also argue that it is their actions in this life, and their commitment to duties such as Salah and Zakah, which determines what will happen in the Hereafter.

A possible conclusion: In conclusion, I think it is clear that Akhirah is certainly an important belief, as it is included in the main tenets of both Sunni and Shi'a Muslim traditions. However, I don't believe it is the most important, as without believing in Allah and doing good deeds, belief in the afterlife would be meaningless.

6.1 The Ten Obligatory Acts

AO1: Here is a possible developed answer: The first reason why the Ten Obligatory Acts are important for Shi'a Muslims is because they are an expression of their core beliefs, and are to be carried out during their life. **(1)** An example of this is Salah – prayer. **(1)**

The second reason is because through practising them, Shi'a Muslims gain nearness to Allah, **(1)** and thereby increase their chance of getting to paradise in the next life. **(1)**

AO2:

For	Against
• All acts come from the Qur'an. • Every act helps Shi'a Muslims gain nearness to Allah.	• Some acts are more difficult to follow. • Sunni Muslims say the Five Pillars are more important.

6.2 Shahadah

AO1: A possible response: Salah, which is praying five times a day. **(1)** Sawm, which is fasting. **(1)** Hajj, which is the pilgrimage to Makkah. **(1)**

AO2: A possible developed answer: Many Muslims may argue that Shahadah is the most important Pillar of Islam because it is the declaration of their core beliefs. The Qur'an says, 'God bears witness that there is no god but Him' (Surah 3:18). They could point to the fact that it is the first Pillar of Islam, highlighting its priority, and argue that you cannot be a Muslim without believing in it.

6.3 Salah

AO1: A possible third point: Ablution (wudu') must be performed before each prayer. **(1)**

AO2:

For	Against
Unlike other Pillars like Sawm and Zakah, Salah is a daily commitment and therefore enables Muslims to connect more frequently with Allah.	Muslims who go on pilgrimage often experience a big change in their life and become more spiritual afterwards.

Compare and Contrast: 6.3 Salah

See the completed table in the Apply section of this Compare and Contrast topic for a sample answer.

6.4 Sawm

AO1: The points have been developed thus: One reason why sawm is important in Islam is because it enables Muslims to develop spiritually. **(1)** Ramadan is a month spent in more worship than normal, so that Muslims can feel even closer to Allah. **(1)**

A second reason is that it teaches Muslims to be more grateful for what they have. **(1)** Going without food and drink for several hours reminds them of how fortunate they are to have these things, as compared with others who might lack them. **(1)**

AO2: A possible counter-argument: However, it could be argued that sawm is not the only way to become a better person. There are other actions that could improve a person's character more, for example Salah, which must be offered five times a day, while sawm is not practised as often. Furthermore, many who perform Hajj seem to become more spiritual afterwards because of the amazing experience they had while in Makkah. Meanwhile, Zakah makes a direct difference to others, and doesn't just benefit the individual paying it. These show that there are many other ways to become better without having to fast.

6.5 Zakah and khums

AO1: A possible second point: Secondly, another purpose of Zakah is to make a positive difference to others. **(1)** By following this Pillar of Islam, the poor and needy are helped directly and benefit from the wealth shared by fellow Muslims. This further makes them feel part of the ummah. **(1)**

AO2: A good evaluation answer shows you have considered different points of view and have been able to give at least one detailed reason why you believe one argument is more convincing than another.

A possible conclusion 'for': In conclusion, although I feel individuals should do their best to reduce poverty, they don't have as much influence and money as the government does. The country's leaders are elected to make fair use of wealth so that all citizens in society have what they need, such as a decent place to live and enough to eat. Therefore I believe it is the government's duty to take care of the less fortunate.

A possible conclusion 'against': Having considered both sides of the argument, I believe that even though governments have a part to play in taking care of the less fortunate, individuals also have a responsibility, especially religious people. This is because their faith teaches them to look out for the poor, and they will be held accountable for this in the next life. Therefore I think that individuals have an important duty to take care of the less fortunate.

6.6 Hajj

AO1: This answer now contains a source of wisdom and authority: One reason why Muslims perform Hajj is because it is a commandment of Allah, **(1)** and one of the Five Pillars. **(1)** This means that it is compulsory for Muslims who meet the criteria. **(1)** As the Qur'an says: 'Proclaim the Pilgrimage to all people.' (Surah 22:27) **(1)**

AO2: A possible counter-argument: However, Hajj may be seen to have more challenges than benefits. This is because it is now very common for millions of Muslims to be together in one place and this is not always safe. There have been several stampedes in Makkah that have caused deaths. This also shows how physically demanding Hajj can be, and is therefore not advised for those who may struggle to keep pace during particular rituals.

6.7 Jihad

AO1: This is a possible developed answer: One Muslim belief about jihad is that it is primarily an internal struggle to become a better person. **(1)** This is why any effort to improve oneself, such as through prayer and fasting, is described as a greater jihad. **(1)**

A second belief is about lesser jihad, which is mainly about protecting Muslims and all oppressed people when there is a threat to their lives. **(1)** The Qur'an teaches: 'Those who have been attacked are permitted to take up arms because they have been wronged' (Surah 22:39). **(1)** This shows that lesser jihad is supposed to be in self-defence rather than for spreading Islam. **(1)**

AO2:

For	Against
• This is what the Prophet Muhammad spent most of his life doing and Muslims are required to follow his Sunnah. • Striving spiritually enables Muslims to get closer to Allah.	• There are circumstances when it is necessary to defend yourself from an attack. Failure to fight could result in a huge loss of life. • The Qur'an praises martyrs who die fighting for Allah.

6.8 Celebrations and commemorations

AO1: A possible developed answer: Commemorations are important for Muslims because it is a chance for them to remember sacrifices made in the past. **(1)** For example, at Id-ul-Adha Muslims are reminded of the story of Isma'il who was ready to be sacrificed by his father Ibrahim (because of a dream seen by Ibrahim in which he was taking his son's life). **(1)** God stopped this from happening and praised them for their willingness to put their faith first, a lesson for all people. **(1)**

Commemorations are also important because they bring Muslims together. **(1)** This helps to strengthen the spirit of love and loyalty within the ummah. **(1)**

AO2: Obviously your thesis could be for or against, as in these possible responses:
For: Both Sunni and Shi'a Muslims share the same six Beliefs and Five Pillars, and therefore have many similarities. There is no reason why they should not celebrate the same events. **Against:** Id-ul-Ghadeer can only be celebrated by Shi'a Muslims because of their belief that Ali should have been the first successor, which Sunni Muslims disagree with.

Chapter 6 Exam Practice

3 mark question

2. Two further features could be: Zakah requires Muslims to give 2.5% of their wealth to the poor. **(1)** It is an act of worship. **(1)**

3. Answers could include: Three Obligatory Acts for Shi'a Muslims include Salah (praying five times a day), **(1)** Khums (giving 20% of one's surplus income), **(1)** and Amr bil Ma'roof (encouraging others to do good). **(1)**

4 mark question

2. Two possible reasons: One reason why Hajj is important to Muslims is because it promotes the bond of unity between Muslims of all colours and cultures. **(1)** This is shown by the wearing of the Ihram, which symbolises the equality of all people, regardless of their background. This is seen at Hajj every year when people from Africa stand shoulder to shoulder with people from Europe, reminding Muslims that no person is superior to another person. **(1)**

Secondly, Muslims believe that the pilgrimage removes all sins as long as they repent with a sincere heart. This is like being born again with a fresh start, and is symbolised with the shaving of the head. **(1)** Only Allah can forgive sins, so by going on Hajj Muslims hope Allah will reward them for their commitment to him. **(1)**

3. Two possible reasons: Muslims believe greater jihad is more relevant to them because it is the everyday struggle to become closer to Allah, which is the highest aim of every Muslim. **(1)** The Prophet Muhammad spent the majority of his time in greater jihad, therefore many Muslims believe they should too. **(1)**

They also believe that greater jihad is more relevant to Muslims because the conditions for lesser jihad are not met today. **(1)** One of these is denying Muslims religious freedoms and stopping them from praying and practising other aspects of their faith. Human rights laws mean that these rights are protected for everyone, including Muslims. **(1)**

5 mark question

2. Explain two reasons why Muslims believe charitable giving is a central part of Islam. In your answer you must refer to a source of wisdom and authority. (5 marks)

A possible response: Islam teaches that wealth is given by Allah for the benefit of human beings and so it should be shared. **(1)** The third Pillar Zakah purifies wealth by Muslims giving a share of it to the poor and needy. **(1)**

The fifth Obligatory Act for Shi'a Muslims is to pay khums, based on Surah 8:41, 'Know that one-fifth of your battle gains belongs to God and the Messenger.' **(1)** Based on this khums, the donation of one-fifth of their surplus income is divided between the Imam in occultation and the poor and orphaned, therefore benefitting the clergy and the community. **(1)**

3. Two reasons could include: One reason why Muslims perform Hajj is because it is a commandment of Allah, and one of the Five Pillars. **(1)** This means that it is compulsory for Muslims who meet the criteria. **(1)** As the Qur'an says: 'Proclaim the Pilgrimage to all people.' (Surah 22:27) **(1)**

Another reason why Muslims perform Hajj is to have their sins forgiven. **(1)** Muslims believe that anyone who performs the pilgrimage with the right intention, and who prays sincerely, will be treated with special mercy by Allah. **(1)**

2. A possible argument for the statement: Many Muslims would agree with this statement because both Sunni and Shi'a Muslims already celebrate two festivals – Id-ul-Fitr and Id-ul-Adha. Id-ul-Fitr is celebrated at the end of the month of Ramadan and is linked to Sawm, which is one of the Five Pillars for Sunni Muslims and one of the Ten Obligatory Acts for Shi'a Muslims. Furthermore, Id-ul-Adha commemorates the occasion that Ibrahim was willing to sacrifice his son Ishma'il and Muslims recount the story as a reminder of their dedication to God, and to inspire them also to put God first. This appears to be a strong argument to favour joint celebrations.

A possible argument against the statement: Other Muslims would disagree because Id-ul-Ghadeer can only be celebrated by Shi'a Muslims because of their belief that Ali should have been the first successor, which Sunni Muslims disagree with. Furthermore, Ashura is a solemn day of remembrance of the martyrdom of the third imam for Shi'a Muslims, Imam Husayn. While he is an important figure for Sunni Muslims too, it is only Shi'a Muslims who hold gatherings when mosques are draped in black and worshippers wear black too, to symbolise mourning.

A possible conclusion: In conclusion, I think it is impossible for all Muslims to celebrate the same commemorations as it is evident that Sunni Muslims would not join Shi'a Muslims in their belief that Ali should have succeeded the Prophet Muhammad rather than Abu Bakr. Many Shi'a Muslims regard Id-ul-Ghadeer as being more important than the other Ids, which Sunni Muslims would disagree with. Both groups interpret Surah 5:3 differently.

3. A possible argument for the statement: Muslims would agree that the benefits of Hajj outweigh the challenges. This is because as one of the Five Pillars of Islam, there must be many blessings associated with it. As the Qur'an says: 'Proclaim the Pilgrimage to all people' (Surah 22:27). Performing the pilgrimage enables Muslims to strengthen their relationship with Allah and brings the ummah together as one united body. These, and the various rituals that take place such as the symbolic stoning of Satan, inspire pilgrims to become better people.

A possible argument against the statement: However, Hajj is also seen as extremely challenging. This is because it is now very common for millions of Muslims to be together in one place and this is not always safe. There have been several stampedes in Makkah that have caused deaths, such as in 2015 when it was reported that around 2000 pilgrims lost their lives. This also shows how physically demanding Hajj can be, and is therefore not advised for those who may struggle to keep pace during particular rituals.

A possible conclusion: In conclusion, I believe there is a more robust case to say that Hajj has more benefits as many pilgrims return home ready to share their experience with other Muslims, which promotes a sense of belonging and community in the ummah.

7.1 The Almighty

AO1: Three characteristics could include: Creator: God created everything in the universe as outlined in Genesis. **(1)** Lawgiver: God gave the Law to Moses on Mount Sinai. **(1)** Judge: God judges how well Jews keep the law that he gave them. **(1)**

AO2:

Oneness is the most important	Something else is the most important
Judaism is monotheistic, which is a central belief. It is found in the Shema which is recited twice daily.	Creator This is the most important, as without creation, there simply would be no universe, no people, and no Judaism.
As there is just one God, this means he is the one Creator, one Lawgiver, and one Judge.	Lawgiver Law is central to life for Jews, and without it, there would be no relationship with God.
The Tenakh makes clear that there is just one God and so he is the only being to whom Jews should offer praise and prayer.	Judge This is linked to the law, but without judgment, there is no point in having laws, making it vitally important.

Conclusion:

Oneness is the most important because Judaism is monotheistic and was founded after Abraham's recognition of this fact.

OR Creator is the most important because as without creation, Judaism would quite simply not exist.

OR They are all equally important because Jews believe the Almighty is all of these things, and without out of these, he would not be the Almighty.

7.2 The Shekhinah

AO1: A possible answer: Secondly, Jews feel the divine presence of the Almighty as they study, worship and pray. **(1)** The Shekhinah is an explanation of this. **(1)**

AO2: Three possible points for 'Agree': **1.** Study is a form of worship for Jews. **2.** Certain prayers can only be said with a minyan. **3.** The Talmud says: 'Whenever ten are gathered for prayer, there the Shekhinah rests.'

7.3 The Messiah

AO1: A possible response: Secondly, Jewish people were reassured by the prophets that a great leader would come to restore their kingdom. **(1)** This was important as they were in exile. **(1)**

AO2:

Agree	Disagree
• Some Jews believe that the Messiah will come when he is most deserved, therefore it is their responsibility to work towards this. • Most Orthodox Jews believe in a Messiah who is come, according to Maimonides' thirteen Principles of Faith. • Even if the focus is not on the Messiah, Jews can actively contribute to bringing about the key ideas of the Messianic Age such as peace and justice.	• The idea of a coming Messiah is not a major focus for many Reform Jews. • Some Jews believe that the Almighty has already set a date for the Messianic Age, so it is irrelevant if Jews try to actively bring it about. • Bringing about a better world is a separate activity from bringing about the Messianic Age.

A possible conclusion: For many Jews, they do not feel it is their responsibility to bring about the Messianic Age and the idea of the Messiah is not a particularly important one. However, observing the Law is.

Another possible conclusion: Some Jews feel that actively pursuing the Messianic Age is important, because there is still oppression of Jews and a need for peace and harmony.

7.4 The covenant at Sinai

AO1: Possible sources of wisdom and authority: **1.** 'God has chosen you to be for Him a treasured people.' (Deuteronomy 7:6) **2.** 'Everything that Hashem has spoken we shall do.' (Exodus 19:8) **3.** An example from the Ten Commandments.

AO2: Four possible reasons: **1.** Identified the Jewish people as the chosen people by God. **2.** Made clear that Jews who followed the agreements would be blessed, and those who did not would be punished (Deuteronomy 28:15–68). **3.** The Torah was given to Moses, which contained 613 laws for Jews to follow. These are still central to Jewish life today. **4.** Every Jewish soul was present at Sinai.

7.5 The covenant with Abraham

AO1: A possible second point: Secondly, prayers for the state of Israel, and for a return to Israel, feature in the Sabbath and festival prayers. **(1)** This shows the importance of this idea for all Jews, even if they are not actively trying to move there. **(1)**

AO2: Four possible reasons: **1.** Abraham was the first one to recognise God as the single creator of the universe. **2.** The promise of a 'great nation' is still central to Judaism today. **3.** Without the covenant with Abraham, there would be no covenant with Moses. **4.** Jews are still circumcised today.

A possible conclusion: In conclusion, it is clear that the covenant with Abraham is the most important as it was effectively the start of Judaism. Without this covenant there would be no relationship between God and the Jewish people.

7.6 The sanctity of life

AO1: One possible example: Firstly, it is clear that protecting human life is important. **(1)** In the Book of Genesis, which is part of the Jewish Torah, it clearly states that God created man in his image. **(1)** The Talmud states that as a result, to take a human life is like destroying the entire world. **(1)**

AO2:

For	Against
• Pikuach Nefesh says the preservation of human life overrides almost all other laws. • If a life is in danger, almost any Mitzvah can be broken. • Example: save a life by organ donation can break law not to desecrate a corpse (Talmud Yoma 83–84). • Other examples: rescue a child from the sea, break apart a wall collapsed on a child, extinguish a fire.	• Some Mitzvah can't be broken, e.g. worshipping another God, saying God's name, or denying God's existence to avoid persecution. • People must not murder, create a dangerous situation (e.g. speed to rush to hospital), or commit adultery. • People cannot give up their life for someone (suicide is forbidden), but they can risk life for someone – but it shouldn't be a higher risk than the other person is in.

7.7 Moral principles and the Mitzvot

AO1: A possible 4-mark answer: One reason is the Mitzvot come from God and this is reason enough to follow them. **(1)** Jews believe that they were given to Moses alongside the Ten Commandments on Mount Sinai. **(1)**

A second reason is Jews believe they are the best way to live their life. **(1)** It enables them to show gratitude to God and deepen their relationship with him. **(1)**

AO2:

For	Against
• Given to Jews from God via Moses on Mount Sinai. • Gift from God and keeping them shows gratitude to God. • Helps bring spiritual significance into daily tasks, such as eating, which deepens the relationship. • This would be the view of most Orthodox Jews.	• Some no longer appropriate such as sacrificing animals. • Inspired Word of God but influenced by culture and history of the time. • Discussion and analysis by Rabbis can help Jews understand better for the modern world. • This would be the view of most Reform Jews.

7.8 Life after death

AO1: A possible source of wisdom and authority: This is based upon Ecclesiastes 12:7, which says: 'Thus the dust returns to the ground, as it was, and the spirit returns to God who gave it.'

AO2:

For	Against
• Most Jews believe there will be an afterlife, and therefore it is a consideration for Jews. • The Torah makes clear that those who do not follow the Mitzvot will be punished (Exodus 31:14). • It is unclear if the afterlife is an instant thing, or something that will only come in the Messianic Age.	• There is very little in the Torah on the afterlife, therefore main focus should be on life. • All souls will reach Gan Eden eventually even if they are deemed unrighteous when dead. • It could be argued that until the Messianic Age, true righteousness will not be established.

Compare and Contrast: 7.8 Life after death

See the completed table in the Apply section of this Compare and Contrast topic for a sample answer.

Chapter 7 Exam Practice

3 mark question

2. Two further answers could be: Well versed in Jewish law. **(1)** A great military leader. **(1)**

3. Three possible answers: Visiting the sick.**(1)** Feeding the hungry. **(1)** Comforting those who are mourning. **(1)**

4 mark question

2. A possible answer: One reason Jews believe that life is holy is that it comes from God. **(1)** In Genesis, it states that 'God created Man in his image'. **(1)**

A second reason is Jews believe that all people are descended from a single person, Adam.
(1) As such, to take a human life is like destroying the whole world. **(1)**

3. A possible response: Firstly, it is the teaching of the Book of Exodus, **(1)**, which says that the Almighty is present among the people of Israel. **(1)**

Secondly, it is the teaching of the Book of Ezekiel, **(1)** which says that the presence of the Almighty dwells in the Temple. **(1)**

Although you don't need one in the 4 mark question, you can use a quote as part of your development of a point.

5 mark question

2. A possible response: Firstly, the Almighty promises Abraham that he will be the father of many nations. **(1)** This means the earth will be blessed through his children, **(1)** as seen in Genesis 17:5–6: 'for I have made you a father of many nations. I will make you very fruitful; I will make nations of you, and kings will come from you.' **(1)**

Secondly, it is a covenant where the Almighty promises the land of Canaan to the Jews, **(1)** which has been a central theme of Judaism throughout history, continuing to today. **(1)**

3. A possible response: One characteristic is the Almighty is considered as Creator. **(1)** This is as only the Almighty could create the universe from nothing, **(1)** as made clear in Genesis 1 and 2. **(1)**

A second characteristic is the Almighty is seen as the Lawgiver. **(1)** This is because he gave the Torah to Moses on Mount Sinai. **(1)**

15 mark question

2. Possible arguments for the statement: This covenant identified the Jewish people as the people chosen by God. It made clear that Jews who followed the agreements would be blessed, and those who did not would be punished (Deuteronomy 28:15–68). The Torah was given to Moses, which contained 613 laws for Jews to follow; these are still central to Jewish life today. Jews believe that every Jewish soul was present at Sinai.

Possible arguments against the statement: The covenant with Abraham was the most important as it was the first one to recognise God as the single creator of the universe. The promise of a 'great nation' is still central to Judaism today. Without the covenant with Abraham, there would be no covenant with Moses. Jews are still circumcised today.

A possible conclusion: In conclusion, it is clear that the covenant with Moses is the most significant covenant for Jewish people as it defines so much about their lives even today. The Law is central to Jews, and this was the gift from God, given on Sinai.

3. Possible arguments for the statement: The Tenakh has many references to the Almighty as judge, for example, Isaiah 33:22. Psalm 9:8 says that the Almighty will ensure the good are rewarded and the evil are punished. Being a judge is a key characteristic of the Almighty for Jewish people.

Possible arguments against the statement: The Messianic Age is still to come and most Jewish people believe that this is when judgement will occur; therefore, in the meantime, Jewish people need to pass some judgements themselves in order to function in society. Jewish courts (Bet Din) make judgements about the Halakhah today.

A possible conclusion: Most Jews would agree with the statement as Judge is a key characteristic of the Almighty. Any judgement that is made by humans is based on Law of the Almighty.

8.1

AO1: Three occasions could include: On the Friday evening at the start of Shabbat. **(1)** For the morning Daily Prayers. **(1)** On Jewish festivals such as Rosh Hashanah. **(1)**

AO2: A possible conclusion: I think it is clear that the public acts of worship that take place in a synagogue are vitally important to Jews. The development of such practice has enabled Jews to be united regularly both locally and globally, which has been particularly important in times of oppression.

8.2 The Tenakh and Talmud

AO1: A possible second way: Secondly, it can be difficult for them to eat out if restaurants are not kosher **(1)** because they may use the same utensils for meat and dairy. **(1)**

AO2:

For	Against
• Why is it important? • Contains teachings and opinions of thousands of early Rabbis • Why do Orthodox Jews agree? (Source of wisdom and authority) • Believe it's oral tradition given to Moses, Perkei Avot says it will help attain eternal life • What practical provision is made for Jews? • Study in the synagogue	• What is the **most** important book? • The Torah • Why may Reform and Liberal Jews disagree? • Feel modern debate is more important • What practical issues might there be? • Incredibly long and not originally in English

8.3 Private prayer

AO1: A possible answer: The first reason is that they believe God instructed them to pray three times a day. **(1)** This allows them to keep the Almighty as an important part of their day. **(1)** It is made clear in Psalms: 'Evening, morning and noon […] He has heard my voice.' **(1)**

Secondly, it allows them to reflect on their day; **(1)** for example, they may say the Modeh ani in the morning to remember their gratefulness of the Almighty's gift of life. **(1)**

AO2:

For	Against
• Psalm 55:16-23; mentions courtyards of House of Hashem. • Can be done at home so it is easy for all to participate; no need to visit synagogue. • It is traditional to recite prayer three times a day; which allows personal time with God.	• Reform Jews may feel it is acceptable to change their practice to match modern living, which may mean not praying three times a day. • Some Jews would say that the quality of prayer is more important than quantity. • The responsibility of all Jews is to read the Torah.

A possible conclusion: In conclusion, I think most Jews would try to pray three times a day, because it is a useful reminder to them of the Almighty's presence in their daily life.

8.4 The Shema and the Amidah

AO1: Other prayers could include: The Amidah is the core part of every Jewish service. **(1)** The Aleinu is recited at the end of every Jewish service. **(1)**

AO2:

The Shema	Makes clear the core belief of one God, plus other important beliefs, therefore it can be considered the most important
The Amidah	Used in every synagogue service
The Aleinu	Used at the end of synagogue services; as the last prayer said, it could be considered the most important
The Kaddish	Prayer of praise which is used regularly
Barkhu	Call to prayer at the start of every service; it is the most important because it comes first

Compare and Contrast: 8.4 The Shema and the Amidah

See the completed table in the Apply section of this Compare and Contrast topic for a sample answer.

8.5 Ritual and ceremony

AO1: A second part of this answer might be: The second feature is that the name for a girl is given in the synagogue, **(1)** while the boy's name is given during Brit Milah when he is circumcised. **(1)**

AO2: Possible arguments against the statement: In an Orthodox synagogue, a Brit Milah is quite different to the Bar Mitzvah, involving different preparation. An exchange of rings only happens in Reform ceremonies, in Orthodox ceremonies the groom just gives one to the bride. Orthodox Jews do not permit cremation while some Reform/Liberal Jews may.

8.6 Shabbat

AO1: A possible developed answer: It is an instruction from the Almighty. **(1)** Genesis makes clear that on the seventh day of Creation, he rested and Jews believe they should do likewise. **(1)** It allows a connection to a Jew's family. **(1)** The Friday night meal is a time for the family to eat, pray and sing together. They will also often spend Saturday together at home or in the synagogue. **(1)**

AO2:

	Orthodox	Reform
Using a mobile phone	Electrical connection seen as 'ignition' – starting a fire was 'work' in the time of Moses.	It may be used to connect to absent family so they are united for Shabbat.
Driving a car to the synagogue	A car requires an 'ignition' when it starts – starting a fire was 'work' in the time of Moses.	Getting to the synagogue is important if you live a long way from it.

Other examples may include: Lights in the house (Orthodox Jews may have timers), watching TV (another 'ignition'), making a cup of tea.

8.7 Festivals

AO1: Festivals could include: Rosh Hashanah is the first day of the Jewish year and remembers the story of Creation. **(1)** Yom Kippur is the 'Day of Atonement' and is the

holiest day of the year. **(1)** Pesach is the first of the three pilgrim festivals; it is also called Passover. **(1)**

AO2:

For	Against
• Rosh Hashanah is specified in the Tenakh, Leviticus 23. • They provide a connection both to the local and global community. Most festivals involve activities in the home and the synagogue. • Link to history of the Jewish people, for example, Pesach and the Almighty 'passing over'.	• May not be possible to celebrate all Jewish festivals, as it would require too much time off work or school. • Most festivals are not specified in the Torah, so are later parts of the Jewish faith. • Regular worship in the synagogue is the most important part of events, or Shabbat each week.

One possible conclusion: Most Jews observe festivals such as Pesach and Yom Kippur, but observance may vary for other festivals depending on whether they are Orthodox or Reform Jews, and where in the world they live.

8.8 Features of the synagogue

AO1:

First feature	The first feature is the bimah, the reading platform in the synagogue.
Development	This represents the altar in the Temple.
Second feature	The second feature is the Ark, where the Torah is stored.
Development	This is a reminder of the Holy of Holies in the Temple, and keeps the Torah safe.

AO2:

For	Against
• Most important features – the Ark and bimah will always be part of the design, and so they are basically designed the same way. • Items are linked to the Temple, and so there should be some similarity. • It would unite different Jewish communities if this was the case, and allow them to worship together.	• Not always practical: a building may have been purchased which does not face Jerusalem, for example. • Orthodox and Reform/Liberal Jews have different traditions, and design will reflect this, such as a balcony for women. • The layout of seats will depend on the position of the Ark, and this varies between traditions, therefore the rest of the design will also vary.

Chapter 8 Exam Practice

3 mark question

2. Possible answers include: Brit Milah is when the boy is circumcised as a baby. **(1)** A Bat Mitzvah is when a girl 'comes of age' at either 12 or 13. **(1)** Misuin is the name for a full marriage. **(1)**

3. Possible answers include: Jews do extra study of the Torah. **(1)** They decorate their homes and synagogues with flowers and greenery. **(1)** They eat dairy food. **(1)**

4 mark question

2. A possible answer: One reason is the Torah contains rules from the Almighty **(1)** and is clear about what Jewish people should and should not eat. **(1)**

Another reason is the Almighty has given humans dominion over the earth **(1)** and this causes minimal suffering to the animals. **(1)**

3. A possible answer: Firstly, it celebrates the Almighty's love for the Jewish people. **(1)** He saved them from slavery in Egypt. **(1)**

Secondly, it is connected to a return to Israel. **(1)** Jews wish that they will celebrate the following year's meal together in Jerusalem. **(1)**

5 mark question

2. A possible answer: Firstly, it is the most special time of the week, when the week ends. **(1)** It is a day of rest and time with the family, including a meal together. **(1)** Jews are remembering the rest that God took after the creation of the world: 'On the seventh day He rested and was refreshed' (Exodus 31:17). **(1)**

Secondly it is a time of prayer and praise when Jews go to the synagogue. **(1)** Jews meet together as a community at the synagogue and hear readings from the Torah. **(1)**

3. A possible answer: One reason private prayer is important is that it is a necessity

for many Jews. **(1)** This is because they cannot get to the synagogue three times a day. **(1)** The Book of Psalms says: 'Evening, morning, and noon, I supplicate and moan; and He has heard me my voice' (55:18) , which is taken as a command to pray three times daily. **(1)**

A second reason is private prayer allows Jews to pray for different intentions. **(1)** This would be important, depending on their current situation; they may want to pray in thanksgiving or asking for something. **(1)**

15 mark question

2. A possible response: Many Jews would agree with this view as Shabbat is seen as such a special time of the week where they relax with family, and as a community in the synagogue. It is clear in Exodus that the Almighty rested on the seventh day after Creation, 'on the seventh day He rested and was refreshed' (31:17), and therefore Jews do the same. Shabbat marks the end of the week. Additionally, it is considered a core part of the Jewish faith, as it featured in the Ten Commandments given to Moses on Sinai. Honouring this is fundamental to many Jews.

On the other hand, some Jews would hold a different point of view and see Shabbat as difficult, if not impossible in the modern world. It is difficult to switch off and not do anything considered 'work'. They may feel that private, daily prayers are the most important thing to do. Psalm 55 makes it clear that 'He has heard my voice' (55:18) when praying evening, morning, and noon. Finally, as there is disagreement about what you can and can't do on Shabbat, some Jews may simply have time with family and friends without keeping to all the laws connected to Shabbat.

Having considered both sides of the argument, I would say that keeping Shabbat is vitally important for Jews, perhaps more so in the modern world. Despite the difficulties, Jews have found ways to overcome them.

3. A possible response: Jews believe that it is important to worship in public with others, originally in the Temple. This is made clear: 'My vows to Hashem I will pay […] in the courtyards of the House of Hashem' (Psalm 116:14–19). Temple worship was a key feature of life for Jews living in Jerusalem at this time. After its destruction in 70CE, public worship moved to the synagogues. Therefore it is a long established part of Jewish life. The synagogue provides an opportunity for Jews to come together as a community, not only to pray, but additionally to socialise, study, and do charitable work.

However, for Jews living in some areas, it may be very difficult to get to a synagogue, therefore they may only be able to attend on special occasions such as Pesach and Yom Kippur. Daily prayers can be said at home, recognising the fact it can be hard to get to the synagogue. They can say the same prayers, and face Jerusalem, from home. Jews who are less observant may still attend the synagogue, just less frequently. They still feel part of the Jewish community, and observe some Mitzvot, but do not worship in public on a regular basis.

A possible conclusion: In conclusion, Jews should worship in the synagogue when possible. However, this must be balanced with their family and work life. It is important to connect with their local community of fellow Jews.

9.1 Revelation

AO1: A possible second point: Secondly, revelation began in the Old Testament when God communicated to the people of Israel. **(1)** An example of this is when he spoke to Moses from a burning bush. **(1)**

AO2: A possible counter-argument: For some Christians, revelation, as contained in the Bible, is not as personal as other religious experiences such as miracles that still occur today. Despite stories of people experiencing revelation, some Christians may feel they need a form of personal revelation to have conviction in their faith. Other arguments for God's existence may feel more convincing as they are more evidenced, such as the design argument.

9.2 Visions

AO1: Here are two possible points: Firstly, visions are important as they may lead to a stronger belief in God. **(1)** They may provide a sense of vocation, for example like Joan of Arc. **(1)**

Secondly, there are many examples of visions in the Bible that help Catholics today interpret their visions. God does reveal himself to people, and so Catholics may feel they too gain insight into the nature of God. **(1)** This happened from the earliest of times, such as in Genesis when God appeared to Abraham. **(1)**

AO2: A possible answer: Some Catholics would argue that as there is a history of visions in the Bible, such as Abraham's and the transfiguration of Jesus, they are an important source of revelation. There is also a history of Catholics having visions, such as Joan of Arc and St Bernadette at Lourdes, which are recognised by the Church. Such visions are in keeping with existing Church teaching.

However, since the Church teaches that full revelation happened through Jesus, for many Catholics, therefore, any vision is only reaffirming this, rather than offering any new revelation. Some Catholics argue that visions are too influenced by personal feelings to be considered important sources. Indeed, the Church does

not force Catholics to believe in visions (outside of the Bible), but gives them freedom to believe in them if they wish, which is a strong argument against their importance.

One possible conclusion: In conclusion, while visions can be hugely important to the individual concerned, I do not believe they offer much proof of God's existence and therefore they cannot be seen as an important source of revelation.

9.3 Miracles

AO1: A possible answer: Firstly, miracles are good evidence as there is no other possible explanation apart from God. **(1)** For example, there have been many medically verified healings at Lourdes. **(1)** God showed his love and healing power through Jesus in the Gospel, such as the blind man healed at Beth-sa'ida. **(1)**

Secondly, miracles make the person who experienced the event feel a connection to God. **(1)** This can transform an atheist or agnostic into a believer, or strengthen the faith of a Christian. **(1)**

AO2: Two possible conclusions: **1.** For Catholics, miracles are in keeping with the characteristics of God – loving and omnipotent. This makes it acceptable to believe they still happen today, as long as they are scientifically and medically researched.

2. Despite a long tradition of miracles, many atheists do not see them as good evidence. The crucial point is that science continues to develop – in the near future miracles may be wholly explainable.

9.4 Religious experiences

AO1:

Two other reasons could include: They may be the result of a hallucination caused by drugs. **(1)** They may be simply wish fulfilment by someone wanting a religious experience to happen. **(1)**

AO2:

For	Against
• They have a big impact on believers, for example 5 million people visit Lourdes each year. • They lead to people of no faith converting to religion. This shows their power. • They are in keeping with God's nature, so they are to be expected and should be recognised.	• There are too many reasons that they may not be genuine: wish fulfilment, hallucinations or stimulants • There is often a lack of physical or scientific evidence; careful research is needed to establish if they did indeed happen. • The reason stories such as Lourdes are so important is because they are so infrequent.

9.5 The design argument

AO1: A possible response: Catholics believe that God is omnipotent, which means all powerful. **(1)** As such he has the ability to be the creator of the universe. **(1)** It is clear just from looking at the universe that this is true, as made clear in Romans 1:20, which says that God's 'eternal power' is shown in everything that he has created. **(1)**

AO2: You may have picked any point, but here is an example of an argument for and against the statement: A key strength of the design argument is that it has universal appeal, since it is evident that there is order and regularity in the world. For example, no one can deny the cycle of the sun, or the patterns of the seasons, linked to so many other aspects of nature.

However, a real weakness of the argument is the fact there is so much evil and suffering in the world. It does seem incompatible with an omniscient, omnipotent, and omnibenevolent God.

9.6 The cosmological argument

AO1: A possible second point: Secondly, even if there is a need for a first cause, it does not need to be God. **(1)** For example, many non-religious scientists may be content with the Big Bang being the first cause. **(1)**

AO2: Two possible conclusions: **1.** In conclusion, it is clear that Catholics are not content with accepting the Big Bang as being the first cause and need to know what caused the Big Bang. As they believe in an omnipotent God, capable of universe creation, it makes sense that God is the cause of the Big Bang, and therefore is the first cause.

2. In conclusion, it seems illogical to a non-religious believer not to accept the Big Bang as the first cause, rather than the claim that God is the cause of the universe. If the claim is that God caused the universe then it is only logical to ask the question, 'What caused God?'

9.7 The existence of suffering

AO1: A possible response: There is bad design, so if God does exist, he is not worthy of worship. **(1)** It is illogical to have belief in God as omnipotent and omnibenevolent while evil exists. **(1)** Natural disasters kill thousands indiscriminately, and God couldn't allow this. **(1)**

AO2: Possible answers could be: Some Christians would say moral evil because it is the direct result of the actions of humans.

Some Christians would say natural evil because it seems like unjust punishment for victims.

9.8 Solutions to the problem of suffering

AO1: Here is a possible second point: Secondly, Catholics may take comfort in the Bible, which provides many stories of suffering. **(1)** They may focus on the stories of Jesus' Passion, where God suffered through Jesus. **(1)** Also in Psalms it states: 'It is good for me that I was afflicted, that I might learn thy statutes' (119:71). **(1)**

AO2:

For	Bible: • Job, who God allowed to suffer as he knew he had strong faith. • God suffered in Jesus, revealing a higher purpose in his suffering. Theoretical: • Suffering may allow people to grow towards goodness. • Using free will positively will be rewarded. Practical: • Prayer and charity.
Against	• Despite high numbers of Christians, some do lose their faith, indicating there is a significant problem. • David Hume called it the 'rock of atheism'. • Free will does not explain natural evil, nor the enormity of the problem.

Chapter 9 Exam practice

3 mark question

2. Two possible further points: Only God is omnipotent with the power to implement design. **(1)** Only God is omniscient with the knowledge to design. **(1)**

3. Examples could include: Healing miracles such as these claimed to have happened at Lourdes. **(1)** Miracles involving nature such as Jesus calming the storm. **(1)** Exorcisms such as when Jesus cast out demons from the man called 'Legion'. **(1)**

4 mark question

2. A possible response: Firstly, the world appears to have regularity and order. **(1)** An example of this would be the way days, weeks, months, years, and seasons work. **(1)**

Secondly, the world appears to have purpose. **(1)** If you consider the complexity of life cycles and ecosystems, nature works in a complex way to enable the survival of all species. **(1)**

3. A possible response: The first way that a miracle may lead someone to belief in God is that if it happens to them, they may feel like a prayer has been answered. **(1)** This could strengthen the faith of even an agnostic as they feel God has chosen them. **(1)**

The second way is that it confirms the characteristics of God – only he is powerful enough to break the laws of nature. **(1)** As a result, it confirms that he is worthy and deserving of worship, leading to increased faith. **(1)**

5 mark question

2. A possible answer: Firstly, as Jesus was the final and complete revelation, any religious experience will not reveal anything new about God. **(1)**. However, the revelation of Jesus could be further explained. **(1)** The Catechism makes this clear in 66–67 **(1)**

The Church has recognised some private religious experiences as being genuine, **(1)** for example, Bernadette's visions of Mary in Lourdes. **(1)** This is suggested in CCC 66–67. **(1)**

3. A possible answer: The first reason is that miracles are understood by Catholics to be a sign of the power of God. **(1)** If someone witnesses the breaking of the laws of nature, they can conclude that God must exist to have such power. **(1)** For example, when Jesus healed an official's son (John 4:43–54), it led to belief in him. **(1)**

The second reason is that the Catechism of the Catholic Church (548) says that miracles are a sign of God's presence, **(1)** which is exemplified by the miracles experienced at Lourdes. **(1)**

15 mark question

2. A possible argument for the statement: God spoke to Moses when he saw the burning bush. This experience confirmed Moses' faith in God as a prophet; he was then able to strengthen the faith of the Israelites by recounting this experience. St Paul encountered God on the road to Damascus, an experience that was powerful enough to bring about his conversion to Christianity. Would-be converts to Christianity were inspired by his conversion to believe and seek baptism, which suggests that religious experience is supported by the philosophical principle of testimony. Christians may believe that people can be brought to belief in God by a sense of awe at God's power. Some have said that they were aware of the presence of God when viewing the beauty of creation, and this has been sufficient to give them a knowledge of God's existence.

A possible argument against the statement: Many non-believers argue that religious experiences are akin to psychological illness; they say it is impossible to prove that the experience is real. They therefore conclude that as a philosophical argument no religious experience can count as proof of the existence of God. Some point out that religious experiences most often come to those who already believe. They argue that such people are already disposed to believe even when the evidence is weak, therefore their testimony is unreliable. Most religious experiences are personal. Some people argue that such an experience could cause a conversion or increase in faith for that person. However, the experience of others is not sufficient to convert those who only hear accounts of that experience.

A possible conclusion: For Catholics that already have faith, I think that religious experiences confirm beliefs and are in keeping with the nature of God. Further, the important thing for many Catholics is the experience in and of itself and the effect that it has on the individual.

3. A possible argument for the statement: The cosmological argument is based around the idea of a need for a first cause. It is persuasive as it fits with scientific thinking that the universe has a beginning in the Big Bang. For Catholics, only God has the power to create something from nothing. It is appealing as humans experience the laws of cause and effect on a daily basis. As such it is natural to believe that the universe itself must have a first cause; it could not have caused itself. Finally, it is the only logical conclusion, given the alternative. Otherwise there would be an infinite regress of cause and effect, which seems impossible.

A possible argument against the statement: However, it has been argued that actually it is impossible to apply our limited understanding of cause and effect to the whole universe. Russell suggested we should just accept the universe as fact – it exists. Additionally, Russell claimed that it is not logical to demand the universe has a cause in the same way that everything inside the universe does. Finally, many non-religious scientists are content with the Big Bang being the first cause, so why can't the first cause be this? It seems odd to claim that the Big Bang cannot be the first cause, but that God can.

A possible conclusion: In conclusion, the idea of the need for a first cause is convincing. For the theist this is clearly going to be an all-powerful God, yet the atheist may claim the Big Bang is satisfactory, making the cosmological argument of only limited success.

10.1 Marriage

AO1: A possible second point:

Secondly, it is lifelong. **(1)** As a result, the Catholic Church does not recognise divorce, despite the legal marriage ending. The couple are still married in the eyes of the Church. **(1)**

AO2: Possible arguments for the statement: Many Catholics believe that marriage should always happen in a church, as it follows the institution that God set out by creating Adam and Eve, as found in Genesis. They argue that church marriage ensures that God is present in the marriage and relationships, believing that this can help ensure it is loving, lifelong, exclusive, and fruitful. Marriage is a sacrament, which is an outward sign of God's grace and love, so should take place in church, according to many Christians.

Possible arguments against the statement: However, some Christians believe that marriage in church is not possible if one of the couple has been married in a church previously as you cannot break the religious vows. In a couple where only one person is a practising Christian, and the other does not agree with the idea of church marriage, then a church service will not be appropriate. Homosexual couples cannot marry in a Catholic church and so would have to have a civil ceremony instead.

10.2 Sexual relationships

AO1: Completed outlines could be: Premarital: having sex before marriage. **(1)** Same-sex: homosexuality is not a sin, but homosexual relationships are. **(1)** Cohabitation: living together before marriage.

AO2:

• Unitive: seals the bond of a couple and ensures they have a unique relationship. • Procreative: an openness to children is a requirement for Catholic marriage and marriage is the appropriate place for their upbringing. • Sex is something to be enjoyed, a source of 'joy and pleasure' (CCC 2362), but as a sign of 'spiritual communion' (CCC 2360).	• Non-religious: as long as consenting and 'moral', it is acceptable. • Same-sex couples are unable to receive sacramental marriage; if their relationship is sexual, it is 'outside of marriage'. • Society has changed and a significant percentage of the population do not wait until marriage.

10.3 The family

AO1: A possible answer: Firstly, the family was created by God. **(1)** Adam and Eve in Genesis were the first family while the Holy Family of Mary, Joseph and Jesus is a further example of family life. **(1)**

Secondly, it is the place where children learn about the faith of how to pray. **(1)** This is in both the home and via parish life. **(1)**

10.4 Support for the family

AO1: Answers include: The priest will be a trained counsellor. **(1)** Catechesis classes can be held for parents while their child is preparing for the sacraments. **(1)**

AO2:

Agree	Disagree
• Catholic families suffer all the same hardships that any other family does – debt, bereavement, relationship breakdown – and need help. • Avoiding divorce, which the Church does not recognise, may be possible through counselling and relationship work through organisations such as Marriage Care. • Charities such as St Vincent de Paul can target and get help quickly to families in need as they are known to the priest.	• Some Catholics may say the provision of sacraments is the most important – the Eucharist is the 'source and summit'. • Some may say it is the responsibility of the government and the Church should focus purely on spiritual issues. • Some may say the parish shouldn't intervene in the private life of parishioners, and maybe the priest is not the best person to advise on such matters anyway – he doesn't have a wife or children so can't understand fully.

10.5 Family planning

AO1: A possible response: Firstly, natural family planning is promoted as it provides a way for Catholic couples to have some control of the number of children they have. **(1)** It uses the menstrual cycle as a way of ensuring the woman is far less likely to get pregnant – this, they believe, is in keeping with God's will. **(1)**

Secondly, artificial contraception is considered unacceptable. **(1)** This is because it separates the unitive and the procreative. It may also be abortive, ending the life, even at the very early stages of the unborn child. **(1)**

AO2:

For	Against
• It allows Catholics to take responsibility over how many children they have. • This is what Church teaching says. Humanae Vitae (1968) outlined the reasons why artificial contraception should not be used. • It is a way of allowing God's will, through the menstrual cycle, without resorting to artificial means that stop the procreative process or can be abortive.	• Other Christians and non-religious people see certain types of contraception as acceptable, such as preventative, rather than abortive, and Catholics may be influenced by this. • Humanists argue that contraception helps couples to be responsible and regulate births. • Some Catholics use contraception as they feel it is appropriate under the concept of 'primacy of conscience'. (Other Catholics would see this as a misuse of conscience, though – the Church is very clear on this issue.)

10.6 Divorce, annulment, and remarriage

AO1: A possible answer: Firstly, a sacrament represents a covenant with God. **(1)** This means that an earthly power, even a court of law cannot end it – it is simply impossible until death. **(1)**

Secondly, it is clear that God does not permit divorce. **(1)** This is made clear in Malachi when it says 'I hate divorce says the Lord', which is reinforced by Jesus. **(1)**

AO2:

For	Against
• Most Christians would agree with this – if the marriage has broken down, especially if there is abuse, divorce is clearly necessary. • Non-religious people do not see marriage as anything more than a legal contract, and so do not see an issue with divorce. As it is more commonplace, this may affect Christian thinking. • Even Catholics may need to get a legal divorce for the benefit of the couple and children, but they cannot get a sacramental divorce – this is not possible.	• The Church teaches that sacramental divorce is not permitted. • However, an annulment may be possible. This says the marriage was never valid. It is not the same as a divorce, but allows Catholics to remarry. • God hated divorce, as made clear in Malachi 2:16 – Jesus reaffirmed this and made clear divorce was only permitted as a result of people stubbornly refusing to obey God.

10.7 Equality of men and women in the family

AO1: A possible response: Firstly, some Christian Churches see equality meaning treating men and women the same. **(1)** As a result they allow women to be ordained, as in the Church of England. **(1)**

However, the Catholic Church sees men and women as equal, but different. **(1)** As Jesus was a man, it only allows men to be ordained. **(1)**

10.8 Gender prejudice and discrimination

AO1: A possible answer: Firstly, the Catechism is very clear: sexual discrimination is 'sinful' (CCC 1938). **(1)** As a result, Catholics will challenge gender prejudice and fight for equal rights. **(1)**

Secondly, Jesus combatted the prejudice and discrimination of his time. **(1)** This gives a clear example to Catholics today. **(1)** One example of this is the Samaritan woman at the well (John 4:4–26). **(1)**

AO2:

For	Against
• Some Baptist and Pentecostal Churches have been ordaining women with great success for over 100 years. • The fact that culture and society have changed dramatically cannot be ignored by Christians today. Women have the same rights as men. • Jesus and his disciples all being male was more a reflection of the time, and its prejudice and discrimination.	• Division was caused by the Church of England ordaining women – some priests left and joined the Catholic Church. • The reason that Catholic and Orthodox Churches do not ordain women is that Jesus was male, and his disciples were also all male. • The Bible is clear that both men and women are 'one in Christ Jesus' (Galatians 3:28), but women have different roles to fulfil. They can do much within the Church, just not be ordained.

Chapter 10 Exam Practice

3 mark question

2. Other features include: It is an exclusive commitment to the marriage partner. **(1)** It should be open to the possibility of new life. **(1)**

3. Reasons include: It contradicts the will of God. **(1)** It can encourage sex outside of marriage. **(1)** There is no need for it as it is possible to avoid pregnancy using natural family planning. **(1)**

4 mark question

2. A possible answer: One reason is that Catholics believe that sex is for procreation. **(1)** They believe that the best place for the procreation of children is within marriage, so that children can be brought up in the faith. **(1)**

A second reason is that the Church views sexual activity as something that should be both unitive and procreative. **(1)** As the Church also believes the nuclear family is the best way to bring up children, it follows that procreative acts should only take place within a marriage. **(1)**

3. A possible response: One way is that there are groups for children to help educate them in the faith **(1)** so that they become responsible members of the community, for example, classes for Confirmation. **(1)**

A second way is family worship, which encourages the whole family to be united in prayer. **(1)** This strengthens the family bond and consequently helps society. **(1)**

5 mark question

2. A possible answer: Firstly, the family has certain rights and responsibilities. **(1)** This is to 'serve life' and educate their children as Catholics. **(1)** This is reaffirmed in Part 3 of *Familiaris Consortio* by Pope John Paul II. **(1)**

Secondly, there is an emphasis on pastoral care of the family provided by the Church. **(1)** This includes support for couples before and after marriage. **(1)**

3. A possible response: Firstly, Catechism of the Catholic Church 1938 teaches that gender discrimination is wrong **(1)** because all people are equal in dignity.**(1)** This means everyone should work for fair and just conditions for all people. **(1)**

Secondly, Jesus had many women followers whom he taught and prayed with. **(1)** Several times Jesus showed that he treated women and men equally. **(1)**

15 mark question

2. Possible arguments in support of the statement: For Catholics, marriage is a sacrament. As such it is considered loving, lifelong, exclusive, and fruitful. There is support for the couple before and after marriage. They usually receive catechesis, sometimes called Pre Cana, as preparation. This may happen via the priest and lay volunteers. The sacrament of marriage only ends when one of the couple dies, that is why the vows say 'Until death do us part'.

Possible arguments supporting a different view: Other Christians do not see marriage as a sacrament. As such, it does not contain promises (vows) made to God in the same sense as matrimony for Catholics. It is therefore easier to break. Most other Christian Churches accept divorce as a necessity in some cases, and allow remarried couples full participation in their services. Non-religious people see marriage as more of a contract that unites two people, but can be broken when necessary.

A possible conclusion: For Catholics, marriage is lifelong, while for other Christians it is able to be broken through divorce. If you believe something is lifelong, you will naturally ensure that careful preparation does take place.

3. Possible arguments in support of the statement: The Catholic Church teaches that one of the natural functions of sex is to reproduce; this means that sexual activity not open to the possibility of reproduction is wrong because it prevents humans from fulfilling God's command to be fruitful. To have sex only for pleasure is viewed by some Christians as sinful; to obtain sexual pleasure only for itself demeans the sanctity of humanity; this means that sexual relations must always be both unitive and procreative. Some Christians argue that artificial contraception has encouraged promiscuity and the spread of sexually transmitted diseases. These views have been upheld and reaffirmed by Pope John Paul II who stated that contraception 'contradicts the will of the Author of life'.

Possible arguments supporting a different view: However, some Christians believe God created sex for pleasure and to provide an experience unique to the married couple. Contraception allows married sex to be free from fear of pregnancy and provides the couple with safe pleasures as there is nothing in the Bible that says that contraception is wrong. Some Christians argue that not all acts of sex need to be open to life; they may recognise that a couple may want to space out their children using contraception. This means they can control the size of their family and look after their children more effectively. Some Christians do not regard contraception as against God's plan as the essence of Christianity is love and contraception can be used to protect a woman's health.

A possible conclusion: The abortive effects of some artificial types of contraception lead me to believe that Catholics should ultimately only use natural family planning.

11.1 The Messiah and the Son of Man

AO1: A completed outline could be: He would also be a descendant of King David. **(1)** Christians believe the Messiah is Jesus who came to earth to save them. **(1)**

AO2:

For	Against
• In Daniel, the Son of Man is a supernatural figure, with cosmic authority.	• In Ezekiel, 'Son of Man' means ordinary human.
• It would have been familiar to Jewish people as a title used in the Old Testament.	• It's suggested that Jesus deliberately used the title to keep things ambiguous until the time was right – he avoided titles such as the Messiah.
• It is used by both Jesus and the author, which suggests a clear meaning that was established.	• The title is not used much after the Gospels, showing it was not used much by the early Church.

A possible conclusion: In conclusion, despite Jesus perhaps intending for this title to be ambiguous, it is hard to deny the divine connotations that it brings. Daniel makes this very clear.

11.2 The baptism of Jesus

AO1: A possible second point: Secondly, it gives an example for Christians to follow. **(1)** For Catholics, it is the first sacrament, and others are not possible without first being baptised. **(1)**

AO2:

For	Against
• It made clear Jesus' origin and divine nature – he was the Son of God.	• Jesus' ministry is best understood in light of his death and resurrection.
• It is so significant that Mark started his Gospel with this event – a dramatic opening to the account of Jesus' life.	• There were other occasions where God affirmed Jesus, such as the transfiguration (see 11.6).
• It indicated his willingness to take on the sins of humanity, which underpins his time on earth.	• Jesus' miracles and teachings spoke for themselves.

11.3 Nature miracles in Mark's Gospel

AO1: A possible answer: Firstly, Jesus walked on water, something that is impossible for a normal human being. **(1)** The wind also ceased as he climbed into the boat. **(1)** This was such an amazing event that the disciples were 'utterly astounded', proving Jesus was clearly divine. **(1)**

Secondly, Jesus fed 5000 people with five loaves and two fish. **(1)** This was clearly impossible, but there was more than enough food leftover, indicating God's supreme power, through Jesus. **(1)**

AO2: Two possible conclusions: **1.** For Christians, it is clear that the nature miracles were signs of the divine nature of Jesus and this led Christians to proclaim Jesus as the Son of God. There is no other explanation for the events recorded, and the lack of a natural explanation confirms their miraculous nature.

2. For non-believers, there is not clear enough evidence. These events have limited evidence and could easily be made up or exaggerated. Therefore, reported miracles are not evidence for Jesus' divine nature.

11.4 Healing miracles in Mark's Gospel

AO1: A possible answer: The healing of Legion clearly shows that Jesus is recognised by the demon. **(1)** He had the power to remove the evil, which could come only from God. **(1)**

The raising of Jairus' daughter shows that Jesus has a power over death. **(1)** This was preparation for the resurrection. **(1)**

AO2: Possible arguments for the statement: When he healed Legion, Jesus showed power over the demon. He was able to cast it out, showing his authority. When Jesus raised Jairus' daughter, he showed his power to overcome death. Jesus' ability to help the woman who has bled for 12 years is another demonstration of his power; all other medical treatment had clearly failed.

Possible arguments against the statement: Nature miracles give a better indication of Jesus' power and authority, for example, calming the storm showed his control over the sea. Feeding the five thousand was witnessed by a large number, highlighting his authority. Walking on water was a powerful act that no one else was able to do.

A possible conclusion: In conclusion, although healing miracles are not the only way of showing Jesus' power and authority, the way in which he dramatically transforms the lives of those who are sick would have been a clear indication of his power and authority to his followers.

11.5 Peter's confession

AO1: A possible development of the first point is: This was because he wanted to avoid misunderstanding of what the Messiah meant. **(1)**

Secondly, some argue that Jesus' vision of being a suffering servant needed to be revealed gradually. **(1)** This was because he knew he would not be the warrior king some thought he would. **(1)**

AO2: Two possible conclusions: **1.** In conclusion, it's convincing to believe that Jesus had a plan about how and when he wanted to reveal himself as a Messiah. Therefore he needed to wait until the time was right.

2. In conclusion, Jesus may have tried to keep it a secret, but there came a point, when enough people had worked it out, that there was little point in trying to keep it a secret.

11.6 The transfiguration

AO1: A possible second point: Secondly, a cloud appeared and God's voice was heard. (1) He said, 'This is my beloved Son; listen to Him!' confirming Jesus as the Son of God. (1)

AO2:

For	Against
• God said, 'This is my beloved Son; listen to him' (Mark 9:7) – clear confirmation of his status. • Moses was present – he represented the Law given by God on Mount Sinai and the covenant with people after the Exodus. • Elias was present – he challenged Kings not true to the religion of Israel. He also was linked to the coming of the Messiah, who was also the Son of God.	• This event happened to just a small group of the disciples, who were confused by the experience. It was not clear to them. • This event seems highly improbable, and therefore it is hard to believe. The disciples may have been experiencing a hallucination or wish fulfilment. • Non-religious people do not accept visions as evidence of Jesus being the Messiah or Son of God.

11.7 The conflicts of Jesus in Mark's Gospel

AO1: Further points include: Jesus healed a paralysed man who was lowered down to him. He said 'your sins are forgiven'. (1) Jesus overturned tables at the Temple and said it had become a 'den of thieves'. (1)

AO2:

For	Against
• Jesus wanted to reward the faith of the men, and heal the paralysed man. Illness and sin were believed to be connected, so it made sense to say 'Your sins are forgiven' (Mark 2:9). • Jesus wanted to point out that the Sabbath was created for man to rest, man was not created for the Sabbath. He also pointed out that he was Lord of the Sabbath (Mark 2:28). • Jesus was angered by those profiteering at the Temple, and felt he needed to take action. The scribes and Pharisees were likely sharing in this profit. • Conflict was needed in order to fulfil the messianic prophecies.	• This led to him being labelled as a troublemaker, and singled him out to be punished. Eventually he was crucified as a result. • The Jewish authorities did not like to be publicly embarrassed, as they were at the Temple. This is why they plotted to 'destroy him' (Mark 11:18). • Jesus was indirectly claiming to be God, by forgiving sins. This was considered blasphemy, as Jesus knew.

11.8 The last days of Jesus' life

AO1: A possible response: Firstly, the Mass, the 'source and summit' for Catholics, was instituted at the Last Supper. (1) Today the priest still uses the same words as Jesus did. (1) He says, 'This is my body' and 'This is my blood' (14:22–24), making the event present. (1)

Secondly, Jesus made a great sacrifice on the cross, giving up his life for the salvation of others. (1) Christians today follow this example, ensuring love is a key part of their life – helping and giving to others in need for example. (1)

AO2: Developed points might include: **1.** The resurrection is more important – it proves once and for all that Jesus is the Son of God and can overcome death.

2. The whole Passion is more important – the resurrection cannot be understood without the other events, beginning with the Last Supper.

3. His birth is the most significant – after all, this is often a bigger celebration and without his miraculous birth, none of the rest of the story of Jesus' life would be possible.

Chapter 11 Exam Practice

3 mark question

2. Two further events could include: Jesus was transfigured and glistened in white light. (1) Moses and Elias appeared. (1)

3. Answers could include: It showed Jesus' divinity through the voice saying 'Thou art my beloved Son'. (1) It revealed the Trinity – father, son, and Holy Spirit. (1) It emphasises the importance of baptism and encourages followers to get baptised. (1)

4 mark question

2. A possible answer: Firstly, it shows that Jesus claimed the authority from God to forgive sins. (1) The teachers of the law thought this power belonged only to God. (1)

Secondly, Jesus seemed to be claiming messianic powers, (1) as healing the man was considered blasphemous. (1)

3. A possible answer: Firstly, it helped the early disciples understand Jesus better. (1) He gradually revealed himself as a suffering servant, rather than a warrior king. (1)

Secondly, it made clear that the plan of salvation was carefully mapped out; (1) Jesus needed to ensure he had provided sufficient teaching to his disciples, and prepared them well enough, before his death. (1)

5 mark question

2. A possible answer: One event is when Jesus healed and forgave the paralysed man who was lowered through the roof. (1) The teachers of Law felt Jesus had committed blasphemy. (1)

A second event is when he allowed his disciples to pick corn on the Sabbath. (1) The Pharisees said they were acting unlawfully, (1), but Jesus responded: 'The Sabbath was made for man, not man for the Sabbath' (Mark 2:27). (1)

3. A possible response: Firstly, it shows only God has power over nature. (1) It shows that Jesus had God-like qualities as the storm obeyed his command to stop. (1) 'He got up, rebuked the wind and said to the waves, "Quiet! Be still!" Then the wind died down and it was completely calm' (Mark 4: 39). (1)

Secondly, the Old Testament taught that the Messiah would be able to perform such miracles, (1) therefore this miracle reinforces the Old Testament prophesies of Jesus as the Messiah. (1)

15 mark question

2. Possible arguments supporting the statement: Some Christians would agree with this statement saying the resurrection proved without any doubt that Jesus was the Son of God; he was able to overcome death. This was the greatest miracle that he performed, and made it very clear that he was the Messiah and everything that he had said and predicted was true. This event made clear the offer of salvation and eternal life. Jesus had begun building the Kingdom of God, but through this moment, it became a reality.

Possible arguments supporting a different view: On the other hand, other Christians may put more focus on the death of Jesus. For them, this event was the dramatic finale to the most terrible suffering. Jesus' death was the moment when he took up the sins of the world, and enabled humanity to receive God's offer of salvation. Others may believe that actually it is hard to pinpoint one part of the Passion story and that the significance lies in the series of events understood as a whole: all the way from the Last Supper to the resurrection.

A possible conclusion: In the light of both sides of the argument, it is clear that while all parts of the last days of Jesus' life are important, Christianity is focused on the resurrection. Indeed, Sunday is the day of Christian worship because of this single important event.

3. Possible arguments supporting the statement: In some people's opinion, engaging in conflict can mean you are just as bad as those you are arguing with. You can be labelled a troublemaker, just like Jesus was by the Jewish leaders. Engaging in conflict can lead to negative consequences; Jesus' outburst in the Temple eventually led to his crucifixion. Jesus always taught his followers to love their neighbours. Was there a way to challenge the Jewish authorities in a more loving way?

Possible arguments supporting a different view: Other people would argue that sometimes it is necessary to engage in conflict to do good. They might say that Jesus was right to prioritise the welfare of his disciples over the details of the law about the Sabbath. It could be argued that sometimes anger is necessary to fight injustice, and anger isn't always wrong. Jesus overturned the tables in the Temple because it was a sacred place to God.

It was important that Jesus forgave the sins of the paralysed man, as not forgiving them would have denied who Jesus was and what he came to earth to do.

A possible conclusion: In my opinion, a good leader often avoids conflict, but sometimes, it is necessary to bring about change or overcome evil. Jesus ended up in conflict when standing up for things that were really important, and Christians may have to do the same.

12.1 The call of the first disciples

AO1: A possible second point: Secondly, he gave them the authority to heal, like he had done. (1) They were also given the authority to cast out demons; (1) Jesus said they had 'authority over the unclean spirits' (Mark 6:7). (1)

AO2:

For	Against

• Christians today are taught that they can share in the healing and confrontation of evil and follow the example of Jesus.
• The work of the Church today is to keep spreading the message:
  ◦ The Catholic Church continues to evangelise.
  ◦ Evangelical Christians will often give public witness to faith.
	• Other Christians may prefer to be disciples by serving others, i.e. charitable work.
	• Some Christians do not feel they are called to announce the Gospel in the way the disciples did – they may see this as reserved for priests.
	• Some Christians do not believe that miracles can happen today.

12.2 Parables

AO1: Features could include: The parable was told to religious leaders, for them to realise and take note of the warning intended for them. **(1)** The owner of the vineyard represents God, his son represents Jesus. **(1)** It meant the Kingdom of God was offered to religious leaders, but they would reject it and then lose it. **(1)**

AO2:

For	Against
• Many Christians link the Kingdom to heaven, which is a place in the future of all living humans. • It is clearly not present now – there is much pain and suffering – even for Christians. Therefore it must be a time to come. • Jesus spoke a lot about the Kingdom but didn't always make it clear what it was physically like, so it is still to be revealed.	• It is clear that the work began with the message Jesus brought – people needed to change their actions and outlook. • If it is not a physical location, more a vocation as many commentators claim; there is no need for it to be just a future event. • The struggles for the Kingdom began from the time of Jesus' ministry, likewise the rewards of the Kingdom must have done so too.

12.3 The story of the rich man

AO1: A possible answer: One lesson is that Christians will need to make sacrifices to follow Jesus. **(1)** However, this does not necessarily mean selling everything as the rich man was told to do – this was his barrier to the Kingdom of God. **(1)**

A second lesson is that the rich man assumed he was righteous; this is something Christians today should avoid. **(1)** Instead, Christians should focus on following the Commandments and building the Kingdom of God as best they can. **(1)**

AO2: A possible conclusion: In conclusion, it is clear that it is not possible for most people, particularly those with families, to live without some kind of income. It is possible to be charitable and giving in many ways without selling everything. However, at first sight the command to 'sell all you have and give to the poor' is a demanding teaching and in a literal sense leaves no room to consider doing anything less. Christians are challenged to work out what this means for them in their own lives.

12.4 The spirit cast out of the boy

AO1: A possible answer: Jesus teaches that prayer and fasting are necessary to experience healing and miracles. **(1)** This is something the disciples seemed to lack, and the father also admitted. **(1)** Jesus said, 'This kind cannot be driven out by anything but prayer and fasting.' **(1)**

AO2: Possible arguments supporting the statement: Jesus rebuked those present for their lack of belief (Mark 9:19); Christians today should have faith. The father cried out, 'I believe; help my unbelief' (Mark 9:24), and the boy was healed, showing that Christians today can grow in faith and be rewarded. Great faith is needed for miracles, as is fasting and prayer.

A possible conclusion: In conclusion, despite not being directly linked to the everyday lives of many Christians today, the message is clear. Faith is needed for miracles, and this is still important for Christians today.

12.5 Jesus' teachings on service

AO1: Points could include: Service would be costly in terms of jobs, family, and friendships. **(1)** Service may end up with suffering and persecution. **(1)** Disciples need to be selfless, servants not leaders. **(1)**

AO2:

For	Against
• 'For the Son of Man also came not to be served but to serve.' Mark 10:45 • Catholic Social Teaching; service to the poor • Sacrifice 'no bag, no money' Mark 6:8	• Prayer and worship of God • 'Take up his cross and follow me.' (Mark 8:34) - not just service, also laying down their lives • Spreading the Gospel is not service

A possible conclusion: In conclusion, service is obviously a very important part of Christian life, Jesus made this very clear in response to the request of James and John, which should still influence Christians today.

12.6 Peter's denial

AO1: A possible answer: Firstly, Peter shows pride, a fault in many human beings. **(1)** At the Last Supper he assures Jesus that he will not betray him. **(1)** He says: 'Even though they all fall away, I will not' (Mark 14:29). **(1)**

Secondly, he shows fear and weakness by denying Jesus. **(1)** He put his own life ahead of loyalty and commitment to Jesus. **(1)**

AO2:

For	Against
• Peter gave an example to Christians; firstly that Jesus should come above anything else, even in times of fear. • Peter himself broke down and wept when he denied Jesus. This demonstrates that denying Jesus does not help towards living a good life. • The experiences of discipleship enable growth – Peter grew to be the leader of the early Church and was later martyred.	• Non-religious people may see discipleship as passive submission; they feel they should use their own conscience instead. • Humanists believe you can live a good life regardless of religion – there is evidence of this in society today. • Religious observances include all kinds of religious behaviour and many activities would be seen as pointless if you didn't believe in God; prayer, worship, festivals etc.

12.7 Women in the ministry of Jesus

AO1: A possible response: The first way is to the Greek woman who asks for her daughter to be healed. **(1)** She is willing to 'eat the crumbs', taking whatever she can. This great faith is rewarded by Jesus healing her daughter. **(1)**

The second way is to the woman who anoints him at Bethany. **(1)** Other people in the room got angry as they thought this was wasteful, but Jesus defends her and makes it clear that her act is one of love and that she is anointing him in preparation for his death and burial. **(1)**

AO2:

For	Against
• Greek woman showed great faith, and as such, even though she was a gentile she was rewarded. Key message in early Church. • Jesus didn't allow criticism of woman at Bethany – in fact commended her on recognising him as Messiah. • The women were key witnesses to the death and resurrection of Jesus – arguably the two most important events of the Gospel.	• The 12 disciples were all male, the women were seemingly secondary to this group. • Peter was picked as the leader of the disciples, and went on to lead the Church. • Miracles and teaching were largely delivered to the male-only 12.

A possible conclusion: In conclusion, it was clear that women did play a key part in Jesus' ministry. His interactions with women were unusual and challenged norms of the time.

12.8 Discipleship in the 21st century

AO1: Further points could be: Living a simple lifestyle. **(1)** Standing up for the oppressed. **(1)** If living in certain areas, suffering persecution and even risk to life. **(1)**

AO2:

For	Against
• Dietrich Bonhoeffer spoke out the Nazi regime and wrote a book called *The Cost of Discipleship*. He was eventually linked to a plot to assassinate Hitler and executed. • Mother Teresa was a Catholic nun who totally dedicated her life to working with the poor in Calcutta. She gave up everything she had to help others. • Christians today still face persecution, even death in some countries. Laying down your life may mean just making sacrifices rather than death to many Christians.	• There are other ways to help the poor and oppressed, rather than laying down your life, such as charitable giving, or praying for the poor and oppressed during Mass or privately. • Spreading the Gospel stops with death; the work of a disciple can be actively continued by avoiding laying down your life.

A possible conclusion: In conclusion, it is not necessary for most Christians to lay down their life for the poor and oppressed. However, it is important that all Christians make sacrifices for these people, through charitable giving, for example.

Chapter 12 Exam Practice

3 mark question

2. Answer could include: By working or volunteering for organisations such as CAFOD or Apostleship of the Sea. **(1)** By being prepared to spread Jesus' message to others. **(1)**

3. Features could include: A man brought his son who had a 'dumb spirit'. **(1)** Jesus seems to criticise the disciples for not having enough faith. **(1)** Prayer and fasting were the way to drive out the spirit. **(1)**

4 mark question

2. A possible answer: Firstly, Jesus made it clear that some people would hear the message but not listen. **(1)** The message does not penetrate their hearts at all, so they would be like the seed eaten by the birds. **(1)**

Secondly, the seeds that fell on the good soil would bear fruit and be like the disciples. **(1)** They have heard and responded to the Gospel. **(1)**

3. A possible response: One reason Jesus told the parable is that it is a story to warn the chief priests who questioned Jesus' authority. **(1)** The tenants are the Jewish leaders who will be excluded from the Kingdom of God. **(1)**

A second reason is it warns the disciples about the risk of persecution and death. **(1)** The servants in the parable are the messengers of God who are abused and killed. **(1)**

5 mark question

2. A possible answer: The first clear challenge is the problem of just having wealth and possessions; something many Christians today have, some in abundance. **(1)** Christians may feel this story is instructing them to sell everything they own, which is not easy in the modern world, especially for those with a family. **(1)** They may feel that they have to do this as Jesus told the rich man, 'sell what you have, and give to the poor' (Mark 10:21). **(1)**

The second challenge is that Jesus makes it clear that rich people cannot easily enter the Kingdom of God. **(1)** This indicates that wealth is a serious problem for those trying to receive the message of the Gospel. **(1)**

3. A possible response: Jesus' first teaching was that there was a price to pay for service, made clear when James and John asked for seats at his left and right in the Kingdom of God. **(1)** Jesus challenged them after acknowledging their ignorance, and made it clear they needed to be ready to suffer; **(1)** he said to them 'the cup that I drink you will drink' (Mark 10:39). **(1)**

His second teaching was that true service and discipleship meant a reversal of society as the disciples knew it. **(1)** He said, 'whoever would be first among you must be slave of all [...] the Son of Man also came not be served but to serve (Mark 10:43–45). **(1)**

15 mark question

2. Possible arguments for the statement: Jesus himself said 'She has done a great thing'. The woman 'anointed' Jesus, therefore recognising him as the Messiah – the Anointed One. There was to be no time for Jesus' body to be anointed when he died and so it was a good thing that she anointed him in advance.

Possible arguments against the statement: On the other hand, some Christians would hold a different point of view because she was a woman, and as Jesus was Jewish he should not have allowed her to touch him. Also, Jesus angered those watching by saying 'She has anointed my body beforehand for burying'. Some believe Jesus should not have allowed such an extravagant waste of money. The perfume was very expensive and the money from its sale could have been given to the poor.

A possible conclusion: Having considered both sides of the argument, I would say that the woman was right to anoint Jesus. Despite it being a controversial act, Jesus was sure that what she was doing was right and proper. If Jesus believed this, it makes sense that Christians would agree.

3. Possible arguments for the statement: Jesus taught that to be a disciple the person must deny themselves and take up their cross and follow him (Mark 8:34). For some Christians this is still true today. Role models for such Christians are people such as Dietrich Bonhoeffer and Mother Teresa who gave up everything to follow Jesus' teaching and work with the vulnerable and those facing persecution in society. James and John gave up family, and Simon and Andrew gave up their jobs. According to this way of thinking, it is necessary to dedicate your life to a cause and deny things such as wealth, marriage, and worldly distractions in order to concentrate on your vocation.

Possible arguments against the statement: Some non-religious people would argue that being a disciple or following religious observance is not necessary to do the work for the poor or vulnerable. The majority of Christians think they can still serve God and be a disciple while continuing to live in comfort and without giving up everything. Some Christians believe it is possible to be a good disciple by living a Christian life, being baptised, going to church, and praying for the world without giving anything up.

A possible conclusion: I believe that this claim is simply not practical and would be irresponsible if you had a family. It is clear that this lifestyle may be appropriate for some people, but not for all.

Glossary

A

'Adl: belief in Allah's justice and fairness

Akhirah: in Islam, everlasting life after death, spent in either paradise or hell

Al-Qadr: predestination, a future already decided by Allah

Altar: a table that is a focal point inside a church

Amr bil-Ma'ruf: encouraging others to do good

Apostolic Tradition: teaching and doctrine that has been passed on from the earliest of times through the Catholic Church

Ascension: the moment the resurrected Jesus is taken up to heaven

Ashura: a day of mourning in Shi'a tradition for the martyrdom of Imam Husayn, the grandson of the Prophet Muhammad

Atheist: a person who does not believe in the existence of God(s)

B

Barzakh: meaning 'barrier'; it is the state between death and the Day of Judgment

Benevolent: loving and good

C

Chalice: a cup for consecrated wine (the 'blood of Christ')

Challah: plaited bread prepared before Shabbat begins

Chametz: foods containing wheat, barley, and oats, left to soak for over 18 minutes; not to be eaten during Pesach

Circumcising: removing the foreskin of the penis; 'Brit Milah' is the name of the Jewish ceremony of circumcision

Cosmological: relating to the history, structure and dynamics of the universe; follows the universal law of cause and effect

Crucifix: a cross with an image of the crucified Jesus on it

D

Day of Judgment: when Allah will decide if a person will go to paradise or hell

Denominations: different groups or churches within Christianity

Discipleship: following the teaching and the example of Jesus

Doctrine: a formal teaching and belief held by the Church

Dominion: humans ruling over the earth

E

Ecumenism: the idea that there should be one unified Christian Church

Efficacious prayer: *efficax* is Latin for powerful and effective; in the funeral rite it is prayer to help and encourage the deceased person

Eschatology: the Christian study of the last things in human life: death, judgement, heaven, hell, and purgatory; Catholic eschatology is rooted in the Paschal Mystery

Eucharist: the sacrament in which Catholics receive the bread and wine that has become the body and blood of Jesus. Also the name given to the consecrated bread and wine that are received; one of the three Sacraments of Initiation

Eucharistic adoration: worship of the presence of Jesus in the bread and wine

Evangelism: to proclaim and live out the Gospel or good news of Jesus

Ex cathedra: means 'from the chair' and refers to the authority the Pope has in inheriting the 'chair' of St Peter; as an heir he would inherit a throne

Exorcism: removal of evil spirits who have possessed a person

Extempore prayer: informal, using one's own words, without planning

F

Five Pillars: five basic acts that form the foundation of Muslim life and belief in the Sunni tradition

Funeral rite: the ceremonies carried out when a Catholic dies

G

Gan Eden: Garden of Eden – not the same place where Adam and Eve lived, but a pure spiritual heaven as a reward for the righteous

Gehinnom: a place for a set time of purification of the soul, similar to the Christian purgatory

H

Hadith: sayings of the Prophet Muhammad. An important source of Islamic law

Haggadah: a Jewish book that sets out the rituals of Pesach

Hajj: the annual pilgrimage to Makkah, which all Muslims must undertake at least once if possible

Halakhah: the list of 613 Mitzvot (commandments) that guide Jewish life

Healing miracles: acts of God that return people to full physical, mental, or spiritual health

Heaven: eternal life with God; a life of love and indescribable joy

Hell: the absence of the love, generosity, and community of God; not a punishment from God

Humanist: A person who prefers non-religious explanations derived from science and reason

I

Id-ul-Adha: a global celebration that remembers the prophet Ibrahim's willingness to sacrifice his son for Allah

Id-ul-Fitr: a festival to mark the end of Ramadan

Id-ul-Ghadeer: a Shi'a celebration of Muhammad's appointment of his nephew Ali as his successor

Imam: 1) Sunni leader of communal prayer; 2) Shi'a religious and political leader, the successor of the Prophet

Imamah: successors to the Prophet Muhammad. The belief that after the Prophet Muhammad there are no more prophets, and no more divine scriptures

Incarnation: God the Son taking human form as Jesus Christ

J

Jihad: to struggle or strive. This could be a spiritual or physical struggle, in particular against evil

Justification: only just (righteous, holy, loving) people can enter into a relationship with God

K

Ka'bah: a building in the centre of Islam's most sacred mosque in Makkah, regarded as the house of Allah

Kaddish: a prayer of praise blessing God's name

Kedusha: the third section of all Amidah recitations

Khums: the payment by Shi'as of one fifth of their surplus income for good causes

Kiddush: prayer of sanctification over the wine at Shabbat

Kingdom of God: the rule of God over all creatures and things

L

Leaven: meaning risen – food that has been fermented with a raising agent such as yeast, prohibited during Pesach

Lectern: book stand from which readings are proclaimed

Liberal: one of the groups within Judaism, believing that the Torah should be understood as a document of its time, and be interpreted in light of modern life and issues

Liturgical worship: the structured public service of worship in Catholic churches

Lord's Prayer: the prayer that Jesus gave to his disciples

M

Magisterium: the teaching authority of the Church, held by the Pope and his bishops

Malaikah: the Arabic word for the angels of Allah

Mass: the central act of worship celebrated nearly every day in Catholic churches; Catholics are expected to attend Mass weekly

Messiah: the anointed one, the King sent from God to save sinners

Mezuzah: a small box set on a doorpost containing a copy of the Shema

Mikvah: ritual bath for purification

Mi'ad: the belief in life after death, resurrection, and accountability after death for the life led on earth

Minyan: a group of ten men (Orthodox tradition) or adults (Reform tradition) over the age of 13

Mitzvot: commandments that set rules or guide action for Jews (singular: Mitzvah)

Modeh ani: 'I give thanks', a prayer recited upon waking

Monotheism: the belief in one God

N

Nahy anil-Munkar: discouraging others from doing bad

Natural Law: a discoverable moral law that never changes and applies to all humans

Nature miracles: acts of God that seem to suspend or change the way nature normally works

Nevi'im: 'Prophets' – the second part of the Tenakh

Nicene Creed: the Christian declaration of faith

Night of Power: when the Prophet Muhammad received his first revelation from Allah through the angel Jibril, in 610CE at the cave of Hira in Makkah

Non-liturgical: worship that does not follow a strict pattern set out by the Church

Nubuwwah: prophethood

O

Olam Ha-Ba: 'The World to Come'; term used for both 1) the Messianic Age and 2) a spiritual afterlife following physical death

Omnibenevolence: unlimited goodness and love

Omnipotence: unlimited power

Omniscience: complete knowledge of all human actions, past, present, and future

Orthodox: traditional beliefs of religion

P

Parables: 'earthly stories with a heavenly meaning', told by Jesus to illustrate his teaching

Paradise: heaven, a place of peace

Paschal Mystery: the Passion, death, resurrection and ascension of Jesus; Paschal is the Hebrew name for Passover (the Jewish celebration of the Israelites being led to freedom by Moses)

Passion: Jesus' arrest, trial, and suffering

Paten: a plate for the consecrated host

Pilgrimage: a journey made for religious reasons

Pontifical: relating to the Pope (the Pontiff)

Popular piety: worship that is not formal Church liturgy

Prayer: communication with God

Primacy of conscience: Catholics have a sacred obligation to follow a conscience informed by the bible and tradition, as interpreted by the magisterium

Prime mover: the first mover or first cause of all other moving things

Purgatory: a place or state of purposeful suffering where the souls of sinners are purified after death before going to heaven

Q

Qur'an: the Holy Book of Islam, as revealed to the Prophet Muhammad by God through the angel Jibril

R

Rabbi: Jewish teacher or religious leader

Reconciliation: the forgiveness of sins

Redemption: the forgiveness of sins through Jesus' sacrifice; redemption is part of salvation

Redemptive efficacy: humans are saved from eternal death and separation from God by the passion and death of Jesus

Reed Sea: some scholars believe a mistranslation led to this originally being called the 'Red' Sea

Reform: one of the groups within Judaism, believing that the Torah should be understood as a document of its time, and be interpreted in light of modern life and issues

Resurrection: Jesus' rising from the dead in a transformed body

Revelation: truth or knowledge revealed by a deity; the way God makes himself known to believers

S

Sacrament: a religious ceremony; a visible sign of God's grace

Sadducees and Pharisees: influential religious groups within the ancient Jewish community

Salah: worship of Allah through regular prayer. The Second Pillar of Sunni and First Obligatory Act of Shi'a tradition

Sarcophagus: a box-like container, usually made of stone, for a corpse

Sawm: obligatory fasting during Ramadan

Secular: concerned with the physical world alone, rather than the spiritual

Shahadah: the Islamic creed or profession of faith. The first pillar of Islam

Shavuot: commemorates the anniversary of the day God gave the Torah to the entire nation of Israel assembled at Mount Sinai

Shema: the main Jewish declaration of faith

Shirk: believing in things other than Allah or as equals to Allah

Siddur: book of daily prayers; literally means 'order' or 'sequence'

Situation ethics: where right and wrong depend on the circumstances of a situation

Son of Man: a title connected with the Messiah used in Daniel 7 in the Old Testament

Stations of the Cross: prayers that honour the suffering and death of Jesus

Stewardship: humans taking care of the earth

Symbolism: using an object to mean something else

T

Tabarra: expressing disdain for the enemies of Allah or evil

Tallit: a fringed prayer shawl

Talmud: the 'Oral Torah', or the Oral laws and traditions passed down from Moses, eventually written down as the Mishnah and the Gemara. There are two versions (Jerusalem and Babylonian)

Tawalla: expressing love for Allah or good

Tawhid: the oneness and unity of Allah

Tefillin: small boxes worn on head and arm containing verses from the Torah, including the Shema

Teleology: the study of a thing's purpose or design

Tenakh: the Hebrew Bible, consisting of the Torah, Nevi'im, and Kethuvim

Ten Obligatory Acts: in Shi'a tradition, the ten key practices that every Muslim should carry out during their life

Teshuva: returning to God; repentance

Theist: a person who believes in the existence of God(s)

Theodicy: a theory/defence of why God permits evil

Tikkun Olam: acts of kindness performed to repair the world

Torah: 1) the Five Books of Moses Bereshit (Genesis), Shemot (Exodus), Vayikra (Leviticus), Bamidbar (Numbers), and Devarim (Deuteronomy); 2) a wider meaning including the written Tenakh plus the Talmud – the oral law and traditions of Judaism

Transfiguration: a change in appearance or form; the unveiling of Jesus as Messiah alongside the support of Moses and Elias

Twelve disciples: the inner group of Jesus' followers who represent the 12 tribes of Israel

V

Virgin Mary: Jesus' mother conceived without sexual activity

Virtue: a moral excellence

Virtue ethics: considering the moral character of a person to help analyse their ethical decisions

Y

Yeshiva: Jewish school of Talmudic study

Z

Zakah: purification of wealth by giving to the poor